The essays in this volume are all original contributions dealing in one way or another with the analysis of prosody – primarily intonation and rhythm – and the role it plays in everyday conversation. They take as their methodological starting-point the contention that the study of prosody must begin with genuine interactional rather than pre-fabricated laboratory data. Through close empirical analysis of recorded material from genuine English, German and Italian conversations, prosody emerges here as a strategy deployed by interactants in the management of turn-taking and floor-holding; in the negotiation of conversational activities such as repair, assessments, announcements, reproaches and news receipts; and in the keying of the tone or modality of interactional sequences.

Studies in Interactional Sociolinguistics 12

General editor: John J. Gumperz

Prosody in conversation

Studies in Interactional Sociolinguistics

Prosody in conversation

Interactional studies

Edited by ELIZABETH COUPER-KUHLEN
University of Konstanz

and MARGRET SELTING
University of Potsdam

CAMBRIDGE
UNIVERSITY PRESS

Published by the Press Syndicate of the University of Cambridge
The Pitt Building, Trumpington Street, Cambridge CB2 1RP
40 West 20th Street, New York, NY 10011-4211, USA
10 Stamford Road, Oakleigh, Melbourne, 3166, Australia

First published in 1996

A catalogue record for this book is available from the British Library

Library of Congress cataloguing in publication data

Prosody in conversation: interactional studies/edited by Elizabeth
Couper-Kuhlen and Margret Selting.
    p. cm.
    Contents: Towards an interactional perspective on prosody and a prosodic
perspective on interaction/Elizabeth Couper-Kuhlen and Margret Selting – On
the prosody and syntax of turn-continuations/Peter Auer – Ending up in Ulster:
prosody and turn-taking in English dialects/Bill Wells and Sue Peppé –
Affiliating and disaffiliating with continuers: prosodic aspects of recipiency/
Frank Ernst Müller – Conversational phonetics: some aspects of news receipts in
everyday talk/John Local – Prosody as an activity-type distinctive cue in
conversation: the case of so-called 'astonished' questions in repair initiation/
Margret Selting – The prosodic contextualization of moral work: an analysis of
reproaches in 'why'-formats/Susanne Günthner – On rhythm in everyday
German conversation: beat clashes in assessment utterances/Susanne Uhmann –
The prosody of repetition: on quoting and mimicry/Elizabeth Couper-Kuhlen –
Working on young children's utterances: prosodic aspects of repetition during
picture labelling/Clare Tarplee – Informings and announcements in their
environment: prosody within a multi-activity work setting/Marjorie Harness
Goodwin.
    ISBN 0 521 46075 1 (hardback)
    1. Prosodic analysis (Linguistics) 2. Conversation analysis.
3. Social interaction. I. Couper-Kuhlen, Elizabeth. II. Selting,
Margret.
P224.P757 1996
414'.6–dc20
                                                       94-48446 CIP

ISBN 0521 46075 1 hardback

Transferred to digital printing 2004

KW

Contents

Contributors

Professor Dr Peter Auer, Germanisches Seminar, University of Hamburg, Germany.

Professor Dr Elizabeth Couper-Kuhlen, Fachgruppe Sprachwissenschaft, University of Konstanz, Germany.

Professor Marjorie Harness Goodwin, Department of Anthropology, University of South Carolina, Columbia, USA.

Dr Susanne Günthner, Fachgruppe Sprachwissenschaft, University of Konstanz, Germany.

Professor John Local, Department of Language and Linguistic Science, University of York, UK.

PD Dr Frank Ernst Müller, Institut für Romanische Sprachen und Literaturen, J. W. Goethe-Universität, Frankfurt/Main, Germany.

Sue Peppé, Department of Human Communication Science, University College London, UK.

Professor Dr Margret Selting, Institut für Germanistik, University of Potsdam, Germany.

Dr Clare Tarplee, Department of Human Communication Science, University College London, UK.

PD Dr Susanne Uhmann, Fachbereich 4, Bergische Universität – Gesamthochschule Wuppertal, Germany.

Dr Bill Wells, Department of Human Communication Science, University College London, UK.

Foreword by John J. Gumperz

Scholars in a number of fields have in recent years turned to everyday talk as the principal source from which to gain insights into both linguistic and social processes. The move is motivated by issues rooted in specific academic traditions and each group or school tends to focus on different aspects of verbal signs. Sociologists, for example, look to the sequential organization of conversational exchanges to learn how conversational involvements are created and sustained: ultimately to deepen their understanding of participant alignments that constitute social relationships and reflect social order. Linguists on the other hand, mindful of the empirical findings indicating that understanding rests on context-bound inferences, and that grammar and semantics cannot alone account for situated meaning, look to everyday talk for evidence of how such inferencing works.

Regardless of these differences in approach, however, it is generally agreed that discourse and conversation have structural characteristics or forms of organization of their own, independent of sentence-level grammar. Moreover, it is evident that prosody plays a key role in discourse-level interpretation: in fact without it there can be no conversing. It is prosody that animates talk and in large part determines its situated characteristics. Only through prosody do sentences become turns at speaking and come to be seen as actions performed by living actors. For example when a reviewer writes about an author's work using the expression, 'You can hear her subjects' intonations. And sometimes you can hear her own–', we know that she is referring to the author's skill in depicting living human beings, not her own or her subject's use of pitch or tone of voice.[1] Yet, while few would question the importance of prosody, discussions of how it enters into situated conversation have been mainly programmatic.

Our knowledge of what prosody is derives largely from utterance-level analyses focussing on what we can call 'the linguistics of prosody'. Recent experimental research by phoneticians and phonologists has, as the editors point out in chapter 1 of this volume, made major advances in identifying the perceptual cues, that is the shifts in intonation, volume, rhythm and tempo, that underlie prosodic assessments, and in explaining their grammatical functions. Yet at the same time they continue to accept the common Saussurian view that words, phrases and sentences make up the core of language and that prosody is somehow derivative, and can be treated as an expressive overlay that supplements or modulates the more basic propositional content. As a result they have encountered difficulties in dealing with other aspects of intonational meaning and attempts to find a resolution have all been unsatisfactory.

The individual papers isolate some of the basic problems and controversies that have plagued both sentence-level linguistic analyses and sequential analyses of conversation, and through their empirical studies suggest how these can be solved by adopting an intermediate perspective that bridges the gap between linguists' and conversationalists' approaches. In this way they bring recent phoneticians' and phonologists' advances in prosodic analysis to bear on conversation.

In contrast to the established linguistic perspective, Couper-Kuhlen, Selting and their contributors argue that, to deal with the communicative role of prosody it becomes necessary to go beyond sentence-level grammar and take an interaction approach to the study of prosodic signs, while at the same time adopting a communicative approach to turn-taking. They set out to construct a basic reorientation in the way we look at prosody that focusses not on words but on continuities and breaks in patterning across turns of speaking. At the same time they suggest that prosody works together with syntax to facilitate the discourse-level co-ordination

---

[1]Gabriele Annan, review of *The Last Duchess* by Caroline Blackwood, *New York Review of Books*, 23 March 1995

of conversational moves and to create the situated understandings on which this co-ordination rests.

This shift to a conversational perspective is a major and in many respects controversial move, which raises fundamental questions of theory and method that cannot possibly be covered in a single volume. The goal of this book is not to try to answer all the questions that arise in terms of interpretation but rather to limit discussion to the place that prosody can play in current work on conversational process.

The incorporation of prosody into conversational analysis is more than simply a methodological addition to the conversational analysts' array of analytical tools. As indexical devices, prosodic signs provide a window into the ways in which context and participants' background knowledge affect their interpretation. We can thus go beyond the generalized analyses of activities of the conversation analytic literature to show how communicative ecologies create meaning, and to assess the communicative effects of the changes in these ecologies that have become so frequent in recent years. Social theorists have long emphasized that today's social institutions are communicatively established and maintained. The papers in this volume take an important step forward in showing how this works through language.

Introduction

MARGRET SELTING AND
ELIZABETH COUPER-KUHLEN

It goes without saying that in spoken interaction we react to a lot more than the words our utterances are made up of: a 'tone of voice', a 'feeling' about the way our partner spoke, the 'atmosphere' of a conversation – these are often more significant cues to the real message than the words themselves. How does this *interactional* meaning (as opposed to the *semantic* or *pragmatic* meaning of words and utterances) come about? What are the cues that help to make social interaction more than the mere exchange of words, namely a real-time encounter between conversationalists who establish and negotiate units of talk as situated meaningful activity? It is our conviction, and the conviction of the contributors to this volume, that at least some of the cues in everyday live speech events are prosodic in nature, involving auditory parameters such as pitch, loudness and duration and the categories they jointly constitute.

As we are concerned with prosody in natural social interaction, in particular conversation in its widest sense, our object of study is on the border between linguistics and the social sciences. In both areas the respective fields – the linguistic study of prosody and the social scientific study of verbal interaction – have long-standing traditions. However, so far they have seldom taken cognizance of one another. Yet if prosody is as important a signalling device in interaction as our everyday intuitions suggest, then the reconstruction of its relevant forms and functions require that it be studied empirically on the basis of data from natural verbal interaction. As surprising as it may sound, this is a very recent insight, one which runs counter to the views and methodologies of much linguistic and social science research as practised today.

The linguistic study of prosody has recently been reinvigorated by new interest in prosodic and intonational phonology within the generative paradigm. Most research in linguistics proper, however, has worked on the basis of introspective, constructed data and has been concerned with the grammatical function of prosody. The categories and methodologies used in this research have been devised to fit this type of data with a grammatical aim in mind. One notable exception is Bolinger, who was convinced that intonation is not fundamentally grammatical but emotional. Yet Bolinger himself worked on the basis of introspective data. Brazil's more recent theory of discourse intonation, although it is based on natural data and seeks discourse rather than grammatical functions, is nevertheless still heavily dependent on traditional structuralist methodology and therefore unable to provide an empirically valid description of prosody in conversation. In sum, despite the long tradition of prosodic research, its categories and methodologies are inappropriate for handling conversational data.

The study of verbal interaction in the social sciences also has a venerable tradition. Here the bridge to linguistics is to be found in sociolinguistic and conversation analytic work. Yet social scientists have been more concerned with aspects of context (setting, genre and role) than with prosody. Recently, however, a controversy has arisen in this field which strikes at the heart of the study of prosody and conversational interaction. Ethnomethodological conversation analysis maintains that interactive meaning is almost exclusively a matter of negotiation between participants on the basis of local management systems such as turn-taking, adjacency-pair sequencing and repair, whereas contextualization theory argues that in the constitution of the same interactive meaning the steering and negotiation of inferential processes via prosodic and other contextualization cues plays a crucial role. For researchers interested in both verbal and non-verbal phenomena, contextualization theory is naturally attractive: it brings together a number of otherwise disparate research endeavours in a single perspective, one which views prosodic and non-verbal devices as metapragmatic resources for the negotiation of social and interactional meaning.

New objects of study require new methodological approaches. Just as in previous approaches descriptive categories were designed to be appropriate for their object of study, so the new object of study *prosody in conversation* will require its own categories and methodology. In the first chapter of this volume ('Towards an interactional perspective on prosody and a prosodic perspective on interaction') we outline a new proposal for the analysis of prosody in natural conversation. This approach is an interactional one, drawing together insights and methodological practices from contextualization theory and conversation analysis. In contrast to previous approaches to prosody, it attempts to reconstruct prosodic categories 'from within' as participant categories, showing how speakers use prosody as a resource for the management and negotiation of interactive meaning. The demonstration that participants do indeed orient to the prosodic features in question is used as a warrant for the analytic decisions made. This procedure, which seeks evidence for its claims in the observable treatment of prosody by participants themselves, frees analysts from the need to rely on intuitions or pre-constructed theories. We argue that the study of prosody in an interactional perspective will enrich and further the development of research in both linguistic and social science fields.

Subsequent chapters deal with some of the recurrent organizational tasks in everyday conversation where prosody can be shown to play an important role, in particular in the organization of turn-taking and the constitution of activity types. Early chapters deal with turn-taking, later chapters with activity types. The individual analyses presented show that conversation as a speech exchange system can take place in a variety of situational settings. Our contributors use data from everyday casual conversation between adults in informal settings, from talk between moderators and callers on radio phone-in programmes, from sociolinguistic interviews, adult–child conversations and work exchanges. For each organizational task, we begin with contributions which analyse informal, private conversation and then move on to those which deal with talk in more specialized, public settings.

The role of prosody in the organization of conversational turn-taking is the object of study for Peter Auer, Bill Wells and Sue Peppé. **Peter Auer** ('On the prosody and syntax of turn-continuations') focuses on the relation between prosodic and syntactic cues for the contextualization of turn-constructional units and the projection of turn completion. In order to study the individual contribution of each of these cues to turn-taking in German conversation, he looks at turns which are expanded beyond a possible syntactic completion point. After first giving a syntactic typology of expansions and then discussing how in principle prosody may be used as a cue to turn completion, Auer analyses the relationship between the two. He shows that syntactically tagged-on material can be presented either as integrated into the prior unit ('camouflaged') or as exposed in a new unit, and that the particular kind of integration or exposure serves to contextualize the status of the material as thematic or rhematic information. Since expansions are vulnerable to overlap, however, the potential conflict between adding or foregrounding new material after a possible syntactic completion point on the one hand, and running the risk of the recipient's taking over the floor on the other, needs to be structurally resolved. This is exactly what the prosodic packaging does. Auer comes to the conclusion that prosody and syntax play independent roles in a 'division of labour' for turn-taking, and that both are monitored by recipients in order to infer when to come in.

Bill Wells and **Sue Peppé** ('Ending up in Ulster: prosody and turn-taking in English dialects') analyse the role of prosodic features in turn-taking in Belfast English. Methodologically, they employ a combination of conversation-analytic techniques and impressionistic phonetic observation. As in previous research on the use of prosodic devices for the signalling of turn-holding versus turn-yielding in London Jamaican and Tyneside, Wells and Peppé start from the assumption that in Belfast too, prosody plays a role in turn delimitation. After first identifying the phonetic features which regularly accompany turn-endings in the clear, i.e. those with smooth transitions between speakers, they search for further evidence of the interactional salience of these features in participants' treatment of more problematic turn exchanges. By systematically recurring to the recipient treatment of turns which display distinctive phonetic shapes, Wells and Peppé warrant their empirical analysis without having to rely on the vague evidence of analysts' or experimental subjects' intuitions. Comparison of their present findings with previous studies in other dialect areas reveals that while the function of each cluster of phonetic cues is phonological since it systematically relates to turn delimitation, the dialects use distinct sets of phonetic features for this task. Dialects can differ both in the locus of phonological prominence as well as in the particular cluster of phonetic cues. As loudness and tempo features are often shared across dialects, the greatest differences are in pitch. Results such as these point to the need for comparative cross-language and cross-dialectal research on the role of phonetic and prosodic features in conversation and their social and interactional consequences for intercultural communication.

On the border between the tasks of turn-taking and activity constitution, the next contributions by Frank Müller and John Local look at conversational objects used to signal different kinds of recipiency: acknowledgement tokens and news receipts. **Frank Müller** ('Affiliating and disaffiliating with continuers: prosodic aspects of recipiency') compares two extracts from Italian radio talk: one in which acknowledgement tokens are used to signal affiliation and another in which they signal disaffiliation. Müller shows that the interpretation of acknowledgement tokens is sensitive both to the token's sequential placement and to its intonational and rhythmic fit with respect to the acknowledgeable. Affiliating tokens, he finds, are more specifically 'in tune' with the talk they acknowledge, whereas disaffiliating ones display little differentiation. They are 'minimal' in the prosodic sense that they show no specific fit to their environment. This means that the signalling of affiliation or disaffiliation via acknowledgement tokens is a highly context-sensitive process, a contingent achievement which involves monitoring the fine details of speech production for possible sequential and prosodic cues. Müller's chapter shows that even as 'mere' recipients of ongoing talk, conversationalists use prosodic resources distinctively and actively in making particular instances of interaction mutual accomplishments.

John Local ('Conversational phonetics: some aspects of news receipts in everyday talk') is concerned with the detailed phonetic analysis of the 'change-of-state' particle *oh*. Using conversation analytic and phonetic techniques, Local shows that this token, which is encountered in a variety of phonetic and prosodic forms and at different locations in conversational talk, can have quite different interactional meanings. He explicitly warns against simplistic intuitive interpretations as found, for instance, in the intonational literature, and against assigning 'meaning' directly to pitch contours. Local argues that the phonetic and prosodic details of conversation can only be made sense of by being situated in an interactional framework where analytic categories are justified by the interactional behaviour of the participants themselves.

The contributions which follow all employ in one way or another a methodology similar to Local's: lexically, syntactically, and in some cases sequentially similar utterances are compared with one another and particular clusterings of prosodic features are shown to distinguish different activity types among them. **Margret Selting** ('Prosody as an activity-type distinctive cue in conversation: the case of so-called "astonished" questions in repair initiation') compares other-initiations of self-repair in German which are identical or similar with respect to linguistic structure and wording but differ in prosody. Prosodically unmarked (inconspicuous) initiations of repair are heard as 'normal', 'non-astonished' initiations, making a recipient's 'normal' self-repair conditionally relevant. Prosodically marked (conspicuous and noticeable) initiations, however, those which display features such as higher global pitch plus greater global loudness and/or louder or higher accent peaks than in surrounding turns, are heard as 'astonished' or 'surprised' initiations of repair. These have quite different sequential implications from their unmarked counterparts: in addition to the problem, the 'astonishment' overtone must be oriented to by the recipient. Selting's paper shows that differential prosody in co-occurrence with the linguistic structure and wording of a sequentially organized activity can signal different activity types and that these make different responses in the next turn relevant. Prosody must therefore be incorporated into descriptions of repair, as it differentiates types of problem-handling *within* repair sequences.

A contrast between prosodically unmarked and marked versions of utterances which are syntactically similar to one another is also the subject of the next chapter. **Susanne Günthner** ('The prosodic contextualization of moral work: an analysis of reproaches in "why"-formats') looks at reproaches in German which are formulated as why-questions. In contrast to 'real' why-questions, in which the questioner is genuinely asking for information, why-questions that are used to contextualize reproaches are, like the 'astonished' questions analysed by Selting, prosodically marked:

they may display a number of features including falling terminal pitch, global increase of loudness, extreme rising–falling or falling–rising pitch movements, falling glides on lengthened syllables, narrow or 'verum' (truth-assertive) focus, staccato accentuation and an increase in tempo. Here too, marked prosody is used in co-occurrence with syntactic, lexico-semantic and rhetorical devices to direct the recipient's attention to a display of affect. An emotive overtone is added to the wording of the utterance which, in the appropriate sequential context, cues the situated interpretation of the utterance as a reproach. Günthner argues that a prosodically contextualized 'reproachful tone' is a highly subtle device due to the inexplicitness, indirectness, reduced referentiality and accountability of prosodic cues. This enables participants to negotiate and exploit a buffer zone for the handling of the reproach in subsequent talk.

Susanne Uhmann ('On rhythm in everyday German conversation: beat clashes in assessment utterances'), drawing in part on the same data as Peter Auer, reconstructs the prosodically marked structure of dense accentuation phonologically as 'achieved beat clashes'. These regularly occur in assessment utterances within stories or in news-informings, but not in assessment pairs (first or second assessments in assessment sequences). Uhmann establishes that the accentuation pattern of so-called elative compounds in German, where one element intensifies the other, serves as a blueprint for the contextualization of 'intensity' or 'emphasis' with a beat clash. She accounts for the distribution of beat clashes in her data as follows: in assessment pairs, the use of beat clashes is too risky, since it systematically increases the risk of receiving a non-preferred, i.e. down-grading, second. Recipients are presumably reluctant to 'outdo' an utterance which is already so emphatic; their second could easily become too strong. In story-telling or news-informing, however, the expressiveness of beat-clashing first assessments is a good packaging device: it provides for the identification of the climax of the story and a display of affect by the speaker, which makes a second assessment from the recipient displaying his or her own emotional involvement relevant.

Verbatim repetitions of a prior turn are the object of study for both Elizabeth Couper-Kuhlen and Clare Tarplee. Their chapters show that the specific prosodic make-up of repetitions makes them do very different interactional work. Elizabeth Couper-Kuhlen ('The prosody of repetition: on quoting and mimicry') examines cases of verbal repetition accompanied by varying degrees of prosodic repetition in a Radio Manchester phone-in programme organized around guessing a riddle. She shows that participants can 'repeat' a prior speaker's pitch register in two ways, relatively with respect to their own voice range or absolutely. The former technique – relative register repetition – is routinely used by the moderator in the data examined when repeating a caller's guess, ostensibly in order to elicit confirmation of the guess from the caller. The latter technique, however – absolute register repetition – is also occasionally encountered. In these cases the moderator is heard to be mimicking the caller, collusively passing comment on some aspect of the caller's guess or manner of speaking. However, mimicry is not exclusively dependent on absolute register repetition as a contextualization cue. Couper-Kuhlen argues that natural voice range and the nature of the critical comment influence how participants cue mimicry prosodically.

Clare Tarplee ('Working on young children's utterances: prosodic aspects of repetition during picture labelling') deals with the familiar situation of young children looking at picture books with their caretakers. Typically the child is expected to label the picture and thus exhibit lexical and articulatory proficiency. Tarplee shows that in such sequences prosody plays an important role. The child's first label is routinely followed by an adult repetition: the repetition may either be affirmatory and close the sequence or instead make a new attempt by the child at labelling the picture relevant. Yet in order for affirmation or correction and re-elicitation to be recognizable by the child, prosody – in particular the intonation and timing of the adult's repeat – is decisive. Only if a repeat is given prosodic contrastivity and/or is withheld until after a gap does the child treat it as a prompt to self-correct or try again. If the adult's repetition – irrespective of the actual degree of articulatory similarity between it and the original – is given without delay and/or the prosodic differences are minimized, the adult version is treated as affirmatory repetition and it closes down the sequence. Tarplee's paper shows that even very young children orient to the prosody of utterances in similar sequential positions as being decisive for interpretation and the projection of an appropriate response.

Marjorie Harness Goodwin ('Informings and announcements in their environment: prosody within a multi-activity work setting') moves into the realm of interaction in a work setting, where communication is largely, though not exclusively, determined by the exigencies of the work process. Goodwin analyses talk in the Flight Operations room of a large airport. In this setting, a variety of different persons, often seated back-to-back at their desks, perform a variety of different tasks simultaneously, producing a 'sonic soup' background noise. Nevertheless, in the initiation of work activity-chains, different kinds of information must be unambiguously transferred, namely *informings* from the Flight Tracker to the Ramp Planner within the Operations room, and subsequent *announcements* by the Ramp Planner in the Operations room to the Ramp crew (in order to prompt the unloading of baggage for incoming planes). To overtone the noisy background of the Operations room and (i) select a particular addressee for the informing, or (ii) ratify a prior informing and make an announcement recognizable as such, prosody, and in particular intonation, is crucial. For each activity, a distinctive chant-like intonation contour is used. Intonation is thus shown to be an important device for cueing specific kinds of work-related activity in this setting. Although Goodwin's data are not 'conversational' in the narrow sense, they nevertheless provide a good example of how prosody is deployed strategically in the organization of routine activity. This deployment has its counterpart in the stylized 'call' intonations of everyday informal interaction.

The aim of the contributions to this volume is to clarify the role of prosody in conversational interaction. As this is a new research area, it is only natural that each author has tried to come to terms with the data in his or her own way. Although the theoretical assumptions and analytic goals of contributors have proved to be uniform enough to warrant this collection of papers, no attempt has been made to achieve uniformity in prosodic representation. Until the basic categories relevant to a prosody-for-conversation are agreed upon, it seems futile to expect notational standardization. The widely diverging prosodic representations encountered here are thus a witness to the varied, if not variegated, past of prosodic research and to the exploratory nature of the present endeavour. We trust that time and future work will lead to greater consensus, at least in representational matters.

Margret Selting   Potsdam
Elizabeth Couper-Kuhlen   Konstanz

Towards an interactional perspective on prosody and a prosodic perspective on interaction

ELIZABETH COUPER-KUHLEN
AND MARGRET SELTING

1 Introduction

If prosody is understood to comprise the 'musical' attributes of speech[1] – auditory effects such as melody, dynamics, rhythm, tempo and pause – then it is surely no exaggeration to state that a large part of this field has been left untilled by modern structural linguistics.[2] Only a few scholars at the most have considered prosody, intonation in particular, worthy of their attention. Moreover, when they have done so, it has been primarily in structuralist terms. Speech melodies and rhythms have been pursued as a part of language competence, analysed in minimal pairs as if they were phoneme- or morpheme-like entities with distinctive functions. More socially oriented approaches to the study of language, by contrast, have openly acknowledged the importance of prosodic phenomena in language-in-use but have not put their words into practice or have done so in an intuitive, pre-theoretical way which does not reflect the state of current prosodic research. In this chapter we shall argue that bringing together these two fields of inquiry, speech prosody and language-in-use, and allowing them to cross-fertilize will help to overcome a number of the weaknesses which have become apparent in the current praxis of each.

In retrospect, it is doubtless the overwhelming influence of literacy on thinking about language which has been responsible for the neglect of prosody.[3] Language, perhaps unconsciously, has been equated with 'prose', those linguistic forms put down in writing and intended to be read. Given that prosodic phenomena (i) are not segment-based, referential units, (ii) are gradient rather than

discrete, and (iii) lack systematic codification in writing, it is perhaps not surprising that they are so often ignored.[4] Without such
features, prosody becomes one of those aspects of language which,
in Silverstein's words, are at the 'limits of awareness' (1976). To be
sure, there have been extenuating circumstances: in the early part of
this century, when the structuralist model was being developed,
spoken language – and with it, prosody – was difficult to
'capture' and make permanent for the purpose of scientific
enquiry.[5] However, with the advent of the tape recorder and,
more recently, the video camera, the stipulation of permanency
can now be met. Auditory and video records are easily obtainable
of events in which the spoken language is used. Too many linguists,
however, still persist in approaching these 'speech events' as if, like
Molière's *bourgeois gentilhomme*, the interlocutors were speaking
prose.

David Abercrombie once wrote that 'what in fact linguistics has
concerned itself with, up to now, has almost exclusively been –
spoken prose' (1965:4).[6] Yet, he points out, spoken prose is an
entirely different mode of language use compared, for instance, to
conversation – in particular with respect to intonation:

if you are reading aloud a piece of written prose, you infer from the text
what intonations you ought to use, even if, as is almost always the case, you
have a choice. The intonation, in other words, adds little information. But if
you try to read aloud a piece of written conversation, you can't tell what the
intonations should be – or rather what they actually were. Here the intonations contribute more independently to the meaning.   (1965:6)

Abercrombie claims that spoken prose has more highly standardized intonation patterns, more evenness of tempo and its pauses
are more closely related to grammatical structure. Thus, he concludes, a prose-based approach to intonation is of little use for
the analysis of conversation.[7] Yet 'spoken prose' is still an apt
characterization of what many modern studies of intonation and
prosody end up examining.[8]

The study of conversation *sui generis* has nonetheless made considerable progress since Abercrombie wrote, above all due to the
efforts of a small group of American sociologists centred around
Harvey Sacks. For Sacks conversation was simply one locus where
social order could be discovered:

conversation analysis . . . seeks to describe methods persons use in doing social life. It is our claim that, although the range of activities this domain describes may be as yet unknown, the mode of description, the way it is cast, is intrinsically stable. (1984:25)

Sacks and his co-workers advocate a special 'analytic mentality' for the discovery of social order in conversation. In their work they emphasize (i) the importance of investigating naturally occurring data, (ii) a view of social interaction as an ongoing, sequentially organized and collaboratively achieved process, and (iii) the necessity for justifying one's analyses by showing the relevance of the categories postulated to the participants themselves. Conversation analysts have called attention to a whole host of phenomena which are often ignored in the study of discourse: hesitation particles, sound stretching, cut-offs, in-breaths, laughter, (micro-)pausing, stressing and intonation. Nominally then, prosody has fared much better in this approach to the study of language as a social phenomenon. Yet, although prosodic events are recorded in the transcripts of interaction, they rarely figure – with the possible exception of pause – in the analyses which conversation analysts have so far offered.

One notable exception to the skirting of prosody by social scientists is to be found in the work of Gumperz (1982, 1992).[9] Gumperz has claimed that participants in verbal interaction employ 'empirically detectable signs' which *cue* conversational interpretation by evoking interpretative schemata or frames. Members of a speech community, he argues, consciously or unconsciously appeal to these frames in drawing inferences about what is being said in interaction or more generally about what is 'going on'. The process whereby participants 'construct' context via such cues in order to make utterances interpretable has come to be known as *contextualization* (see also Auer and di Luzio 1992). Foremost among the means which speakers use to contextualize language are prosodic features; others include code-switching and non-verbal elements such as body position, gesture and gaze (Auer 1992). Gumperz (1992) argues that contextualization cues affect interactants' inferencing at three levels of generalization: (i) conversational management, e.g. in turn-taking and signalling degrees of informational relevance; (ii) sequencing, e.g. in cueing implicatures and disambiguating speaker intent in utterances; (iii) framing, i.e. in generating expectations about the nature of the interaction and in keying its mood or atmosphere.

The interactional approach to prosody which we advocate here is in effect inspired by the theoretical insights of contextualization theory coupled with the methodological procedures of conversation analysis. However, before filling in the details, we shall discuss some of the problems, as we see them, in the field of prosodic and especially intonation research as currently practised (§2). We shall then outline an interactional perspective, showing how it can resolve some of these difficulties (§3). In the last section of the chapter (§4), we shall argue that not only does prosodic analysis stand to gain from an interactional perspective but that a proper consideration of prosody will also enrich conversational research.

2 Current problems in prosodic research

There are three central questions which lack satisfactory answers in traditional prosodic work. They concern formal, functional and methodological issues respectively.

2.1 Prosodic categories: phonetic or phonological?

Much of prosodic, and especially intonation, research has centred around the concept of the *tone group* or *tone unit*.[10] (We shall use these terms interchangeably.) In this tradition a tone group is defined as a phonological unit which has *one* prominent pitch movement beginning on an accented syllable and optionally extending over any following unaccented syllables.[11] This accented syllable is called the *tonic syllable* or the *nucleus* of the tone group or unit; the pitch movement selected here is known as a *tone* or *nuclear tone*. When there are several accented syllables in a unit, the nucleus is typically the last, most prominent one. The boundaries between phonological tone units are said to be expounded by phonetic cues such as a pause, final syllable lengthening, a rhythmic break and/or a pitch upstep or downstep in unstressed syllables. More recent prosodic models (e.g. Pierrehumbert 1980, Selkirk 1984, Nespor and Vogel 1986) share many of these premises but call the tone group an *intonational phrase* and refer to the pitch movements on prominent syllables as *pitch accents*. Despite acknowledged prob-

lems in delimiting tone groups and identifying tone-group boundaries (see Brown, Currie and Kenworthy 1980), much recent
research has addressed questions concerning the identification and
description of nuclei and their functional interpretation (e.g. Brazil,
Coulthard and Johns 1980, Ladd 1980, Gussenhoven 1983; for
overviews see Couper-Kuhlen 1986, Cruttenden 1986).

The traditional tonetic approach runs into trouble, however,
when phonetic and phonological criteria conflict in the identification of tone groups. For although phonetically oriented prosodists
have tried hard to narrow the gap between phonology and phonetics, the tone group remains a phonological unit which is not
necessarily delineated by phonetic boundary cues. Even though
there may be no phonetic evidence of a tone-unit boundary, the
analysis of a prominent syllable carrying one of the nuclear tones
forces the postulation of a boundary. Similarly, the presence of
several nuclear tones in succession usually imposes a tone-unit
boundary between them,[12] although there may be no phonetic
cues signalling it (see also Selting 1993). In cases like these intonologists will tend to fall back on syntax when pressed to locate the
boundary. For instance, assuming pitch accents on *Wales* and
Cardiff in the sentence under (1), the boundary is likely to be
drawn between *Wales* and *is* rather than between *is* and *visiting*
or between *visiting* and *Cardiff*, on syntactic grounds:

(1)   The Prince of Wáles // is visiting Càrdiff tomorrow

(Cruttenden 1986:38)

Yet such a procedure shows greater affinity with the analysis of a
syntactic entity 'S' into units of constituent structure than with
'integral melodic patterns' (Bolinger 1978:474) which are used for
communicative and interactional purposes.

If 'zero' realization of tone-unit boundaries creates a problem for
intonational phonology, so pauses and hesitation render the phonetics of tone-unit analysis difficult. Consider, for instance, the
utterance recorded in Figure 1.1 from a San Francisco radio
phone-in programme during the war in the Persian Gulf.
Applying the phonetic criteria for tone-unit delimitation mentioned
above, we obtain relatively clear boundaries following *down, I did,
today* and *upsets me*.[13] Yet should *and uh*, clearly separated from
following talk by a rhythmic break and a pause, be considered part

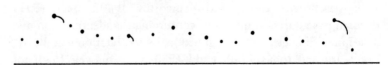

it was real:ly nice to go down: and be with people who felt the same way that I did (0.4)

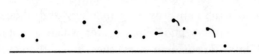

and uh (0.4) what I'm seeing today: really upsets me hhh

(Small dots represent unstressed syllables, large dots represent stressed syllables with no audible pitch movement, tadpole-like tails represent pitch glides.)

Figure 1.1

of the tone group *what I'm seeing today*? If not, is it a tone group of its own with, say, a level nucleus on *and*? Similar problems arise when speakers lengthen a pre-pausal segment as a holding device and then resume the pitch and loudness of this segment after the pause. Should these segments be thought of as belonging to two separate tone units although the speaker clearly signals the continuation of one melodically cohesive unit?

The conflict between phonetic and phonological criteria in tone-group analysis can be avoided if prosodic phrasing units are identified in an interactional perspective. To see this, let us draw a parallel with lexico-syntactic structure in language. The units of traditional linguistic analysis are grammatical entities such as sentence, clause, phrase, word. Yet taking a discourse perspective on language, we speak of 'acts' or 'moves' whose basic units are *utterances*. These are units which derive their specific characteristics from their occurrence in turns. By analogy, the basic *prosodic phrase* in speech, when viewed interactively, is likely to be *not* the prosodic counterpart of a grammatical sentence or clause, but rather a unit defined with respect to the utterance as a turn-constructional unit, a 'phonetic chunk' which speakers use to constitute and articulate turns-at-talk. Utterances are subject to constraints which derive from properties inherent in interaction: the exchange of (and competition for) turns-at-talk, changing deixis, emergent and negotiable meaning.[14] The same sorts of constraint are likely to apply to the basic prosodic phrase in verbal interaction. That is, its shape will derive from the interactive need of participants to project turn completion. It will be sensitive to interactive requirements such as recipient design and local fit. And it will be subject to repair. Ultimately, interactionally grounded categories for prosodic and intonational analysis may correspond only loosely – or not at all – to traditional tonetic categories.[15]

2.2 Prosodic function: distinctive or not?

Henry Sweet, one of the pioneers of modern phonetics, claimed as early as 1877, that, in intonation languages like English, *intonations* or *tones* such as *level, rising, falling, compound rising* and *compound falling*, are functionally *sentence-tones*: 'In all these cases the tones . . . modify the general meaning of the whole sentence' (1877:95). Elsewhere, the sentence-tones are explicitly linked to sentence-types: 'The interesting question now arises, how do such languages express these general ideas (interrogation, affirmation, etc.), which it is the function of the English tones to express?' (*Collected Papers of Henry Sweet*, cited in Henderson 1971:179). Thus, in one of the oldest traditions of British prosodic analysis, the tone group is thought of as corresponding to the grammatical unit of sentence and the primary tones, fall vs rise, as corresponding to the grammatical sentence-types 'affirmative' (*statement*) vs 'interrogative' (*question*).

The grammatical approach to intonation reaches its apex in Armstrong and Ward (1926), where the melodies of English sentences are reduced to two (Fig. 1.2). Tune I (with final falling pitch) is said to be used in 'ordinary' statements, in questions requiring an answer other than 'yes' or 'no', in commands and in exclamations (1926:8ff.), while Tune II (with final rising pitch) is said to be called for in 'indefinite' statements, questions requiring the answer 'yes' or 'no' and requests (1926:19ff.).[16] The procedure in this and other grammar-based approaches to intonation is thus to associate tunes with different grammatical sentence-types and to treat excep-

Tune I   Tune II

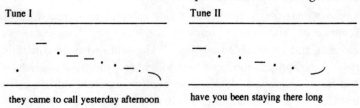

they came to call yesterday afternoon   have you been staying there long

Figure 1.2

tions as conveying attitudinal modifications such as 'indifferent',
'polite', 'surprised', etc.

Some intonologists have preferred to segment melodic tunes like
those Armstrong and Ward identify into their component parts, a
procedure inspired by phonemic analysis. Here the pitch of each of
the small constituent parts of a melodic whole is said to create a
distinctive meaning opposition. Pike (1945), for instance, postulates
four pitch phonemes for English intonation: extra-high (1), high (2),
mid (3) and low (4), which articulate the intonation contour
(1945:26). The following minimal pairs illustrate:

(2) (A raised degree mark precedes the first stressed syllable of the
     contour.)
  a He's gone
     3-   °2-4
  b He's gone
     3-   °2-3
  c He's gone
     3-   °1-4
  d He's gone
     3-   °3-4

In terminal position a falling contour to pitch level 4 as in (a) is
claimed to have the meaning of finality, whereas one which falls to
pitch level 3 (b) is said to be incomplete and to suggest an addition
such as 'but he's coming back' (1945:45). A falling terminal contour from pitch level 1 (c) is claimed to be more intensely contrastive, often insistent, and may have an element of surprise, as
compared to a falling terminal contour from level 3 (d), which is
said to be much milder and detached (1945:47f.).

Halliday (1967, 1970) is also at pains to demonstrate the distinctiveness of intonational features, although he does not 'segment' intonation to quite the extreme of the American structuralists. He argues, for instance, that presence or absence of a tone-group boundary will change a sentence with one 'information unit' as in (3a) below into a sentence with two 'information units' as in (3b):[17]

(3) a   // he washed and brushed his hair//
    b   // he washed // and brushed his hair//

(adapted from Halliday 1967:36)

Furthermore, according to Halliday, the variable location of tonic prominence will result in different 'information foci', as in:[18]

(4) a   // I saw him//
    b   // I saw him//

(adapted from Halliday 1967:38)

Finally, he states that the substitution of, for instance, rising for falling pitch on a tonic syllable will change a statement as in (5a) into a question (5b):

(5) a   //John hàs//
    b   //John hás//

(adapted from Halliday 1967:41)

The claim is that because such choices are systematically and distinctively related to meaning, intonation is *grammatical* in function. However, as any linguist who has looked seriously at naturally occurring data will know, the problem is that intonational patterns – in contrast to morphemes, with which they have been compared – do not always carry this kind of functional load in language use; in fact they do so so rarely that to treat them as 'intonemes' is arguably rather meaningless.

Two specific difficulties compound the problem of identifying intonational functions based on distinctive oppositions. First, *co-varying lexico-syntax*: with very few exceptions, it is hard to prove distinctive function for intonational features because it is nearly impossible to control all variables but one and still have plausible examples. This is why O'Connor and Arnold (1973), for instance, must match their prototypical tone groups with different (non-overlapping) sets of sentences. Compare, for example:

(6)   THE SWITCHBACK (unemphatic)
      You can ˇtry.

(7)   THE JACKKNIFE (unemphatic)
      It's riˇʼdiculous.

                          (adapted from O'Connor and Arnold 1973:42)

When the Switchback is now glossed as 'grudgingly admitting'
(170) and the Jackknife as 'censorious' (214), O'Connor and
Arnold are left open to the criticism that it is the lexico-syntactic
content, and not the intonation, of their sentence+tone-group combinations which invites each interpretation. If lexical content co-
varies with intonational tune, then in strict structuralist terms, minimal pairs are not possible and no distinctive function can be established.

   Second, *iconicity of intonation*: this difficulty can be put in a
nutshell by Bolinger's observation that 'intonation has more in
common with gesture than with grammar' (1986:xiii). Although
an elaborate argument can be constructed to show that a gesture
which originates iconically (i.e. is non-arbitrary) can nevertheless
become part of a structural system used conventionally, the fact is
that intonational iconicity is not just rudimentary and overlaid by
other structurally organized features. It is quite ubiquitous and
therefore constantly in danger of 'interfering' with rigorous structuralist demonstration. Consider, for instance, the following
O'Connor and Arnold examples:

(8)   *(It's six o'clock)* ↑Hèavens!

(9)   *(You've passed your exam)* What wonderful ↑nèws!
                          (adapted from O'Connor and Arnold 1973:57, 75)

In cases like these, the high and widely falling tone (represented here
as ↑ˋ) is said to convey an emotive element of *surprise*. Yet what is
the structural value of high pitch and wide pitch movement as
conveyors of surprise when the level of physiological arousal associated with this state quasi-automatically produces a sudden fluc-
tuation in vocal-fold vibration, and consequently in pitch?

   In sum, there appears to be, on the one hand, little or no con-
stancy between intonational form and meaning: in the worse case,
the same tune 'means' something different with each different

lexico-syntactic carrier. On the other hand, there is no final proof, on a more general level, that pitch ultimately functions by way of nurture (cultural convention) and not by way of nature.[19] As long as intonologists pursue a grammar-based, structuralistic approach, there is little hope of solving such problems.

An interactional perspective, however, offers a way out. Here intonation is linked up to functions which derive from the situated use of language to accomplish interactional goals. Placed in its context of use, language 'means', i.e. suggests interpretations, through a complex interaction of verbal forms with contextual and situational factors. Arguably, the discourse functions of intonation are more likely to relate to this kind of *pragmatic* 'meaning' (situated, inference-based interpretation) rather than to the semantic meanings of decontextualized linguistic forms.[20] In an interactional perspective, analysts are consequently not looking for minimal pairs and distinctive functions. Instead they typically find that intonation and prosody have a *contextualizing* function (Gumperz 1982, Auer 1986, Auer and di Luzio 1992). This means that they cue frames for the situated interpretation of utterances. In other words, they constitute *how* something is said, not what is said, and they ultimately influence only what participants *infer* is the meaning. Prosodic contextualization cues are not referential, but indexical, signs (Silverstein 1992). They stand in a reflexive relationship to language, cueing the context within which it is to be interpreted and at the same time constituting that context. Their iconicity facilitates (rather than interfering with) this function (see Auer 1992). In this sense, the 'problems' referred to above (covarying lexico-syntax, iconicity) are not problems at all for intonational function in an interactional perspective; they are rather merely reflections of the nature of this function.

2.3 Prosodic methodology: what data? what proof?

'Discourse' intonologists have been somewhat more successful in avoiding the lexico-syntactic trap described above. Brazil (1981, 1982), for instance, postulates two distinctive tones for English discourse, a 'Referring' tone, which falls and then rises, and a 'Proclaiming' tone, which simply falls. Compare, for example:

(10) a when I've finished VMIDDlemarch // I shall read Adam \BEde //
     b when I've finished \MIDDlemarch // I shall read Adam VBEde //
                       (Brazil, Coulthard and Johns 1980:13)

The falling–rising tone in both these examples is said to *refer* (r) to a piece of information as part of the common ground, the falling tone, to *proclaim* (p) a piece of information as new. In addition, three 'keys' are postulated – High, Mid and Low – which apply to the tones and describe their relative pitch height within the speaker's voice range. Compare:

(11)
   high   eventually
a *mid // r*   // p we gave it our neighbours // p
   low   the Robinsons//

   high   eventually   Robinsons//
b *mid // r*   // p we gave it our neighbours // p the
   low
                       (Brazil, Coulthard and Johns 1980:30)

Low key as in (11a) is said to mark an *equivalence* relation between items in successive tone groups, i.e. here between *neighbours* and *Robinsons*. High key (11b) marks a *contrast* between two items.[21] Thus, both tone and key are claimed to be responsible for (minimally) distinctive oppositions in English discourse. However, the crucial point here is that they cannot be predicted from lexico-syntax: 'Tone choice, we have argued, is not dependent on linguistic features of the message, but rather on the speaker's assessment of the relationship between the message and the audience' (Brazil, Coulthard and Johns 1980:18). The model employed by Brazil, Coulthard and Johns thus has the salutary effect of uncoupling intonation from lexico-syntax. Once intonation is seen as a quasi-independent signalling system, it becomes a powerful means of creating interactional meaning, in alignment or non-alignment with verbal forms.

Yet the analytic interpretations which this model offers have a methodological weakness: they are warranted only by the analyst's own intuitions (see also Local, Kelly and Wells 1986). Although Brazil's theory is based on data from classroom interaction, we are given no independent evidence that interactants do indeed interpret, for instance, low key as marking an equivalence relation and

high key as marking a contrastive one. Instead, Brazil, Coulthard
and Johns seem to rely on our implicit recognition of the validity of
these claims. Yet without some proof of speakers' 'indigenous'
interpretations, the analyst risks assigning interpretative labels
'from without', labels which may lack cross-contextual and cross-
linguistic validity.

The same criticism can be levelled at Bolinger (1986, 1989), who
has also stressed the independence of intonation as a signalling
system. Rather than seeing the major thrust of intonational meaning
in relation to information, as do Brazil, Coulthard and Johns,
Bolinger emphasizes its emotional contribution: 'Intonation is part
of a gestural complex whose primitive and still surviving function is
the signaling of emotion' (1986:195). The intonational system is in
principle independent of lexico-syntax: 'even when it interacts with
such highly conventionalized areas as morphology and syntax, intonation manages to do what it does by continuing to be what it is,
primarily a symptom of how we feel about what we say, or how we
feel *when* we say' (1989:1).

Bolinger's 'primary profiles' – A, a relatively high pitch on an
accented syllable followed by a jump down, and B, a pitch jump
up to or up from an accented syllable – have abstract meanings that
ultimately derive from the metaphors of falling or 'down' vs rising
or 'up'. In context they take on more specific meaning by under-
going metaphorical transformations. For instance, 'down' may
come to mean termination or demarcation for separate importance.
'Up' extends to meanings of incompletion and 'keyed-upness'
(1986:341).

Yet here too we are given no evidence that actual participants in
verbal interaction do indeed orient to 'down' as being associated
with rest and relaxation and 'up' as being associated with tenseness
and effort. As intuitively pleasing as Bolinger's interpretations may
be, the final proof has yet to come that they are relevant in this way
to interactants in real conversations. Moreover, the data upon
which Bolinger's analysis is based are for the most part constructed
by himself. While there can be little objection to the sporadic use of
artificial examples for the purpose of argumentation, to build one's
intonational theory on the basis of these alone is rather risky. As
those who have worked with genuine data will know, reality often
bears more surprises than fiction. From an interactional perspective,

only genuine real-time communication can provide context-rich data. As we shall demonstrate below, it is participants' own handling of prosodic cues within this context that enables empirical proof procedures for the validation of analytic categories. In other words, the theory relies crucially on the way prosody is deployed in real interaction.

3 Prosody in an interactional perspective

Our argument so far has been that problems of the sort sketched above have prevented a breakthrough in the study of prosody in discourse and that they can be avoided by adopting a different perspective, one we have provisionally dubbed *interactional*. Methodologically, this perspective is inspired by the practices of conversation analysis, a sociologically grounded approach to verbal interaction which developed from the application of ethnomethodological principles (Garfinkel 1963, 1967) to the analysis of everyday conversation.[22] One of the fundamental assumptions of conversation analysis (henceforth CA) is that verbal interaction is structurally organized and that traces of this organization can be found in the interaction itself. Consequently, as Heritage puts it, 'no order of detail can be dismissed, *a priori*, as disorderly, accidental or irrelevant' (1984:241). In fact, CA studies have revealed conversational interaction to be a surprisingly orderly accomplishment, brought about by speakers who rely for its management on the local use of context-free and context-sensitive organizational systems such as turn-taking and repair.

One of the characteristics of CA work is its strictly empirical stance: hypotheses are generated from close analysis of audio- or video-recorded, naturally occurring, conversation. Like ethnomethodologists, conversation analysts attempt to reconstruct social (conversational) interaction as the collaborative endeavour of 'members' (the participants of a culture, group or other social category). They seek to describe and systematically account for the practical methods which members employ in the production and interpretation of conversational activity. These methods are viewed as means or devices designed to resolve specific interactional tasks (Levinson 1983:319). Yet the idea is not to describe conversational sequences in terms of well-formedness but to reconstruct the unmarked expectations which underlie interlocutors' inferential processes. Deviations from expected sequences may also systematically steer inferences: 'Conversationalists are . . . not so much constrained by rules or sanctions, as caught in a web of inferences' (Levinson 1983:312).

The point that we wish to make here is that prosody can be seen as one of the orderly 'details' of interaction, a resource which interlocutors rely on to accomplish social action and as a means of steering inferential processes. Prosodic features, we suggest, can be reconstructed as *members' devices*, designed for the organization and management of talk in social interaction. They can be shown to function as part of a signalling system which – together with syntax, lexico-semantics, kinesics and other contextualization cues – is used to construct and interpret turn-constructional units and turns-at-talk (Selting 1992a, 1995). Viewed as a member's device, prosody is amenable to CA methodology. That is, some of the same techniques which have been used to expose the orderliness of conversational organization can be applied to the analysis of prosody in conversation. In the following we shall show how a selection of conversation-analytic research 'maxims' can be adapted to prosodic research.

3.1 Give priority to the analysis of naturally occurring talk

CA's rigorously empirical stance for the study of conversation transfers quite naturally to prosodic investigation. Close inspection of prosody in large quantities of everyday conversational data should make it possible to reconstruct members' prosodic devices for achieving their conversational goals. Ethnomethodological experiments of course need not be ruled out.[23] Conceivably, the controlled use of 'deviant' prosodic features by well-trained speakers in everyday conversational encounters can help to generate working hypotheses. Additional insight into members' common-sense reasoning about prosody can be gained from interviews with experimental subjects.[24]

3.2 Treat the data as an integral part of the context in which it occurs

Conversation analysts have emphasized that speaker's utterances in interaction are context-sensitive, i.e. that they are especially constructed to fit the particular location and occasion of their use. Transferred to the study of prosody, context-sensitivity means recognizing that prosodic features may be selected with regard to the particular verbal forms which 'carry' them. The prosody associated with a given interactive function, for instance, may be sensitive to whether the accompanying syntax is complete or not (Selting 1995; Auer, this volume). Or it may be sensitive to whether the carrier is a syntactic adjunct ('post-completer') (Local, Kelly and Wells 1986: 423).

Viewing prosody context-sensitively also means paying attention to the fact that its carrier is a turn at talk (or part of one) which itself has a sequential location. Just as Schegloff states that a syntax-for-conversation must 'recognize that its sentences will be in turns and will be subject to the organization of turns and their exigencies' (1979a:281), so a prosody-for-conversation must recognize that its basic unit – whether expounded by intonational, rhythmic, pausal or dynamic means – co-occurs with, and will be interpreted in relation to, a turn-constructional unit. Similar to turn-constructional units, which may be situated parts of larger 'projects', prosodic units will be sensitive to their location in a series. And similar to turns, which occur in sequence, prosodic units can be expected to demonstrate sensitivity to their sequential location (cf. Müller, this volume). As Schegloff concludes for syntax: 'all the types and orders of organization that operate in and on turns in conversation can operate on the sentence' (1979a:282). Substituting 'basic prosodic unit' for 'sentence', the same applies to prosody: all the types and orders of organization that operate in and on turns in conversation can operate on the basic prosodic unit.

By way of illustration, consider prosody in the *decontextualized* English utterance in Figure 1.3. Considered out of sequential context, the combination of low and suppressed pitch range, low volume and relatively fast tempo plus a carrier which refers to an event as *upsetting* might evoke a functional interpretation of, say, 'repressed concern'. Nor is this interpretation necessarily wholly

low

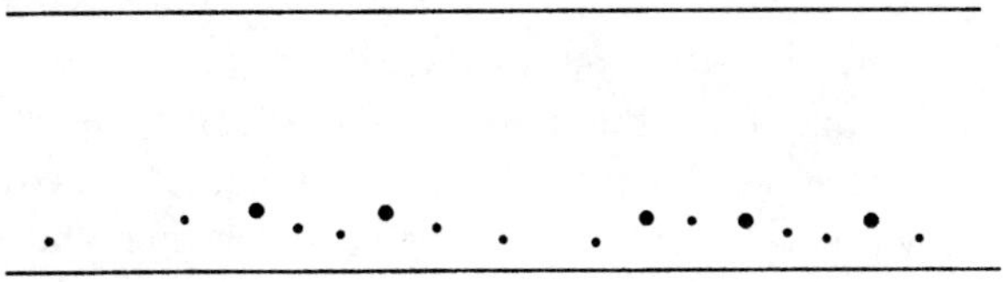

<uh (tʃi:) that guy I just listened (to)> that really really upsets me   <p, acc>

(Deviations from normal volume are marked in angled brackets as *ff, f, p* or *pp*; deviations from moderate tempo are indicated with *acc* or *dec*; *high* or *low* to the left of the interlinear transcription indicates that the whole intonational clef is at an extreme in the speaker's voice range.)

Figure 1.3

wrong. Yet considered in its actual sequential location, the prosody appears to be doing more:

(12) *A San Francisco radio phone-in programme during the Persian Gulf war; callers have been encouraged to make their opinions known and share their feelings about the war. There has just been an on-the-spot report from an anti-war demonstration, the reporter having described how he is momentarily boxed in by angry demonstrators and police-men about to use tear gas.*

   (This fragment is transcribed in conventional CA notation, with the addition of /;/ for terminal falling pitch ending at a mid level in the speaker's voice range.)

1   L: we continue to take calls=Debbie on the line from San Jose, you're on the Giant 68 KNBR. I'm Leo Laporte.
     D: hi Leo.
     L: hi Debbie.
→ 5 D: uhm.(0.3) uh [tʃi:] *that guy I just listened (to) that really really upsets me.*
     L: [°why°]
     D: [uhm;] (0.4) well the reason why I called; is I was uh (0.1) in San Jose, on Monday, downtown at the the uh (0.4)
10   demonstration that was going on then, and it (0.5) was such a different feeling; than from what I'm seeing these last two days. it was so peaceful, (0.4) uh (0.1) you know; people were down there to really support each other. (0.3) and wha(h)t I'm seeing now; I I think you know is just uh; (0.3) goes against what these people are trying to demonstrate for.

   From conversation analytic work on telephone calls (Schegloff and Sacks 1973, Schegloff 1979b), we know that one of the main concerns of a caller is placing some 'mentionable' in a way that it

will be recognized as the 'reason for the call'. In private telephone
conversations, it may be in the participant's interest to delay such
an announcement, especially if the reason is to request a favour. In
radio talk, however – as here – the constraints on time and topic
are such that callers can generally be expected to introduce the
reason for the call with few or no preliminaries.[25] Yet the first
complete utterance by the caller in (12) (lines 5f.), although it is
preceded by an *uhm* which begins high and loud as if to announce
an upcoming reason, is not hearable as the reason for the call.
Instead it comes across as an 'aside' directed to an aspect of the
hic et nunc of this telephone call: *that guy I just listened (to)* manifestly refers at this point in talk to the endangered on-the-spot
reporter. The fact that this comment is not the reason for
Debbie's call is made explicit in her next turn, where she verbally
labels the concern presented there as the reason for calling (lines
8ff.). Thus, retrospectively, the unit *that guy I just listened (to) that
really really upsets me* is confirmed as not being the reason for the
call.

Yet the 'aside' character of Debbie's turn in line 5 is not produced
only retrospectively. Debbie's turn bears in it prosodic cues signalling its subsidiary status: low pitch, soft dynamics and fast tempo.
This prosody stands in marked contrast to the high, loud and slow
prosody of subsequent utterances such as *it was such a different
feeling* (lines 10ff.) or *it was so peaceful* (line 12). The latter are
verbally labelled and treated as relevant and topical. Thus it stands
to reason that the markedly contrasting prosody in *that guy I just
listened (to)* is contextualizing its turn as less relevant and off-topic.
In addition to its emotional overtones, the prosody of Debbie's
utterance in lines 5f. can be thought of as a feature of the design
and fit of her turn in its particular context. As such, it has a substantial contribution to make to the situated interactional meaning
of talk.

3.3 Treat the data as emergent in the real time of ongoing interaction

In contrast to much text and discourse analysis, which tends to
regard spoken data *ex post factum* as a finished product or the
'behavioral realization of a preplanned cognitive unit' (Schegloff

1982:71), conversation analysts stress that discourse must be treated as being accomplished over time. In Schegloff's words: 'Good analysis retains a sense of the actual as an achievement from among possibilities: it retains a lively sense of the contingency of real things' (1982:89). The notion of emergence also transfers to prosody: just as a multi-unit turn is, in the default case, not produced as a monolithic, preconceived whole but grows incrementally

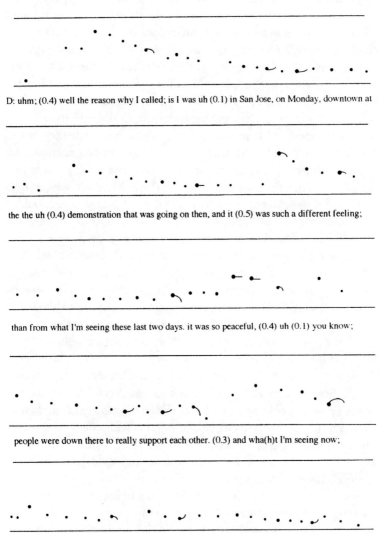

D: uhm; (0.4) well the reason why I called; is I was uh (0.1) in San Jose, on Monday, downtown at

the the uh (0.4) demonstration that was going on then, and it (0.5) was such a different feeling;

than from what I'm seeing these last two days. it was so peaceful, (0.4) uh (0.1) you know;

people were down there to really support each other. (0.3) and wha(h)t I'm seeing now;

I I think you know is just uh; (0.3) goes against what these people are trying to demonstrate for

Figure 1.4

and anew at each transition relevance place (TRP) as the result of an interactive achievement, so prosodic units carried by turns or turn-constructional units may emerge as a contingency of the moment-to-moment decisions speakers make to continue or not and, if so, *how* to continue.

By way of illustration, consider Debbie's multi-unit turn in (12), reproduced here in full with prosodic notation (see Fig. 1.4).

If we are to regard this turn as emergent discourse, then we must think of it as an incremental product achieved by both participants collaboratively. This means realizing that at each and every TRP which arises, Leo has the opportunity to take over the floor himself. When he passes up this option, Debbie's continuation is as much a product of Leo's pass as of her own speaking plan. Assuming, hypothetically, that TRPs in this variety of English are signalled by a combination of complete syntactic structure (whether word, phrase or clause) and semantic (topical) unit, in conjunction with a fall-to-low pitch and an isochronous rhythmic pattern,[26] the first place at which a floor switch could occur would be following *people were down there to really support each other.*[27] At this point, Debbie has completed an idea: she has established a contrast between the demonstration in San Jose and the deictically given one in San Francisco, between the *then* of the former and *these last two days* of the latter, between the *so peaceful* nature of the former and the deictically implied nature of the latter. As the pause after *support each other* indicates, Debbie *stops* at this point, long enough to allow Leo time to come in.[28] However, Leo does not take up the option, where-upon the floor reverts to Debbie. Debbie now has the option to take over the floor again or to pass it back to Leo. If she does the latter, a lapse would presumably result, since Leo has just indicated no desire for the floor himself. Debbie continues instead. Yet her 'continuation' is not a prosodic continuation (Local 1992): there is a break in rhythm between the regular beats on *really*, *support* and *other* and the next stress on *what*. There is also a declination reset, a shift up to a high onset on *what*, from which subsequent stresses descend anew.[29] Debbie thus designs the prosody of her turn to contextualize it as a new contribution to talk (not a continuation of her former turn), and in doing so she retrospectively displays that the prior stretch of talk was complete. A prosodically 'informed' transcription of this passage as emergent discourse would be as follows:

(13) *Revised transcription of (12) as emergent discourse*
1   D: uhm; (0.4) well the reason why I called; is I was uh (0.1) in San
        Jose, on Monday, downtown at the the uh (0.4) demonstration
        that was going on then, and it (0.5) was such a different feeling;
        than from what I'm seeing these last two days. it was so peaceful,
5.   (0.4) uh (0.1) you know; people were down there to really support
        each other.
     L: (0.3)
     D: and wha(h)t I'm seeing now; I I think you know is just uh; (0.3)
        goes against what these people are trying to demonstrate for.

An emergent perspective on the prosody of this multi-unit turn
suggests that it was not conceived as a whole with two prosodic
'paragraphs' but that it grew into its ultimate shape as a result of
on-the-spot local decisions made by participants in the process of
negotiating talk.

3.4 Ground analytic categories in the data itself

Sacks, Schegloff and Jefferson have stressed that the sequential
organization of conversational interaction serves as a means for
interactants to display their understanding of prior talk to each
other. At the same time, they point out, this mutual display of
understanding can be used by analysts as a 'search procedure' in
order to discover 'what a turn's talk is occupied with' (1974:728f.).
Applied now to prosody, it should be possible to refer to the
sequential organization of conversation in order to discover what
a turn's prosody is doing. Wootton (1989) has pointed out that
conversation analysts can be shown to rely on several different
types of evidence for the discovery of members' devices: (i) relationship to just prior turns, (ii) co-occurring evidence within the turn,
(iii) subsequent treatment in interaction, (iv) discriminability, and
(v) deviant cases.[30] In fact, each of these types of evidence can be
brought to bear on prosodic analysis.

(i) The relationship of the device to just prior turns. Prosodic categories can be discovered by examining the relationship between a
prior turn and/or its prosody and the prosody at the beginning of a
new turn. To illustrate: Local (1992) shows that a speaker may
signal that a new turn is actually a continuation of a foregoing
interrupted or discontinued turn by gauging pitch level, loudness

and tempo at the beginning of this turn to match those at the end of
the turn broken off. Thus:

(14) *Prosodic continuation (spelling standardized)*
1   LOTTIE: where'd you get the turkey.
     EMMA: up at the Balbo Market
     LOTTIE: oh y[eah.]
     EMMA: [°hhh] it had a little bla:ck spot though on the
5   white skin I wonder if it was brui::sed. h
                         (.)
     LOTTIE: [ye:ap]
→   EMMA: [blood]
                         (.)
10   LOTTIE: probably [wa::s,
     EMMA: [°hh
→   EMMA: blood coagulated but uh

                                              (Local 1992:283)

According to Local, there is nothing in the prosody of Emma's talk
at drop-out (line 8) which projects continuation, and yet, following
Lottie's *probably was* (line 10), Emma's resumption with *blood
coagulated* (line 12) has the same pitch and loudness characteristics
as her first *blood* (line 8). Local argues that matching the prosody of
prior interrupted talk in this way is a means conversationalists have
of 'doing continuation'.

A second example of this type of evidence being used in prosodic
analysis can be found in Couper-Kuhlen and Auer (1991), where it
is shown that in English conversation the timing of the first prosodic prominence in a new turn with respect to the last two
prosodic prominences of a prior turn may display the degree of
cohesion between turns – and metaphorically, the degree of
momentary speaker affiliation or disaffiliation with an interlocutor.
Consider, for example:

(15) *Lack of rhythmic cohesion*
      (Left-hand slashes precede prosodic prominences; vertical alignment
      indicates that the prominences come at perceptually regular intervals
      in time.)
1   DJ: /whereabouts in/
           /Bolton do you /
           /work.
→   G: (0.5) eh -I

5   /don't; I'm unem-/
                               /ployed – well a   /
                               /student;   /
                               /part-time.

                                                          (1991:11)

Here DJ sets up a clear 'rhythm' at the end of his turn by timing the last prosodic prominences to come at quasi-equal intervals in time. G, however, 'misses his cue' by not picking up the established rhythm and coming in on the next beat. Instead, the first prosodic prominence of G's turn is late with respect to the pulse, although he establishes a rhythm of his own thereafter. Given the fact that DJ's question (lines 1–3) appears to be making an unwarranted assumption about G (see below), it can be argued that the timing of G's subsequent incoming (line 4) is a quasi-iconic 'document' of the gap in understanding between himself and his interlocutor.

(ii) Co-occurring evidence within the turn. The interpretation of prosodic categories may be discoverable from verbal evidence in the turn or in surrounding talk. Thus, in cases like the above, when cues are used cumulatively, the interpretation of prosody is suggested by the wording of the turns concerned. In (14), for instance, Emma repeats her prior turn, this repetition being consistent with the interpretation that the prosodic cues signal 'resumption' and 'continuation'. In (15) G formulates an answer which explicitly contradicts the presupposition of DJ's question; the content of his turn thus suggests the interpretation of the rhythmic break as a sign of disaffiliation.

(iii) Subsequent treatment of the interactional device in question. Prosodic categories may be discoverable by inspecting following talk to see how a turn-constructional unit or a turn and its prosody are treated there. Selting (1995), for instance, shows that in standard German when speakers use mid-level pitch on the final accented syllable of a turn-constructional unit, this is treated by recipients as a signal that current speaker has not finished the turn. Potential next speakers hold off their entries at this point, as the example in Figure 1.5 illustrates. Here I's answer reaches points of potential syntactic/semantic completion after each individual turn-constructional unit. Yet the absence of next-speaker incomings – despite pauses – following *because everyone needs an education,* and *and I'm not going to worry about it any more,* and the

N: aber KUNST is aber nich kein gutes ANgebot hier oder
       but there's not much offered in art here is there

I: (0.5) ES GEHT NEE:: (0.3) NICH so SONderlich GUT
       it's alright no   not so very good
       (0.5)

N: mhm
       (1.0)

-> I: a:ber ich mach das jetzt hier zuENde (0.7)
        but I'm going to finish this now here
        <f>

I: WEIL: eine ausbildung BRAUCH der mensch (1.4)
       because everyone needs an education

I: aso s HAB ich mir jetzt so geSA:GT (0.2)
       or so I've said to myself now

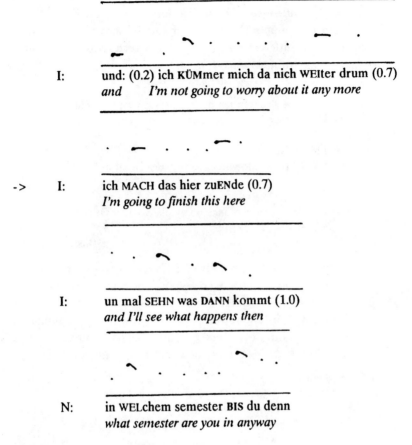

I: und: (0.2) ich KÜMmer mich da nich WEIter drum (0.7)
    and   I'm not going to worry about it any more

-> I: ich MACH das hier zuENde (0.7)
        I'm going to finish this here

I: un mal SEHN was DANN kommt (1.0)
    and I'll see what happens then

N: in WELchem semester BIS du denn
    what semester are you in anyway

(Selting 1995; CAPS denote primary, CAPS secondary, accented syllables.)
Figure 1.5

two occurrences of *I'm going to finish this here* suggests that mid-
level pitch on a final accented syllable in a turn-constructional unit
is functioning as a prosodic turn-holding device here.
(iv) Discriminability of the interactional device. Systematic comparison of the prosodic configuration in question with other configurations may help to reveal the specific role which a prosodic
device plays. For instance, the mid-level terminal pitch in standard
German referred to above can be compared with final falling or
final rising terminal pitch configurations in similar contexts,
which do not routinely block entries by next speakers.

Similarly, with respect to the notion of prosodic continuation illustrated in example (14) above, it can be shown that speakers sometimes use different prosody on a new turn following an interrupted or discontinued one:

(16) *Prosodic re-starting*
1   w: ... this was about ten o'clock at night on the London
            Underground and there was a whole carriage in
            stitches
→   LT: I must [say y[ou do sound a bit
5   w: [°hhh [do you have any idea [what a- * * *
     PR: [* * *
                        (.)
→   LT: you do sou:n:d disconcertingly like an alternative theatre
            group
                                                (Local 1992:285)

According to Local, the prosody of LT's repeat *you do sound* (line 8) is higher in pitch than the corresponding part of his prior turn (line 4). Thus he can be heard as not continuing but 'starting anew'.

By contrast with (15) above, it can be shown that the timing of an answer to an out-of-the-blue question like *whereabouts do you work* or *what do you do in life* need not be late and arhythmic:

(17) *Rhythmic cohesion*
1   DJ: what d'you
                    /do in life   /
                    /John?   /
→   J: /uh `well I'm   /
5   /off` sick at   /
                   /present,   /
                                      (Couper-Kuhlen and Auer 1991:14)

Although here too DJ's question (lines 1–3) appears to be making an unwarranted assumption about his interlocutor and the second speaker J formulates an answer which is not the preferred or expected one, in doing so he picks up DJ's rhythm by placing the first prosodic prominence of his turn such that it coincides temporally with the next pulse (line 4). Thus, the timing of J's turn onset is rhythmically well-coordinated with the prior turn and the sequence as a whole comes off cohesively.

(v) Deviant cases in the use of the device. Using evidence such as that cited above, conversation analysts typically proceed on a case-

to-case basis assembling an 'analytically coherent set of cases' (Schegloff 1982:80). With a set of like cases, systematic features in interaction can be more reliably identified. Of course deviant cases may appear in which the hypothesized regularity seems to break down. However, close analysis of such deviant cases often reveals that what appears to be a contravention of the 'rule' at first sight is actually a confirmation of it on a deeper level.

It was precisely such deviant-case argumentation which we employed above to underline the context-sensitivity of prosody in the Gulf War phone-in example (12).[31] Recall that Debbie's *that guy I just listened (to)* initially appeared to deviate from the routine placement of the reason for the call in telephone conversations on radio phone-ins. Without taking prosody into consideration, this example would constitute a deviant case. However, with proper consideration of its prosody, example (12) can be shown to confirm a deeper generalization: routinely, on-topic turns in this sequential position are reasons for the call, a status confirmed by corresponding prosodic treatment (non-low pitch register and volume, non-fast tempo). Off-topic turns in the same position, on the other hand, are prosodically contextualized as 'misplaced'. Their contrasting prosodic treatment thus indirectly confirms the routine understanding of similarly positioned (and appropriately contextualized) turns.

There is one well-known study in which deviant cases, or 'hitches' (Levinson 1983:319), have been used to discover prosodic regularity. Beattie, Cutler and Pearson (1982) set out to investigate turn delimitation, and in particular the numerous interruptions found to occur in formal interviews with the then Prime Minister Margaret Thatcher. Based on close analysis of one interview, they find that turn-taking hitches – in which the interviewer was invariably heard to be interrupting his interviewee – were regularly accompanied by current speaker's (i.e. Thatcher's) use of rapid or steep pitch falls which reached a mid point in her voice range. By contrast, in clear speaker switches in the same interview, current speaker used steep falls but ones which regularly ended quite low in the voice range. The authors conclude that the turn-taking hitches in this interview were due to a conflicting set of cues: a pitch fall to non-low typically found in turn-medial utterances but a steep gradient as found in turn-final utterances. These conclusions are substantiated via traditional social-scientific methods such as polling independent judges for judgements of finality/non-finality and statistical tests. However, it was the study of hitches which originally led to hypothesizing the regularity behind prosodic turn delimitation in these interviews.

3.5 Validate analytical categories by demonstrating participants' orientation to them

As Sacks, Schegloff and Jefferson point out, the fundamental sequential organization of conversational interaction can also be appealed to for the validation of analyses (1974: 729). That is, via an inspection of turns at talk directed at a prior turn's talk, analysts can access participants' displays of understanding directly, the latter serving as warrants for analytic decisions. Here too, there is a straightforward application to the analysis of prosody. One study which demonstrates this is Kelly and Local's (1989b) investigation of test-word repetition by interviewees in the Tyneside Linguistic Survey. Their hypothesis is that speakers' use of a rapidly falling pitch contour (from high to low) with marked loudness on a repeat following interviewers' proffering of a word for recognition counts as an understanding check, designed to verify that the word has been heard correctly. For example:

```
(18)  Understanding check (McN is the interviewer, Eir the interviewee)
1     MCN:  er (0.2) varnigh
            (3.5)
→     Eir:  varnigh (high falling pitch to low, marked loudness)
            (0.4)
5     MCN:  aye (1.5) you know for nearly
            (1.5)
      Eir:  w I've never heard it I've heard me mother use it
                              (adapted from Kelly and Local 1989b:267)
```

Kelly and Local's argument in support of this hypothesis is based on sequential evidence: the following turn by the interviewer routinely contains some acknowledgement or confirmation token (here *aye* in line 5), and the interviewee does not offer any sign of recognition (as here in line 7) until this acknowledgement is given. Moreover, when the hypothesized prosodic cues are not present, i.e. when speaker's falling pitch stops mid-way, or does not begin high and is realized with a breathy, soft voice, the sequential treatment is different. In the latter case, rather than immediately confirming or disconfirming the speaker's rendition of the word, the interviewer routinely withholds a turn until the speaker has offered some appreciation of it. Kelly and Local suggest that this kind of prosody signals that speakers are 'mulling over' the word. Compare:

(19) *Mulling over* (McN is the interviewer, GSh the interviewee)
1   MCN: er (0.8) varnigh
              (0.9)
    GSh: varnigh (flat falling pitch from mid, quiet voice)
              (1.0)
5   oh yes I've sometimes said varnigh
    MCN: aye (.) uh (.) yeah
                                        (adapted from Kelly and Local 1989b:274)

Thus the interactional and prosodic categories which this study proposes are warranted by demonstrating that participants to the interaction orient to them in predictable ways.[32]

4 Interaction from a prosodic perspective

The preceding discussion has demonstrated how the methodology of conversation analysis can be profitably transferred to the study of prosody within an interactional framework. Ultimately, we believe, this kind of prosodic analysis will also enrich the study of conversation. Among current approaches to spoken interaction, three come to mind which acknowledge in one way or another the prosodic make-up of talk: standard conversation analysis,[33] the 'information-flow' model (Chafe 1980, 1988) and contextualization theory (Gumperz 1982; Auer and di Luzio 1992).[34] These approaches differ widely with respect to the importance they attribute to prosodic form and function. Yet all stand to benefit from advances in the field of interactional prosody, we shall argue, in two ways: systems for the transcription of prosody can be made more sensitive to interactionally relevant features, and analyses of conversational discourse can be made more revealing of participants' methods by incorporating interactional prosodic functions.

4.1 The transcription of prosody

With one or two minor exceptions, the conventions for prosodic transcription in current approaches hark back to a single model, that developed over a number of years by Gail Jefferson (see the surveys in Schenkein 1979, Atkinson and Heritage 1984, Psathas and Anderson 1990). Newer systems, e.g. DuBois, Schuetze-Coburn, Cumming and Paolino (1993) and Gumperz and Berenz (1993), may advocate slightly different symbols in order to facilitate computerized word-processing, but the categories themselves tend to remain on the whole the same. The following discussion takes CA conventions as its point of departure, as these are most widely known. However, our remarks apply as well to similar systems of prosodic transcription.

Traditionally, conversation analysts have used a largely ad hoc notation system for the representation of segmental-phonetic and prosodic detail. These conventions are justified with respect to the aim of making transcripts 'accessible to linguistically unsophisticated readers' (Sacks, Schegloff and Jefferson 1974:734). High priority is given to the readability of transcripts by non-linguists. Dialectal or other noticeable deviations from standard pronunciation are typically indicated by adopting English spelling conventions in a kind of 'folk-phonetic' representation 'to get as much of the actual sound as possible into our transcripts' (Sacks, Schegloff and Jefferson 1974:734). Such transcripts inevitably rely on the reader's familiarity not only with (implicit) spelling conventions but, more generally, with the speech variety at hand (cf. also Gumperz and Berenz 1993).

In the domain of prosody and intonation, a minimal notation system has been proposed which, in one of the more recent compilations, provides for the use of a period /./ for a 'stopping fall in tone', a comma /,/ for 'continuing intonation', a question mark /?/ for a 'rising inflection', a combined question mark/comma /¿/ for 'rising intonation weaker than that indicated by the question mark', upward and downward arrows /↑,↓/ for 'rising or falling shifts in intonation immediately prior to the rise or fall' and exclamation point /!/ for 'animated tone' (Psathas and Anderson 1990:94). Pitch change within the word is to be notated by the combination of underscoring for stress in relation to the prolongation marker /: /.

The stress-mark (underscoring) is placed on the 'first letter' of a stressed (and prolonged) syllable if there is no change in pitch: /venee:r/ (sic); on the vowel immediately preceding the colon in case of a pitch drop: /venee:r/; and on the prolongation in case of a rise: /venee:r/ (Psathas and Anderson 1990:94f.). As for timing, it is recommended that the onset of overlapping talk be represented with double obliques (//) or right-hand brackets, that 'no interval' between turns be indicated with an equal sign (=), and that silent intervals in the stream of talk (within and between utterances) be timed in tenths of a second and indicated in parentheses (Psathas and Anderson 1990:93).

Yet current notation conventions will be found lacking with respect to two general principles of design for systems of discourse representation (see also Edwards 1993). First, prosodic symbols should allow readers without access to the original data to recapture important features unequivocally. However, the use of punctuation marks, for instance, for the representation of phrase-final intonation depends on stereotypical associations between sentence-type and intonation which are misleading, especially for the non-linguist. Clearly, not all questions have rising intonation, nor do all utterances with rising intonation function as questions. Although most current transcription systems explicitly warn users against such simplistic equations, nonetheless the use of written-language devices for the transcription of spoken language invites misunderstanding.[35] This could be avoided with the use of less functionally loaded and more iconic symbols.

Furthermore, the notation of pitch change within the word by variable underlining in the graphic word is problematic because of the frequent lack of correspondence between phonics and graphics in language. In addition, to mark a pitch change (or lack of it) by underlining the syllable onset or coda is unfortunate because it suggests optically that it is consonants which carry pitch. (Phonetically speaking, presence or absence of pitch change should be marked on the syllable peak.) Moreover, when a pitch change is marked on the syllable coda, this suggests, by virtue of the implicit iconicity between space and time, that there is a delay in the temporal alignment of pitch peak and syllable core. Such delays do occur in intonation but are generally recognized as producing different tones (e.g. a rise–fall instead of a fall; cf. Ladd 1983).

Of course the exact wording of the transcription conventions may not warrant these implications, but the point is that the pitch and stress conventions invite an iconic reading where none is called for. In actual fact, the symbols would benefit from being made more mnemonic.

Third, as notation conventions stand now, it is unclear what the domain of the pitch changes recorded with punctuation marks is. A plausible guess would be that they extend from the last stressed syllable over any and all following unstressed syllables. Yet this assumption is not made explicit, nor is stressing systematically marked in all phrases.[36] A related problem concerns where exactly the pitch of terminal intonation changes. Does a final question mark refer to a rising inflection on the last stressed syllable or on the last (unstressed) syllable? If the former, how can a change in pitch direction on an unstressed tailing syllable following the last stressed syllable be captured? In traditional intonation analysis, such a pattern would correspond to a falling–rising (nuclear) tone as opposed to a simple falling one, a contrast which has been attributed a distinctive function in English.[37] In Brazil's discourse-analytic approach to English intonation, the difference is fundamental (recall the Referring vs Proclaiming tone). Local (1992) provides conversational evidence that falling–rising pitch at the end of a turn is projective of more talk to come (1992:275). Arguably then, an additional category for falling–rising phrase-final intonation must be introduced if it can be shown to be functionally different from a simple rise.

This brings us to a second and all-important design principle with respect to systems of prosodic notation. They should make it possible to represent especially those prosodic features which are relevant to conversationalists. Here too, current systems are often lacking. For instance, the provision for two categories of rise as opposed to one for falls suggests that the *kind* of fall used is irrelevant for the organization of talk. Yet Lehiste (1975), Yule (1980) and others have shown that speakers of English use differing degrees of falling intonation to signal something akin to 'paragraph' non-finality vs 'paragraph' finality. Kelly and Local (1989b) find that speakers of Tyneside English use low falling pitch for finality, non-low falling pitch (i.e. fall to mid) for non-finality in turn construction. Since how low a contour falls may have both a discourse-structural and an interactive function, it can be argued that transcription conventions should provide for two kinds of fall: low (full) vs non-low (truncated). Furthermore, there is a certain amount of evidence accumulating that the relative pitch level at which a speaker *begins* an intonation phrase (called *onset* or *head* in tonetic research and *key* in discourse-analysis studies) may have a discourse-structural function (Brazil, Coulthard and Johns 1980, Couper-Kuhlen 1983, Wichman 1991). High onsets, for instance, typically accompany topic initiations. In oral narratives they may be used to signal a return to the foreground following excursions into the background or evaluative commentary. Low onsets tend to be associated with intonational parentheses. Yet current transcription conventions make no systematic provision for notation of onset level.

Whereas tonal categories in current systems tend to be underdeveloped, conventions for the notation of timing are often overly 'exact'. With respect to the transcription of pauses, for instance, they imply an objectivity which is unwarranted in two senses. First, in relation to accuracy of measurement: Jefferson (1989) reports originally having used a stopwatch to time breaks exceeding approximately 0.2 sec. Yet the method now recommended is slow and regular counting: 'no one thousand, one one thousand, two one thousand . . . ' (Jefferson 1989). Psathas and Anderson (1990) also recommend this method over clock-time accuracy, provided the transcriptionist is internally consistent. However, the problem is that pauses measured this way continue to be expressed in tenths of a second. This not only incorrectly implies real-time objectivity; it also makes cross-transcription comparison hazardous and prevents meaningful generalization.[38]

The objectivity implied by timing conventions is also unwarranted with respect to pause identification. According to pause-perception research, observed pauses do not always correspond to actual silences and, vice versa, actual silences need not be heard as pauses (see e.g. Duez 1985, Carpenter and O'Connell 1988). Consequently, when analysts set out to transcribe pauses as accurately as possible, they are not making an objective record of silence (absence of phonation over some specified interval of time) but of what *they* consciously *perceive* as silence. These (transcriber) perceptions are not necessarily the same as what interactional participants hear and/or orient to.

This is by no means to say that the lay notions of long and short pause or of coming in 'too late' or 'too early' are irrelevant for interaction. On the contrary, they are highly relevant, but the point is that they are not based on absolute time. Empirical studies of naturally occurring English conversation suggest, for instance, that it is the *rhythm* and *tempo* of surrounding talk which determine whether some absolute length of silence is perceived as long or short. As for turn-taking, the timing of (minimally) the last two prominent syllables in a speaker's turn appears to serve as a metric for the next speaker's entry (Couper-Kuhlen 1991, 1993). Yet in current transcription practice, no provision is made for indicating this perceptually more relevant *rhythmic* timing. By virtue of recording 'objective' time, transcribers misleadingly imply potential relevance for it. Moreover, its (pseudo-)objectivity suggests parallels where none are called for and obscures perceptually relevant likenesses.

As they stand then, current notation conventions are not easily readable nor precise enough to retrieve crucial aspects of the original – and, most importantly, they do not necessarily capture those prosodic categories which are of potential interactive relevance for conversational participants. In place of ad hoc categories, we would advocate the introduction of interactionally grounded ones for the transcription of prosody in conversation. By interactionally grounded categories, we mean ones which have been discovered and warranted according to the methodological principles outlined above. What exactly these categories are must be worked out in interactional studies. We thus take an analytic stance similar to that of Gumperz and Berenz (1993), who advocate a *functional* approach to the recording of prosodic phenomena, one in which transcription becomes an integral part of the analysis: 'In rendering prosodic, intonational and paralinguistic phenomena, we . . . concentrate on just those features of pitch, tune, and accent that can be shown to affect situated interpretation at the interactive or relational level as well as at the level of content' (1993:92). The goal of prosodic transcription in our view is not an objectivistic, etic notation of the original,[39] but a record of those prosodic details which may be of relevance for the inferential work of participants. One sets down on paper 'all those perceptual cues that past research and on-going analyses show participants rely on in their online processing of conversational management signs' (Gumperz and Berenz 1993:92). To a certain extent then, adequate prosodic notation requires prior analysis.

On the other hand, we recognize that some guidelines must be available in performing this preliminary prosodic analysis. Here a plea can be made for detailed *phonetic* observation of an 'impressionistic' sort (Kelly and Local 1989a). ('Impressionistic' is a phonetician's term used to refer to the record of all auditory sound distinctions without reference to their function.) In Kelly and Local's words, 'at the beginning of work on language material we can't, in any interesting sense, know beforehand what is going to be important. Consequently we must attend to and reflect everything we can discriminate' (1989b:26). Behind the notion of impressionistically recording everything one hears is a healthy 'fear' of pre-established notation systems, which may bias and restrict researchers' perception and analysis. In this sense, Kelly and Local are implicitly warning against premature phonologization of categories. Presumably, however, once impressionistic records have been functionally interpreted and the relevant prosodic categories extracted, the latter can be generalized for a given speech community. Then, for the study of conversation as social interaction, only those functional categories shown in interactional analysis to be relevant for conversational inferencing need be retained in the final transcript. Thus both phonetic *and* functional approaches to prosody are relevant to the analysis of conversation, each in its own way.

4.2 The contribution of prosody to interactive meaning

Current approaches to spoken interaction range from nominally attributing some relevance to prosody to assigning prosody a central role in the production and understanding of interactive meaning. Conversation analysts, for instance, have openly attested to the relevance of intonation for turn construction. The basic unit of a turn, the so-called turn-constructional unit, they point out, cannot be fully described in syntactic terms, as 'any word can be made into a "one-word" unit-type, . . . via intonation' (Sacks, Schegloff and Jefferson 1974:721f.). This formulation suggests that speakers and recipients make use of intonation or better, prosody, to delimit the basic unit of conversational interaction.

However, on the whole conversation analysts pay little attention to prosodic phrasing. In transcription, the end of something similar to a phrasing unit is presumably represented by a punctuation mark. Yet this only implicitly suggests that the material between two punctuation marks is indeed an integral prosodic phrase. In fact, CA attention has focussed more on the sequential aspects of conversational organization, key notions being 'conditional relevance' and the 'sequential implications' that a first turn creates for the next. The prosody of a turn, however, has tended to be taken for granted: how it contributes – along with sequential location – to steering conversationalists' interpretations is not made explicit. Despite an impressive arsenal of transcription symbols for the representation of prosody, it figures surprisingly little in CA reconstructions of speakers' methods for doing conversation.

In the work of Chafe and his associates, by contrast, the intonation phrase is treated as the fundamental unit of discourse production (Chafe 1979, 1980). It is also therefore a unit in terms of which major research questions are formulated. In Chafe's model the intonation unit has a cognitive counterpart: it corresponds to a focus of consciousness (originally called an 'idea unit'), or the amount of information to which one devotes central attention at a given time. Its phonetic description has evolved over time (cf. Chafe 1980, 1988, 1993). However, major effort is now being invested to specify its characteristics and make explicit strategies for its identification (DuBois, Cumming and Schuetze-Coburn 1988; DuBois, Schuetze-Coburn, Paolino and Cumming 1992; DuBois, Schuetze-Coburn, Cumming and Paolino 1993).

Yet for all the importance attributed to this unit of intonational phrasing in Chafe's approach, surprisingly little attention is paid to other prosodic phenomena, although provision is made for noting stress, loudness and speech rate in transcription. As for intonation, the main functional distinction is between final (or 'period'), continuing ('comma') and appeal ('question mark') transitions between intonation units (so-called *transitional continuity*). Reminiscent of the American structuralists' terminal juncture, transitional continuity is said to signal 'whether the discourse business at hand will be continued, or has finished' (DuBois, Schuetze-Coburn, Paolino and Cumming 1992:28). The functional classes of transitional continuity may have different phonetic contour realizations cross-linguistically, but presumably have a constant realization within one speech community. The distinction between continuing and finished intonation plays a crucial role in Chafe's theory of levels of linguistic processing. A 'finished' intonation contour signals the end of a spoken 'sentence' and is expected when a thought or centre of interest is complete.

In contrast to Chafe's rather limited focus on intonation unit, pause and terminal continuity, Gumperz envisages a much broader range of prosodic features which enter into speaker inferencing. His attention has focussed on stress, pitch direction and register, timing, and loudness, as well as on paralinguistic and kinesic features as situated cues to the (mis-)understanding of speakers' interactional meanings in (intercultural) communication (1982, 1992).[40] Yet such analyses can only be carried out against the background of speakers' unmarked prosodic expectations in discourse, and, given the present stage of research, these can often only be guessed at.

On the whole then, both with respect to turn construction and to activity-related inferencing, the contribution of prosody in the organization of conversational interaction and in the negotiation of interactional meaning needs more explicit recognition and detailed attention. The interactional approach to prosody outlined above will benefit current conversational and discourse research by drawing attention to a wide range of interactive functions in which prosody is implicated.

5 Conclusion

In proposing an interactional perspective on prosody as a 'remedy' for formal, functional and methodological problems in current research, we have taken a doubly empirical stance: (i) the approach advocated takes empirical data as its object of study, and (ii) it seeks empirical evidence for the validation of its analyses. While the analysis of empirical data is arguably not new in prosodic studies, the kind of empirical validation suggested here is often absent from other approaches. It is true that the term 'discourse' is beginning to appear in mainstream work on prosodic and intonational phonology.[41] Nevertheless, this kind of work is not oriented towards the empirical analysis of natural data. Other recent studies clearly set out to investigate intonation in natural settings.[42] This attests to the growing awareness that the study of prosody should be based on empirical data from natural interaction. What is absent, however, is evidence that participants in real interactions do indeed interpret prosody and/or intonation in the way the researcher models it. In contrast to most other empirical approaches, an interactional perspective emphasizes the necessity of empirically warranting prosodic categories and descriptions. And in contrast to structuralist approaches and their offspring, an interactional perspective does not simply aim at pattern recognition and description, but at the reconstruction of patterns as cognitively and interactionally relevant categories which real-life interactants can be shown to orient to.

In suggesting ways to improve the formal and functional analysis of conversation by incorporating a prosodic perspective, we have taken a step towards the reconstruction of what Silverstein (1992) calls the 'interactional text'. The interactional text is 'laid down in realtime discursive interaction' (1992:58); it contains not only all the referential sign-forms which participants in interaction use (these comprise the 'denotational text') but also all those indexical ones which contribute to meaning and inference in the widest sense. If the interactional text is strategic and maximally transparent, i.e. gives a plausible reconstruction of 'moves' in interaction based on participant understandings, it can be 'studied transcriptionally in vitro with confidence that the in vivo reality is close to hand' (1992:74). It is our contention that prosody furnishes some of the indexical sign-forms which contribute to the establishment of interactional text.

Notes

1   In defining prosody this way, we align ourselves within the Firthian tradition, where prosody is understood to comprise the syntagmatic properties of syllables, words and phrases as opposed to the paradigmatic, phonematic properties of single sounds (Firth 1957/1969).
2   See Auer, Couper-Kuhlen and Müller (to appear) for a discussion of how Saussurian linguistics has 'detemporalized' language.
3   For the same reason repair phenomena have been excised from the sentences with which linguists and syntacticians have concerned themselves (Schegloff 1979a; also Müller 1993).
4   *Context* shares a number of these features and has likewise been overlooked in modern, especially formal, linguistics (Goodwin and Duranti 1992).

5 See Auer 1993 for a historical survey of technical recording and speech analysis aids and the way linguists have made use of them.

6 *Prose* is defined as 'essentially language organized for visual presentation' (Abercrombie 1965:3).

7 We might add that the emergent nature of conversation (see below) makes it radically different from prose, a finished product.

8 E.g. Liberman and Sag 1974 or Pierrehumbert and Hirschberg 1990.

9 Others who deserve mention here include folklorists working in the Tedlock/Hymes 'ethnopoetic' tradition (see, e.g., Sherzer and Woodbury 1987) and sociologically oriented literary critics in the Bakhtin circle (see, e.g., Vološinov 1976).

10 Halliday 1967, 1970 and Crystal 1969 represent two well-known British schools.

11 Under certain conditions a tone unit may have *two* prominent pitch movements in Crystal's model, but only provided the directions of these pitch movements are complementary and there is no rhythmic or melodic break between them. Halliday allows for similar 'compound tones', stipulating that there can be no pretonic segment in between.

12 Barring (in Crystal's model) tonal subordination.

13 The falling pitch movements on the two occurrences of *really* would presumably be treated as superordinate to those on *down* and *upsets* respectively in Crystal's system.

14 See also Local and Kelly (1986:185), who make this point cogently.

15 See French and Local (1983), Local and Kelly (1986), Local, Kelly and Wells (1986) and Local, Wells and Sebba (1985) for a selection of phonetic and prosodic parameters which have proved to be relevant for the analysis of speech as verbal interaction.

16 Armstrong and Ward list as a fourth use for Tune II 'incomplete groups', a first step towards the recognition that tunes need not coincide with sentences.

17 The problem with the notion of 'information unit' is one of circularity: there are no means independent of intonation for identifying this unit.

18 Recent work on focus assignment and realization has shown that the relation between 'sentence accent' and focussed constituent is much more complex than Halliday's description suggests (cf. e.g. Gussenhoven 1983 and Uhmann 1991).

19 The case for nature appears to be substantiated by universally valid patterns of intonation such as those reported in Bolinger 1978. The case for nurture, on the other hand, is strengthened by language-dependent rules of e.g. focus realization (Uhmann 1991).

20 As Gumperz (1992) points out, contextualization cues channel or constrain interpretations, which then must be negotiated and confirmed interactively. Meaning in interaction is never a 'one-shot go'.

21 The meaning of (11b) would then be approximately 'the Robinsons, of all people'.

22 See, e.g., Sacks 1992, Schegloff and Sacks 1973, Sacks, Schegloff and Jefferson 1974, Schegloff, Jefferson and Sacks 1977, for early, influential work in the field of conversation analysis.

23 Ethnomethodologists have been known to conduct 'breaching experiments' by e.g. purposefully adopting alienating methods in order to study the routine grounds of everyday interaction (cf. Garfinkel 1963, 1967).

24 See, e.g., Erickson and Shultz (1982), who use a combination of CA-inspired microanalysis of selected interactional sequences as well as post-hoc viewings of videotapes of these sequences with participants to generate and validate hypotheses.

25 Radio phone-in programmes appear to have individual codes of conduct; some provide for an initial exchange of greetings between callers and anchor-person, while others do not; in the former case routine greetings may be one-way or two-way, and may allow for a *how are you* sequence or not. On this programme, callers regularly exchange only greetings with Leo and then proceed immediately to the reason for the call.

26 Strictly speaking, this assumption would first have to be proved. We make it here hypothetically for expository purposes.

27 Arguably the mid-high sustained pitch on *peaceful* (line 12) is a prosodic turn-holding device, although Debbie does pause here long enough for some recipient signal from Leo.

28 According to a rhythm-based metric for turn-taking (Couper-Kuhlen 1991, 1993), an unmarked floor entry at this point would be timed so that its first stress coincided with the regular beat established by the stresses on *really*, *support* and *other*. The fact that the next beat is silent indicates that Leo has not made use of his option to become the next speaker.

29 In other words, the 'declination line' of prior talk does not continue here.

30 Wootton works these out based on CA investigations of tokens such as *oh* and *uh-huh*.

31 Thanks to John Gumperz for drawing our attention to this.

32 For other studies in which this kind of argumentation is used, see Local, Wells and Sebba (1985), Local, Kelly and Wells (1986) and Selting (1987a b; 1992a, b).

33 See, e.g., the contributory volumes by Schenkein 1979, Atkinson and Heritage 1984, Psathas 1979, Button and Lee 1987, Zimmerman and West 1980, Button, Drew and Heritage 1986 and Boden and Zimmerman 1991; also Heritage 1989.

34 This list is not intended to be exhaustive.

35 As Edwards herself states (albeit arguing for the opposite point): 'strategies based on reading habits are not necessarily subject to conscious awareness and may be difficult to suspend when reading a transcript, even if it is desirable to do so' (1993:6).

36 'Emphasis' tends to be recorded more systematically, using italics and/ or large letters to signal higher degrees of stress (Psathas and Anderson 1990:94).

37 Cf. *She has a lovely vòice* vs *She has a lovely vóice* ('but I don't think much of her as an actress') (O'Connor and Arnold 1973:68ff).

38 O'Connell and Kowal (1990a, b) make a plea for the use of physical time as measured acoustically in the transcription of timing despite (or perhaps because of) its non-participant-oriented, alienating effect.

39 *Pace* early work on CA (e.g. Sacks, Schegloff and Jefferson 1974), which advocates 'special care' in order to maximize the detail and precision of transcription. Psathas and Anderson (1990) take a more moderate stance, demanding merely that the transcript 'captures/displays those features of the interaction that are of analytic interest' (1990:76).

40 Cf. Tannen 1984, 1989 for applications of contextualization theory to the analysis of American conversational discourse.

41 See, e.g., Pierrehumbert and Hirschberg 1990.

42 McLemore 1991, for example, gives a 'pragmatic interpretation of English intonation' based on naturally occurring sorority speech.

References

Abercrombie, D. 1965. *Studies in Phonetics and Linguistics*. Third impression, 1971. London: Oxford University Press.

Armstrong, L. E. and I. S. Ward 1926. *Handbook of English Intonation*. Leipzig: Teubner.

Atkinson, J. M. and J. Heritage (eds.) 1984. *Structures of Social Action. Studies in conversation analysis*. Cambridge University Press.

Auer, P. 1986. Kontextualisierung. *Studium Linguistik*, 19: 22–47.
   1992. Introduction: John Gumperz' approach to contextualization. In Auer and di Luzio 1992, pp. 1–38.
   1993. Über ↘. *Zeitschrift für Literaturwissenschaft und Linguistik*, 90/91: 104–138.

Auer, P. and A. di Luzio (eds.) 1992. *The Contextualization of Language*. Amsterdam and Philadelphia: Benjamins.

Auer, P., E. Couper-Kuhlen and F. Müller (to appear). *Language in Time: the rhythm and tempo of spoken interaction*.

Beattie, G. W., A. Cutler and M. Pearson 1982. Why is Mrs Thatcher interrupted so often? *Nature*, 300: 744–747.

Boden, D. and D. H. Zimmerman (eds.) 1991. *Talk and Social Structure. Studies in ethnomethodology and conversation analysis*. Cambridge: Polity Press.

Bolinger, D. L. 1978. Intonation across languages. In J. P. Greenberg, C. A. Ferguson and E. A. Moravcsik (eds.) *Universals of Human Language*, Vol. II *Phonology*. Stanford University Press, pp. 471–524.

1986. *Intonation and its Parts. Melody in spoken English.* Stanford
University Press.

1989. *Intonation and its Uses. Melody in grammar and discourse.*
London: Edward Arnold.

Brazil, D. 1981. The place of intonation in a discourse model. In M.
Coulthard and M. Montgomery (eds.) *Studies in Discourse Analysis.*
London: Routledge & Kegan Paul, pp. 146–157.

1982. The place of intonation in the description of interaction. In D.
Tannen (ed.) *Analyzing Discourse: Text and talk.* Washington, D.C.:
Georgetown University Round Table on Language and Linguistics, pp.
94–112.

Brazil, D., M. Coulthard and C. Johns 1980. *Discourse Intonation and
Language Teaching.* London: Longman.

Brown, G., K. L. Currie and J. Kenworthy 1980. *Questions of Intonation.*
London: Croom Helm.

Button, G. and J. R. E. Lee (eds.) 1987. *Talk and Social Organisation.*
Clevedon: Multilingual Matters.

Button, G., P. Drew and J. Heritage (eds.) 1986. Interaction and Language
Use. Special double issue, *Human Studies,* 9(2–3).

Carpenter, S. and D. C. O'Connell 1988. More than meets the ear: some
variables affecting pause reports. *Language & Communication,* 8: 17–
27.

Chafe, W. L. 1979. The flow of thought and the flow of language. In T.
Givón (ed.) *Discourse and Syntax.* New York: Academic Press, pp.
159–181.

1980. The deployment of consciousness in the production of a narrative.
In W. L. Chafe (ed.) *The Pear Stories.* Norwood, N.J.: Ablex, pp.
9–50.

1988. Linking intonation units in spoken English. In J. Haiman and S. A.
Thompson (eds.) *Clause Combining in Grammar and Discourse.*
Amsterdam and Philadelphia: Benjamins, pp. 1–27.

1993. Prosodic and functional units of language. In J. A. Edwards and
M. D. Lampert (eds.) *Talking Data: Transcription and coding in discourse research.* Hillsdale, N.J.: Lawrence Erlbaum, pp. 33–43.

Couper-Kuhlen, E. 1983. Intonatorische Kohäsion. Eine makroprosodische
Untersuchung. *Zeitschrift für Literaturwissenschaft und Linguistik,*
49: 74–100.

1986. *An Introduction to English Prosody.* London: Edward Arnold and
Tübingen: Niemeyer.

1991. A rhythm-based metric for turn-taking. *Proceedings, 12th International Congress of Phonetic Sciences,* Vol. I. Aix-en-Provence:
Université de Provence, pp. 275–278.

1993. *English Speech Rhythm. Form and function in everyday verbal
interaction.* Amsterdam and Philadelphia: Benjamins.

Couper-Kuhlen, E. and P. Auer 1991. On the contextualizing function of
speech rhythm in conversation: question–answer sequences. In J.

Verschueren (ed.) *Levels of Linguistic Adaptation*, Vol. II. Amsterdam: Benjamins, pp. 1–18.

Cruttenden, A. 1986. *Intonation*. Cambridge University Press.

Crystal, D. 1969. *Prosodic Systems and Intonation in English*. Cambridge University Press.

DuBois, J. W., S. Cumming and S. Schuetze-Coburn 1988. Discourse transcription. In *Santa Barbara Papers in Linguistics*, Vol. II, *Discourse and Grammar*. Santa Barbara: Department of Linguistics, University of California, pp. 1–71.

DuBois, J. W., S. Schuetze-Coburn, S. Cumming and D. Paolino 1993. Outline of discourse transcription. In J. A. Edwards and M. D. Lampert (eds.) *Talking Data: transcription and coding in discourse research*. Hillsdale, N.J.: Lawrence Erlbaum, pp. 45–89.

DuBois, J. W., S. Schuetze-Coburn, D. Paolino and S. Cumming 1992. *Santa Barbara Papers in Linguistics*, Vol. IV, *Discourse Transcription*. Santa Barbara: Department of Linguistics, University of California.

Duez, D. 1985. Perception of silent pauses in continuous speech. *Language & Speech*, 28: 377–389.

Edwards, J. A. 1993. Principles and contrasting systems of discourse transcription. In J. A. Edwards and M. D. Lampert (eds.) *Talking Data: transcription and coding in discourse research*. Hillsdale, N.J.: Lawrence Erlbaum, pp. 3–31.

Erickson, F. and J. Shultz 1982. *The Counselor as Gatekeeper. Social interaction in interviews*. New York: Academic Press.

Firth, J. R. 1957. Sounds and prosodies. In Firth 1969, *Papers in Linguistics 1934–1951*. London: Oxford University Press, pp. 121–138.

French, P. and J. K. Local 1983. Turn-competitive incomings. *Journal of Pragmatics*, 7: 17–38.

Garfinkel, H. 1963. A conception of, and experiments with, 'trust' as a condition of stable concerted actions. In O. J. Harvey (ed.) *Motivation and Social Interaction*. New York: Ronald Press, pp. 187–238.

1967. *Studies in Ethnomethodology*. Englewood Cliffs, N.J.: Prentice-Hall.

Goodwin, C. and A. Duranti 1992. Rethinking context: an introduction. In A. Duranti and C. Goodwin (eds.) *Rethinking Context. Language as an interactive phenomenon*. Cambridge University Press, pp. 1–42.

Gumperz, J. J. 1982. *Discourse Strategies*. Cambridge University Press.

1992. Contextualization revisited. In Auer and di Luzio 1992, pp. 39–53.

Gumperz, J. J. and N. Berenz 1993. Transcribing conversational exchanges. In J. A. Edwards and M. D. Lampert (eds.) *Talking Data: transcription and coding in discourse research*. Hillsdale, N.J.: Lawrence Erlbaum, pp. 91–121.

Gussenhoven, C. 1983. *On the Grammar and Semantics of Sentence Accents*. Dordrecht: Foris.

54   Elizabeth Couper-Kuhlen and Margret Selting

Halliday, M. A. K. 1967. *Intonation and Grammar in British English*. The Hague: Mouton.

1970. *A Course in Spoken Intonation*. London: Oxford University Press.

Henderson, E. J. A. (ed.) 1971. *The Indispensable Foundation. A selection from the writings of Henry Sweet*. London: Oxford University Press.

Heritage, J. 1984. *Garfinkel and Ethnomethodology*. Cambridge: Polity Press.

1989. Current developments in conversation analysis. In D. Roger and P. Bull (eds.) *Conversation. An interdisciplinary perspective*. Clevedon: Multilingual Matters, pp. 21–47.

Jefferson, G. 1989. Preliminary notes on a possible metric which provides for a 'standard maximum' silence of approximately one second in conversation. In D. Roger and P. Bull (eds.) *Conversation. An interdisciplinary perspective*. Clevedon: Multilingual Matters, pp. 166–196.

Kelly, J. and J. K. Local 1989a. On the use of general phonetic techniques in handling conversational material. In D. Roger and P. Bull (eds.) *Conversation. An interdisciplinary perspective*. Clevedon: Multilingual Matters, pp. 197–212.

1989b. *Doing Phonology: observing, recording, interpreting*. Manchester University Press.

Ladd, D. R. 1980. *The Structure of Intonational Meaning. Evidence from English*. Bloomington: Indiana University Press.

1983. Phonological features of intonational peaks. *Language*, 59: 721–759.

Lehiste, I. 1975. The phonetic structure of paragraphs. In A. Cohen and S. G. Nooteboom (eds.) *Structure and Process in Speech Perception*. Berlin: Springer, pp. 195–203.

Levinson, S. C. 1983. *Pragmatics*. Cambridge University Press.

Liberman, M. and I. Sag. 1974. Prosodic form and discourse function. *Chicago Linguistic Society*, 10: 416–427.

Local, J. K. 1992. Continuing and restarting. In Auer and di Luzio 1992, pp. 272–296.

Local, J. K. and J. Kelly 1986. Projection and 'silences': notes on phonetic and conversational structure. *Human Studies*, 9: 185–204.

Local, J. K., J. Kelly and W. H. G. Wells 1986. Towards a phonology of conversation: turn-taking in Tyneside English. *Journal of Linguistics*, 22: 411–437.

Local, J. K., W. H. G. Wells and M. Sebba 1985. Phonology for conversation: phonetic aspects of turn delimitation in London Jamaican. *Journal of Pragmatics*, 9: 309–330.

McLemore, C. 1991. *The pragmatic interpretation of English intonation: sorority speech*. Ph.D. diss., University of Texas at Austin.

Müller, F. E. 1993. Das audiovisuelle Defizit der cartesianischen Linguistik. *Zeitschift für Literaturwissenschaft und Linguistik*, 90/91: 157–177.

Nespor, M. and I. Vogel 1986. *Prosodic Phonology*. Dordrecht: Foris.

O'Connell, D. C. and S. Kowal 1990a. A note on time, timing, and transcriptions thereof. *Georgetown Journal of Languages & Linguistics*, 1(2): 203–208.

1990b. Some sources of error in the transcription of real time in spoken discourse. *Georgetown Journal of Languages & Linguistics*, 1.4: 453–466.

O'Connor, J. D. and G. F. Arnold 1973. *Intonation of Colloquial English* (2nd edn). London: Longman.

Pierrehumbert, J. B. 1980. *The Phonology and Phonetics of English Intonation.* Ph.D. diss., Cambridge, Mass.: MIT.

Pierrehumbert, J. B. and J. Hirschberg 1990. The meaning of intonational contours in the interpretation of discourse. In P. Cohen and J. Morgan (eds.) *Intentions in Communication.* Cambridge, Mass.: MIT Press, pp. 271–311.

Pike, K. L. 1945. *The Intonation of American English.* Ann Arbor: University of Michigan Publications.

Psathas, G. (ed.) 1979. *Everyday Language. Studies in ethnomethodology.* New York: Irvington.

Psathas, G. and T. Anderson 1990. The 'practices' of transcription in conversation analysis. *Semiotica*, 78: 75–99.

Sacks, H. 1984. Notes on methodology. In Atkinson and Heritage 1984, pp. 21–27.

1992. *Lectures on Conversation.* 2 vols., ed. E. A. Schegloff and G. Jefferson. Oxford: Blackwell.

Sacks, H., E. A. Schegloff and G. Jefferson 1974. A simplest systematics for the organization of turn-taking for conversation. *Language*, 50: 696–735.

Schegloff, E. A. 1979a. The relevance of repair to syntax-for-conversation. In T. Givón (ed.) *Discourse and Syntax.* New York: Academic Press, pp. 261–296.

1979b. Identification and recognition in telephone conversation openings. In G. Psathas 1979, pp. 23–78.

1982. Discourse as an interactional achievement: some uses of 'uh huh' and other things that come between sentences. In D. Tannen (ed.) *Analyzing Discourse: Text and talk.* Georgetown University Round Table on Languages and Linguistics 1981. Washington, D.C.: Georgetown University Round Table on Language and Linguistics, pp. 71–93.

Schegloff, E. A. and H. Sacks 1973. Opening up closings. *Semiotica*, 8: 289–327.

Schegloff, E. A., G. Jefferson and H. Sacks 1977. The preference for self-correction in the organization of repair in conversation. *Language*, 53: 361–382.

Schenkein, J. (ed.) 1979. *Studies in the Organization of Conversational Interaction*, New York: Academic Press.

Selkirk, E. O. 1984. *Phonology and Syntax. The relation between sound and structure.* Cambridge, Mass.: MIT Press.

Selting, M. 1987a. *Verständigungsprobleme. Eine empirische Analyse am Beispiel der Bürger-Verwaltungs-Kommunikation.* Tübingen: Niemeyer.

1987b. Reparaturen und lokale Verstehensprobleme – oder: zur Binnenstruktur von Reparatursequenzen. *Linguistische Berichte,* 108: 128–149.

1992a. Prosody in conversational questions. *Journal of Pragmatics,* 17: 315–345.

1992b. Intonation as a contextualization device: case studies on the role of prosody, especially intonation, in contextualizing storytelling in conversation. In Auer and di Luzio 1992, pp. 233–258.

1993. Phonologie der Intonation. Probleme bisheriger Modelle und Konsequenzen einer neuen interpretativ-phonologischen Analyse. *Zeitschrift für Sprachwissenschaft,* 11(1): 99–138.

1995. *Prosodie im Gespräch. Aspekte einer interaktionalen Phonologie der Konversation.* Tübingen: Niemeyer.

Sherzer, J. and A. C. Woodbury (eds.) 1987. *Native American Discourse. Poetics and rhetoric.* Cambridge University Press.

Silverstein, M. 1976. Shifters, linguistic categories, and cultural description. In K. H. Basso and H. A. Selby (eds.) *Meaning in Anthropology.* Albuquerque: University of New Mexico Press, pp. 11–55.

1992. The indeterminacy of contextualization: when is enough enough? In Auer and di Luzio 1992, pp. 55–76.

Sweet, H. 1877. *A Handbook of Phonetics.* Oxford: Clarendon.

Tannen, D. 1984. *Conversational Style.* Norwood, N.J.: Ablex.

1989. *Talking Voices. Repetition, dialogue, and imagery in conversational discourse.* Cambridge University Press.

Uhmann, S. 1991. *Fokusphonologie. Eine Analyse deutscher Intonationskonturen im Rahmen der nicht-linearen Phonologie.* Tübingen: Niemeyer.

Vološinov, V. N. 1976. Discourse in life and discourse in art (concerning sociological poetics). In *Freudianism. A marxist critique,* transl. by I. R. Titunik. New York: Academic Press, pp. 93–116.

Wichman, A. 1991. A study of up-arrows in the Lancaster/IBM spoken English corpus. In S. Johansson and A.-B. Stenström (eds.) *English Computer Corpora. Selected papers and research guide.* Berlin: Mouton de Gruyter, pp. 165–178.

Wootton, A. J. 1989. Remarks on the methodology of conversation analysis. In D. Roger and P. Bull (eds.) *Conversation: An interdisciplinary perspective.* Clevedon: Multilingual Matters, pp. 238–258.

Yule, G. 1980. Speakers' topics and major paratones. *Lingua,* 52: 33–47.

Zimmerman, D. H. and C. West (eds.) 1980. Language and Social Interaction. Special double issue, *Sociological Inquiry,* 50/3–4.

2

On the prosody and syntax of turn-continuations

PETER AUER

1 Introduction

According to Sacks, Schegloff and Jefferson (1974), smooth turn-taking in conversation is based on participants' recognition of certain stretches of talk as 'turn-constructional units', the completeness of which occasions the possibility of turn-transition. The turn-allocation component of the turn-taking system, assigning turns according to certain ordered options to another or the same speaker, thus depends crucially on the 'visible' production of such turn-constructional units. It is these units that determine turn-transition places.

Sacks, Schegloff and Jefferson remain somewhat vague – as does subsequent conversation analytic research – about the structural bases according to which turn-constructional units are recognized. They seem to conceive of them basically in syntactic terms (as 'sentences' or smaller syntactically independent structures). The notion of syntactic closure is left up to linguists to investigate. At the same time, the role of prosody (intonation) is mentioned in determining turn-constructional units. From research on gaze, it is additionally known that turn-yielding is regularly indicated by speaker-gaze at the recipient as a possible (intended) next speaker.[1] It also seems obvious that semantico-pragmatic aspects of completeness enter into the recognition of turn-constructional units as well. For a non-speaking participant in a conversation to know where speakership may change, i.e. when it may be 'his (or her) turn', it is therefore necessary to monitor on-going speech production together with its accompanying non-verbal activities in a very comprehensive manner, taking into account not only syntax, but

also, minimally, prosody, gaze and the content of the utterance
against the background of what is being talked about.

As 'contextualization cues'[2] for the production and recognition
of possible turn-transition places, syntactic, prosodic, semantico-
pragmatic and visual parameters share the typical characteristics
of these cues: in particular, their 'meaning' is not that of decontextualized (transcontextually stable) referential symbols, but rather
that of indices which must be interpreted in and specific to, a
local environment; they may (and indeed often do) co-occur (i.e.
there is often a certain amount of redundant signalling); and their
interactive effect cannot be taken back or 'interactionally denied'.[3]

From this it follows that the projection of a turn's possible completion (i.e. of a potential transition relevance place) is a highly
interpretative issue; the correlation between syntactic, semantico-
pragmatic, prosodic, gestural and other visual cues on the one
hand, and the possibility of transition from one speaker's turn to
another's on the other, is anything but unequivocal. Syntax, the
various components of prosody, gaze, semantico-pragmatics and
other possible verbal and non-verbal parameters represent independent resources for signalling that a turn is approaching its end or is
terminated. This means (i) that speakers may choose a combination
of these parameters (with semantico-pragmatics, syntax and prosody always being present but sometimes 'neutral', i.e. not predictive) for contextualizing turn completion, (ii) that they may use
contradictory parameters, and (iii) on the side of the recipient/
listener, that monitoring these parameters may lead to inconclusive
interpretations. Thus, the recognition of a turn-construction unit is
in itself a complex multi-faceted interactional task. (The claim that
syntax, intonation, etc. are independent resources for signalling
turn transition should of course not be taken to mean that conversationalists are necessarily or usually conscious of these sets of
parameters as distinct. Instead, as with all contextualization cues,
what may be brought to consciousness is at best the holistic
outcome of an interpretative process, the details of which remain
completely unconscious.)

The present chapter will deal with syntax and prosody as two of
the omnipresent, yet independent signalling resources for contextualizing turn-constructional units. How much can participants rely
on syntactic, and how much on prosodic, features in on-going talk

for successful turn-taking? It is difficult to answer this question as long as syntactic and prosodic means indicate termination of some (turn-constructional) unit at the same point in time. More interesting are cases in which the two (sets of) parameters may be 'out of phase'. Here, we will primarily focus on one of these cases, i.e. syntactic expansions of a turn *beyond a possible syntactic completion point* in German conversations.

The analysis requires a conception of syntax which may appear somewhat unusual to those linguists who are used to dealing with syntactic structures as a product of grammatical rules, or as a correlate of semantic structures only. As the above characterization of syntax as a 'contextualization cue' for turn-taking may have indicated already, we are less interested here in syntactic structures as the potential output of some abstract grammatical system, than as communicatively and cognitively real events in time. To underline this approach, we will speak of syntactic *gestalts* instead of syntactic structures. In particular, a 'possible syntactic completion point' will be defined as one in which a syntactic gestalt is closed. The gestalt approach to syntax and the notion of syntax as a contextualization cue are linked to each other in decisive ways. Indeed, syntax can only contextualize turn-completion and turn-yielding because of its projecting potential, which in turn is due to its real-time perception in terms of emergent gestalts. During the emergence of a syntactic gestalt, the chances for predicting (correctly) the not-yet-produced remaining part (and therefore, its termination) continually increase. Thus, the production of a gestalt in time starts with a phase of minimal projectability, implying a high load of perceptual–cognitive work on the part of the recipient and of productive–cognitive work on the part of the speaker, and ends with a phase of maximal projectability in which the speaker profits from the quasi-automatic terminability of already activated patterns and the recipient from the low informational load of the remaining utterance. Syntax as a contextualization cue for turn-taking capitalizes on precisely this feature of the increasing predictability of gestalts in time: while turn completion itself is not predictable, gestalt closure with respect to syntax (usually) is. And since the termination of a turn-constructional unit is regularly made to coincide with the closure of syntactic gestalts, the latter may be used as a cue for the first.

A possible syntactic completion point has been reached when a structure has been produced which is syntactically independent from (i.e. does not project into) its following context. (Obviously, such syntactic independence is not to be equated with pragmatic or conversational independence.) Marking such a syntactic completion by a right-hand square bracket], the syntactic expansions 'x' may be represented as

$$[\ldots]_1 \, x \,]_2.$$

It will be noted that possible syntactic completion is not a syntactic *category* (such as 'sentence'[4]) but a syntactic boundary or *juncture*. It relates to the 'sentence' just like the 'possible turn completion point' as introduced by Sacks and colleagues relates to the 'turn'.[5] Since the structure up to the first syntactic completion point $]_1$ and the structure up to the second completion point $]_2$ must both be syntagmatically independent, 'x' itself is not a projected continuation of an open syntactic gestalt; instead, it will be heard as a non-projected expansion of an already closed syntactic gestalt, which, in an act of restructuring, is transformed by the hearer/recipient into an element of another gestalt, superimposed on, and incorporating, the previous one.

For practical reasons, the discussion here will be restricted to expansions in size below the level of the clause, particularly to noun or adverbial phrases; clause-level coordination and subordination will be neglected, although they share important characteristics with phrase-level expansions. Falling within the scope of the present chapter are therefore continuations such as (1) or (2), but not (3), where the continuation is an explanatory *because*-phrase.

(1)   MERCEDES 12
       M: dann=zahl=i nomal zehndausend Mark drauf,=
          (na)=hab=i=n fantastischn (.) h Gä Tä í (.) gell,
       F: m:,=
->   M: =absolut néu. -
       M: *in that case I pay another ten thousand marks in addition,=*
          =and I get a fantastic (.) h GTI [a car] (.) you know,
       F: *m:,=*
->   M: *=absolutely new, -*

(2) SEGLERINNEN
    A: und ich hab nur heut morgen noch n Arzt geholt
->   oder heut mittag,
    A: *and I only got a doctor this morning*
->   *or this afternoon*

(3) SPATEN 5
    A: ja der muß früh wieder héim
->   weil der hat abns Termíne
    A: *yes he has to go home early*
->   *because he's got appointments this evening*

In cases of syntactic expansions such as in (1) or (2), the interesting problem is to see if, and under what conditions, syntactic completion is an indicator for potential turn transition. In particular, the following questions may be asked: is an expansion beyond a syntactic closure related to or indicative of a 'problem' in turn-taking? If not, are there prosodic cues that counteract an interpretation of syntactic closure as indicative of a turn-transition place? If so, does the expansion address this problem in any way?

We will first give a syntactic typology of expansions beyond possible syntactic completion in German,[6] then sketch some of the ways in which prosody may be used for contextualizing turn completion and, finally, discuss the relationship of and interaction between the two.

2 Syntactic resources for turn-expansion

A context-free, purely syntactic definition of a closed syntactic gestalt is difficult, even impossible, to give. There is a certain temptation to define a minimal syntactic gestalt as consisting of a finite verb plus its obligatory arguments (in full or anaphorically abridged form).[7] However, it is not clear that what is obligatory can be stated in ways which do not recur to semantics or pragmatics (in the sense of the informational structure of a text). Furthermore, a wider conception of syntax seems necessary in order to deal with the structural ellipsis of obligatory constituents, one which goes beyond the limits of the traditional sentence. This can be seen most clearly in question–answer sequences:[8] answers, of course, can (or must) be formulated such that certain rules of ellipsis are applied; these may even prescribe dropping of the finite verb. Nevertheless, they are surely syntactically complete structures. Similar problems are faced in the case of so-called 'verbless sentences'; in German, and presumably in many other languages as well, one can find an array of such structures which do not obey the rules of 'core syntax' (but instead those of one or more 'marginal syntaxes'); see German complete syntactic gestalts such as *ich und CDU wählen!, du Esel! Einfahrt freihalten* (Fries 1987).

Therefore, only in a given co-text, it seems, can potentially complete syntactic structures be detected and distinguished from non-complete structures. Syntax – in the sense of a contextualization cue for turn-taking – is a context-sensitive ability to tell ongoing from completed syntactic gestalts.

Given this restriction, it is nevertheless possible and necessary to formulate rules for the production and detection of syntactic gestalts which may be used – in a given context – to decide on the syntactic independence of a given structure. In German, one particularly important syntactic rule which enables speakers to cue completion is the so-called *Satzklammer* ('sentence brace'), which indicates closure (the 'right brace' of a clause coinciding with completion). Subject to this grammatical rule are, first of all, all verb-second clauses (main declarative or w-interrogative clauses) which contain a composite verb form, i.e. an auxiliary or modal finite verb plus an infinitive or past participle, a verb with a separable prefix, or a *Funktionsverbgefüge* (an idiomatic combination of a semantically neutral verb such as *bringen* 'bring' or *kommen* 'come' with a noun, e.g. *in Erfahrung bringen* 'bring into experience, ascertain', *in Betracht kommen* 'come under consideration, be possible', etc.). In these structures, the finite verb represents the left brace, the infinitive, past participle, separable prefix or noun phrase the right brace. The right and left braces enclose the so-called inner-field (*Mittelfeld*), while the front-field (*Vorfeld*) precedes the left brace in declarative (verb-second) clauses (the rules of standard German syntax allow only one argument of the verb to appear in this position) and the end-field (*Nachfeld*) follows the right brace. (In written standard German, there are heavy restrictions on the use of this position in the sentence.) Here are some examples for standard German syntax:

The notion of *Satzklammer* also applies to verb-first sentences such as yes/no-interrogatives. In this case, the left brace (finite verb

[n gutes Datum] *a good date*	[kann] *can*	[natürlich] *of course*	[der sechste März] *the 6th of March*		[sein] *be*
NP	V_{fin}	AdvbP	NP		$V_{infinitive}$
[die] *they*	[ham] *have*	[wahrscheinlich] *probably*	[gestern] *yesterday*	[zuviel] *too much*	[geschnapselt] *schnaps–drunk*
NP	V_{fin}	AdvbP	AdvbP	AdvbP	$V_{participle}$
[der] *he*	[liegt] *lies*	[schon] *already*	[den ganzen Tag] *all the day*		[flach] *on his back*
NP	V_{fin}	AdvbP	AdvbP		Prefix

Vorfeld   Mittelfeld

form) is sentence-initial (the front-field is empty; e.g. *Liegt er schon den ganzen Tag flach?* 'does he lie on his back all day?' *Kann der 6. März ein gutes Datum sein?* 'Can the 6th of March be a good date?' etc.). Finally, verb-final clauses (e.g. subordinated clauses) display the sentence brace structure as well. Here the left brace is the subordinating conjunction, the right brace the verbal complex (including the finite verb). Declarative sentences with no 'sentence braces' in the traditional sense are more complicated to handle; yet even in such cases, there are a number of reliable, yet flexible and context-sensitive ('pragmatic') rules as to which constituent comes last, and thereby marks gestalt closure.[9]

Given these constraints, it is quite easy in many cases to predict the possible completion of a syntactic gestalt: according to the rules of German syntax, the closure of a syntactic gestalt is very often tied to the occurrence of the right brace. The emergence of syntactic gestalts will therefore be monitored by conversationalists in order to locate possible syntactic completions which might qualify as turn-transition places in German conversations. By the same token, any expansion of a syntactic gestalt beyond such a visible and recognizable closure is of foremost interest for analysing the relationship between syntax, prosody and turn-taking.

Before proceeding, it will be useful to describe these expansions in syntactic terms. It should be kept in mind for the following discussion that, from a purely syntactic point of view, it does not matter if expansions are separated from the gestalt they orient to by some recipient's 'continuer', and that preceding gestalt and expansion may even be produced by different speakers.

In a *first type*, representing the largest group of instances, one constituent which 'ought to' have been placed earlier is produced after the first locatable syntactic closure, i.e. in the post-field of the sentence.[10] (Just where exactly the structure 'ought to' have been produced is sometimes difficult to say. Frequently, there are various possibilities.) Examples are the *de facto* realizations of two of the above-mentioned clauses:

(4) SEGLERINNEN (Square brackets indicate overlap)
     B: die ham gestern @ zuviel geschnápselt. -
     -> ⌈wahrscheinlich.
     A: ⌊ja:,
     B: *they had too much schnaps yesterday.-*
     -> ⌈*probably.*
     A: ⌊*yes,*

(5) SEGLERINNEN
     A: der liegt also @ flách
     -> schon den ganzen Ta:g,
     A: *he's been lying in bed*
     -> *already all day,*

@ marks the canonical location of the expanding structure within the sentence frame according to standard written grammar.

It is a matter of dispute whether post-closure continuations of this type should be regarded as altogether normal, as exceptional, as marked or even as ungrammatical in spoken German (the question will be taken up again below). Yet even if one takes the extreme stance that spoken (in contrast to written) German permits post-field constituents without any restraint, there can be no doubt that the sentence adverbial *wahrscheinlich* and the temporal adverbial phrase *schon den ganzen Tag* are produced after a possible syntactic completion in examples (4) and (5), i.e. after the right braces *geschnapselt* and *flach*.

In (6), the first example for the German *Satzklammer* above, the issue is different:

(6)   AKTIENBERATUNG

    M: ich mein n gútes Dátum kann natürlich @ sein, -
-> der sechste März;
    M: *I mean a good date of course could be, -*
-> *the sixth of March;*

Here, *der sechste März* is an obligatory argument, the subject of the clause, which would not be complete before its production. No possibility for turn transition arises before the complete utterance of this constituent. Although 'debraced', the subject noun phrase is not an expansion of a complete syntactic gestalt, but brings this gestalt to closure. Thus, 'debraced' material is not necessarily indicative of an expansion beyond syntactic closure; it is only so under the proviso that it is not an obligatory argument which is placed in the post-field of the German sentence.

The following two extracts exemplify post-positioned syntactic constituents which 'ought to' have been placed before a closure-marking final element in syntactic contexts slightly different from (4) and (5). In (7), the temporal adverbial phrase *vierzehn Tage* (Alemannic *vierzehn Da:g*) is placed after the right brace of a subordinated *ob*-clause (*if*-clause), i.e. after the verbal complex *mitkann*; in (8), the right 'brace', although that of a main declarative sentence, is a predicative adjective, after which the adverbial *dann* is placed in the post-field:

(7)   TÖRN

    F: hab=ich=denkt jetz ruf den an ob der vielleicht (.) jetzt
        nächst Woch scho @ mitkann;
-> =vierzehn Da:g;
    F: *so I thought give him a ring if maybe he can come with us now*
        next week;
-> *for a fortnight;*

(8)   BÖRSIANER

    A: jajá. da bín ich @ nich (.) (h)ni(h)ch so kl(h)éinlich
-> ⌈ dann;
    B: ⌊ ja oke
    A: *yes yes. I won't be so small-minded about that*
-> ⌈ *then;*
    B: ⌊ *yes o.k.*

Again, the stretches of talk indicated – *vierzehn Da:g* and *dann* – are 'too late' according to standard German syntax, since a syntactic closure has already been reached.

A *second type* of expansion beyond a syntactic completion point may be called paradigmatic and thereby distinguished from the first type, which could be called syntagmatic. While syntagmatic expansions add (or insert) an additional constituent (in)to a syntactic gestalt, paradigmatic expansions replace a constituent in it. Among these, replacements for pro-forms may be singled out as a group of their own for functional reasons. This (often referred to as 'right dislocation')[11] is exemplified by (9); (10) is an instance of repair of a full form (paradigmatically related constituents are underlined with dots):

(9) SPATEN
     K: dú: des däd i it mogeln;
     K: hey that I wouldn't do chéat;

(10) SEGLERINNEN
     B: i muß da éhrlich sage i ⌈ hab scho seit zwéi Stunden
     A: ⌊ ((räuspert sich))
     B: Máttscheibe. - ganz blöden ⌈ Kopf,
     A: ⌊ ((räuspert sich))
     B: to tell you the truth I' ⌈ ve had a blackout for two hours. -
     A: ⌊ ((clears throat))
     B: real dull feeling in my ⌈ head.
                                ⌊ ((clears throat))

Note that in (10), the expansion *ganz blöden Kopf* has case marking for a direct object and therefore visibly fulfils the same syntactic role/function as the constituent it replaces (*Mattscheibe*). This is the decisive cue for differentiating retrospective syntagmatic expansions from the following, third type.

While both the first and the second type of expansion after syntactic completion imply a retrospective orientation (they insert material into the previous structure or replace one of its constituents), the *third type* of expansion lacks this retrospective orientation entirely. Such *continuations* are possible when none of the above-mentioned syntactic boundary cues (right-hand braces) occur. Continuations may appear in various shapes. One is an internal expansion of the constituent which closes the gestalt. Such an expansion, e.g. within a noun phrase, adds material after the possible completion of this lower-level constituent, which leads to another completion, the completion of the lower-level constituent coinciding with that of the constructional unit. Thus, in example (11) *so von Kuantan hoch* expands/modifies the noun phrase *die Ostküste* into a more complex noun phrase and thereby expands the syntactic structure as a whole by continuation:

(11) CHINA 18

    s: ehm (.) un was halt tóll is is die Óstküste: (.)

  -> so- (.) d- von Kúantan hó:ch;

    s: *ehm (.) and what is fantastic is the east coast (.)*

  -> *like (.) from Kuantan upwards;*

Another way to expand a syntactic gestalt non-retrospectively (another type of continuation) is to add parenthetical material which semantically modifies some prior constituent but has no formal syntactic relationship with it (viz., no grammatical agreement). This case of what could be called *asyndetic appositionals* is exemplified in extract (12), where *rund* modifies *Hülse* but is not a postpositioned element that would somehow fit into the preceding syntactic structure *auf der éinen Seite is also áußen sonne Hülse.*[12]

(12) ANTENNENKABEL

    M: des[13] auf der éinen Seite is also áußen sonne Hülse,=

    F: =j⌈ a,

  -> M: ⌊ rund,

    M: *that's on the one side is you know outside a kind of sheath,=*

    F: =ye ⌈ ah,

  -> M: ⌊ *round,*

Summarizing this section, we may say that there are at least three syntactically different ways to expand a closed syntactic gestalt: syntagmatic-retrospectively, paradigmatic-retrospectively (by right dislocation or repair proper) and syntagmatic-prospectively (by continuation). In all of these cases, the expanding structure may be said to suspend and postpone the previous syntactic completion point, incorporating further material into the first gestalt, which is thereby reorganized in terms of a second one, until another possible syntactic completion point is reached.

3 Prosodic resources for signalling turn completion and turn-continuation

Is there anything comparable to syntactic expansion in prosody? Does prosody (in particular, intonation) build up gestalts independent from those in syntax? In order to investigate the means by which prosodic expansions might be accomplished, we must ask first if prosodic structures display predictable closure at all. The available research on the role of intonation in conversation is scarce and the terminology underdeveloped. Nevertheless, particularly Selting (1995) for German, and Local and collaborators for some British varieties of English,[14] offer important insights.

According to Selting, prosodic units are defined in the first place by intonation in spoken German. An 'intonation contour' in her sense is made up of one or more accent units, each of which shows falling, rising, level, falling–rising or rising–falling pitch. In the case of several accent units, the sequence is hearably cohesive because the pitch accents integrate into some pattern (i.e. their 'global intonation'), such a globally falling, rising, high, mid or low.[15] The global pattern in combination with loudness and duration often singles out one pitch movement as the most salient one of the contour; such a 'phrasal accent' may be the end-point or the beginning of a globally falling or rising contour, the widest pitch movement, etc. The sequence of accent units may be preceded by one or more unstressed syllables (*Vorlauf*, roughly equal to 'anacrusis' in Anglo-American research on intonation). These are often marked by an intonational upstep or downstep, which sets them off from the last syllables of the previous contour, and they may be spoken with faster tempo than the preceding stretch of talk.

It is not easy to spell out the conditions under which intonation contours in this sense form recognizable gestalts, and, by consequence, to evaluate their potential for making the closure of a prosodic unit predictable. For Selting, contours are such gestalts if they are globally, or at least from some point onwards, steadily falling or rising. Such a prosodic gestalt would reach closure as soon as a 'highest' or 'lowest' pitch accent has occurred. If this is true, we may ask why such a global pattern has a predictable point of closure. One possible explanation would be that interactants have, or develop during the interaction, a feeling for the range in which global falls or rises take place in a co-participant's speech, provided they are produced in an 'unmarked' key (i.e. excluding the intonational display of 'surprise', 'anger', etc., or of textually/conversationally problematic items such as repairs or contrasts). This range would make it possible for interactants to forecast the termination of a contour by guessing when it will reach its limits. For instance, in example (13), the contour contains three consecutive accent units (the beginnings of which are marked by accented syllables, ') which combine into a rising overall pattern. This pattern has reached its climax with the third accent unit; impressionistically, this also seems to be the upper end of the intonational range for that speaker in unmarked key (see dotted line).[16]

(13)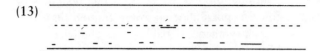

Note that in a prosodic gestalt of this type, the number of non-accented syllables after the final pitch accent is unpredictable; therefore, the right-hand end of the gestalt is underdetermined. However, we would be able to predict the first possible point of prosodic closure in such a contour, which would be the occurrence of the 'highest' or 'lowest' pitch protrusion, notwithstanding the possibility of an indeterminate number of further non-accented syllables to follow. Thus, comparable to syntactic gestalts, such an intonational gestalt could be expanded by continuation.

Unfortunately, globally falling or rising contours (particularly those in which the limits of a speaker's range are reached) are relatively infrequent. In other, more complex global contours made up of global rises *and* falls, it is difficult or impossible to predict how many accent units (or syllables) are still to follow. They therefore cannot be said to be gestalts in the sense discussed for syntax in the preceding section, since their predictive value is small. What can be predicted for a prosodic 'gestalt' of this type is not much more than that it must contain at least one (pitch) accent. (Therefore, the hearable beginning of a new contour is incomplete up to the occurrence of the first pitch protrusion.) However, compared to syntax, prosodic structures are not typically suitable for projecting very far into the future. Selting (1995) states that in contrast to syntax (where, for instance, the requirement that all obligatory arguments of a verb be present allows relatively far-reaching projections), intonation is basically confined to small-scale predictions, often not beyond the range of a single accent unit (see also Grosjean and Hirt, in press).

It should be noted, however, that precisely this 'disadvantage' is responsible for the easy expandability of intonational contours. In this respect, prosody fares much better than syntax; for while many syntactic structures simply cannot be expanded beyond a syntactic completion point without showing some kind of backwards orientation (see our 'retrospective expansions' of the last section), any material may be included into a potentially closed intonational contour as a prosodic continuation.[17] It will be shown in the following sections how the different possibilities (advantages and disadvantages) of prosodic and syntactic signalling are combined in a 'division of labour' for the construction of turn-construction units.

In order to display some syntactically tagged-on material as part of the preceding intonation contour (*prosodic integration*), or in order to display it as a new prosodic unit (*prosodic exposure*), the following resources are available in conversational German:

(i) *Integration/exposure by pitch.* Two techniques for smooth continuation must be differentiated. The first is a simple addition of further unstressed syllables to the last accent unit of the contour. Their pitch then will start at the level of the last syllable in the 'old' contour, or slightly below (see example (14)).

(14)

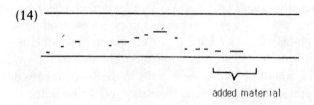

added material

Pitch remains at approximately the low level it has reached at the end of the final accent unit before the expansion; the expansion shows only a very slight fall since the 'base line' has almost been reached already. Within such a sequence of unaccented syllables, some may be slightly foregrounded by lengthening or loudness; they do not bear a pitch accent, however (i.e. they are, in a somewhat misleading but nonetheless widespread turn of phrase, 'destressed').

A second way to expand an existing contour beyond a possible completion point is to add another accent unit, i.e. a (pitch) accent plus non-accented syllables ad libitum. This happens, for instance, in example (15). Again, the contour that finally emerges bears no traces whatsoever of an expansion, as long as the segmental level is disregarded.

(15)
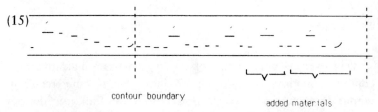
contour boundary

added materials

While in (15) the accent units added are very similar to the previous ones – i.e. the addition works on the principle of repeating existent pitch movements – this is not necessarily so. For instance, a L(ow) pitch accent may be added to a H(igh) pitch accent just as well.

Non-integration into an existing contour, i.e. *prosodic exposure*, can be marked by a pitch jump between the last unaccented syllables of the preceding and the anacrustic syllables of the new contour. For example, in example (16) the jump is downwards on the anacrustic syllables of the added accent unit, when compared to the upward slur on the last syllable in the old unit, which bears a secondary accent (the final word is *Éiscafé* 'ice parlour').

(16)
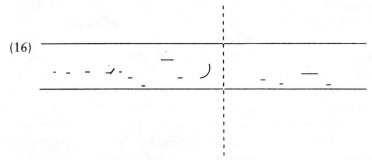

When the preceding contour ends and/or the added material begins with an accented syllable, it is difficult to judge if a possible

pitch jump is contour-internal or contour-delimiting (see example
(17)).

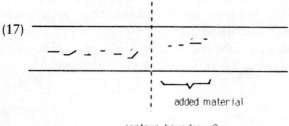

(17)

added material

contour boundary ?

Very extreme pitch jumps of this type may be indicative of a
contour boundary but, since pitch jumps occur quite regularly
within or between accent sequences as well, this indicator alone is
a rather vague one in most varieties of German.[18] In the usual case,
other prosodic cues for contour boundaries have to be present
in combination with such pitch jumps before or after accented
syllables in order to permit a more conclusive interpretation.

(ii) *Integration/exposure by tempo and loudness.* In addition to
pitch, integration or exposure of added material may be marked by
tempo. If there is a change towards faster tempo, this may be heard
as the beginning of a new contour. The same function of exposing
or camouflaging boundaries at the segmental level may be taken
over by loudness: for smooth integration, loudness will not change
or will only decrease gradually through the final part of the
(expanded) contour; for exposure, loudness will be increased or
diminished abruptly on the anacrustic syllables of the new contour.
(It should be kept in mind, however, that both tempo/rate of speech
and loudness primarily serve other functions, particularly for information processing: more loudness and reduced tempo/rate of speech
may be indicative of 'more central' (more relevant) information,
less loudness and faster tempo/rate of speech of 'less central'
information.[19] Loudness and tempo seem to link up to contour
delimitation only indirectly via these functions.)

(iii) *Integration/exposure by pausing.* The boundary between
two contours can further be established by a 'pause'. However,
'pauses' also occur within contours. For a period of perceptual
silence to be interpreted as a contour-delimiting device, additional
requirements need to be met. In particular, it seems to be necessary

that no articulatory gestures occur during the silence. Local and Kelly (1986) have in fact shown that not interrupting articulatory gestures such as glottal constriction during a pause is an interactionally relevant phenomenon: perceptual silence of this type is oriented to as a 'holding pause', which does not indicate the end of a contour, nor (*a fortiori*) that of a speaker's turn. 'Holding' of a turn during and over a period of perceptual silence can also be signalled by some anticipatory articulation movement on the segment preceding the pause. For instance, French (1988) has shown that non-vocalization of /r/ in British non-rhotic accents ('linking /r/') may be used to indicate that 'something more', i.e. a vowel, is going to follow after the pause. For English, it has also been shown that stress shift may be used as a floor-holding device signalling more to come following a period of silence which might otherwise be heard as contour-terminal.

For a silence to be interpretable as contour-delimiting, the articulatory gesture has to be interrupted entirely and anticipatory articulations must be absent. Of course, so-called filled pauses ('ehms') do not satisfy these requirements. If, on the other hand, additional material is to be integrated into an existing contour, 'pauses', if they occur at all, must be 'holding' or 'filled' pauses.

(iv) *Integration/exposure by rhythm.* According to the conception of rhythm followed here,[20] this implies in the first place integration into an existing isochronous pattern (if existent).[21] A smooth integration of additional material will therefore entail adding a new accent unit such that its stressed syllable is isochronous with the preceding stressed syllables. By contrast, exposure of new material may be achieved by interrupting an existing isochronous pattern. (Again, it should be added that isochronous rhythmic patterns often stretch over more than one intonational contour. The persistence of a rhythmic pattern therefore does not automatically entail that no boundary intervenes. Nevertheless, rhythmic patterns sometimes do begin and end within intonational phrases. The general point is that rhythm, and other prosodic cues such as loudness and tempo, are not foolproof indicators of prosodic boundaries. On the contrary, as with all contextualization cues, their interpretation is in itself context-dependent and, to use a conversation analytic term, dependent on 'local' surroundings.)

In the transcripts, rhythm will be represented by brackets below the intonational contour linking isochronous stresses. (15)′, a revised version of (15), shows a rhythmically integrated addition of material.

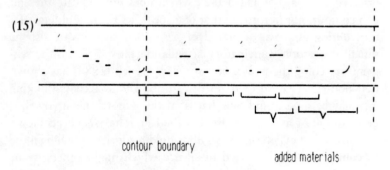

contour boundary

added materials

4 Syntax, prosody and thematic relevance

As the preceding sections have shown, both syntax and prosody offer ways to expand existing structures. In syntax, expansions come either in the shape of progressive expansions (continuations), or in the shape of (paradigmatically or syntagmatically) regressive expansions. In each case, a point of syntactic gestalt closure is suspended and postponed until completion of the expansion. In prosody, 'continuations', i.e. additive expansions of existing contours, may be integrated into preceding talk by adding new syllables to the last accent unit, by adding another accent unit within the contour (without an upstep or downstep), by incorporation into an isochronous rhythmic pattern, and/or by continuing with (approximately) the same loudness and tempo, without a (noticeable) pause.

We will now look at the interplay between syntax and prosody. This is an area in which the positions taken by various schools of linguistic thinking widely diverge. In the older generative approaches to the phonology of intonation, prosodic phrasing is usually derived from syntax, as a kind of shallow 'interpretation' of the information contained in the central syntactic component of grammar. In such an approach, intonation is entirely dependent on syntax. From the discussion in this section, it will become clear that such a position is untenable: we will see that for each syntactic type of expansion, prosody offers the possibility of either getting it done smoothly (by integrating the added material into the previous contour), or exposing it as an expansion of the already completed turn via packaging in a distinct contour.

A number of more recent theories, e.g. 'Prosodic Phonology', assume instead that syntactic constituents are the basis of prosodic phrasing (e.g. division into intonational contours), but that the prosodic component of grammar is independent enough from syntax to allow combining two (or more) syntactic constituents into one larger prosodic unit when necessary (for instance, when the syntactic units are too small to each form independent intonational contours), thus obliterating syntactic boundaries in prosodic representation.[22] Yet the opposite case is also observed: one syntactic unit may be split into various components by prosodic means, for reasons of emphasis (e.g. A: *what's new?* B: *Susy, is, pregnant!* uttered in three distinct intonational contours: fall–rise, fall–rise, rise–fall); or, prosody may be used for marking the closure of a grammaticalized anacoluthon (e.g. *and if I told her?* with 'question intonation' to indicate that the second part of the conditional is not to follow).

If, then, the independence of prosody from syntax is considerable, the priority of syntax nonetheless cannot be denied either. The discussion in the previous sections suggests a model in which syntax and prosody cooperate in very delicate ways, each of them on the basis of its particular semiotic possibilities. Into this model of a division of labour, syntax brings its capacity to build relatively far-reaching gestalts, the completion of which becomes more and more projectable in time; prosody, particularly intonation, brings in its local flexibility to revise and adjust these gestalts while they are being 'put to speech'. Thus, syntax retains its priority, but prosody/intonation is nevertheless independent from it.

The syntactic expansion types will now be considered in turn with regard to the way in which prosody operates on/packages them. Although all of them may be camouflaged or exposed by prosody, there are certain empirical imbalances between these two possibilities.

When *syntactic continuations* are prosodically integrated into the previous prosodic gestalt, there is no indication of an expansion at all. Although a syntactically defined completion point has been reached (marked by]), the continuation of the structure is neither a kind of regressive operation on the previous syntactic structure, nor prosodically (the beginning of) a new one:[23]

(18) CHINA 20

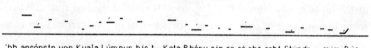

'hh ansónstn von Kuala Lúmpur bis t- Kota Bháru sin so séːchs acht Stúndn] mim Bús -
  {più forte   } {decrescendo   }

'hh apart from that from Kuala Lumpur to Kota Bharu it takes about six or eight hours by bus

(19) (=13) ALTWEIBERFASNACHT

det is fúrchbare fúrchbare Stimmung hier] im Hauːs

there is a horrible horrible atmosphere here in the house

However, it also happens that syntactic continuations are 'exposed' as expansions by prosody, as in the following two examples:

(20) CHINA 18

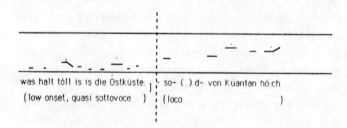

was halt tóll is is die Ostküste:] ¦ so- (.) d- von Kúantan hóːch
  {low onset, quasi sottovoce   } ¦ {loco   }

what is fantastic is the east coast - like - from Kuantan upwards

(21) (=1) MERCEDES

M: dann=zahl=i nomal zehndausend Mark drauf,=

(na)=hab=i=n fantàstischn (.) h Gä Tä í⌉ (.) géll,⌉

F: m:,=

⌐__ _ ⌐✓

M: =absolut néu, -

M: *in that case I pay another ten thousand marks in addition,=*
=and I get a fantastic (.) h GTI (.) you know,
F: *m:,=*
M: <u>*=absolutely new,*</u> *-*

On the basis of the available data it seems that asyndetic appositionals are typically 'exposed' by prosody (as in example 21). This seems plausible, for the added section always contains new information about a referent, i.e. it is highly rhematic. For other continuations, both options are equally available.

Among the *regressive, paradigmatic expansions, right dislocations* behave differently from the rest. As in examples (22) and (23), they seem to be formatted prosodically as 'smooth' more often than not. By integrating them into the previous intonational contour, the speaker gives a kind of cataphoric reading to the pronoun which is elaborated in the expansion (such as the *das* in (22) and the *des* in (23)), although the entity referred to by the pronoun has usually been mentioned in the conversation (just) before.

(22) CHINA 3

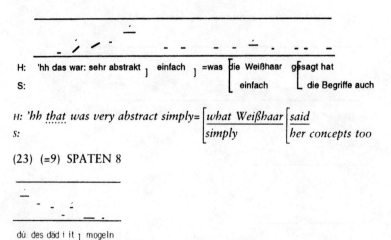

H: 'hh das war: sehr abstrakt] einfach] =was [die Weißhaar g]sagt hat
S: [einfach   [die Begriffe auch

H: 'hh *that* *was very abstract simply*= [*what Weißhaar* [*said*
S: [*simply*   [*her concepts too*

(23) (=9) SPATEN 8

dú des däd i it] mogeln

hey that I wouldn't do chéat;

In the case of (22), integration of *was die Weißhaar gesagt hat* into *das war sehr abstrakt einfach* (with an additional possible syntactic completion point: *einfach* is a regressive, syntagmatic expansion) is achieved by the absence of a pitch movement between *einfach* and *was*, and the unchanged tempo and loudness. In (23), a very short expansion (the infinitive *mogeln* 'cheat', substituting for *des* in the prior structure) is – despite its syntactic status – integrated so well into the contour as a sequence of two unstressed syllables after the (originally contour-final) second pitch accent, that exactly the same prosodic shape could be used if *mogeln* were to be replaced by a transitive verb such as *machen* 'do', which would then be the right brace of an entirely 'normal', non-expanded syntactic unit (*des däd i it mache* 'that I wouldn't do').[24]

The other paradigmatically regressive expansions (which are termed *repairs* more properly) behave in just the opposite way: often, they present themselves as prosodically 'exposed', constituting an intonation contour of their own:

(24) CHINA 15

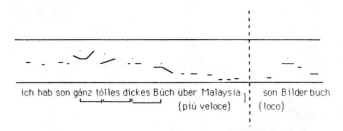

ich hab son gánz tólles díckes Búch über Malaysia] son Bílderbuch
(più veloce) (loco)

I've got a kind of really wonderful big book about Malaysia a kind of picture book

(25) CHINA 13

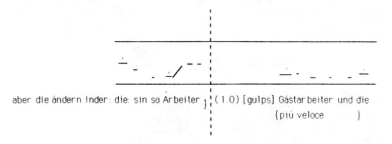

aber die ándern Inder: die: sin so Árbeiter] (1.0) [gulps] Gástarbeiter und die
(più veloce)

but the other Indians they are kind of workers (1.0) guest workers and they . . .

(26) CHINA 17

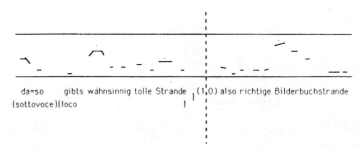

da=so gibts wáhnsinnig tolle Strande] (1.0) also richtige Bilderbuchstrande
(sottovoce)(loco)

there=kind=of are incredibly fantastic beaches (1.0) you know real story-book beaches

The beginning of the new contour in (24) is marked primarily by a return to average tempo after a stretch of *accelerando*; the pitch of the first syllable in the new contour is exactly at the level of the last syllable in the old contour and cannot serve as an indicator for prosodic exposure in this case. In (25), the new contour is signalled by a pause (and gulping), the upward pitch movement on *Arbeiter* followed by a lower onset on *Gastarbeiter*, as well as the faster tempo. In (26), a pause, a slight upstep on the anacrustic syllables of *also*, and the new global contour are responsible for the auditory impression of an exposed expansion.[25]

The last syntactic type, *syntagmatically retrospective expansions*, seem to occur equally frequently in either prosodic packaging. Thus, they may be smoothly integrated into an existing contour, which is done most unambiguously when they are added as low pitch syllables without further notable pitch movement ('de-stressing', see above):

(27) CHINA 2

als die sie auf den Vortrag á:ngesprochen hat] =während der Ta:gung

{decrescendo}

when she spoke to her about her talk during the conference

(28) (=22) CHINA 3

'hh das war: sehr abstrákt] einfach

'hh that was very abstract simply

The 'destressed' syllable, i.e. the one that could have received a pitch accent in another context, had prosody been used to expose the expansion, may be made somewhat more prominent by increased duration as in *Tagung* in (27).

Also integrated are expansions with an additional pitch movement which is added onto the existing contour, as in the following example:

(29) FASCHING 1

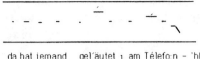

da hat jemand   gel'äutet ⌐ am Télefo:n - 'hhh
{very emphatic, high onset}

somebody rang on the telephone

Finally, the same type of syntactic expansion can be prosodically 'exposed' by being packaged into an intonational contour of its own. It is this constellation of syntactic and prosodic features that has sometimes been called an 'afterthought' (*Nachtrag*) in the literature:

(30) CHINA 1 (=16)

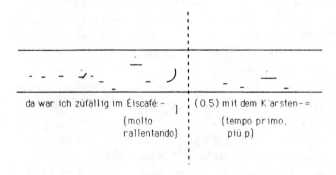

da war ich zúfällig im Éiscafé:- ⌐   (0.5) mit dem K'arsten-=
                    {molto   {tempo primo,
                    rallentando}   più p}

I happened to be in the ice parlour (0.5) with Karsten

(31) CHINA 6

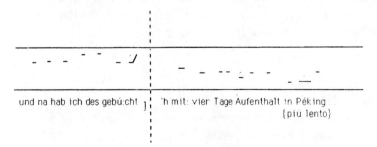

und na hab ich des gebú:cht ⌐ 'h mit: vier Tage Aufenthalt ın Péking
                                          {più lento}

and then I booked it 'h with four days in Peking

Since retrospective syntagmatic expansions appear in all possible prosodic packagings with some frequency (integrated/'destressed', integrated/new accent unit, exposed/new contour), they are well suited to show that, pragmatically, these alternatives are not equivalent.

'Destressing' added material downscales its relevance to thematic or subthematic status, while adding a new accent unit or even intonational contour with a pitch movement of its own attributes more, even rhematic, relevance to the addition. Thus, (29) may be said in a context in which it is not clear what is meant by *geläutet* (i.e. what it was that rang, the telephone, the door-bell, etc.), while a version in which *am Telefon* is added without further pitch movement is only adequate in a 'universe of discourse' in which the speaker can take it for granted that the recipient will know that it could only have been the telephone that rang. In the same way, prosodically independent expansions contextualize their pragmatic status as rhematic information. For instance, in (30), which is the beginning of a narrative, the fact that the teller was 'with Karsten' is new information added in the format of a side-remark, i.e. its status is that of rhematic material. No such interpretation would be possible if *mit dem Karsten* was prosodically integrated into the preceding intonation contour and 'destressed': in this case, prior mentioning of 'Karsten' would be presupposed.

The role of the prosodic packaging of an expansion with respect to its thematic/rhematic status is further supported by the way in which obligatory syntactic arguments are handled (which, as we have seen above, are not expansions, since a possible syntactic completion point has not been reached.) If such obligatory arguments are placed in the end-field, they are uttered in the shape of a new intonation contour as in (32), or they at least constitute a pitch movement of their own (as in example (33)):

(32) (=15) VERTRETUNG 2

    A: hallo?

    L: Hau:f

    A: ja grüßgott mein Name is Be::mann in Mü:nche:n

    L: grüß=sie Gott Herr Bemann=

    A: =ah:: Herr Hauf der Herr:: ahm: (.) Cemann der is nücht im Hause gei?

L: im: Moment nicht würd aber sam=ma in der nechsten
halb.n Stunde; also=er=wollte=an=und=für=sich schón m
(.) vórmittach da sein; ' ⌈th
A: ⌊ ja:, j ⌈ a:
L: ⌊ a:ber: eh: würd auf
jedn Fall in Kürze eintreff.n;
A: i:ich frage aus folgndn Grúnd=°eh°=mein=Name is Be:mann in
                            ((acc.))   ((loco))
München:?
L: ja:,=

wir hattn uns amal unterhóitn wegn=a éventuellen Vertrétung in Báyern oder Südbayern
                            ∟____∥∟_____∥∟____∥∟____∣

(A = caller)
A: hello?
L: Hau:f
A: yes good afternoon my name is Beman in Munich
L: good afternoon Mr Beman=
A: =ah Mr Hauf Mr ehm: (.) Ceman is not in is he?
L: at the moment he isn't but he will be in half an hour;
you see actually he wanted to be back in
the (.) morning; 'th ⌈
A   ⌊ yes ⌈ yes
L: ⌊ but: eh: he will arrive here very soon;
A: the reason I ask is this = eh = my name is Be:man in Munich?
L: yes,=
A: we once talked about a possible sales representation in Bavaria
or Southern Bavaria

(33) (=22/28) CHINA 3
H: das war sehr abstrákt einfach;=
=was   die ⌈ Weißhaar g ⌈ esagt hat.
S: ⌊ °einfach°   ⌊ die Begriffe auch (mit)
Metápher un Met ⌈ onymie un=un °Metonymie° (.) eh (0.5)
H: ⌊ °ja°   ((clapping noise))
S: schréiben un=wéiblicher=schrei ⌈ ben°
H: ⌊ °ja°
S: °und=solche=Sachen°=un=
vielleich=ein ⌈ fach, wenn se nícht in der Diskussion
H: ⌊ s=war f:-
S: drin ist.
H: °ehm° (0.3)

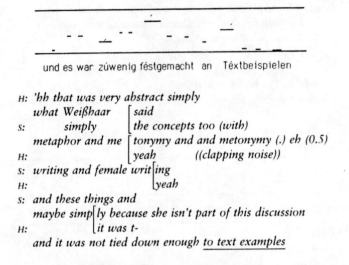

und es war zúwenig féstgemacht an   Téxtbeispielen

H: *'hh that was very abstract simply*
   what Weißhaar ⎡ *said*
S: *simply*   ⎣ *the concepts too (with)*
   metaphor and me ⎡ *tonymy and and metonymy (.) eh (0.5)*
H: ⎣ *yeah*   *((clapping noise))*
S: *writing and female writ*⎡*ing*
H: ⎣*yeah*
S: *and these things and*
   maybe simp⎡*ly because she isn't part of this discussion*
H: ⎣*it was t-*
   and it was not tied down enough <u>*to text examples*</u>

A full noun phrase as an obligatory argument cannot contain presupposed (or subthematic) information. Our interpretation of the effect of prosodic integration or exposure on the thematic/rhematic status of expansions predicts that obligatory arguments in the end-field will not be prosodically integrated and destressed. This is in fact the case.

The findings of this section can be summarized as follows: in principle, every syntactic expansion may be prosodically integrated and thereby 'camouflaged', or 'exposed' by being uttered in a new intonational contour.

From the point of view of information processing (or thematic relevance), the prosodic treatment of syntactic expansions gives them either rhematic or (sub)thematic value. The distinction between rhematic and (sub)thematic prosodic contextualization does not coincide with that between integration and non-integration, however: while non-integrated expansions are always rhematic, integrated expansions which add a new accent unit to the contour are rhematic as well; only 'destressed' expansions serve to contextualize clearly (sub)thematic information. What counts for the contextualization of rhematic/thematic information, then, is not so much the question of one or two intonational contours (which, as we shall see in the following section, is of primary importance for turn-taking), but instead the question of whether another pitch accent is added or not.[26]

5 Syntax, prosody and turn-taking

Up to this point, we have been concerned with the issue of how prosody either exposes or camouflages an expansion beyond a possible syntactic completion point. We must now become more precise on the role of prosody and syntax (and their interaction) for turn-taking. From the discussion in the preceding section, it would seem that prosody provides (some of) the contextualization cues which help participants bridge the gap between possible syntactic completion and possible turn completion. One model of how this happens would see prosody as a 'filter' between syntax and turn-taking. The filter would be used by participants to decide which possible syntactic completions may be heard as possible turn completions. It would have the effect of confirming or suspending the relevance of syntactic information for turn-taking, by underlining or cancelling the relevance of a syntactic completion point for turn transition. According to the 'filter model', speakers re-phrase syntactic constituents via prosody, and recipients process this prosodic surface information (disregarding syntax) for turn-taking cues.

This model is intuitively plausible and receives some prima facie support from another area in which intonation is important for turn-taking, but which is not the focus of the present chapter: the proposal that the type of pitch movement in the final part of the contour indicates whether a possible syntactic completion point, which also coincides with the end of an intonational contour, is turn-transition relevant. In a non-regional variety of German, good cues for indicating turn closure are global pitch movements that fall either throughout the contour or in its final accent unit to the speaker's 'base-line' (see examples (13), (14)). Level or (slightly) upward moving contours indicate turn-continuation instead (see examples (15), (16), (17))[27] – although certainly not always.[28] The 'filter model' states that it is enough to monitor the contour-final pitch movement to decide if a contour boundary is transition-relevant.

Applied to the problem at hand, i.e. the integration or non-integration of expansions into an existing contour, the 'filter model' leads to the assumption that integrated expansions are heard as suspending and postponing a possible turn-transition relevance, while exposed ones are not, i.e. they imply and define an intervening possible transition place. This is so because the model assumes that prosody 'lets pass' only its own phrasing, and obliterates syntactic boundaries (the]). As a consequence, prosodic integration would result in one turn-constructional unit (equivalent with any other, non-expanded syntactic structure), but prosodic exposure would result in two turn-constructional units. The unit-internal syntactic boundary] would be irrelevant to turn-taking in the first case, and no turn-taking turbulence would be expected around this place. The prosodically exposed syntactic boundary before the expansion in the second case would occasion all those possible turn-taking disturbances which may occur around possible transition places.

Analysis of the data reveals that these predictions are not borne out and that the filter model is not adequate. Although there is a large group of camouflaged expansions which are not 'problematic' with respect to turn-taking in any way (and are thus congruent with the 'filter model' predictions), next turns (or continuers, indicating recipient passes in turn-taking) are also regularly observed to be produced simultaneously with prosodically fully integrated (camouflaged) expansions, where these do not add a further accent unit to the intonational contour. This, as we have argued in the preceding section, happens particularly in the case of the syntagmatic regressive type (*Ausklammerungen*, see note 10), for instance in the following extracts:

(34) SEGLERINNEN

A: könn ma nomal (.) zusamm sprechn] ⌈morgn
B: ⌊ja::

A: *we can talk about that again* ⌈ *tomorrow*
B: ⌊ *yes*

(35) (=8) BÖRSIANER

A: da bin ich nich (.) (h)ni(h)ch so kl(h)einlich] ⌈dann
B: ⌊ja oke

A: *yes yes. I won't be so small-minded about that* ⌈ *then;*
B: ⌊ *yes o.k.*

(36) CHINA 7

H: das kannste dir auch (.) sélber anles⌈en] (.) vorher
S: ⌊mitm Stadtführer

H: *you can read that by yourself (.)* ⌈ *beforehand*
S: ⌊ *with a city guide*

Contrary to the predictions of the 'filter model', these overlaps are evidence for the relevance of syntax *and* prosody for the production and interpretation of possible turn-transition places. By overlapping material around the final brace (*sprechen, kleinlich* and *anlesen* in the above examples), participants orient to the completion of the *syntactic* gestalt represented by this brace as indicative of a possible turn completion. Post-brace material is thereby treated as added to a full syntactic gestalt, and at the same time, to the speaker's turn. (It may be noted that recipients' attention to possible syntactic completion points preceding 'debracing' is also evidence for the continued markedness of this construction, even in spoken German; contrary to the contentions of some grammarians, this construction has not become a regular pattern of spoken German syntax. It still has the status of a syntactic expansion.)

Recipients' monitoring of a possible syntactic completion point and the ensuing simultaneous talk is also related to the issue of rhematic relevance and its contextualization through prosody. By taking over the floor around the first possible syntactic completion point (or by passing it on with a continuer), next speakers display an understanding of the propositional content of the speaker's utterance. Prosodically contextualized non-rhematic, low-relevance expansion matches this: since the recipient has already displayed or signalled understanding, added material has low relevance on the propositional level. Also, if overlap occurs, the reception of the overlapped material may be impeded. A speaker has to take into account that expansions are vulnerable to overlap, even when produced within an intonational contour. By adding low-relevance material without a further accent, a speaker is on the safe side: even if overlap occurs, it will not jeopardize the reception of a central piece of information. By adding high-relevance material, however, s/he runs the risk of the material being 'deleted' by next speaker's talk.[29]

The inherent risk of adding rhematic, high-relevance material in an expansion (with appropriate, non-integrative prosody) leads to a noticeable conversational problem in example (37):

(37) CHINA 12

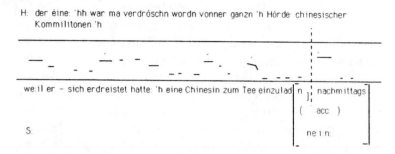

H: der éine: 'hh war ma verdróschn wordn vonner ganzn 'h Hórde: chinesischer Kommilitonen 'h

we:il er – sich erdreistet hatte: 'h eine Chinesin zum Tee einzulad| n ,| nachmittags
{ acc }

S.   ne:1:n:

H: *one of them [sc., the African students in China] had been beaten up by a whole gang of Chinese fellow students because he - had dared to invite a Chinese woman for te[a in the afternoon*
S: [no

H, the teller of the story about the racist Chinese, runs into trouble here, since the expansion of the main line of her story (Chinese mob beats up a black person who has 'dared to invite a Chinese woman for tea') is focal to the understanding of the gist of the story (i.e. that the invitation was 'in the afternoon', not in the evening, and that there was therefore no violation of decency rules). Recipient S starts her evaluation of the story slightly before the beginning of the expansion (*nachmittags*); although H tries to 'rush through' the possible turn-completion point after *einzuladen* by accelerating on the last (already overlapped) syllable of this word and the first syllable of the following *nachmittags*, this does not prevent S from delivering her emphatic exclamation *ne:i:n:*. Due to its very high onset, the expansion is clearly presented as an intonational contour of its own, thereby displaying its high informational value. Yet it is uttered in competition with the recipient's evaluation of the story, which starts at a point where she has hardly been able to grasp the full relevance of the telling, and which threatens the decodability of the very information that she would need to do so.

Extract (37) exemplifies a speaker's dilemma which, in the specific context of a narrative, is exacerbated by the obligations this genre puts on the recipient. The speaker's dilemma is the following: on the level of turn-taking, it would be appropriate and situationally adequate to package an expansion, if it is to be produced at all, as low-relevance material as soon as recipient starts simultaneous talk around the possible syntactic completion point. On the level of marking textual relevance, however, an expansion provided with an accent of its own can serve to foreground a phrase in a way that would not have been possible had it been placed within the inner-field of the sentence (cf. the discussion above). In the particular case of the present telling, H has two 'sensational' points to make: one is that the black student invited the Chinese woman for tea (and nothing else); the second is that this invitation was for the afternoon. Had H placed the constituent containing the second information (*nachmittags*) before the verbal complex (*zum Tee einladen*), this double point would have been spoiled and the information about the time of the day downgraded in relevance with respect to the information 'invited for tea'. The dilemma for the speaker then is that there may be contexts in which an expansion would be a very handy instrument for foregrounding information so that two noun phrases have equal rhematic status; but the same technique which is useful on the level of information structuring has its specific risks from the perspective of turn-taking.

What is more, there are structural constraints on the recipient to behave as she does in the present case and thereby thwart her interlocutor's attempts to highlight a second piece of information. These structural constraints are due to the fact that ('sensational') stories should receive an adequate (expressive) evaluation *as soon as* they can be heard as such. In the present instance, this is the case at the possible syntactic completion point which is reached after the teller has produced the first of her two points, i.e. after *einzuladen*. S, being a supportive co-conversationalist, duly makes use of this possible syntactic completion point to deliver her evaluation at this earliest possible moment, starting even slightly before it. This over-lap, however, turns out to be a problematic one, threatening to prevent as it does the teller's second sensational revelation from being interactionally successful.

One solution to the problems inherent in high-relevance expan-sions is to delay them until recipient has finished his or her next activity. In particular, speakers may delay expansions until after continuers; such expansions then have to be contextualized as non-integrative. See example (21), above, and the following (38):

(38) CHINA 1

H: da-=aber=da hab ich also jedenfalls áuch gemerkt,

daß die únheimlich únsicher is] uber únsere Gef´uhle ihr gegenuber `hh

S: aha
(piano)

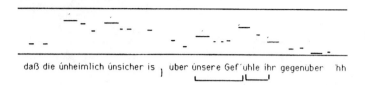

H: oder`?(.)`?uber   unsere Éinstellungen
(quasi sottovoce)

H: *then but anyway then I also realized that she is terribly unsure about our feelings towards her 'hh*
S: *I see*
H: *or (.) about our attitudes*

The sequentially different placement of the expansion in (38) reflects a process of constructing conversational meaning which is different from that in (34)–(36), but it also avoids the problems of (37): the speaker elaborates on, repairs, corrects, etc., a piece of information which has already been ratified interactionally by her recipient.[30]

In order to avoid the risk of having high-relevance expansions overlapped, speakers may produce them in an exposed intonational contour and withhold this second contour for some time; in this 'gap', recipients have the possibility of delivering an utterance of their own (as in (38)). If they don't, the expansions will be seen as being due to recipient's delay of a next utterance, possibly indicating some kind of 'problem' with speaker's utterance:

92 Peter Auer

(39) (=26) CHINA 17

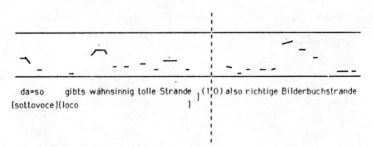

da=so gibts wåhnsinnig tolle Strände (1.0) also richtige Bilderbuchstrande
(sottovoce)(loco)

*there=kind=of are incredibly fantastic beaches (1.0) you know real story-
book beaches*

(40) (=3) SPATEN 5

A: ja der muß früh wieder héim

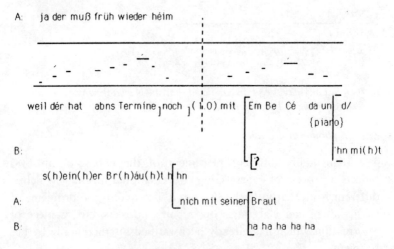

*A: yes he [a co-present colleague of A] has to go home
early because he's got appointments this evening still (1.0)
with MBC and*
B: ?   'hn wi(h)th h(h)is
girl h hn
A: not with his girl
B: ha ha ha ha ha

The two expansions *also richtige Bilderbuchstrände* and *mit Em
Be Cé da* – one a syntactic repair, the other a continuation – are
uttered as independent intonational contours. In both cases, the
preceding contour is marked as possibly turn-final by a final falling

pitch on the last unstressed syllable(s);[31] the non-holding silence
before the beginning of the expansion, as well as its internal prosodic make-up (pitch accent) signal its prosodic independence.

In extract (40), the interactional relevance of the withheld expansion is particularly evident for, in this case, both the present speaker
and the recipient offer expansions after a period of silence. The
situation is this: A and B are business partners engaged in a telephone conversation; A's colleague C (mentioned in this extract) is
with him in the same room. All three know each other well; talk is
about their respective plans for the day. A says that C won't be
staying long in the office because he has further appointments later
in the evening. The mentioning of appointments in the evening
reminds B of a former meeting in which C had used this same
argument as an excuse to get away from A and B and meet his
girl-friend.

In the extract, B withholds response to A's – somewhat vague –
account of why C has to go home early in the evening. A thereupon
adds another turn component which specifies what kind of an
appointment C has; by doing so, he retrospectively attributes to B
a reason for his non-response, i.e. that his own formulation was not
enough to account for C's plans. In order to correct this attribution
(which has face-threatening correlates, since B is not in a position to
question C's plans for the evening), the recipient now provides an
expansion of his own, formulating in a joking manner (see the
laughter underlying his utterance and framing it) his suspicion
that, once again, C is concealing from him (them) the true reason
why he cannot stay on in the evening. Both expansions are clearly
rhematic, adding information not contained in the previous clause
and, at least in B's case, central to the allusion he is trying to
make.[32]

The extracts discussed in this section have shown that prosody
and syntax are both monitored by recipients in order to decide
when it may be their turn to take the floor, and that a 'filter
model' for the interaction between the two is inadequate. They
also demonstrate in various ways that the prosodic packaging of
an expansion is not at the speaker's disposal alone: since expansions
are overlap-vulnerable, speakers and recipients cooperate in their
construction, and thereby in the construction of the speaker's turn.
This cooperation is most successful for overlapped low-relevance

expansions and exposed high-relevance expansions after an intervening silence, which minimizes the risk of recipient's talk during
the expansion itself. More difficult to handle are expansions without such intervening silence and which show pitch movement (i.e.
add another accent unit to the contour). In this case, recipient's
overlapping of the high-relevance material marked by this prosodic
treatment (as in example (37)) cannot be excluded.

6 Conclusion

We have tried to outline some of the complex ways in which syntax
and prosody contribute to the construction of turns in conversation,
focussing on syntactic expansions of an already closed syntactic
gestalt. It has been argued that the various types of such expansions
can be treated as part of an existing intonational contour or as a
new intonational contour, i.e. they can be prosodically 'exposed' or
'camouflaged'. Although these two possibilities are basically available for all types of expansion, there seem to be certain preferences:
right dislocations tend to be camouflaged, asyndetic appositionals
and repairs in the strictest sense seem to be more often exposed.

On the level of information processing, expansions that contain
at least one accent unit have a pragmatic status that is different
from camouflaged expansions without further pitch movement:
the former present themselves as rhematic, or highly relevant, the
latter as (sub)thematic, or of low relevance. This differing pragmatic
status and the fact that all expansions are vulnerable to overlap can
lead to a conflict. In particular, although there are good pragmatic
reasons for foregounding a constituent by placing it after a possible
syntactic completion point and marking it prosodically, the same
constituent is in danger of being 'deleted' by simultaneous talk in
this position. It has been shown how speakers and recipients can
cooperate to achieve a pattern which avoids this conflict. Either the
first point of syntactic gestalt closure is interpreted as a 'recognition
point' for turn-taking by recipient, after which speaker adds only
low-relevance material, contextualized prosodically by the addition
of unstressed syllables without further pitch protrusion and delet-
able by overlap; or, high-relevance (rhematic) material is added as a
new intonational contour after a small 'gap', or after a recipient's

continuer, which frames it as a response to the recipient's initial withholding of a next activity.

Notes

I wish to thank Elizabeth Couper-Kuhlen, Aldo di Luzio, Susanne Günthner, Margret Selting and Susanne Uhmann for their often extensive and helpful comments on previous versions of this chapter.

1 See Kendon 1967, 1973: Goodwin 1981; for an early comprehensive treatment see Duncan 1972.
2 See Gumperz 1982 as well as various papers in Auer and di Luzio 1992.
3 The term is borrowed from Silverstein 1992.
4 The notion of a 'sentence' will be avoided; for a discussion of the difficulties associated with this term, see Crystal 1979, Auer 1992.
5 See Auer 1992.
6 A more detailed discussion on this issue may be found in Auer 1991.
7 See the approach to French spoken syntax along these lines in Blanche-Benveniste, Bilger, Rouget and van den Eynde 1991.
8 See Klein 1984.
9 Some of these preferences or rules may be found in Heidolph, Flämig and Motsch 1981, 702–764; also see Uhmann 1993 for a discussion.
10 Expansions of this type are known as *Ausklammerungen* ('debracing') among German grammarians. 'Debracing' is a well-investigated phenomenon (historically and, somewhat less, synchronically). The interested reader is referred to Lambert 1976 and the more recent work by Zahn 1991 for a more extensive review of research. From an interactional point of view, there is no reason to treat *Ausklammerungen* differently from other types of post-closure expansions (sometimes called *Rechtsherausstellung*; see Altmann 1981).
11 Paradigmatic substitution (replacement) is a syntactic operation and must be strictly separated from the semantic operation performed by it. In particular, it does not imply (error) correction. In fact, 'right dislocations' are never such error corrections, and 'repairs' are so only occasionally. More usually, they are 'elaborations' or 'clarifications'.
12 As a syntactically retrospective Type 1 expansion, i.e. an insert before *Hülse, rund* would have to agree with the noun in case and gender (*(eine) runde*). Pragmatically it would do the same job, but its syntactic status would be quite different.
13 *Des* is an allegro contraction of *das ist*. The whole construction is a syntactic pivot (sometimes called *apo koinu*).
14 See Local and Kelly 1986, Local 1992, Local, Wells and Sebba 1985, and in particular Local, Kelly and Wells 1986.
15 According to Selting, these five types are frequent and prototypical, but the list is not exhaustive. In fact, the contours found in the data used for

the present investigation show a wider variety of global contours than
the five types mentioned.

16 Examples in this paragraph are actually encountered intonation contours taken from conversational transcripts. Their segmental basis has
been left out so that syntax and semantics will not bias an appreciation
of their prosodic shape. The melody may be underlaid by any sequence
of syllables, each dot or line conforming to a shorter or longer syllable.
(Length iconically represents phonetic duration.) Pitch movements were
transcribed auditorily, but checked instrumentally for all transcripts in
the extract series 'CHINA'. (For measurement, the Kay Elemetrics
model 5500 Signal Analysis Workstation at the Phonogrammarchiv
of the University of Zürich was used. My thanks to Elizabeth
Couper-Kuhlen for providing me access to this laboratory.)

The scale implicit in this kind of transcription does not correspond
directly to numerical fundamental frequency values, but only via a log-
transformation. It should be read rather like music, the musical intervals being much closer to human perception of pitch change than
differences in Hz values.

17 Expansions of prosodic gestalts (intonational contours) are usually of
the prospective, syntagmatic type. Retrospective paradigmatic expansions, i.e. repairs on previous contours, may occur as well but seem to
be rare.

18 Future comparative research will have to decide if (some) varieties of
German and English show different prosodic structure with respect to
the status of pitch jumps on non-accented syllables in the immediate
context of accented ones. Most analyses of English intonation suggest
that unaccented syllables within a contour usually follow on from a
prior accent syllable; i.e. pitch jumps such as in example (15) are rare.
For the German data used in the present study (which are mainly from
southern Germany), this does not seem to be the case.

19 On the contextualizing functions of tempo/speech rate cf. Uhmann
1992, Barden 1991 and Couper-Kuhlen 1992.

20 See Couper-Kuhlen 1993; Auer, Couper-Kuhlen and Müller (to
appear).

21 A rhythmic pattern is said to be isochronous when at least three stresses
(phonetic prominences) follow each other at a pace even enough to be
perceived as regular.

22 E.g. Nespor and Vogel 1986.

23 In this and the following figures, prosodic parameters are placed in
curly brackets, with p = piano, acc = accelerando, loco = return to
normal, etc.

24 Some analysts of spoken language (e.g. Zimmermann 1964) have interpreted right dislocations as a particularly efficient way of negotiating
the fit between speaker's amount of verbalization and recipient's background knowledge. The argument is that by using a pronoun first,
speakers can test out if shared background knowledge alone is suffi-

cient for the recipient in order to achieve propositional understanding, with the result that the dislocated phrase need not be uttered if recipient signals such understanding beforehand. An interactive analysis of right dislocations as recipient-initiated repairs does not seem to be adequate for the German data investigated here, where prosodically independent right dislocations (in the shape of a new contour) are the exception rather than the rule. The data present evidence, then, for a certain degree of grammaticalization of such constructions in present-day spoken German.

25 It will be noted that in (26), insertion of the 'repair marker' *also* encourages the prosodic separation of the two contours.

26 In this context, the explanation given by Uhmann 1993 for the occurrence of expansions in spoken German is of interest. She argues that accented expansions always have 'narrow focus' while the same constituent placed in the central field of a German sentence would be open to a reading of either 'narrow' or, more likely, 'wide focus'. In this sense, putting a stressed constituent in the post-field of a sentence would serve to exclude the latter interpretation. However, wide and narrow focus for the interpretation of a constituent in the central field are alternatives only as long as there is just one 'sentence stress' in the contour. Thus, the utterance

eine Chinesin zum Tée einzuladen, náchmittags

has two foci, the second of which is identical with the expansion. The alternative version

eine Chinesin nachmittags zum Tée einzuladen

is indeed ambiguous between a narrow focus (*zum Tee*) and a wide one (presumably the whole subordinated clause). However, if both *nachmittags* and *Tee* receive a pitch accent, as is perfectly possible in spoken German, both are independent rhematic pieces of information just as in the expanded version, and each of them defines one focus constituent:

eine Chinesin náchmittags zum Tée einzuladen

Thus, Uhmann's explanation rests on the questionable assumption that a prosodic contour may contain only one 'sentence accent'.

27 I believe that the so-called progredient intonation contours of German (slightly bent upward) cannot be differentiated unambiguously from 'questioning intonations', i.e. upward contours implying turn completion, without taking into account syntax and content. (In fact, I know from syntax that, in (17), a question is implied, while the upward contours in (15) and (16) are not turn-final. From the contours alone, however, no such information can be taken.) It seems that only level and base-line fall contours are good indicators for turn (in)completion.

28 See Cutler and Pearson 1986, who show that intonation alone is not
    sufficient to cue turn completion in English discourse.
29 The recurrence of simultaneous talk around syntactic completions post-
    poned by syntactic expansions may also shed some light on the defini-
    tion of 'recognition points'. (In Jefferson's terms, the transition between
    the 'old' syntactic structure and its expansion is a 'recognitional term-
    inal overlap', see Jefferson 1980.) Close inspection of the internal gram-
    matical and prosodic context of such recognition points reveals that
    one structurally defined locus for which this categorization is justified is
    precisely that of a possible syntactic (but not prosodic) completion.
30 Some of the interactional details of such 'delayed' repairs or expansions
    are also investigated in Schegloff 1992.
31 In (40), the final adverbial *noch* is itself an expansion of the prosodi-
    cally integrated type (*Ausklammerung*).
32 It will be noted that the silence around the first transition-relevant
    gestalt closure (a 'gap' in the terminology of Sacks, Schegloff and
    Jefferson 1974) is not transformed into a 'pause' (i.e. an intra-turn
    event) by the expansion, as has been claimed occasionally in the litera-
    ture, at least not into a 'pause' as usually produced within a turn-
    constructional unit (e.g. Bergmann 1982). Since the passage before
    the expansion shows none of the features preparing a holding silence
    (see above), the transition relevance of such a silence remains visible.

References

Altmann, H. 1981. *Formen der 'Herausstellung' im Deutschen*. Tübingen:
    Niemeyer.
Auer, P. 1991. Vom Ende deutscher Sätze. *Zeitschrift für Germanistische
    Linguistik*, 19(2): 139–157.
    1992. The neverending sentence: rightward expansion in spoken lang-
    uage. In M. Kontra and T. Váradi (eds.) *Studies in Spoken Languages:
    English, German, Finno-Ugric*. Budapest: Linguistics Institute/
    Hungarian Academy of Sciences, pp. 41–59.
Auer, P. and A. di Luzio (eds.) 1992. *The Contextualization of Language*.
    Amsterdam and Philadelphia: Benjamins.
Auer, P., E. Couper-Kuhlen and F. Müller (to appear). *Language in Time:
    the rhythm and tempo of spoken interaction*.
Barden, B. 1991. Sprechgeschwindigkeit und thematische Struktur. *KontRI
    Working Paper* 15, Dept. of Linguistics, University of Konstanz.
Bergmann, J. 1982. Schweigephasen im Gespräch. Aspekte ihrer interakti-
    ven Organisation. In H. G. Soeffner (ed.) *Beiträge zu einer empirischen
    Sprachsoziologie*. Tübingen: Narr, pp. 143–184.
Blanche-Benveniste, C., M. Bilger, C. Rouget and K. van den Eynde 1991.
    Le français parlé. Paris: Centre National de la Recherche Scientifique.

Couper-Kuhlen, E. 1992. Contextualizing discourse: the prosody of inter-active repair. In P. Auer and A. di Luzio 1992, pp. 337–364.

1993. *English Speech Rhythm. Form and function in everyday verbal interaction.* Amsterdam and Philadelphia: Benjamins.

Crystal, D. 1979. Neglected grammatical factors in conversational English. In S. Greenbaum, G. Leech and J. Svartvik (eds.) *Studies in English Linguistics.* London: Longman, pp. 153–166.

Cutler, A. and M. Pearson 1986. On the analysis of prosodic turn-taking cues. In C. Johns-Lewis (ed.) *Intonation in Discourse.* San Diego: College Hill Press Inc., pp. 130–155.

Duncan, S. 1972. Some signals and rules for taking speaking turns in conversation. *Journal of Personality and Social Psychology,* 23(2): 283–292.

French, P. 1988. Word final /r/ in a Northern English accent: an interac-tional account of variable production. In P. Auer and A. di Luzio (eds.) *Variation and Convergence.* Berlin: de Gruyter, pp. 124–132.

Fries, N. 1987. Zu einer Randgrammatik des Deutschen. In J. Meibauer (ed.) *Satzmodus zwischen Grammatik und Pragmatik.* Tübingen: Nie-meyer, pp. 75–95.

Goodwin, C. 1981. *Conversational Organization.* New York: Academic Press.

Grosjean, F. and C. Hirt (in press). Using prosody to predict the end of sentences in English and French: Normal and brain-damaged subjects. *Language and Cognitive Processes.*

Gumperz, J. J. 1982. *Discourse Strategies.* Cambridge University Press.

Heidolph, K. E., W. Flämig and W. Motsch (eds.) 1981. *Grundzüge einer deutschen Grammatik.* Berlin: Akademie-Verlag.

Jefferson, G. 1980. Notes on some orderlinesses of overlap onset. In V. d'Urso and P. Leonardi (eds.) *Discourse Analysis and Natural Rhetorics.* Padova: Cleup Editore, pp. 11–38.

Kendon, A. 1967. Some functions of gaze-direction in social interaction. *Acta Psychologica,* 26: 22–63.

1973. The role of visible behavior in the organization of face-to-face interaction. In M. v. Cranach and I. Vine (eds.) *Social Communication and Movement. Studies of interaction and expression in man and chimpanzee.* London and New York: Academic Press, pp. 29–74.

Klein, W. 1984. Bühler Ellipse. In C. F. Graumann and T. Herrmann (eds.) *Karl Bühlers Axiomatik.* Frankfurt: Klostermann, pp. 117–141.

Lambert, P. 1976. *Ausklammerung in Modern Standard German.* Ham-burg: Buske.

Local, J. K. 1992. Continuing and restarting. In P. Auer and A. di Luzio 1992, pp. 272–296.

Local, J. K. and J. Kelly 1986. Projection and 'silences': notes on phonetic and conversational structure. *Human Studies,* 9: 185–204.

Local, J. K., J. Kelly and W. H. G. Wells 1986. Towards a phonology of conversation: turn-taking in Tyneside English. *Journal of Linguistics*, 22: 411–437.

Local, J. K., W. H. G. Wells and M. Sebba 1985. Phonology for conversation: phonetic aspects of turn delimitation in London Jamaican. *Journal of Pragmatics*, 9: 309–330.

Nespor, M. and I. Vogel 1986. *Prosodic Phonology.* Dordrecht: Foris.

Sacks, H., E. A. Schegloff and G. Jefferson 1974. A simplest systematics for the organization of turn-taking for conversation. *Language*, 50: 696–735. Revised and enlarged version in J. Schenkein (ed.) 1978, *Studies in the Organization of Conversational Interaction.* New York: Academic Press, pp. 7–55.

Schegloff, E. A. 1992. Repair after next turn. The last structurally provided defence of intersubjectivity in conversation. *American Journal of Sociology*, 97: 1295–1345.

Selting, M. 1995. *Prosodie im Gespräch. Aspekte einer interaktionalen Phonologie der Konversation.* Tübingen: Niemeyer.

Silverstein, M. 1992. The indeterminacy of contextualization: when is enough enough? In P. Auer and A. di Luzio 1992, pp. 55–76.

Uhmann, S. 1992. Contextualizing relevance: on some forms and functions of speech rate changes in everyday conversation. In P. Auer and A. di Luzio 1992, pp. 297–336.

1993. Das Mittelfeld im Gespräch. In M. Reis (ed.) *Wortstellung und Informationsstruktur.* Tübingen: Niemeyer, pp. 313–354.

Zahn, G. 1991. *Beobachtungen zur Ausklammerung und Nachfeldbesetzung in Gesprochenem Deutsch.* Erlangen: Palm & Enke.

Zimmermann, H. 1964. *Zu einer Typologie des spontanen Gesprächs.* Bern: Francke.

Ending up in Ulster: prosody and turn-taking in English dialects

BILL WELLS AND SUE PEPPÉ

1 Introduction

Although great strides have been made recently in the phonetic analysis of prosodic features as a result of technological developments, the advances in phonological analysis have arguably been less impressive, at least with respect to the phonology of intonation systems. This is evident if one considers a traditional concern of phonologists: the comparison of related languages or dialects. A great deal of work has been done on comparative phonology at the segmental level, and a good deal also on comparing lexical tone, stress and accent, yet there is strikingly little published research that systematically compares the intonational systems of related languages, dialects or accents. For example, in John Wells' compendious study of English accents, intonation is given little space (Wells 1982). Cruttenden (1986) notes that, although there have been scattered individual studies of different accents, these have not been used as a basis for systematic comparative work. This is somewhat surprising, given the increasing recognition, within the world of speech technology as well as more traditional applications of linguistics, that prosodic features of intonation are centrally involved in the comprehension of speech and the management of conversational interaction. Surely the ability to handle dialectal prosodic variation will be a *sine qua non* of a successful speech recognition system, and, one would hope, of an acceptable speech synthesis system too.

This omission is not happenstance, but derives from a general unwillingness on the part of linguists to treat 'intonation' with due phonological respect. In particular, there has been a failure to recognize the importance of warranting, from the observable behaviour of naive native speakers, the functional categories that intonational features are held to be exponents of. Conversation analysis (CA) has a great deal to offer to intonation studies in this regard, since its practitioners have been centrally concerned with the warranting of interactional categories from the observable behaviour of participants in the talk (see Atkinson and Heritage 1984). The present study describes the role of prosodic features in turn-taking in Belfast English, using an approach that combines CA with impressionistic phonetic observation. The description is followed by some suggestions as to how such an approach to prosodic description can provide a principled basis for comparative phonological statements.

2 Turn delimitation

One candidate function of prosodic features in English is to handle the exchange of speaking turns. General mechanisms of turn-taking have been outlined by Sacks, Schegloff and Jefferson (1974); but there are clearly language-, dialect- and accent-specific factors involved in the ways in which conversationalists convey that they have finished a speaking turn, are continuing the current turn, or are claiming a new turn.

There is no *a priori* reason to assume that prosodic features are centrally involved in the handling of turn transition: Sacks, Schegloff and Jefferson do not refer to them, and most descriptions of English intonation do not consider its turn-signalling functions explicitly. Brazil (1978:33) suggests that there may be a relationship between 'discourse units' and 'pitch sequences' but the discourse units in question are topic units (called 'transactions') which are bigger than speaker turns (Coulthard and Brazil 1979:46). Brazil does not in fact account for any aspects of prosodic patterning in terms of speaker's intention to signal turn completion: the transition of turns presumably 'falls out' from the interaction of the phonological systems of key, termination and tone which were established by reference to other functional criteria. Brown, Currie and Kenworthy (1980) do include turn transition in their list of intonational functions, under 'interactive structure', asserting that speaker's choice of pitch direction on the final stressed syllable of a pause-defined unit indicates whether or not the speaker intends to continue his turn (1980:24), although in their final statement of the Edinburgh intonational system, it appears that the choice of tone determines continuation of topic rather than of turn (1980:190), and the presence or absence of a tone on the last stressed syllable of the pause-defined unit belongs to an optional system of *syntactic* delimitation (1980:158), rather than turn delimitation. In suggesting that prosodic features are involved in an optional system of syntactic delimitation, Brown, Currie and Kenworthy follow Trubetskoy's lead: 'each language possesses specific, phonological means that signal the presence or absence of a sentence, word or morpheme boundary at a specific point in the sound continuum. But these means are only ancillary devices' (Trubetskoy 1969; cited in Brown, Currie and Kenworthy 1980:158). Local, Wells and Sebba (1985), by contrast, propose that the domain of those delimitative features sometimes associated with the sentence is not in fact the sentence itself but the turn – an interactional unit – and that in conversation the sentence is delimited just in the case where it is coextensive with the turn. The 'optional' nature of sentence delimitation can then be accounted for by the fact that one sentence may constitute a turn, but a turn may consist of more than one sentence.

Although there is no *a priori* reason to assume that turn delimitation is realized prosodically, there is a distinct theoretical advantage in treating turn delimitation as a candidate function of prosodic features: it is a relatively straightforward matter to identify turn transitions in conversation, and, having identified them, the analyst can identify recurrent linguistic features which accompany them and show the relevance they have for participants in the conversation. Techniques for identifying the phonetic features specifically associated with the delimitation of speakers' turns have been developed in studies of two very different varieties of English, the findings of which are summarized later in this chapter (Local, Wells and Sebba 1985; Local, Kelly and Wells 1986). At no point do these techniques require an appeal to the intuitions of the native speaker. It is implicit in the findings of the two turn-delimitation studies that in each variety an accentual system operates to delimit stretches of talk as phonological entities. These accentual systems are phonological, since they relate phonetic exponents (of pitch, loudness, tempo and other parameters) to the functional category of turn delimitation. Since the functional category remains constant in the analysis of different varieties (London Jamaican, Tyneside, and Ulster presented below), phonological categories and phonetic exponents can be compared and contrasted across dialects.

2.1 Prosodic aspects of turn delimitation in Ulster English

Ulster English is of particular interest to students of English intonation since it is one of the accents that is characterized by a rising pitch pattern for declaratives (Jarman and Cruttenden 1976). It thus provides an obvious challenge to any approach that starts out from the Southern British 'standard' variety, which is characterized by a falling pitch pattern for declaratives. At the same time, it bears a prima facie resemblance to some other accents of British English, such as those of Tyneside (Local 1986) and West Midlands (Wells 1989), which also have a characteristic rising pattern. The data analysed here were collected as part of a sociolinguistic study conducted in Belfast in the mid-1970s, in the course of informal interviews (Milroy 1987). The analysis focusses initially on a single extended extract from one conversation, in order to identify those phonetic features which regularly accompany turn-endings. Some contributions are not included for consideration, e.g. those made by the non-Ulster interviewer, or those that produce a response from her: although her turns come across as appropriate and seem unproblematic for co-participants, it is possible that she is not orienting to all the features available to speakers of the variety of English in question. The interviewer's participation in the conversation was very limited, and has not been used to warrant any of the major claims of the analysis. (See appendix for transcription conventions.)

CONVERSATION

MA 01   he was the first one to smack a gi:rl (0.9)

           {alleg.........}   {< >}

MB 02   ┌ yes/
F? 03   └ aye/

MA 04   smacked a wee: woman=

                  {dim..........}

FA 05   =(we) had an American minister and that though (0.5)

                       {dim....{ral.................}}

?   06   oh (   )

M? 07   from Lo:s Angeles (0.5)

?   08   (giggles)

?   09   (   )=

FI 10   =what did he make of it all (1.3)

M?   11   he li:ked it=
             {p, alleg..< >;......}
?   12   =(   )=

FA   13   =he liked them he liked both sides of the community
             {alleg.............................. < >.....................................}
FI   14   yeah
FA   15   when he (.) when he (0.4) when he got (0.3) he says he's seen
     16   no difference you know ⎡what I/ mean (0.6)
MA   17   ⎣yeah/

MA   18   I mean (.) you know he wasn't like a minister that sits
             {alleg...}

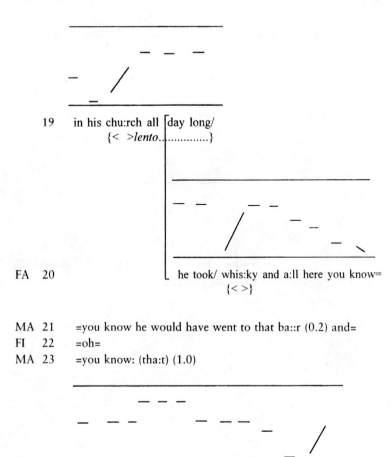

19   in his chu:rch all ⌈day long/
                        {< >*lento*..⌊............}

FA   20   ⌊ he took/ whis:ky and a:ll here you know=
                                        {< >}

MA 21   =you know he would have went to that ba::r (0.2) and=
FI   22   =oh=
MA 23   =you know: (tha:t) (1.0)

MB 24   there was another one come over that night too
            {*f,⌊alleg*..

25   there was two ministers that night wasn't there (0.5)
               .... f }{dim...}}

FA 26   ah but there was only one come in he:re=
               {alleg.. < >}

MB 27   =there was one we met (but the man has) another frie::nd
               {alleg..................................< >..

28   was a minister:: another frie:nd that came down later on
               ....< >...

```
29    that night and (this) friend was a minister (.)
      ............................<>{dim...............}}
?     30    m
```

2.1.1 Phonetic features

Phonetic features that occur at turn-endings in the clear (i.e. where there is a smooth transition between speakers, without overlapping talk) include:

(i) *swell*: a sudden increase and decrease in loudness during the ictus syllable of the last foot of the turn (shown as < >);

(ii) *lengthening*: appreciable duration on the ictus syllable of the last foot of the turn, whatever the phonological length of the vowel;

(iii) *rallentando*: a general slowing down in tempo to the end of the turn: the domain being, minimally and usually, the last two feet of the turn;

(iv) *pause* at the end of the turn;

(v) *pitch contour*: the overall pitch pattern of the turn is generally 'bowl'-shaped, although not symmetrically so (see fig. 3.1a, the Bowl). It tends to start high, with the pitch-level of each succeeding syllable slightly lower than the last, until a rising ictus syllable in the final foot brings the pitch steeply up to a peak which generally reaches or exceeds the level of the previous one. These two peaks stand out as prominent features and have been identified as:

    (a) *final pitch peak*, i.e. denoting the highest point of the utterance, present in the last (usually two) feet;

    (b) *onset pitch peak*, i.e. a high point occurring near the beginning of the utterance.

(vi) *rise* designates the last on-syllable rising pitch movement of the turn. Often the location is the final ictus syllable of the turn. However, in some cases the final rise occurs well before

the end of the utterance, being located on the lexically
stressed syllable of the word of focal importance in the utterance, which also shows more of the other salient phonetic
features (such as swell, wide pitch-movement, lengthening)
than any subsequent syllable. In such cases, the pitch on
subsequent syllables may (a) be sustained (continue at the
final high peak of the utterance) or (b) step gradually
down, without pronounced movement or other features
such as swell and lengthening, and without reaching the
bottom of the speaker's pitch-range. In the latter case, the
impression is of a 'spout' being added to the 'bowl'-shape:
an optional variation on the basic shape (see fig. 3.1b, Bowl-
with-spout). Variant (a) would appear to correspond to
Jarman and Cruttenden's Tone 2 (High Rise), whilst variant
(b) seems to correspond to their Tone 3 (Rise–Fall).

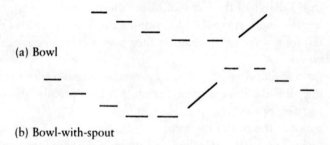

(a) Bowl

(b) Bowl-with-spout

Figure 3.1

(vii) *drop* (see Crystal 1969): the pitch pattern that precedes the
final rise can take slightly different forms, in part depending
on the phonological context. There is sometimes a 'kink' in
the pitch contour before the final rise: the pitch on the syllable immediately before the main rise sometimes drops lower
than is predicted by the contour described in (v) above, and is
then brought immediately back up to start the final rise (see
fig. 3.2a, the Dip: clear examples of this can be seen in the
transcript at lines 19, 24, 26); sometimes the syllable immediately before the syllable carrying the main rise continues the
contour shape, but then the pitch is dropped for the start of
the syllable carrying the main rise (see fig. 3.2b, the Dive:

lines 5, 11, 13, 20, 29). This characteristic, in both manifes-
tations, is here described as 'drop'.

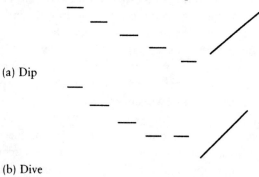

(a) Dip

(b) Dive

Figure 3.2

Not all the features listed are present at every turn transition, but
most non-problematic turn transitions display a cluster of them, as
the following examples show:

in line 4, there is lengthening and rise to final pitch-peak on
wee, sustained over *wo-*, and there is a bowl-shaped pitch-
pattern (although the starting-point, *smacked*, is relatively
low). The bowl is thus not symmetrical: the pitch-peak on
wo- is higher than that on *smacked*. There is also *diminuendo*, and a tiny step-down at the end, in that the last
syllable is slightly lower than the peak. There is no pause.

in line 5, there is no lengthening or swell on the ictus syllable,
min-, but there is *rallentando* and *diminuendo* on *and that
though*. There is onset pitch-peak on the first word, *we*,
followed by a smooth stepping down to *-can*; then a drop
(dive) to the start of *min-*, with a steep rise to *-ster* at about
the level of *had*. Stepping down is apparent on *and that
though*: this is therefore an example of the 'bowl-with-
spout' shape. There is a brief pause before the next speaker
(who produces about five unrecoverable syllables).

in line 20 there is onset peak on *he took*, and a drop (dive) to
the start of *whisky*. There is swell on *whi-*, and the lengthening happens on the /s/ of *whisky* rather than on the
stressed vowel /i/; for this reason there is more pitch-jump
than rising pitch-movement between the first and second

syllables of *whisky*. Final pitch-peak, slightly lower than onset, is maintained over *-sky and*; some slowing is achieved by the lengthening of the vowel of *all*, and there is stepping down over *all here you know*. There is no pause before the next speaker begins with *you know*.

in line 26 the utterance is pitched at the lower end of the speaker's range; it starts mid-height at *ah but*, steps up slightly to *on-*, then down smoothly as far as *come*; *in* is dropped below adjacent syllables; *here* has swell and lengthening, and rises probably to the level of the onset pitch-peak (the next speaker's turn is so closely latched at this point that the final pitch of *here* cannot be heard). There is effectively a *rallentando* by virtue of the lengthened vowel of *here*. There is no pause before the previous speaker takes up again.

The pitch shapes of turn-endings are mainly rising, or rising-and-stepping-down; and we have not been able to identify contexts in which, for turn-taking considerations, one of these two pitch-patterns (rise or rise plus step down) may be preferred to the other. This is in line with Jarman and Cruttenden, who also identify two related contours (High Rise and Rise–Fall). They go on to claim that the latter is a more emphatic version of the former, i.e. contextually conditioned, though in our data there is no evidence to suggest the two are not in free variation (Jarman and Cruttenden 1976:9).

There is one other pitch pattern that occurs, albeit very rarely, at turn-endings in the clear elsewhere in the conversation. This is an on-syllable falling pitch with no previous rise as in the following extracts:

(1)
MA 77   you know: woman (a)cross the road there (0.3) and she was
    78   goin through the barrier yesterday and (another and Ellie)
    79   took diarrhoea (hehheh.hehhehheh)

```
          ___  ___  ___

                    \
    _____
```

FA   80   **hey Ellie who**
                {{ *f,alleg*} {p.......}}
MA   81   Ellie Hartley

Here *hey Ellie* is at one level and high; there is a considerable step-down; *who* has falling pitch.

(2)
MB   199   turned it over and set fire to it (.) then the army couldn't
       200   say no more then the army had to come in you know (.)

```
    _____

                ___  ___  ___

                        \
    _____
```

MB   201   **(re)member that Sunday**
                {<   >}   {*ral*..........}

```
    _____

    \

            ___
    _____
```

FA   202   **mhm**
                {*p...*}

In line 201, *re-* is barely there, but *-mem-* is high, with swell and main accent. Much lower are *that* and *Sun-*, and *-day* moves down to the bottom of the speaker's pitch-range with *rallentando*.

One possibility is that this pattern has a different function inter-actionally: in the few examples we have found, such falling con-tours are associated with questions. In example (1) (line 80) the word *who* projects either a question or a relative clause, and MA's response in line 81 indicates that he is treating *who* as a question; in example (2) (line 201) the syntax suggests an ellipted question and FA's response is appropriate for that.

2.2 Interactional salience

Following Local, Kelly and Wells (1986), four different kinds of evidence are now presented to show that the phonetic features identified have relevance for the conversational participants.

2.2.1 Turn-endings displaying these features are designed and treated as complete

The non-problematic turn transitions instanced above are evidence that turns displaying these features are designed as complete: having displayed the cluster of features, the first speaker does not continue the turn at talk in overlap with the next speaker. Furthermore, at least in three out of the four instances quoted (lines 4, 20 and 26), the next speaker starts up without an intervening pause, suggesting that the second speaker orients to the prior turn as being complete.

2.2.2 Turn transition does not happen at potential syntactic completion points where the phonetic features are absent

This can be seen in line 13, where there is a (potentially) syntacti-cally complete utterance *he liked them*. The previous speaker iden-tifiable (line 11) used almost precisely these words (*he liked it*), and that utterance was designed and treated as complete, in that turn transition followed smoothly and prior speaker made no attempt to regain the turn:

(3)

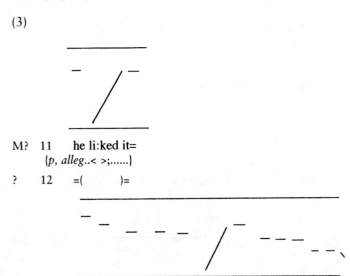

M?   11   he li:ked it=
           {p, alleg..< >;......}

?   12   =(   )=

FA   13   =he liked them he liked both sides of the community
           {alleg............................. < >....................................}

In line 11, *he* is high; there is a drop (dive) to the start of *liked*; there is swell, slight lengthening and a steep rise on *liked*; and *it* can be heard at the same height as the end of *liked* (more or less the same pitch as *he*): i.e. the 'bowl'-shape is there, though it is steep (V-shaped) due to the shortness of the utterance. In sum, line 11 displays a cluster of features that have been identified as occurring at turn-endings. In line 13, by contrast, although *he* is high and there is a slight step down from it to *liked*, there is no swell or lengthening and no movement, rise or otherwise, on *liked* to make a bowl-shape: the pitch stays at this level for *them he liked* before dropping (diving) to *both*. Thus although *he liked it* and *he liked them* are, on syntactic grounds, equal candidates for turn-ending, phonetically they are different, and turn transition only happens following the one with the phonetic features that have been identified.

   In line 29 there is a potential syntactic completion point (...*night*) but, apart from slight swell and lengthening on *friend* (l.28, long before *night*), there is a lack of the phonetic features associated with turn-endings. Following this there is, by contrast, a slight *diminuendo*, swell and lengthening on *friend*, the character-

istic bowl-with-spout pitch-pattern, and a short pause; whereupon
another speaker says *m*:

(4)

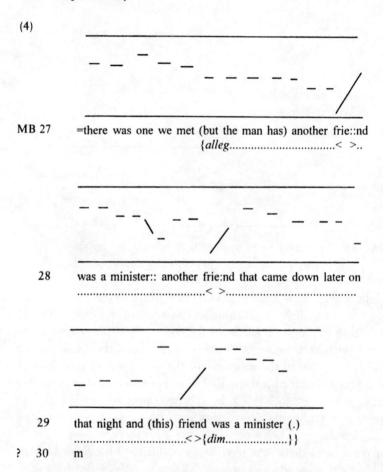

MB 27   =there was one we met (but the man has) another frie::nd
                         {*alleg*....................................< >..

28   was a minister:: another frie:nd that came down later on
         ....< >....................................

29   that night and (this) friend was a minister (.)
          ....< >{*dim*....................}}
?   30   m

Occasionally a syntactic completion point is reached, accompanied by some of the turn-yielding phonetic features, but the speaker
nevertheless retains the turn. Immediately before the example
already quoted in lines 28–29 (*another friend that came down
later on that night*), there is a syntactically complete utterance –
(*but the man has*) *another friend was a minister* (lines 27–28) –
which shows most of the pitch features we have identified as occurring at turn transition, and some dynamic ones: there is lengthening

and swell on *friend*, an early pitch-peak on *one*, a slight drop
feature (dive) before *friend*, a steep rise to peak on *friend*
which is maintained over *was a mini-*, and a fall on *-ster*: i.e. a
V-shaped bowl with a long spout.

However, the speaker also employs a salient phonetic feature
that has the effect of overriding the turn-delimitative features: the
-er of *minister* is very much lengthened, and there is no break at all
between it and the start of his next sentence. The current speaker
thus lays claim to a continued turn by phonetic means.

2.2.3 Where turn transition happens without the cluster of phonetic features, the second speaker displays that his intervention is designedly competitive

In the following examples, the interrupting speaker demonstrates
his awareness that the prior turn has not yet ended by producing
speech with some very salient phonetic features, notably high pitch
and loud volume – two features that research has shown to be the
crucial attributes of talk that is treated as turn-competitive (French
and Local 1983).

(5)

| MA | 90 | say the wrong thing in that area | (|) |

| FA | 91 | | oh: I: (hea:rd) i:t |
| | | | {ff.....................} |

MA's speech steps down from *say the wrong* to *thing in that . . .*
and continues at this level with no swell, slowing, lengthening or
any other indication of turn completion, whereas FA's speech is

particularly high and loud; in addition, her vowels are all lengthened, which gives an impression of slow speech.

(6)

MB   250   send kids home cos they haven't (any) uniform and all (0.2)
FI   251   yeah=

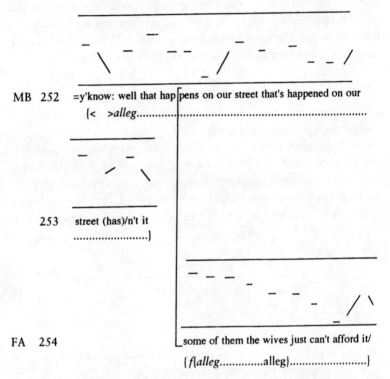

MB   252   =y'know: well that hap|pens on our street that's happened on our
                         (<   >*alleg*...

     253   street (has)/n't it
                ....}

FA   254 |some of them the wives just can't afford it/
                                  {*f*{*alleg*...............*alleg*}.........................}

In line 254 FA starts very high and fast and fairly loud, and
continues fairly high and loud although she stops speaking fast
when it becomes apparent that MB is not going to relinquish the
turn. That MB was not ready to relinquish the turn is clear from the
fact that he repeats himself from where he was interrupted (see
French and Local 1983).

This suggests that when the cluster of phonetic features identified
above is absent, talk in overlap is designed and treated as com-
petitive. There is, however, one example in the transcribed text
which suggests that overlap can happen non-problematically:
where a next speaker anticipates correctly that the current speaker's
turn is coming to an end:

(7)

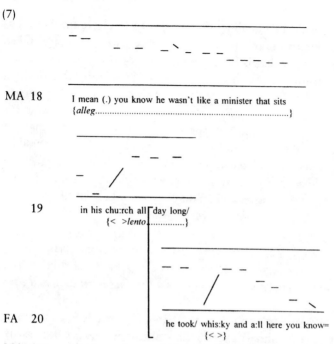

MA 18   I mean (.) you know he wasn't like a minister that sits
         {*alleg*...}

19   in his chu:rch all ⌈day long/
         {< >*lento*.............}

FA 20   he took/ whis:ky and a:ll here you know=
                               {< >}

MA 21   =you know he would have went to that ba::r (0.2) and=

That MA's turn at lines 18–19 is designed and treated as complete is supported by the fact that he lets FA finish her turn (which
started by overlapping MA's); moreover, when MA speaks again
(line 21), the content of his turn, in its reference to the minister's
trips to the bar, builds on FA's mention of his taking whisky: MA
does not treat FA's turn as a violative interruption by ignoring it or
repeating himself, as in the previous example. The overlap here
belongs to Jefferson's category of 'recognitional onsets', in which
the second speaker comes in once she has recognized what is being
said, but before it is in fact completed (Jefferson 1986).
Furthermore, in lines 18–19 the main phonetic events associated
with turn-ending have already happened by the time FA starts
speaking: there has been an early peak (*wasn't*), a smooth stepping
down to *in*, a dropped (dipped) *his*, steep rise, swell and lengthening
on *church*, and final peak on *all*. By contrast, in the previous example (extract (6)), FA starts her (interruptive) turn while MB is at the
start of a bowl-shape (slight downward glide on *that* before step
down to *hap-*) but is not far enough through it for FA to have

phonetic evidence signalling that MB will soon have finished, thus making interruption unnecessary. These two examples taken together suggest that it is because she has oriented to the relevant phonetic features in (7) that on this occasion FA is able to start up in overlap with no problem either for herself or for the other participants. For speakers of this accent, it may be surmised that, after the rise with peak has occurred, speakers feel free to assume that the rest may be taken as 'given' and that overlapping talk is permissible: prosody thus provides one resource for listeners in enabling them to recognize that the informational content of the turn is for all practical purposes complete, and on that basis to take their turn without being heard as turn-competitive.

2.2.4 *When first speaker's turn displays the relevant cluster of phonetic features but is not treated as complete, there is evidence in the subsequent talk that the turn had in fact been designed as complete*

Although turn transition does not happen at syntactic completion points where the phonetic features are absent, it does not necessarily follow that when the phonetic features are present at syntactic completion points, turn transition invariably happens. If however turn transition does not happen, at points where the speaker has designed his talk as complete with the expectation that it will be treated as complete by another participant, subsequent talk by the speaker might be expected to display evidence that he is treating his original turn as having been completed. Evidence to support this is provided by instances where (i) the speaker's talk is syntactically and semantically complete and spoken with the phonetic features we have identified, but (ii) the 'offer' of a turn is not taken up, and (iii) the speaker's subsequent talk, in recycling the syntax and content of the original turn, displays that he is still awaiting a response.

These characteristics can be seen in lines 1 and 4:

(8)

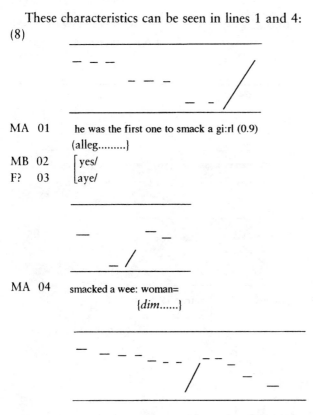

MA   01   he was the first one to smack a gi:rl (0.9)
                   (alleg.........)
MB   02   ⎡yes/
F?   03   ⎣aye/

MA   04   smacked a wee: woman=
                   {dim......}

FA   05   =(we) had an American minister and that though (0.5)
                   {dim...{ral...........}}

The ending words *the first one to smack a girl* (line 1) are followed by a noticeable pause; a minimal response (in the form of *yes*
and *aye*) does eventually come, but meanwhile the speaker (MA)
has begun to present the same remark in a different way (line 4):
smacked a wee woman, uttered with similar phonetic features. In
fact it is said with a pitch-pattern similar to the original, but in a
lower key and more quietly: what is described as 'trail-off' in Local,
Kelly and Wells (1986). This time he succeeds in yielding the turn:
he is followed immediately (in latched transition) by a contribution
from another speaker (FA).

MB is less lucky in line 160 below. He repeats *worry about him*
twice, each time with a cluster of phonetic features (drop to steep
rise and swell on *wo-*, high peak on *-rry about* and slight pause after

the second repetition). Despite several minimal responses of *yeah*
(line 161), he repeats himself a third time until at last a full response
is forthcoming:

(9)

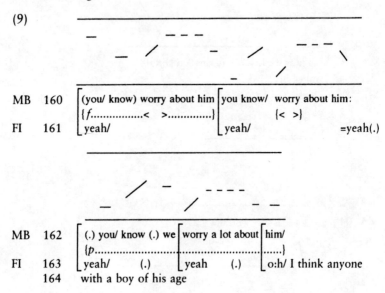

```
MB   160   ⎡(you/ know) worry about him ⎡you know/  worry about him:
           {f.................< >.............}              {< >}
FI   161   ⎣yeah/                        ⎣yeah/                     =yeah(.)
```

```
MB   162   ⎡(.) you/ know (.) we ⎡worry a lot about ⎡him/
           {p....................................................}
FI   163   ⎣yeah/       (.)   ⎣yeah    (.)  ⎣o:h/ I think anyone
     164   with a boy of his age
```

3 Comparison with other English dialects

In this section, the findings reported for Ulster speakers will be
compared to two other dialects spoken in the UK. Local, Wells
and Sebba (1985) investigated turn delimitation in London
Jamaican. The delimitation of speaker turns ending in declarative
structures was studied in two conversations involving teenage Afro-
Caribbeans born and living in London. Examination of turn-
endings 'in the clear' (i.e. not overlapping with next speaker's
turn) revealed that the following phonetic features routinely accompanied turn-endings:

  (i)   narrow falling pitch movement to the bottom of the speaker's
        normal pitch range on the final syllable, with accompanying
        creaky phonation;
  (ii) the starting point of this pitch movement is never higher than
        the preceding syllable;

(iii) absence of *decrescendo* on the final syllable, in spite of frequent *decrescendo* over the preceding portion of utterance,
leading to an impression of resurgence of loudness;

(iv) absence of greater dynamic pitch movement earlier in the
utterance.

The authors were able to show that these features are oriented to
as exponents of potential turn completion even when the current
speaker in fact continues speaking after they occur. The delimitative
role of these features is further attested by the fact that syntactic
completion points that are *not* accompanied by the features are not
treated by either current speaker or co-participant as interactively
complete.

Local, Kelly and Wells (1986) developed this type of analysis in
an investigation of turn delimitation in Tyneside English, again
using audio recording of conversational talk. Here, two classes of
turn-ending were identified. Each is characterized by a cluster of
phonetic features which do not occur, as a cluster, elsewhere in the
course of turns. Listed below are the features accompanying Class 1
turns, which include 83 per cent of turn transitions in the clear:

(i) a general slowing down in tempo to the end of the turn, the
minimal and usual domain being the last two rhythmic feet;

(ii) a sudden increase and decrease in loudness during the ictus
syllable of the last foot of the turn;

(iii) appreciable duration on the ictus syllable of the last foot of
the turn (whatever the phonological length of the vowel);

(iv) centralized quality in the vowel(s) of the last foot of the turn;

(v) a pitch step up at the end of the turn, which is usually greater
than any other pitch step up in the turn and which always
attains a higher point than any other step up in the turn. (The
pitch patterning associated with this type of turn-ending has
to be further subclassified, with respect to the rhythmic structure of the final two feet of the turn.)

The phonetic features associated with turn delimitation in the
three dialects are set out in Table 3.1.

The three dialects are similar in that each has a definable phonological unit that constitutes the domain of the turn-delimitative
system. This unit is thus the correlate, at the phonological level of

Table 3.1. Phonetic features associated with turn delimitation

Feature	London Jamaican	Tyneside	Ulster
Pitch	narrow fall on last syllable, start no higher than previous syllable; no greater pitch movement earlier	step up at end of turn; ends higher, and is no narrower, than any earlier step up	bowl-shape pattern; drop may precede final rise; following syllables level or slight fall; earlier peak usually not higher than final peak
Tempo		slowing over last two feet approx.	slowing over last two feet approx.
Loudness	resurgence on last syllable	swell on last ictus	swell on last ictus
Duration		extra on last ictus	extra on last ictus
Other	creaky voice on last syllable	centralized vowel quality on last ictus	

analysis, of the turn-constructional unit at the interactional level. It would be premature to designate it a 'tone unit', since that designation presupposes a phonological system of tones, of which the tone unit is the domain (see Halliday 1967). A more neutral designation for a prosodically complete unit seems appropriate, for example the metrical term 'line'. In each dialect the turn-delimitative line can be seen to be in system with other lines which do not project turn completion: the analysis of each dialect has shown that there are stretches of talk that do not manifest the cluster of (dialect-specific) turn-delimitative features, and that such stretches of talk are not treated by co-participants as turn-delimitative.

The prosodic character of the turn-delimitative line differs across the three dialects, as is evident from Table 3.1, and this represents one of the most striking differences between these (and other) dialects of British English. For instance, London Jamaican has a characteristic falling pitch contour, ending at the base of the speaker's normal pitch range (as indeed does the most frequently described variety of British English, Southern British Standard); whereas both Tyneside and Ulster (together with other dialects such as that of the

Black Country in the English West Midlands, see Wells 1989) are characterized by a contour that ends relatively high in the pitch range. Within this broad classification further distinctions have to be made: thus in Ulster there is a characteristic bowl-shaped contour ending with a steep rise, generally on the last ictus syllable, whereas the most common Tyneside contour generally ends with a step up, the precise form of which is determined by the metrical structure of the line-end (Local, Kelly and Wells 1986:420).

A major difference between London Jamaican on the one hand, and Tyneside and Ulster on the other, is that in London Jamaican it is the final syllable of the line that provides the principal locus for phonetic features of turn delimitation. In the other two dialects, the main locus for these features is often the final ictus syllable of the line. This may also be the final syllable of the line, e.g. (for Ulster) in line 1 of the conversation, *girl*; but there are often remiss (unaccented) syllables that follow, e.g. *it* in line 11. Furthermore, in many cases there is a considerable stretch of material, sometimes constituting extra feet, after the main locus of the delimitative features. Sometimes this represents a semantically empty tag, e.g. *and that though* in line 5, or *and all here you know* in line 20. On other occasions, this material is semantically empty because it represents 'old' information, recoverable from the linguistic or non-linguistic context, e.g. *sides of the community* in line 13 and *was a minister* in lines 28–29. This is characteristic not only of Ulster and Tyneside, but also of Southern British English, and probably of all indigenous accents of British English, and is of course a consequence of the fact that in these accents the main point of prosodic prominence is associated with the main information focus of the sentence. In London Jamaican, by contrast, 'old' information and tags can constitute the locus of phonetic prominence, when they occur in line-final position. In line 2 of the following extract (from Local, Wells and Sebba 1985), the biggest pitch movement is on the second word of the tag *you know*; and in line 3 the final word *law* has the turn-delimitative features, even though it is clearly 'old' information.

(10)

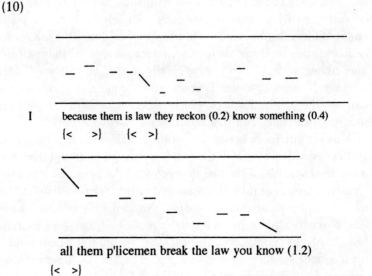

I   because them is law they reckon (0.2) know something (0.4)
      {<   >}   {<   >}

all them p'licemen break the law you know (1.2)
{<   >}

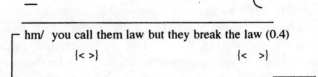

      hm/ you call them law but they break the law (0.4)
            {< >}   {< >}

F   hh/   mm

This difference sets London Jamaican typologically apart from
other accents of English in terms of its intonation system (cf.
Sutcliffe 1992, ch. 8): in London Jamaican, the phonological systems relating to information focus and to turn delimitation are
independent (Wells 1992), whereas in indigenous accents the two
systems interact.

4 Conclusion

This brief comparison of English dialects from the standpoint of the phonetics and phonology of turn delimitation has shown that dialects can differ phonologically in quite major ways, e.g. with regard to the main locus of phonological prominence (London Jamaican vs the rest). Such a difference clearly has implications for the exponency of systems at other levels, notably information focus, and indeed there is some anecdotal evidence that the London Jamaican system causes considerable difficulties for English listeners from other dialect backgrounds who are not familiar with it. Other dialects, e.g. Tyneside, Ulster and probably Southern British Standard, differ more at the level of phonetic exponency: turn delimitation is associated with a particular cluster of phonetic features located at a particular place, and though the system for assigning that place is shared by these accents, each uses a somewhat different cluster of features. An outsider to one of these dialects will therefore have to learn what is the particular cluster of features associated with turn completion, as opposed to turn-continuation, if they are to participate unproblematically in conversational interaction. It would appear that the greatest differences are in pitch features, since features of loudness and tempo are shared, at least by Ulster and Tyneside (Table 3.1). Future researchers may wish to investigate such social and interactional consequences of dialect differences in intonation. We suggest that such research will be that much easier if it grows from descriptive and comparative studies which themselves take as their starting point the analysis of conversational interaction, and which derive their interactional and phonological categories inductively from that analysis.

Appendix

Transcription notation

Detailed phonetic transcription is confined to parts of the conversation referred to in the discussion.

Within text

[	start of overlapping talk
/	end of overlapping talk

(0.1)	pause, measured in tenths of a second
(.)	pause too short to measure
=	talk continues without a pause between one speaker and the next (i.e. is 'latched')
(word)	transcriber uncertainty about words
( )	unrecoverable words, lasting as long as the speech overlapped by the space in parentheses
MA, MB, I, F in margin:	denotes identity of speaker; M=male, F=female, FI=interviewer
?	speaker cannot be identified

Above text

Relative pitch-height and on-syllable pitch-movement are represented impressionistically, within staves designating the limits of the speaker's normal pitch-range.

Below text

IPA symbols and extensions are used (Duckworth, Allen, Hardcastle and Ball 1990): they are shown in labelled braces which span the amount of speech to which the feature applies.

< >	swell
lento	slow
alleg	fast
f	loud
p	soft
rall	getting slower
accel	getting faster
cresc	getting louder
dim	getting softer

Note

This research was supported by a Leverhulme Personal Research Fellowship to Bill Wells. Thanks are due to Lesley Milroy for access to data, which were collected as part of SSRC project no. HR3771.

References

Atkinson, J. M. and J. Heritage (eds.) 1984. *Structures of Social Action. Studies in conversation analysis.* Cambridge University Press.

Brazil, D. 1978. *Discourse Intonation II.* Discourse Analysis Monographs 2. University of Birmingham: English Language Research Unit.

Brown, G., K. L. Currie and J. Kenworthy 1980. *Questions of Intonation.* London: Croom Helm.

Coulthard, M. and D. Brazil 1979. *Exchange Structure.* Discourse Analysis Monographs 5. University of Birmingham: English Language Research Unit.

Cruttenden, A. 1986. *Intonation.* Cambridge University Press.

Crystal, D. 1969. *Prosodic Systems and Intonation in English.* Cambridge University Press.

Duckworth, M., G. Allen, W. Hardcastle and M. Ball 1990. Extensions to the International Phonetic Alphabet for the transcription of atypical speech. *Clinical Linguistics and Phonetics*, 4: 273–283.

French, P. and J. K. Local 1983. Turn-competitive incomings. *Journal of Pragmatics*, 7: 17–38.

Halliday, M. A. K. 1967. *Intonation and Grammar in British English.* The Hague: Mouton.

Jarman, E. and A. Cruttenden 1976. Belfast intonation and the myth of the fall. *Journal of the International Phonetic Association*, 6: 4–12.

Jefferson, G. 1986. Notes on 'latency' in overlap onset. *Human Studies*, 9: 153–183.

Local, J. K. 1986. Patterns and problems in a study of Tyneside intonation. In C. Johns-Lewis (ed.) *Intonation and Discourse.* London: Croom Helm, pp. 181–198.

Local, J. K., J. Kelly and W. H. G. Wells 1986. Towards a phonology of conversation: turn-taking in Tyneside English. *Journal of Linguistics*, 22: 411–437.

Local, J. K., W. H. G. Wells and M. Sebba 1985. Phonology for conversation: phonetic aspects of turn delimitation in London Jamaican. *Journal of Pragmatics*, 9: 309–330.

Milroy, L. 1987. *Language and Social Networks* (2nd edn). Oxford: Basil Blackwell.

Sacks, H., E. A. Schegloff and G. Jefferson 1974. A simplest systematics for the organization of turn-taking for conversation. *Language*, 50: 696–735.

Sutcliffe, D. 1992. *System in Black English.* Avon: Multilingual Matters.

Trubetskoy, N. 1969. *Principles of Phonology*, trans. by C. A. M. Baltaxe. Berkeley: University of California Press.

Wells, J. C. 1982. *Accents of English 1: An introduction.* Cambridge University Press.

Wells, W. H. G. 1989. Prefinal focus accents in English: a comparative study of two varieties. In D. Bradley, E. J. A. Henderson and

M. Mazaudon (eds.) *Prosodic Analysis and Asian Linguistics: To honour R. K. Sprigg.* Canberra Pacific Linguistics C-104.

1992. Phonetic aspects of focus in London Jamaican. Paper presented at the Colloquium of the British Association of Academic Phoneticians, Cambridge, April.

4

Affiliating and disaffiliating with continuers: prosodic aspects of recipiency

FRANK ERNST MÜLLER

1 Introduction

A task for any description dealing with the use of spoken language in natural situations is to account for the radical interdependency of speaking and listening. Speakers, in the very act of speaking, i.e. when holding a turn, are at the same time also listeners. They perceive the responses coming from listeners and may instantly, in their speaking, react to them and modify their course[1] (see Jefferson 1973). Listeners, on the other hand, even though maintaining their stance as recipients of the developing turn of a current speaker, act at the same time to some degree as speakers: listening is an activity that has a global ecology, comprising facial, proxemic, gestural and bodily signals as well as purely verbal ones. Yet it also has a vocal, verbal and linguistic side: with small tokens like 'hm', 'uh huh', 'yeah', 'yes', 'right', etc., which a 'listener may get in edgewise' (Yngve 1970), which 'may come between sentences' (Schegloff 1982) or which act as 'bridges between turn-constructional units' (Goodwin 1986), recipients track the course of emerging talk in discourse, and display, in brief, their current understanding of that talk, co-constituting its continuation. It is in this limited sense, restricted to the small but still hearable, linguistic tokens inserted into the ongoing talk of a current speaker, that the term 'recipiency' will be used in the following.[2]

To do the 'intermediate' work they do, the tokens of recipiency must remain brief and unobtrusive – they are designed to fit into slight gaps of ongoing talk and usually avoid obliterating parts of the ongoing talk to which they refer. They are thus small tokens and include vocalizations such as 'hm' or 'uh huh', which, taken in isolation, do not have a distinct lexical content. More so than with properly lexical items, they acquire meaning locally and indexically by the precise sequential location where they occur. A consequence of this in research literature has been to gloss the local meaning by paraphrasing it. One famous paraphrase, going beyond local meanings and generalizing to a class of usages, has been given by Schegloff (1982), who introduces the term 'continuer':

Perhaps the most common usage of 'uh huh', etc. (in environments other than after yes/no questions) is to exhibit on the part of its producer an understanding that an extended unit of talk is underway by another, and that it is not yet, or may not yet be (even ought not yet be), complete. It takes the stance that the speaker of that extended unit should continue talking . . . 'Uh huh', etc. exhibit this understanding, and take this stance, precisely by passing an opportunity to produce a full turn at talk. When so used, utterances such as 'uh huh' may properly be termed 'continuers'. (1982:81)

The 'understanding' or 'stance' described by Schegloff has both a retrospective aspect – incompleteness of the unit reached, as seen by the recipient and documented by his/her continuer symbol – and a prospective 'instruction' to the current speaker ('Go on, say more'), but it remains neutral as to the many other possible qualities of the continuation work in question. In fact, for the smallest and most unobtrusive continuer tokens, the monitoring, neutral or polyvalent stance has been found to be the most prevalent; see Laforest (1992:194): 'The most simple forms ('humhum', 'yes', 'ok') and the most common ones are the most polyvalent ones' (my translation – FM). It seems evident that the neutral or 'polyvalent' stance of continuers is of great importance for what may be the most usual type of intermediate response in spoken interaction. In documenting the state of talk reached, one small token may thus fulfil three functions at once: recipient acknowledges the receipt of previous talk until that moment in a neutral way, recognizes its character as extended talk, talk to be continued and completed by current speaker, and, third, withholds a more expanded 'terminal' response, to be formulated only at turn completion.

Yet recipiency, vocalized with these small tokens, is more diversified and more complex than this. Thus the very minimalism of the tokens, an important functional property of their non-interference with current talk, may also be used as a contingent achievement to display a more specific stance of the recipient – e.g. that of non-interfering with current talk in the sense of visibly/hearably withholding a more differentiated (within-turn) response although it may be called for, agreeing to further continuation of the turn in progress, although manifestly not supporting the position formulated at this moment by the current speaker. More generally, when following the track of continuers as they 'punctuate' the progress of extended turns in conversational data, we often note that recipients, merely by their use of continuers, recognizably 'take sides' in relation to current talk in ways more specific than merely acknowledging receipt and agreeing to its continuation. The same tokens that may document a mere monitoring stance may also be used to display a more substantial 'agreement' (Schegloff 1982) or 'alignment' (Goodwin 1986) with the current speaker's talk, or to display non-aligning attitudes – doubt, scepticism or hostility. It is this rough distinction of three basic semantic values – neutral, affiliating and disaffiliating in relation to current talk – which will be investigated more closely in the following.[3]

Short tokens, 'long' prosody. As we mentioned above, continuers, given their size and their scant lexical content, are highly indexical contingent achievements. As responses constructed to 'fit' into the continuing discourse of a current speaker, they acquire specific meaning locally, not only by their precise sequential placement, but also by the particular 'fit' they show in relation to the prosodic features of their immediate environment. This obviously concerns intonation, in particular those intonational features indicating cohesion, the provisory completeness or incompleteness of units in progress,[4] but also other features such as e.g. correspondences in loudness/intensity, recipient's use of 'slots' opened up by micropauses occurring in the current speaker's turn construction, rhythmic integration (i.e. the continuation – by the continuer – of a regular rhythmic pattern initiated by the current speaker[5]). Prosodic features of these kinds will be given detailed consideration in the following analysis.

In past research on continuers, the relevance of prosody has been suggested, but it has not been of central interest. Some of these suggestions and related questions will be presented in a brief discussion in section 2. Section 3 will characterize the set of conversational data selected for the present study of the 'biased' use of continuers. One longish fragment of extended discourse will be used for the presentation of evidence, and the discussion, of affiliating usages (section 4), and one for disaffiliating uses (section 5). Results and a comparison/summary will be given in section 6.

The specific stance a continuer may display remains yet to be analysed as a contingent achievement. The data selected for discussion include usages of continuers whose supportive work in the emergence of further talk from the current speaker is doubtful. Therefore, without casting doubt in principle on the generalization quoted above from Schegloff (1982), the more neutral term of 'acknowledgement token', which leaves the specific local meaning of an item open, will be preferred here.

2 Previous suggestions concerning the role of prosody

Several of the early studies in CA have at least hinted at the relevance prosody must have in the description of continuation work. Acknowledgement tokens may be solicited, i.e. current speakers may interrupt the further progression of an initiated turn and make its continuation dependent on eliciting a continuer from the recipient. In their study on the preference for 'recognitionals', Sacks and Schegloff (1979) describe sequences where speakers suspend further continuation of an initiated turn in an effort to 'achieve recognition'. Speakers here introduce and specify ('recipient-design') an object of reference in such a way as to make this object, person or place a 'recognitional'. In other words, the description is designed to allow, and even invite, the present recipient to find, from the reference form or proper name selected, 'who, that recipient knows, is being referred to' (1979:17).

Sequences where speakers try to achieve recipient-designed recognition (see the example in (1)), are characterized prosodically by 'try-markers':

(1)
```
->   A: ...well I was the only one other than than the uhm tch Fords?,
->      Uh Mrs Holmes Ford? You know uh ⌈the the cellist?
     B:                                  ⌊Oh yes. She's the cellist.
     A: Yes
     B: Ye⌈s
     A:   ⌊Well she and her husband were there....
```
                                    From Sacks and Schegloff (1979:19)

The referential description is produced with an upward intonational contour and is followed by a brief pause, a 'slot' which the referring speaker leaves open for the recipient to insert, in the case of success, a token of recognition. The token solicited in this way can be an explicit 'yes', as in (1), but also 'an "uh huh" or a nod can be used to do this' (1979:18). Further tries, produced with basically the same prosodic features, may follow the first one, engendering a sequence until either recognitional success is reached or the search is given up.

The approach to 'recognitionals' as outlined by Sacks and Schegloff (1979) raises a number of interesting questions. One of them concerns the difference between 'weak' tokens, such as the 'yes' in (1), and 'stronger' ones, such as the 'oui' reiterated three times in (2) (line 4), and the different stances a recipient may indicate by their use. The 'recognitional' in (2) is an exhibition at an art museum which recently opened.

(2)
1   A: (..) j'ai vu qu'il y avait l'exposition: au Musée des
         (..) I saw there was an exhibition at the Art
2   Beaux-arts ça je vais y aller. C'est pas: ça vient
         Museum I'm going to go there. It's not: it just
3   d'ouvrir aujourd'hui là.
         opened today.
4   B: Oui oui oui
         yes yes yes
5   A: Ça je vais y aller ça dure tout' l'été, (continues)
         I'm going to go it's on all summer (continues)

From Laforest (1992:163)

According to the notation of intonation in the transcript, A's turn ends with a descending intonation (line 3), a cue indicating turn completion; the referential description given is not 'try-marked'.[6] This sequence demonstrates that 'recognitionals' may also be constituted retrospectively, i.e. by the recipient, using e.g. a 'strong' token of recognition to indicate a specific, here 'recognitional' stance towards the object just introduced, although prosodically it is not presented as a recognitional by the current speaker.

The same example also illustrates the 'directive' influence ('Go on, say more') which tokens of acknowledgement can have on continuation in discourse. The 'strong' token in (2) can be 'heard directively' (Sacks 1971:5).[7] That is to say, a fairly inconspicuous fact – same-topic continuation by current speaker in the next turn – is not a projection recognizably initiated by that speaker in her preceding turn, but generated only by the recipient and by the particular type of recipiency given to the turn. By strongly affirming that she knows the object and event just referred to, the recipient can be heard to suggest that the speaker should continue to talk on this topic. As the sequence occurs in an interview – recipient B in (2) is the interviewer – this also shows a technique available for eliciting further talk from the informant, 're-lancing' (Laforest 1992) talk in the interview from the position of recipient. Recipiency may thus not only act on current talk, but even be a resource to elicit continuation and direct its further course.

The reiterated use of a 'continuer' has been considered to make it 'prosodically salient' (Bublitz 1988:180). Prosodic salience gives it additional affirmative value, but the difference between weaker and stronger tokens is not only a subtle shade of difference in meaning. As mentioned above, the unobtrusive weak tokens tend to be used prevailingly as neutral monitoring responses and 'generalized acknowledgers' (West and Zimmerman 1982:531), displaying active listenership but acknowledging a recognition of the emergent speech object only and thus remaining limited to a 'de dicto' reading ('Yes I hear you and follow what you are saying'). In this usage they do not contain further commitments, e.g. affiliation or disaffiliation with a position which the speaker is currently developing, beyond what is necessary to acknowledge its development until now, see that it is still in course of progression and agree to its further development by the current speaker. By making acknowledgement tokens 'prosodically salient', a recipient may then signal an understanding that goes beyond a display of 'de dicto' recognition and assume a more differentiated stance, e.g. a 'de re' recognition of the object, place, person or event current speaker is talking about ('Yes, I know what/whom you are talking about'), an affiliation with an evaluative judgement or with the appropriateness and truth of what has been said. This is the case in the following example, taken from the present set of data (see section 3 below for details; transcription conventions listed in appendix).

(3)   Gabriella (39:11)
1   A: quindi nel momento in cui non c'è più accelerazione ma in
          well in the moment when there is no more acceleration but to
2   qualche misura la vita dece:lera (.)
          a certain degree life slows down (.)
3   G: sì
          yes
4   A: allora ci si sofferma (.) e si comincia a guardare indietro
          then you hold on (.) and you start to look back to the past
5   G: è ve:ro ve:ro proprio così
          that's true very very true

In (3) we have first a weak token, documenting a 'de dicto' acknowledgement (line 3), and then a strong terminal one (line 5), reinforced both lexically and 'prosodically' (reiteration) and affiliating with the current speaker's position. The weak token is located within the emergent turn, at a constituent boundary which is saliently marked as a turn-internal juncture by a number of co-incident cues (both syntactic and intonational ones, as well as 'rhetorical' micropausing by current speaker to 'involve' the recipient[8]). The strong token follows at the end of a list-like syntactic period. It is obvious that an inverse sequential order of weak and strong tokens here would hardly be imaginable. Further instances of merely monitoring, weak, within-turn tokens and strong terminal ones can easily be found. Yet, once more, recipiency is more complex. And although it is apparent that we need prosody to distinguish the value of tokens, it is clearly not sufficient to limit 'prosodic salience' to reiterated usages.

3 Data and data selection

The data discussed below come from an Italian radio phone-in. An institutional radio setting of this kind is not neutral as to recipiency, but has a number of implications. Formulated more strongly, the particular type of recipiency prevailing in an institutional setting may be an important part of linguistically 'achieving' the genre in question.[9] This is not a subject to be developed here extensively, but in examining the data below their institutional situatedness in a radio setting must be kept in mind. To mention briefly a few points: callers as a rule are expected to develop, in an extended turn which closely follows the opening section, the 'reason for the call' autonomously and without recipiency tokens from the moderator, who intervenes with recipiency tokens only in subsequent interaction. The moderator, on the other hand, in particular when confronted with callers who display timidity when entering onto the 'stage' of public speaking, may deviate from the highly ritualized pattern of the usual opening section and initiate 'affiliative openings' (see Hutchby 1991), engaging in more 'familiar' turn-by-turn talk with the caller before launching him or her into the task of exposing 'the reason for the call'.

The institutional radio setting and the prerogatives of the moderator within this setting also result in 'hearing rules', i.e. the talk of the moderator is received by the callers in a manner that differs from that in which talk of the callers is received by the moderator. The following example of a 'category-bound' reception by the moderator in acknowledging talk by a caller will illustrate this. ('A' – here and in the following transcripts – stands for the moderator.)

```
(4)   Roberta (16:22)
1     R:  anche per il lavoro che ho fatto preferisco non dirlo
          also as to the job I have had I prefer not to tell it
                    ⌐
2         perché
          be⌐use
3     A:  │ certo certo⌐non c'è problema
          └ certainly certainly no problem
4     R:            │ecco           communque:
                    └o.k.           any way (continues)
```

The caller, mentioning a preference not to talk about a topic and going on to give a reason for this, is heard here by the moderator to be pleading for a 'licence' to do this and is accorded an acknowledgement (line 3). The acknowledgement is a 'continuer', but distinctly not a mere 'de dicto' receipt of current talk: it is distinguished by 'prosodic salience' (reiteration) and a following brief lexical expansion. The token granting the 'licence' stops the initiated reasoning of the caller, who then continues her turn (line 4) but modifies its course.

From the many instances of the use of acknowledgement tokens occurring in the phone-in data a narrow set has been selected for close observation and discussion. A first and obvious criterion for selection has been the evidence they contain for the 'affiliating' and 'disaffiliating' alignments which participants may display in relation to current talk by the placement and prosodic design of small tokens of acknowledgement.

A second consideration has been to select extended discourse and to proceed via an in-depth analysis of longish fragments rather than to collect a greater number and broader range of single cases, pairing speech objects with specific tokens acknowledging them. The latter procedure entails a more de-contextualizing approach and unavoidably separates recipients' behaviour further from its 'natural' environment, viz. extended discourse. (See the criticism of the 'back channel' approach in Schegloff (1982) and Goodwin (1986).)

For these reasons the discussion in the following will be centred around the observation and analysis of two extensive fragments, following in detail the 'track' of acknowledgement tokens in sequential placement and prosodic design throughout the extended talk. Both fragments are taken from the closing sections of calls, i.e. analysis can start with the initial assumption – to be specified subsequently – that continuation and extension of talk is a matter of special attention for the parties concerned.

In the first fragment, illustrating 'affiliative' uses, the current speaker is prevailingly the moderator and it is the moderator who extends, with a long and elaborate summary assessment, the closing section beyond its usual format. His talk is received and acknowledged by a caller who aligns with the assessing and summarizing as it emerges in an approving and appreciating manner. The interaction of this closing gives the impression of being a smoothly or even happily coordinated 'duet'.

The second fragment, illustrating 'disaffiliating' uses, documents a closing section where a caller 'moves out' (see Button 1987) of a closing initiated by the moderator and continues topical talk beyond it. Here it is the caller who is responsible for the unusual extension of the closing section of the call and it is the moderator who is prevailingly recipient. He receives the continuing talk of the caller in a disaffiliating way, i.e. does not encourage its further continuation, but rather attempts to bound it and minimize its further extension. Rather than being a harmonious 'duet', the interaction gives the impression of being a strained and disharmonious one.

The two fragments are presented textually in each section in a transcription inspired in part by Selting (see Chapter 6 of this volume). A transcript containing intonational contours, indicated by superscribed numerical indices, is added in the appendix (see also the transcription conventions there). In the analytic comments, intonation contours are indicated only as far as they are relevant for the argument being developed.

4 Affiliating

4.1 Background

Most of the closings in our data are initiated by summary assessments which 'bound' the further progression of topical talk in the call: the moderator reformulates in a summary what the position of the caller has been in the preceding talk and presents this reformulation for confirmation to the caller and 'author'. Confirmation of the summary then is the warrant for the moderator to enter into closing of the call.

In the present closing, the last one before a scheduled break in transmission, the summarizing and assessing is expanded and elaborated. Within a stepwise and continuous 'incremental turn construction' (see below), where each further progress is turned into an 'acknowledgeable' and is acknowledged by the caller, the moderator leaves room for an extended turn of the caller, who introduces a brief story (line 17). At completion, the story is acknowledged, evaluated and again summarized by the moderator. This second 'formulation of gist' (28–32), well adapted to summarize the immediately preceding story but also to stand as a final boundary, a 'signature' (Schegloff and Sacks 1973) to the whole of the call, is again proposed for acknowledgement to the caller and this is warrant to enter into closing terminals.[10]

4.2 Transcript

(5)   (Anna 29:02; A=moderator; a=caller)
1   A: quindi LEi (.) in qualche modo (.) **NON** rifiuta
          in conclusion (.) in a way (.) you don't refuse

2   il passato⌐ rifiuta i LUO:GHI e i VO:LTI⌐del passato
        the past you refuse the places and the faces of the past
3   a: ⌐no   ⌐sì
                ⌊no   ⌊yes
4   A: ma vuole un paSSAto DENtro di LEi=
        but you want a past within yourself=
5   a: =SOno d'aCCORdo
        =I agree
6   A: come una specie di (.) caLOR viTA:le=
        like a sort of (.) vital energy=
7   a: (h)(h) sì
            yes
8   A: di (.) fuo/focoLA:re LE:Nto che BRU:cia DE:Ntro
        from (.) fi/from a small slow fire that burns inside
9   che da VI:ta fuOri
        that gives life outside
10 a: certo qualcosa di MI:o in ogni caso
        certainly something that is mine anyhow
11 A: (.) certo e questo è importante che ci SIa questa sorta (.)
        (.) certainly and it is important that there is this kind (.)
12   di: (.) .hhh e: come dire (.) più riPOSta identiTÀ no
        of (.) .hhh eh how shall I say (.) more secret identity right
13 a: SÌ (?⌐?)
        yes
14 A: ⌐che salvaguarda⌐dalle in=TEM=PE:rie
            ⌊*that protects you from adversities*   ⌐
15 a: ⌐*sì*   *sì*
                    ⌊*yes*   ⌊*yes*

16 A: e che non è contamiNA:ta da sguARdi indisCRE:ti
        and that is not contaminated by indiscreet looks
17 a: sì (.) tra l'altro (introduces a STORY)
        yes (.) by the way
.   (in the STORY she tells how she shares her
.   past with her husband; last part of STORY:)
26 a: lo riscopro nel suo passato che a POco a POco
        I discover him in his past which bit by bit
27   LUI mi racconta (.) e la STEssa COsa FAccio io
        he reveals to me (.) and I do the same
28 A: insomma (.) una formiCHI:na del passato NON una
        in sum (.) a little ant of the past not a   ⌐
29 a: ⌐SÌ
                                        ⌊*yes*

30 A: ciCA:la
        cicada

```
31   a:   (h)⌐ (h)   (h)   (h)
32   A:    │che SPERde TUTTo in una noTTA:ta di GRA:Nde voCI:o=
           └that expends everything in one night of grand singing=
33   a:   =d'aCCORdo
           =I agree
34   A:   grazie a Lei⌐Anna FI:ne della PRIma PARte
           thank you Anna   end of the first part
35   a:             │prego
                    └you're welcome
```

4.3 Response to emphasis

Observing now in more detail the 'where' and the 'how' of recipiency tokens, a first observation is that the caller immediately
responds to and 'follows' the prosodically most salient contrast in
the moderator's first summary. Acknowledgement tokens precede
the factual completion of the turn and are placed contiguously, i.e.
at the earliest recognition point(s) of the emergent structure of the
contrastive pair (see the two tokens in line 3).

(6)

```
                                        4+    3 2 2 2
1    A:   quindi LEi (.) in qualche modo (.) NON rifiuta il
          in conclusion (.) in a way (.) you don't refuse

          2  3 2  2 2 2 2   4+    3 2 2   4 ⌐3   2 2   3 2
2         passato rifiuta i LUO:GHI e i VO:LTI del passato
          the past you refuse the places and the faces of the past

                    │32              │23
3    a:             │no              │sì
                    └no              └yes
```

The contrastive pair (non rifiuta X, rifiuta Y), prosodically the most
strongly marked episode in the fragment, is made salient by a high
pitch range and by pitch peaks where the moderator goes beyond
his usual range. The segments that carry the contrast, furthermore,
are made salient by increased intensity and, in part, also by vowel
lengthening and decreased speech rate. Although situated within the
(factual) turn, the two acknowledgement tokens which occur in line
3, given the descending intonation and potential syntactic completion point in current speaker's turn, may be heard to occur at a
point of potential transition relevance. A more clearly marked transition relevance place (TRP) is reached by A in line 4.

(7)

```
          2   2  2    2   3 2   3    2 2   32
4    A:   ma vuole un paSSAto DENtro di LEI=
          but you want a past within yourself=
          3   2   2    3  1
5    a:   =SOno d'aCCORdo
          =I agree
```

Although the clause in line 4 does not have a strongly descending
intonational contour, it conveys a strong impression of closure for
syntactic and rhetorical reasons: the contrastive pair is expanded
and closure is reached with the third of three constituents, marked
by a parallel strong local accent (*vuole Z*). The third constituent
thus closes a global stylistic and rhetorical pattern (*non rifiuta X,
rifiuta Y, ma vuole Z*).

The caller responds at this point (line 5), with a more expanded
acknowledgement token which 'echoes', i.e. closely reproduces, the
main part of the immediately preceding contour on *dentro di lei*
(3-2-2-3-2, 3-2-2-3-1) and also 'aligns' lexically with the preceding
summary of the moderator. Although more expanded, the token in
line 5 remains a token of recipiency: with its briefness and intonational closure it displays an 'analysis' of the preceding turn as a turn
still in progress and is thus to be heard 'directively'.

One main point to be retained from this brief consideration of
the first three acknowledgement tokens is that the caller affiliates
with the moderator's talk by responding immediately to the emphasized and prosodically most salient parts of the emerging turn. We
will return to this point of acknowledging emphasis when dealing
with the 'disaffiliation' fragment below, where the moderator as a
recipient, even though producing acknowledgement tokens, withholds responses to prosodically marked salience.

4.4 Incremental turn construction

It is true in an elementary and very general sense that discourse is
produced 'incrementally' (see Schegloff 1982). In a more specific
sense, this term can also be applied to a state of talk where a current
speaker, although still holding the turn and displaying that he or she
is going to continue it, articulates and segments it in a number of
singularized steps which are presented separately for acknowledge-

ment. It is from this kind of 'incremental' progression in turn construction that the 'duet' we find in our fragment arises: the caller is recurrently accorded within-turn slots for acknowledgement and she reinstates with her acknowledgements the current-speaker status of the moderator. In other words, the whole of the interaction, up to the story introduced by the caller in line 17, must be considered not as turn-by-turn talk, but as interaction carried on within one continued turn by the moderator, who expands the first summary of the call gradually – and incrementally – into a more abstract position, but takes care to 'negotiate' the several steps with the caller by making them acknowledgeable.

Prosody is essential to delimit and single out the parts in emerging discourse which are presented or offered for acknowledgement by the recipient. A set of several distinct procedures is involved, including, as a rather obvious case, the standard format for response solicitation in Italian, tag questioning with *no?*. It is applied in lines 12–14, where the appropriateness of the selection of a lexical item, try-marked also by other preceding features, is proposed to the recipient as an 'acknowledgeable'. Intonationally, the soliciting, rising part of the contour is realized uniquely on the tag item itself:

(8)

```
                              2  2   3 2 3 3  3   1  4
12   A:  .hhh e: come dire (.) più riPOSta identiTÀ no
         .hhh eh how shall I say (.) more secret identity right

              3   ⌜
13   a:  Sí (?   ?)
         yes │
14   A:       │ che salvaguarda (...)
             ⌞ that protects you (...)
```

Intonational phrasing can be considered as another and more subtle way of singling out and demarcating emerging parts as items to be specifically acknowledged by the recipient. It is used in conjunction with micropausing and an 'additive', right-branching syntax[11], i.e. yet another constituent is added – e.g. by coordination, by prepositional adjunction or relative clause – after one constituent has been acknowledged and in this way also 'negotiated' with the recipient. The 'incremental' elaboration of the moderator's turn is evident in the syntactic construction reaching from line 1 to line 9 and can be represented schematically as:

(9)   quindi non rifiuta X
       in conclusion you don't refuse X
       - acknowledgement -

       rifiuta Y
       you refuse Y
       - acknowledgement -

       ma vuole Z
       but you want Z
       - acknowledgement -

       come una specie di X
       like a sort of X
       - acknowledgement -

       ...di Y, che da Z (syntactic completion)
       ...of Y, which gives Z
       - acknowledgement -

The same type of incremental construction with interspersed acknowledgements prevails also in other parts of the fragment (lines 11–16) and, following the story of the caller, lines 28–34.[12]

The singled-out constituents thus figure ambivalently: as possible 'closure pieces' (see Local and Kelly 1986) at first and retrospectively, when presented as 'acknowledgeables' to the recipient; when acknowledged they are then revealed as parts prospectively (and already) involved in a continuing structure. Acknowledgements accompany the parsing and pave the way to further, additional completion.

Intonationally the singled-out constituents are presented with the cohesiveness of an overarching intonational phrase[13] which recurrently has a moderately falling pitch movement at its end, cf. the tokens in lines 5, 7, 15, 17 and their preceding contours.

(10)
                              3   2   2   3 2
4   A: ma vuole un paSSAto DENtro di LEi=
           but you want a past within yourself=

5   a: =SOno d'aCCORdo
         =*I agree*

                                    3   2 3 2
6   A: come ⌈una specie di (.) caLOR viTA:le=
         like a sort of (.) vital energy=
7   a: (h)(h) ⌈sì
                ⌊*yes*

(11)

                              ⌈   2   3   4 2⌈
14   A: che salvaguarda dalle in=TEM=PE:rie
         that protects you from adversities
15   a: ⌈*sì*   ⌈*sì*
                     ⌊*yes*   ⌊*yes*

                                  3   2 2 2   3 2
16   A: e che non è contamiNA:ta da sguARdi indisCRE:ti
         and that is not contaminated by indiscreet looks
17   a: sì (continues)
         yes

Only once, at the end of the syntactic construction reaching from
lines 1 to 9, do we find a level pitch-holding (line 9).[14]

(12)

              3   3   3 3
9   A: che da VI:ta fuOri
         that gives life outside
10   a: certo (continues)
         certainly

Ideally the level pitch-holding of a 'suspended intonation'[15] could
be expected to correspond best to the retrospective–prospective
ambiguity mentioned, indicating at the same time provisory closure
and finality of the constituent and its non-finality and 'openness' as
part of a projected continuation. The moderately falling contours
that we find to prevail at the provisory closures nevertheless are in
neat contrast with finality as it is indicated in tokens by the caller
(cf. line 10). (The falling contour here coincides with a 'fading out',
i.e. the last syllable is hardly audible.)

(13)

                   3   1 1   1 2 1
10   a: certo qualcosa di MI:o in ogni caso
         certainly something that is mine anyhow

The moderately falling contours as described above for the provisory closures are also in contrast with closure as it is indicated at a major interactive boundary of the call (line 32), the last topical contribution of the moderator, projecting imminent closing of the call.

(14)

```
                                    3   2  2 3 1
32   A:  che SPERde TUTTo in una noTTA:ta di GRA:Nde voCI:o=
         that expends everything in one night of grand singing=
33   a:  =d'aCCORdo
         =I agree
34   A:  grazie...
         thank you...
```

It is a major boundary of the call which is initiated and proposed here and the strong intonational marking of closure in line 32 coincides with several other closures: of a syntactic construction, of a turn and of a metaphorical 'gestalt'. It is thus also a rhetorically achieved 'poetic closure' (see Smith 1968) of the call.

4.5 Further discussion of acknowledgement tokens by the caller

Although it is not possible to discuss every single item, prosodic features and their 'indexical' meaning will be discussed in the case of tokens which seem to have a somewhat deviant status in the fragment (cf. the tokens in lines 13, 15 and 17).

(15)

```
                            3  2  3   3 3 1   4
12   A:  .hhh e: come dire (.) più riPOSta identiTÀ no
         .hhh eh how shall I say (.) more secret identity right

         3      ⌐
13   a:  SÌ (? └ ?)
         yes     │
                 │
         2   2 2   3 2 2 2 2   3    4   2
14   A:          che salvaguarda⌐dalle in=TEM=PE:rie⌐
                 that protects you from adversities
15   a:                         │*sì*           │*sì*
                                └yes            └yes

         2  2   3 3 2  2 2  3 2  2   3  2 2  2   3 2
16   A:  e che non è contamiNA:ta da sguARdi indisCRE:ti
         and that is not contaminated by indiscreet looks
```

```
          1        2    3  3
17   a:  sì (.) tra l'altro (introduces a STORY)
         yes (.) by the way
```

Lines 13/14 show the only overlap in the otherwise perfectly well-coordinated interaction: the moderator here resumes his interrupted turn as soon as he receives the acknowledgement solicited. Yet, as acknowledgement tokens often prefigure the starting of a turn (see, e.g., line 17), and may even be a very common turn-entering strategy,[16] the possible start of a more extended turn by the caller, as in fact occurs in line 17, seems to be curtailed at this point.

A closer look at the caller's subsequent tokens supports this: the tokens in lines 15 and 17, in strong contrast with line 13, are produced with reduced loudness, on a low pitch level and without pitch movement. The first token in line 15 furthermore is manifestly 'displaced' in relation to the current turn, i.e. there is no speech object to be acknowledged at the point where it occurs. The second one – and the one in line 17 – are sequentially appropriate, but are 'out of tune' (see below), i.e. they do not relate to the emphasis just being formulated in the utterances they follow. These tokens, rather than acknowledging current talk, can be heard as 'precursors' or 'probes': the recipient displays, by audibly ignoring or neglecting important sequential and/or prosodic details of current talk in progress, that (s)he is preoccupied prospectively, preparing a turn and waiting for a completion point in current talk in order to be able to start it. Current speaker, as a recipient of tokens which announce a turn 'in store', may give room to it and cede the floor, in particular when realizing retrospectively that (s)he may just have curtailed the initiation of a turn, as is the case in our example.

The tokens just mentioned, hearably out of touch with important details of current talk, are exceptional in this fragment. The other tokens display their particular 'fit' to the contingent speech object they acknowledge in placement and prosodic design. As mentioned, this includes echoing intonational aspects of preceding talk, but may also involve non-correspondences, notably on the level of speech rate. A salient non-correspondence in speech rate (not noted in the transcript) will be commented on for the token in line 10.

(16)

```
        2    2  2 2 3  3  3   3 3    3   3  3    2
8    A:  di (.) fuo/focoLA:re LE:Nto che BRU:cia DE:Ntro
        from (.) fi/from a small slow fire that burns inside

        3  3   3 3    3 3
9    che da VI:ta fuOri
        that gives life outside

        3  1   1 3 2  2   3 1 1  1 1   2  1
10   B:  certo qualcosa di MI:o in ogni caso
        certainly something that is mine anyhow
```

The caller in line 10 goes beyond the minimal format of an acknowledgement token and displays a 'down to earth' understanding of the more abstract poetic metaphor of the 'fire slowly burning inside' just proposed to her, conveyed and 'staged' by the moderator with an 'iconic' prosody, i.e. a strongly repetitive intonational contour maintaining the same pitch level, repeated vowel lengthening and a neatly perceptible slowing down of speech rate. The caller, in her onset in line 10, 'echoes' the high pitch level but does not orient to the 'tempo rubato' mode of its presentation: she produces her acknowledgement with a high speech rate. High speech rate may be related to recipiency and be a display of not expanding a token, designing it to remain a brief intermediary token. The 'in-between' or 'bridging' status of line 10, inserted to fit in 'edgewise', is thus conveyed prosodically not only by an unmistakably clear intonational indication of closure, but also by a high speech rate. Minimization in temporal extension can display a recipient's stance, documenting that (s)he hears the preceding as an ongoing turn, to be continued and not to be obstructed by 'long' utterances that may make the legitimate current speaker wait for space to continue.[17] Further properties of the caller's tokens will be mentioned below when comparing the two fragments.

5 Disaffiliating

5.1 Background

Acknowledgement tokens can be noticeably absent or they can be 'out of tune', 'out of place' and 'out of rhythm'. As mentioned above, there is a cumulative dynamic in the interactive effects of recipiency. Just as the moderator, in the previous fragment, can be increasingly assured of pursuing a common 'line of thought' with the caller, there is also a reverse effect and we need not be astonished to find illustrations of several 'misuses' all within one fragment. Illustrations of several of these are found and discussed in the following fragment, taken from a call which also has an unusually extended closing section. In this case it is the caller who is responsible for the extension – she 'moves out' (cf. Button 1987) of a closing initiated by the moderator. The moderator, in consequence, has to manage a situation where the caller continues topical talk and retards the projected closing (and the opening of the next call). It is his recipiency which will be inspected more closely below.

The transcript sets in when the call has been going on for a comparatively long period and is 'ripe' for closing. Roughly, the sequence of events in the fragment is as follows: in line 7 the caller finishes a story. It is 'only' a story about the weather, the fog in her home town in Piedmont, yet it is told with much involvement[18] by the narrator and is received with much distance by the moderator (see below). The moderator subsequently (line 11) attempts to initiate closing in the usual way by summarizing the 'gist' of the caller's position in the call, but fails – the caller retopicalizes material from the summary and continues topical talk. Yet, although continuing, the caller still orients to the fact that closing has been initiated: the topic she introduces, a complimenting and appreciating sequence (lines 22–36), is in fact conventionally a 'last' topic, i.e. it is sequentially implicative of closing (see Button 1987). By clearly demarcating the end of this topic (line 36), the caller signals that she is now 'ready' for closing. Topic bounding, usually an activity by the moderator, thus is done here exceptionally by the caller. Closure of this topic then is a sufficient warrant for the moderator to enter immediately into closing terminal formulation (line 37).

5.2 Transcript

(17) (Mirella 23:24f; A=moderator; M=caller)
1   M: mi ricordo che c'erano (.) quelle giorNA:te pie:ne di NE:bbia
         I recall that there were (.) these days full of fog
2   una nebbia TERRI:bile (.) .hhh
         a terrible fog (.) .hhh

3 che non si veDEva da un MEtro di disTA:Nza (0.5)
so that one could not see at a metre's distance (0.5)
4 e con tutto ciò::: m:: scenDE:vo dalla mia CA:sa
and with all that m:: I left my house
5 dovevo=andare (.) m:: in una boTTE:ga (.) che=era poco distante (.)
I had to go (.) m:: to a grocery store (.) which was not far away (.)
6 e conTA:vo le PO:Rte delle (.) delle varie CA:se perchè non si
veDE:va
*and I counted the doors of the (.) of the various houses
because one could not see*
7 (.) le conTAvo e arriVAvo coSÌ al neGO:zio .hhh
(.) I counted them and thus arrived at the store .hhh
8 (0.8)
9 A: bene
fine
10 M: e QUEsto mi: (h)(.) e: sono (.) ricordi beLLISSimi dottor
GuerZO:ni=
*and this (h)(.) and these are (.) the most beautiful
memories doctor Guerzoni*
11 A: =certo quindi mi pare Mirella (.) che potremmo riassumere
*=certainly well then it seems to me Mirella (.) that we can
sum up*
12 la sua telefonata nel se:gno della nostalgia=
your call under the sign of nostalgia=
13 M: =MO::Lto MO::Lto
=very much⌈indeed
14 A: ⌊(? va bene?) (h)
⌊(?allright?) (h)
15 M: e sono MOLto leGA:ta=ancora=alle MIe=aMI:che
and I'm still very much attached to my friends
16 A: ⌈questo
⌊*that*
17 M: ⌈qualCU:na
⌊*there is one*
18 ci scriviamo anCO:ra
we keep writing to each other
19 A: certo
certainly
20 M: a naTA:le così PA:Squa sa
well⌐at Christmas at Easter you know
21 A: benë
fine
22 M: ⌐dottor Guerzoni io le voglio fare compliME:Nti per le sue
⌊*doctor Guerzoni I want to compliment you on your*
23 trasmissiON .hhh (.)
programmes .hhh (.)

24   per le sue (.) **TU:TTE** le sue trasmissioni che sono MO:Lto=
        for your (.) all your programmes which are very=
25   imporTANti e ci=inSEgnano MO:Lto
        important and teach us a great deal
26 A: bene
        fine
27 M: ma le più BEL:Le (.) mi creda almeno per ME (.) sono QUE:ste (.)
        but the nicest ones (.) believe me at least for me (.) are these (.)
28 A: hm
        hm
29 M: coSÌ SENza: (0.5) speciaLI:sti specialiZZA:ti doTTO:ri
        ones without (0.5) specialists specialized people doctors
30 A: bene
        fine
31 M: | per quanto sono la:/e:: (.) ripe:to
        | *they rather are worle:: (.) I repeat*
32 A: | interessanti anche QUELLe (.) certo=
                                         | *those are also interesting (.) surely=*
33 M: =anche QUELLe ci VOgliono ma QUEste sono più sponTA:Nee
        =those are useful too but these are more spontaneous
34   VENGono da:
        they come from
35 A: certo
        certainly
36 M: da delle perSONe COMe ME ECCo=
        from people like me that's it=
37 A: =bene gra:zie tante Mirella=
        =fine thank you so much Mirella=
38 M: =e: s'iMMA:gini arriveDERla
        =eh you're welcome goodbye

5.3 Incremental turn construction

In this fragment as well, the caller's continued turn is basically constructed 'incrementally' and the emerging turn-parts, the 'partes orationis', are presented as provisorily complete steps, singled out by coherent intonational phrasing as individual propositions to be acknowledged by recipient (and, mostly, to be modified and connected within a continuing syntactic structure afterwards). Yet the 'negotiation' of the several steps in the progression of the turn takes on a different shape, as will be described in more detail below. A first difference from the previous fragment, to be noted here only in brief: not all of the propositions presented as 'acknowledgeables' are also acknowledged by recipient. In the series of caller's propositions (followed by moderator's acknowledgements) which begins in line 15, a token of acknowledgement is noticeably absent following lines 22–23, where the caller introduces, as yet a further topic to be treated within the call, her proposal to 'compliment' the moderator on his radio programmes.

(18)

```
        2   2     2  3 2 2 2  2 2   2 2  2    2  4   2  2  2 32
22  M:  dottor Guerzoni io le voglio fare compliME:Nti per le sue
        doctor Guerzoni I want to compliment you on your

           2     2  1
23      trasmissiON .hhh (.)
        programs .hhh (.)

           2  2 3 1       4  3   2  32  2  2   3 2 2   2  2   3   2
24      per le sue (.) TU:TTE le sue trasmissioni che sono MO:Lto=
        for your (.) all your programs which are very=

           2    2  3 2 2   2   3    2  2  3   1
25      imporTANti e ci=inSEgnano MO:Lto
        important and teach us a great deal

            2  1
26  A:  bene
        fine
```

Prosodically the proposition in lines 22/23 is again presented as an 'acknowledgeable' – cf. its intonational closure – and the subsequent micro-pausing offers a slot for acknowledgement. We may even see the subsequent modification of *le sue trasmissiON*, i.e. the emphatic upgrading which follows in line 24, in relation to the absence of a token in line 23 and as also being an upgraded solicitation for acknowledgement.

5.4 Minimal response to emphasis

The caller's story, although performed with hesitations within, is closed with a unit clearly demarcated as a 'last line', reformulating the main point of her story. (It is by counting the doors that she arrives, in the opaqueness of the fog, at her goal.) As a 'closure piece' (Local and Kelly 1986), the last line is intonationally – and iconically – characterized by a gradual 'stepping down' on the stressed syllables, arriving at the *neGO:zio* also at the lowest pitch point (see line 7).

(19)

```
        4         3       2    1-
7  (M:)  (.) le conTAvo e arriVAvo coSÌ al neGO:zio .hhh
         (.) I counted them and thus arrived at the store .hhh
```

In spite of its clearly marked gestalt-like closure, the moderator
acknowledges the story in a rather distant manner, producing in a
neutral voice only one token, which has only a weakly perceptible
pitch accent (line 9), and which also comes late.

(20)

```
          3 3  4   2 22  2 3  2  2 21 1  1- 1
7  (M:)  (.) le conTAvo e arriVAvo coSÌ al neGO:zio .hhh
         (.) I counted them and thus arrived at the store .hhh
8        (0.8)

           2 1
9  A:    bene
         fine

         2   3 2  3      2 3 2   2 3 2 2  4 3 2 2  2
10 M:    e QUEsto mi:(h) (.) e: sono (.) ricordi beLLISSimi dottor

           2  3  1
         GuerZO:ni=
         and this (h)(.) and these are (.) the most beautiful
         memories doctor Guerzoni

           2 1
11 A:    =certo quindi mi pare Mirella (.) che potremmo riassumere (...)
         =certainly well then it seems to me Mirella (.) that we can sum
         up (...)
```

Uttered in this way and at this point, i.e. merely acknowledging
receipt and passing the floor at story completion, this token can
be heard to 'delete' the narrative work of the story and to withhold
a more differentiated evaluation. The absence of a more differentiated response is noticed by the caller, who formulates in her next
turn (line 10), a (self-)evaluation of the story, using an address
term and an emphasized superlative assessment (sono ricordi
beLLISSimi dottor GuerZO:ni) to elicit evaluative comment from
the recipient.[19]

Superlative assessments have been claimed to attract 'newsmarks' (Jefferson 1978:243) or other responses 'in tone' that will
respond to the involvement documented by current speaker and
display the recipient's participation in the high-graded assessment.
Viewed prosodically, it seems plausible to assume that superlatives

may often be, as in our case above, those parts in a turn which are demarcated – by pitch movement and/or duration and intensity – as being the most salient cues, orienting and directing the recipient's attention to them and inviting acknowledgements as documents of participation in the 'superlativization'. It is evident that there is great variety in the way speakers have of expressing super-latives – cf. a simple case and an elaborate one taken from Cosnier and Kerbrat-Orecchioni (1991),[20] both 'attracting' acknowledgement tokens.[21]

(21)
52 F: les garçons font extrêmement::. attention à la façon
        boys pay extreme attention to the way
    H: oui'
                                                   yes
    F: dont i=sont habillés:" (continues)
        they dress

                                                        (1991:377)

(22)
80 F: (mais) y a une chose' qui m=choque' à propos du
        but there is one thing that shocks me about
        vêt=ment' c'est le::. les sommes' que les gens peuvent
        clothes that's the the amount of money that people
        claquer là-d=dans,,
        throw away on them
    H: c'est vrai,
        that's true
    F: ça c'est incroya:ble, les gens:, (continues)
        that's incredible people
    H: ouais
            yes

                                                        (1991:378)

The 'attracting' is evident in the simple case (line 52): the acknowl-edgement token displaying recipient's alignment to the high-graded assessment *extrêmement* has to 'wait' for the predicate noun *atten-tion* to emerge after the superlative term, but it still comes in 'spontaneously', i.e. without the delay of waiting for the turn to be completed. Judging from the transcript, the prosodic salience of the superlative seems to be constituted here mainly by duration.

In the more elaborate case, prosodic salience in the superlative assessment is conveyed in a different manner. The assessment has an intonation contour descending from a fairly high pitch level, on

3
sommes

to a particularly low one, reaching below the usual range of the speaker:

```
1   3        1  2   1     2  2  1    1-
les sommes que les gens peuvent claquer là-dedans
```

This also orients and directs the recipient's display of participation in a different manner. The expression of superlative assessment and corresponding alignment by recipient is commented on by Fontaney as follows:

F does two things: she affirms that people throw lots of money away on clothes, and she expresses her feelings about this behaviour ('shocks me'; 'throw away' (*claquer*) is also a verb which carries an evaluation). The falling tone corresponds to an affirmation, but the especially low level to which it falls has an affective value and expresses her indignation. H reacts with

3   2
/c'est vrai/

'that's true' also with a falling tone. By his words he indicates that he agrees with the affirmation ('people throw away a lot of money'), by his tone, which in a way echoes the tone used by F, he indicates his agreement with the feeling of indignation expressed by F. (Cf. also the repeated and renewed alignment of H in the next sequence.) (1991:240; my translation – FM)

Acknowledgement tokens thus may be 'attuned' to the prosodically most salient features of the speech object they follow and acknowledge. Depending on the specifics of their object, there are several possible ways for such an 'attunement' to be expressed in conversation (e.g. by contiguity or 'spontaneous' placement, by correspondence in intonational contour and/or matching in 'animation'/loudness).

Yet, as is evident from our 'disaffiliation' fragment, they may also be 'out of tune'. Returning to our fragment, this is the case with the moderator's token, cf. the

2   1
certo

in line 11, which closely follows a prosodically salient superlative
assessment by the caller (*ricordi beLLISSimi*) and which prefaces an
initiation to closure. Produced 'monotonously', i.e. with a low pitch
range and only slight internal pitch movement, and with fairly high
speech rate, the token acknowledges the preceding turn, but does so
in a formal and distant manner: it disregards the prosodically most
salient features of prior talk and disaffiliates from the orientation
projected by current speaker's prosody.

We recurrently find the same kind of minimal response by recipient, disproportionate in relation to the prosodic 'maximizing'
of resources employed by current speaker, in the appreciation
sequence, where the caller assesses – and praises – the moderator's
different types of radio programmes, going again to extremes (lines
24f.).

(23)

```
              2  2  31      4  3  2  32   2  2 3   2   2 2 2    3  2
24   (M:)  .hhh per le sue (.) TU:TTE le sue trasmissioni che sono MO:Lto=
           .hhh for your (.) all your programs which are very=

           2  2   3   2 2   2    3  2  2   3   1
25         imporTANti e ci=inSEgnano MO:Lto
           important and teach us a great deal

           2  1
26   A:    bene
           fine

           2 2   2  4   2    1  2 1  1  2 1  1    3    2  2    4 1
27   M:    ma le più BEL:Le (.) mi creda almeno per ME (.) sono QUEste (.)
           but the nicest ones (.) believe me at least for me (.) are these (.)
28   A:    hm

           2 3  3   2       2 2  2 2   2   2 2   2 2 2    2   1
29   M:    coSÌ SENza: (0.5) speciaLI:sti specialiZZA:ti doTTO:ri
           ones without (0.5) specialists specialized people doctors

           2  1
30   A:    bene
           fine
```

The caller here uses several procedures to formulate high-grade
assessments: universal and intensifying quantifiers (lines 24–25), a
grammatical superlative (27) and listing (29). These carry either the
most salient pitch peaks in the intonational contours or, as in line
29, strong, intensity-marked local accents on the propositions presented for acknowledgement. Each proposition of praise is followed

by a minimal token of acknowledgement, appropriate as to sequential placement, but manifestly not 'attuned' to the specific, prosodically salient features of the 'acknowledgeable'.

Minimally responding to the praise, the moderator responds more explicitly to the criticism potentially implied: as it happens, the caller's praise of one type of programme, that 'without specialists', entails the criticism of another, the type including the experts and 'doctors', and the moderator comes in in a next turn – produced partly in overlap with the caller – with a 'repair', *interessanti anche quelle* (line 32), rejecting the implied criticism and thus contributing once more to his prevailing stance of disaffiliation in this fragment.

5.5 Out of place

An 'out of place' token occurs in the 'disaffiliation' fragment at the moment where the caller retards, with sound-stretching and level intonation, the completion of an utterance manifestly still in progress and not yet acknowledgeable (line 35).

(24)
```
33   M: =anche QUElle ci VOgliono ma QUEste sono più sponTA:Nee
        =those are useful too but these are more spontaneous

            3  2  2  2
34      VENGono da:
        they come from

           2  1
35   A: certo
        certainly

        2  2  2  2  3  2  3  3   3 3   1
36   M: da delle perSONe COMe ME ECCo=
        from people like me that's it=
37   A: =bene gra:zie tante (...)
        =fine thank you so much (...)
```

At the point where the token (*certo*), which has the falling contour of an assertion, occurs, there is no possible speech object to be acknowledged or asserted. Judging by the subsequent reaction of the caller and the way she completes the utterance, the misplacement may have a situated meaning that reverses the usual 'directive' instruction of continuers ('Go on, say more'). The completing part of the caller's utterance turns out to be her last topical contribution to the call and is marked by intonational, syntactic and lexical (*ECCo*) cues as a 'last line' of topical closure. The misplaced token can thus be considered as one more – and a more open and less polite – instance of disaffiliation within the series of several that have occurred since moving out of closing (see line 15 of transcript) by the caller. The moderator and reluctant recipient withdraws recipiency and signals a more decisive stance of not being available to listen to further talk from the caller. The token thus may be intended to 'hurry up' the caller and have the effect of inducing her to close down topical talk.

6 Comparing rhythmicity

Continuers that come 'between sentences' (see Schegloff 1982) may also continue the rhythm, if there is a locally established regular rhythmic pattern in the 'sentence' they follow. In the smoothly coordinated 'dueting' realized in the first fragment, but not in the second, acknowledgement tokens tend to be rhythmically integrated, i.e. the 'affiliating' recipient tends to affiliate on the level of rhythm as well. This can be shown in a brief comparison of rhythmic structures in the two fragments. (The conventions for rhythmic transcription will be found in the appendix.)

In the disaffiliation fragment, caller Mirella closes her story with a regular rhythm:

```
(25) (Mirella, 7f.)
     M:         le con=
          /=TAvo e arri=    /
          /=VAvo co=        /
          /=SÌ al ne=       /
          /=GO:zio .hhh
     A:   (0.8)
          bene
```

Regular rhythmic patterns make temporal projections for well-coordinated next-turn responses (see Couper-Kuhlen 1993). In the present case it makes the moderator's first and scant recipiency of the story all the more visible as a response which is both delayed and 'off beat'.

The onset of the moderator's initiation to closing on the other hand – the *certo* in (26) below – is rhythmically integrated.

(26) (Mirella, 10f.)
```
    M:      sono ri=
            /=cordi beL=    /
            /=LISSimi       /
            /dottor Guer=   /
            /=ZO:ni         /
    A:  /certo quindi...
```

As was shown above, *certo* is intonationally 'out of tune', i.e. does not correspond to and avoids responding to the preceding high-graded self-assessment of the caller, who attempts to re-negotiate the evaluation of the story she has just told. The acknowledgement token of the moderator thus rejects the caller's attempt to re-negotiate the evaluation of the story and prefaces an initiation for closure of the conversation instead. Acknowledgement tokens may thus be 'out of tune', but nevertheless 'in time', i.e. rhythmically integrated. Rhythmic integration at this point can be seen to serve as a 'camouflage' (see Couper-Kuhlen 1992). It permits the moderator to insert the proposal for topical rupture and closure of the conversation in an inconspicuous manner at a position where it would be inappropriate in natural, non-institutional conversation and thus mitigates and 'naturalizes' the inappropriate next-positioning of such a proposal.

In (27) the moderator's token follows a preceding regular rhythm and is followed by caller's continuation in the same rhythm.

(27) (Mirella, 24f.)
```
    M: le sue trasmissioni che sono
            /MO:Lto impor=    /
            /TANti e ci=in=   /
            /SEgnano          /
            /MO:Lto           /
    A:  /bene             /
    M:  /ma le più        /
            /BEL:Le (.)
```

Continued sequences of this type, however, are exceptional in the fragment and in other sequences the moderator is 'out of rhythm' with his tokens of recipiency.

As mentioned above, speakers, although they continue to speak, i.e. hold their turn, are at the same time also recipients of the incoming tokens of recipiency. A case in point is apparent in (28), where the moderator's token continues the rhythm saliently established by the caller with a list structure.

(28) (Mirella, 29f.)
    M: specia=
        /=**LI**:sti speciali**Z**=   /
        /=**ZA**:ti do**T**=   /
        /=**TO**:ri=   /
    A: /ben⌈e
    M: ⌊per quanto sono...

Yet the caller obliterates the rhythmicity of this continuation by coming in now too early and 'off beat' in order to (incrementally) continue her turn beyond the completed list structure. List structures (see Jefferson 1990) frequently occur as 'closure pieces' of turns. Thus, in this fragment, there are 'three' parties – the caller as the current speaker who does not often maintain a regular rhythm for long periods, the moderator as the main recipient, who is not always 'on the beat' with his tokens, and the caller as a 'recipient' of intermediate tokens of recipiency – all of whom contribute to preventing much of a common rhythm from arising in this interaction.

After all this, it is astonishing to note that the terminal sequence of the call is coordinated, with a surprising 'désinvolture', in perfect rhythmic order:

(29) (Mirella, 37f.)
    A: /bene   /
        /gra:zie   /
        /tante Mi= /
        /=rella   /
    M: /e: s'iM= /
        /=**MA**:gini /
        /arrive= /
        /=**DER**la

By comparison, maintenance of a common rhythm is an essential part of the dueting in the 'affiliation' fragment. The prevailing type of sequence (presentation of a proposition to be acknowledged –

acknowledgement token – 'incrementally' continued turn construction) repeatedly occurs as a rhythmically integrated process:

```
(30)  (Anna, 4f.)
      A:      un paS=
              /=SAto              /
              /DENtro di          /
              /LEi
      a:          SOno d'aC= /
              /=CORdo
      A:  /come una           /
      a:  /specie di           /
              /^ (.) ca=        /
              /=LOR vi=         /
              /=TA:le           /
      a:  /(h) (h) sì
```

Note also, in contrast with the 'disaffiliating' fragment, the rhythmically integrated reception of this caller's story (31). Here the last line of the story (*la STEssa COsa FAccio io*), the first reception and evaluation by the moderator as well as the evaluation again received and acknowledged by the caller in the process of its 'incremental' construction are all carried out within a regular rhythmical framework, shared by current speaker and recipient. The regular rhythm is then maintained until topical closure of the call. Talking, as was once remarked by John Gumperz, can be like ballroom dancing.

```
(31)  (Anna, 27f.)
      a:          la
              /STEssa            /
              /COsa              /
              /FAccio            /
              /io                /
              /^                 /
      A:  /^            in=      /
              /=somma    (.)     /
              /^ una formi=      /
              /=CHI:na del pas=  /
              /=sato             /
      a:  /Sì                    /
      A:  /NON una ci=           /
              /=CA:la            /
      a:  /(h) (h) (h) (h)
      A:              che
              /SPErde            /
```

```
        /TUTTo (.)        /
        /^  in            /
        /una noT=         /
        /=TA:ta di        /
        /GRA:Nde vo=      /
        /=CI:o
  a:             d'aC=    /
        /=CORdo
```

A comparison of the rhythm of the two fragments does not reveal an all-or-nothing difference in presence vs absence of rhythm, but a rhythmicity more pervasively maintained in the affiliating fragment, where the acknowledgement tokens are integrated elements. Given this proviso, detailed rhythmic analysis supports an audible 'prima facie' impression of the 'happiness' of this interaction.

7 Conclusion

When attempting to generalize features of the recipiency tokens found and described in the two fragments, a rough distinction can be made between variation vs monotony. In the fragments analysed, the affiliating tokens are more varied – in intonation, in lexical selection and also in length, i.e. there are occasional brief expansions. Affiliating tokens respond more specifically to important details and to salient prosodic features in the talk they acknowledge. They are more 'matched' responses, hearably more in touch, 'in tune' and 'in rhythm' with the emerging talk of their environment than are their disaffiliating counterparts. Taken out of context and compared, many of the moderator's tokens in the disaffiliating fragment resemble each other prosodically: recurrently we find an assertory

```
    2  1
    bene
```

on a low pitch register and with only slight internal (falling) pitch movement. That is to say, except for their sequentially appropriate placement, these tokens do not display a specific design to fit the particular speech object which they follow and acknowledge, but they maintain a distance and display 'ex negativo', by their minimalism and lack of differentiation, a stance of disaffiliation, of non-involvement, of low or absent participation in current speaker's highly involved assessment or other orientation, of non-interference with current talk or of other types of non-supportive attitude.

It has been stated that continuers and acknowledgement tokens provide 'aperçu-glosses' of the talk of the moment (Fries 1952; Laforest 1992). By the graded and nuanced use of these 'glosses in a nutshell' recipients are able to express intricate and subtle stances of participation vis-à-vis current talk. Prosody opens up new possibilities for studying the fine-grained calibration of speaking and listening in conversation.

Appendix

Transcription conventions and transcripts

Textual representation

NON rifiuta il passato	extra strong/loud accent
un paSSAto DENtro di LEi	primary accentuated syllables
i VO:LTI	sound stretching
fuo/focoLA:re	restart of a unit
in=TEM=PE:rie	(within unit) syllabic articulation
ci=inSEgnano	(between vowels) *liaison vocalique*
=	(between utterances) latching
(.)	micropause
(0.8)	timed pause
(h) (h) (h)	laughing
.hhh	audible breathing
si	*sotto voce* (undertone)
(introduces a story)	comments
(??)	transcriptionist doubt

Intonation

Intonational contours have been established on a purely auditory basis and verified by 'judging' co-auditors. (I am grateful to Christine Bierbach, Fabio Messori and Flavia della Valle for their assistance.) Indicating contours with the use of numerical superscripts which refer to pitch levels has some tradition in Romance linguistics. (For a recent approach orienting to conversation structure, see Fontaney (1991).) The present transcription has focussed primarily on the relational structure of pitch movements indicating finality, 'line-holding' and continuation or suspension ('tonia sospensiva', see Canepari (1988)). It does not indicate high, mid, or low range within which this occurs except in the rare, but important, cases where speakers go to pitch peaks either in an extra high or extra low register.

The notation by superscripting as well as the notation of extremities surpassing the usual range of levels is evident from the following illustration.

(i)

```
                °
4 -
3 -          °           °
2 -             ° ° ° °      °
1 -
        NON rifiuta il passato


                 °
4 -                          °
3 -       °      °              °      °
2 - ° ° ° °              ° °       ° °   °
1 -
        rifiuta i LUO:GHI e i VO:LTI del passato
```

The contours in (i) can be represented linearly as in (ii).

(ii)

^{4+ 3 2 22 2 3 2}
NON rifiuta il passato

^{2 2 22 3 4+ 3   22 4   3 2   2 3 2}
rifiuta i **LUO:GHI** e i **VO:LTI** del passato

A low extremity appears in (iii) and is noted as in (iv).

(iii)
```
4 -
3 -       ° °
2 - ° °        ° °
1 -          ° °     °
                  °
        arriVAvo coSÌ al neGO:zio
```

(iv)

^{2 2 3 3 2 2 1   1 1-   1}
arriVAvo coSÌ al neGO:zio

The two fragments in this notation:

Transcript 1

(Anna, 29:02; A=moderator; a=caller)

^{2 2 3   2   2 2 3 2   4+   3 2 2}
1 A: quindi LEi (.) in qualche modo (.) **NON** rifiuta
   in conclusion (.) in a way (.) you don't refuse

```
        2   2  32   2 2 2 2   3  4+  3   2 2   4    3   2   2    3 2
2       il passaⸯo rifiuta i LUO:GHI e i VO:LⸯTI del passato
        the past you refuse the places and the faces of the past
                    ⌈32                          ⌈23
3    a:             |no                          |sì
                    |no                          |yes
                    ⌊                            ⌊
        2   2  2 2   2   3 2  3   2   2 32
4    A: ma vuole un paSSAto DENtro di LEi=
        but you want a past within yourself=

         3  2   2    3    1
5    a:  =SOno d'aCCORdo
         =I agree

        2  2 2 2   3   2 2     2 3    2 3 2
6    A: come una specie di (.) caLOR viTA:le=
        like a sort of (.) vital energy=

7    B: (h)(h) sì
        yes
         2     2 2 2 3  3   3   3   3    3   3 3     2
8    A: di (.) fuo/focoLA:re LE:Nto che BRU:cia DE:Ntro
        from(.) fi/from a small slow fire that burns inside

          3  3   3   3  3 3
9       che da VI:ta fuOri
        that gives life outside

         3  1    1  3 2  2   3 1 1  1   1 2 1
10   B: certo qualcosa di MI:o in ogni caso
        certainly something that is mine anyhow

           3  1 2   2  2 2 2  2  3  2   2  2 32   2 2  3  2
11   A: (.) certo e questo è importante che ci SIa questa sorta (.)
        (.) certainly and it is important that there is this kind (.)

         2        3   3 2 2 2     2 2 3  2 3 3 3  1    4
12      di: (.) .hhh e: come dire (.) più riPOSta identiTÀ no
        of (.) .hhh eh how shall I say (.) more secret identity right

         3 ⌈
13   a: SÌ (?   ?)
        yes
        |                2  2   2   3  2 2 2 2   3    4 ⸯⸯ
14   A: |               che salvaguarda⌈dalle in=TEM=PE:rie
        |               that protects you⌊from adversities
        ⌊               ⌈*sì*                  ⌈*sì*
15   a:                 |yes                   |yes
                        ⌊                      ⌊
        2   2  3   3 2  2   2   3 2  2    3   2 2  2    3 2
16   A: e che non è contamiNA:ta da sguARdi indisCRE:ti
        and that is not contaminated by indiscreet looks
```

```
        1    2  3  3
17   a: sì (.) tra l'altro (introduces a STORY)
        yes (.) by the way
        (in the STORY she tells how she shares her
        past with her husband; last part of STORY:)
        2  2  3  2  2  32  2  3 2  2 2  4 2 2  4 2
26   a: lo riscopro nel suo passato che a POco a POco
        I discover him in his past which bit by bit
        3  2 2  3  1    3 3   3 3   3 3  3    2 21
27   LUI mi racconta (.) e la STEssa COsa FAccio io
        he reveals to me (.) and I do the same
        3  3  1    2 2 2  2   3 2 2  2  3 2   4    3 2
28   A: insomma (.) una formiCHI:na del passáto NON una
        in sum (.) a little ant of the past not a  |
                                                    |   3
29   a:                                             |  SÌ
                                                    |  yes
        2  3  2                                     |
30   A: ciCA:la
        cicada
31   a:   (h) (h) (h) (h)
        |      2   3  2  3  2 2  2 2  2   3 2  2    3   2  2 3 1
32   A: |  che SPERde TUTTo in una noTTA:ta di GRA:Nde voCI:o=
        |  that expends everything in one night of grand singing=
        3   2   1
33   a: =d'aCCORdo
        =I agree
        3 2 2  3 3   2 3  2   2 2   3  2  3  1
34   A: grazie a Lei Anna FI:ne della PRIma PArte (continues)
        thank you Anna end of the first part
                            |  2  1
35   a:                     |  prego
                            |  you're welcome
```

Transcript 2
(Mirella, 23:24f; A=moderator, M=caller)

```
        2  2   3 2   2  3 2 2    2 2  2  3 2  3  2 2  4   2
1    M: mi ricordo che c'erano (.) quelle giorNA:te pie:ne di NE:bbia
        I recall that there were (.) these days full of fog
        2  2  2  2   3  42 1
2    una nebbia TERRI:bile (.) .hhh
        a terrible fog (.) .hhh
        2  3  2  2 3 2 2 2    3 2 2 2   1  1
3    che non si veDEva da un MEtro di disTA:Nza (0.5)
        so that one could not see at a metre's distance (0.5)
```

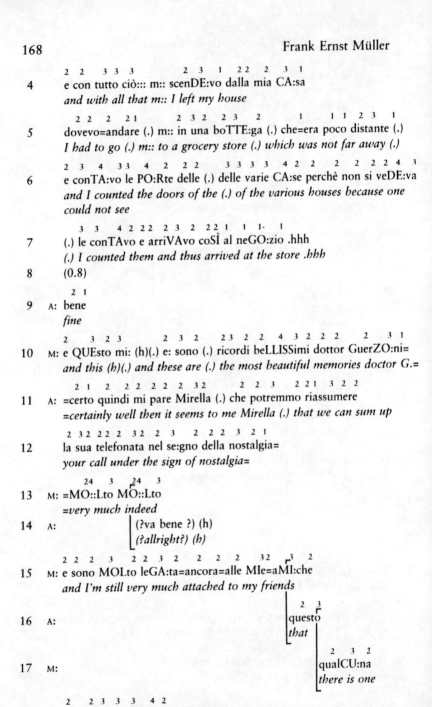

      2 2   3 3 3   2 3 1 22 2 3 1

4   e con tutto ciò::: m:: scenDE:vo dalla mia CA:sa
       and with all that m:: I left my house

      2 2   2 21   2 32   2 3   2   1   1 1 2 3   1

5   dovevo=andare (.) m:: in una boTTE:ga (.) che=era poco distante (.)
       I had to go (.) m:: to a grocery store (.) which was not far away (.)

      2 3   4 33   4   2   2 2   3 3 3 3   4 2 2   2   2 2 2 4 3

6   e conTA:vo le PO:Rte delle (.) delle varie CA:se perchè non si veDE:va
       and I counted the doors of the (.) of the various houses because one
       could not see

         3 3   4 2 22 2 3 2 22 1   1 1-   1

7   (.) le conTAvo e arriVAvo coSÌ al neGO:zio .hhh
       (.) I counted them and thus arrived at the store .hhh

8   (0.8)

      2 1

9   A: bene
        fine

      2   3 2 3   2   3 2   23 2 2   4 3 2 2 2   2   3 1

10 M: e QUEsto mi: (h)(.) e: sono (.) ricordi beLLISSimi dottor GuerZO:ni=
       and this (h)(.) and these are (.) the most beautiful memories doctor G.=

      2 1   2   2 2 2 2 32   2   2 3   2 21 3 2 2

11 A: =certo quindi mi pare Mirella (.) che potremmo riassumere
       =certainly well then it seems to me Mirella (.) that we can sum up

      2 32 2 2 2   32 2 3   2 2 2 3 2 1

12   la sua telefonata nel se:gno della nostalgia=
       your call under the sign of nostalgia=

      24   3   24   3

13 M: =MO::Lto MO::Lto
       =very much indeed

14 A: │ (?va bene ?) (h)
                 └ *(?allright?) (h)*

      2 2 2   3   2 2 3 2   2   2   2   32   2

15 M: e sono MOLto leGA:ta=ancora=alle MIe=aMI:che
       and I'm still very much attached to my friends

                                                          2 3

16 A: questo
                                        that

                                              2   3   2

17 M: qualCU:na
                                          there is one

      2   2 3 3 3   4 2

18   ci scriviamo anCO:ra
       we keep writing each other

```
            2  1
19   A:  certo
         certainly

         3  3  33 3 3  3   2  2
20   M:  a naTA:le così PA:Squa sa
         well at Christmas at Easter you know

            2 1
21   A:  bene
         fine
             ┌
            │ 2  2    2  3 2 2 2  2 2    2 2  2   2   4   2  2  2 32
22   M:     │dottor Guerzoni io le voglio fare compliME:Nti per le sue
            └doctor Guerzoni I want to compliment you on your

            2    2 1
23        trasmissiON .hhh (.)
          programmes .hhh (.)

          2  2  31     4   3  2 32  2  2  3 2   2 2 2   3  2
24        per le sue (.) TU:TTE le sue trasmissioni che sono MO:Lto=
          for your (.) all your programmes which are very=

          2    2 3  2 2  2   3   2  2   3   1
25        imporTANti e ci=inSEgnano MO:Lto
          important and teach us a great deal

            2 1
26   A:  bene
         fine

          2  2   2   4   2    1   2 1 1  2 1  1    3     2  2    4   1
27   M:  ma le più BEL:Le (.) mi creda almeno per ME (.) sono QUE:ste (.)
         but the nicest ones (.) believe me at least for me (.) are these (.)
28   A:  hm
         hm

          2  3 3   2      2  2 2 2   2  2 2  2  2    2  2   1
29   M:  coSÌ SENza: (0.5) speciaLI:sti specialiZZA:ti doTTO:ri
         ones without (0.5) specialists specialized people doctors

            2  1
30   A:  bene
         fine
            ┌
            │ 2    3   2 2  2  2 2   ┌2 3 2
31   M:     │per quanto sono la:/e:: (.) │ripe:to
            └they rather are worle (.)  │I repeat
                                        │
                                        │2 2 2  3 2 2  2    3  2    2 1
32   A:                                 │interessanti anche QUELLe (.) certo=
                                        └those are also interesting (.) surely=

          2   2   3 2  2 3  3  3   2   3 2 2  2   2  2   3  3 2
33   M:  =anche QUELLe ci VOgliono ma QUEste sono più sponTA:Nee
         =those are useful too but these are more spontaneous
```

```
          3    2  2  2
34        VENgono da:
          they come from

          2 1
35   A:   certo
          certainly

          2  2  2  2  3  2   3  3    3 3     1
36   M:   da delle perSONe COMe ME ECCo=
          from people like me that's it=

          3 1   3  2 3 2   2 3 1
37   A:   =bene gra:zie tante Mirella=
          =fine thank you so much Mirella=

          2  2    3  2 2 2 2 2 3  1
38   M:   =e: s'iMMA:gini arriveDErla
          =eh you're welcome goodbye
```

Transcription of rhythmic patterns

The notion of rhythm used here has been developed by Peter Auer and
Elizabeth Couper-Kuhlen and is based on the regular recurrence, perceived
to be isochronous, of stressed syllables, i.e. syllables that may be prominent
by greater relative length, greater relative loudness and/or higher relative
pitch. In the notation (see Couper-Kuhlen and Auer 1991), left-hand slashes
are placed in front of those tokens of stressed syllables in the sequence that
constitute the regularly recurring rhythmic beats of a continuous pattern.

```
M:            specia=
         /=LI:sti specialiZ=      /
         /=ZA:ti dot=             /
         /=TO:ri                  /
A:       /bene
```

The regularity of the recurring beats in time is thus represented by lining up
successive left-hand slashes underneath one another on the page. Right-
hand slashes are used quasi-iconically as an indication of the relative duration of an interval (a 'cadence') between the rhythmic beats. By definition,
at least three beats recurring at perceptually isochronous time intervals are
said to constitute a rhythmic pattern. For a detailed description, see
Couper-Kuhlen (1993).

Notes

1   That is to say, react without delay and with 'precision placement'. For
    the technical capacity for precision placement, basic to conversational
    interaction, see Jefferson (1973:49): 'A recipient of some ongoing talk
    has the technical capacity to produce his talk with precision in relation
    to that ongoing talk . . . The precise placement of a recipient's talk can
    then entail alternative possible actions'.

2 A broader conception of recipiency ('back channel'), initiated in particular by work of Yngve (1970), Duncan (1974), Duncan and Fiske
(1977), includes a number of other more extended phenomena such
as e.g. requests for clarification, echo-questions, repetitions, reformulations, cooperative sentence completions; see Bublitz (1988), Laforest
(1992). For a criticism of the earlier 'back channel' approach, see
Schegloff (1982), Goodwin (1986).

3 The distinction has also been mentioned in other terms in the research
literature. Gaulmyn (1991:221) distinguishes three types of continuer
('régulateur') or of 'continuation work' ('régulation'): 'continuation
work which *acknowledges ('enregistre')* the mere fact that current
speaker is talking *without ratifying* the utterance or its uttering...;
continuation work which *approves* of the current speaker's utterance
...; continuation work which *disapproves* of or puts in doubt the current speaker's utterance' (my translation, FM). Gaulmyn also agrees
that selection among these alternatives is a matter of prosody
(1991:218).

4 For intonational research relating to conversational structure see Local,
Wells and Sebba (1985), Fontaney (1991), Selting (1995).

5 For the role of rhythmic patterns in conversation see Couper-Kuhlen
(1993), Couper-Kuhlen and Auer (1991).

6 This is at least true for intonation. The self-interruption and post-
positioned information on the opening of the museum, however, indicates that A may have expected recognition but not fully achieved it at
this moment, as has been suggested by E. Couper-Kuhlen (personal
communication).

7 'One party to a conversation can employ "uh huh" when the other
party has no intention of going on. Hearing "uh huh" they are then
in a position of seeing that they said something that the other party
figures to be as yet incomplete, and then proceed to find that they ought
to go on. So that "uh huh" can be heard directively.' I quote Sacks
following Laforest (1992:23).

8 It is only at moments not liable to be taken as transition relevance
places (TRPs), i.e. when turns are manifestly still incomplete and display this incompleteness by some set of cues – e.g. syntactic ones as in
our example – that speakers may exploit pausing as a rhetorical
resource to create suspense and attain the direct attention of recipients.
In our example the two rhetorical pauses – in lines 2 and 4 – unmistakably occur at within-turn junctures and, as part-and-parcel phenomena, also contribute to making these junctures salient. The rhetorical
pauses mark the two prior components as point-laden and preface the
third, syntactically and list-structurally final, component which brings
home the point.

9 See the contributions in Drew and Heritage (1992).

10 The closing sections are in many ways an important resource for the
moderator. In particular it is here, in the summarizing assessments, that

he may interpret globally the preceding talk, 'formulate' the call and its 'cumulative import' (Heritage and Watson 1979) specifically for the overhearing audience as well. It is apparent in the following section, but also in others, that the moderator here tends to select 'poetic' formulations, metaphors, generic truths, etc. – in other words, the occasion to formulate 'last words' to the caller furnishes at the same time the occasion to formulate 'big words' to the audience. For a description of the 'radio-rhetorical' usage of closing sections, see Müller (1992, 1994).

11 For the specific appropriateness of right-branching syntax for purposes of turn construction, see Auer (1991) and, more generally on the role of syntax, Auer (1992; this volume).

12 According to the type of interaction in which it is situated, incremental turn construction, as a contingent achievement, can be a resource for various forms of common work. See, e.g., the stepwise 'negotiated' progress in the practice of oral lay interpreters, translating syntactically and cognitively complex turns for their recipients, as described in Müller (1989).

13 For the difficult question of how to determine the global cohesion of intonational phrases, a question not addressed in this paper, see Selting (1995). Although based on a concept of 'phonemic clause' which is criticized by Couper-Kuhlen and Selting (this volume, ch. 1), intonational cohesion and intonational phrasing have been considered in a psycholinguistic perspective (Dittmann and Llewellyn 1967) to be of basic importance for the placement of acknowledgement tokens.

14 This finding may not be as paradoxical as it seems at first glance: intonation can 'counteract' syntactic completion and project an 'openness' of the turn for further development across a point of syntactic completion.

15 See the description of the 'tonia sospensiva' in Italian as given in Canepari (1988).

16 For a description of such usage of acknowledgement tokens, see Gaulmyn (1991:214f).

17 In our example the 'legitimate' current speaker is at the same time the institutionally legitimate person, a professional on the public floor of 'talk-radio' and sufficiently 'at home' there to expand his talk with more ease and leisure and, for example, to take the time for a rhetorical effect that relies on a *ritardando*. In contrast the callers are guests and may speak only at rare occasions in public, and without professional experience and skill.

18 For the prosodic description of features of emphasis and involvement, see Selting (1993). Questions raised in my present paper have been influenced by Selting's study, which focusses on emphasis as a resource for current speakers.

19 When stories are 'deleted' by recipients, post-story activities of tellers are a common feature: 'teller will search for ways to elicit recipient talk deploying story components' (Jefferson 1978:228).

20 The transcription conventions employed by Cosnier and Kerbrat-Orecchioni include a representation of intonation as follows:

'   ton assez haut ou montant (*rather high or rising tone*)
"   ton plus haut ou ton ascendant (*higher tone or rising tone*)
^   intonation descendante de haut à moyen (*intonation falling from high to mid*)
,   descendant d'un ton moyen (*falling moderately*)
„   intonation descendante finale (*final falling intonation*)

(1991:374)

21 See also Goodwin (1986), Goodwin and Goodwin (1987) for the expression and recipiency of other high-graded assessments. When formulating high-graded assessments, speakers tend to leave room for intermediate or concurrent participation displays by recipients. Recipients tend to respond 'spontaneously' and without delay to emerging high-graded assessments, i.e. 'while the object being commented on is still present' (Goodwin 1986:211). Participation displays by recipients occurring here in overlap are not treated as intrusions into the current turn. See also Müller (1993); Schwitalla (1993).

References

Atkinson, J. M. and J. Heritage (eds.) 1984. *Structures of Social Action. Studies in conversation analysis.* Cambridge University Press, and Paris: Editions de la Maison des Sciences de l'Homme.

Auer, P. 1992. The neverending sentence: rightward expansion in spoken language. In M. Kontra and T. Váradi (eds.) *Studies in Spoken Languages: English, German, Finno-Ugric.* Budapest: Linguistics Institute/Hungarian Academy of Sciences, pp. 41–59.

Bolinger, D. L. (ed.) 1972. *Intonation. Selected readings.* Harmondsworth: Penguin.

Bublitz, W. 1988. *Supportive Fellow-speakers and Cooperative Conversations.* Amsterdam: Benjamins.

Button, G. 1987. Moving out of closings. In G. Button and J. Lee (eds.) *Talk and Social Organisation.* Clevedon: Multilingual Matters, pp. 101–151.

Canepari, L. 1988. Intonazione e prosodia. In G. Holtus, M. Metzeltin and C. Schmitt (eds.) *Lexikon der Romanistischen Linguistik, Vol. IV: Italienisch, Korsisch, Sardisch.* Tübingen: Niemeyer, pp. 13–19.

Cosnier, J. 1988. Grands tours et petits tours. In J. Cosnier and C. Kerbrat-Orecchioni (eds.) *Echanges sur la conversation.* Paris: Editions du Centre National de la Recherche Scientifique, pp. 175–184.

Cosnier, J. and C. Kerbrat-Orecchioni (eds.) 1991. *Décrire la conversation.* Lyon: Presses Universitaires.

174   Frank Ernst Müller

Couper-Kuhlen, E. 1992. Contextualizing discourse: the prosody of interactive repair. In P. Auer and A. di Luzio (eds.) *The Contextualization
of Language*. Amsterdam: Benjamins, pp. 337–364.
1993. *English Speech Rhythm. Form and function in everyday verbal
interaction*. Amsterdam: Benjamins.
Couper-Kuhlen, E. and P. Auer 1991. On the contextualizing function of
speech rhythm in conversation: question–answer sequences. In J.
Verschueren (ed.) *Levels of Linguistic Adaptation*, Vol. II. Amsterdam:
Benjamins, pp. 1–18.
Dittmann, A. T. and L. G. Llewllyn 1967. The phonemic clause as a unit of
speech decoding. *Journal of Personality and Social Psychology*, 6(3):
341–349.
Drew, P. and J. Heritage (eds.) 1992. *Talk at Work: Interaction in institu-
tional settings*. Cambridge University Press.
Duncan, S. 1974. On the structure of speaker–auditor interaction during
speaking turns. *Language in Society*, 3: 161–180.
Duncan, S. and D. W. Fiske 1977. *Face-to-face Interaction: Research,
methods and theory*. Hilldale, N.J.: Lawrence Erlbaum.
Ehlich, K. 1979. Formen und Funktionen von 'HM'. Eine phonologisch-
pragmatische Analyse. In H. Weydt (ed.) *Die Partikeln der deutschen
Sprache*. Berlin and New York: de Gruyter, pp. 487–509.
Erickson, F. 1986. Listening and speaking. In D. Tannen and J. Atlatis
(eds.) *Languages and Linguistics: The interdependence of theory,
data and application*. Washington, D.C.: Georgetown University
Press, pp. 294–319.
Fontaney, L. 1991. L'intonation et la régulation de l'interaction. In J. Cos-
nier and C. Kerbrat-Orecchioni (1991), pp. 225–268.
Fries, C. 1952. *The Structure of English*. New York: Harcourt, Brace and
World.
Gaulmyn, M.-M. de 1991. Les régulateurs verbaux: contrôle des récep-
teurs. In J. Cosnier and C. Kerbrat-Orecchioni (1991), pp. 203–225.
Goodwin, C. 1986. Alternative sequential treatments of continuers and
assessments. *Human Studies*, 9: 205–218.
Goodwin, C. and M. Goodwin 1987. Concurrent operations on talk. *IPRA
Papers in Pragmatics*, 1: 1–54.
Grosjean, M. 1992. Les formes vocales de l'engagement. In A. Borzeix and
B. Gardin (eds.) *Langage et activités de service*. Langage et Travail 4,
pp. 69–86.
Heritage, J. 1984. A change-of-state token and aspects of its sequential
placement. In Atkinson and Heritage (1984), pp. 299–345.
Heritage, J. and D. R. Watson 1979. Formulations as conversational
objects. In G. Psathas (ed.) *Everyday Language. Studies in ethno-
methodology*. New York: Irvington, pp. 123–162.
Hutchby, I. 1991. The organization of talk on talk radio. In P. Scannell
(ed.) *Broadcast Talk*. London: Sage, pp. 119–138.

Jefferson, G. 1973. A case of precision timing in ordinary conversation: overlapped tag-positioned address terms in closing sequences. *Semiotica*, 9: 47–96.

1978. Sequential aspects of storytelling in conversation. In J. N. Schenkein (ed.) *Studies in the Organization of Conversational Interaction*. New York: Academic Press, pp. 219–248.

1990. List-construction as a task and resource. In G. Psathas (ed.) *Interaction Competence. Studies in Ethnomethodology and Conversation Analysis* 1. Lanham, Md.: University Press of America, pp. 63–92.

Laforest, M. 1992. *Le back channel en situation d'entrevue*. Quebec: Département de langue et linguistique, Laval University.

Local, J. K. and J. Kelly 1986. Projection and 'silences': notes on phonetic and conversational structure. *Human Studies*, 9: 185–204.

Local, J. K., W. H. G. Wells and M. Sebba 1985. Phonology for conversation: phonetic aspects of turn delimitation in London Jamaican. *Journal of Pragmatics*, 9: 309–330.

Müller, F. E. 1989. Translation in bilingual conversation. Pragmatic aspects of translatory interaction. *Journal of Pragmatics*, 13: 713–739.

1992. *Mariuccia, Mariella and many more. The interactive management of callers in an Italian radio phone-in program*. KontRI Arbeitsberichte Nr 19, University of Konstanz.

1993. Interaction et syntaxe – Structures de participation et structures syntaxiques dans la conversation à plusieurs participants. To appear in R. Vion and D. Veronique (eds.), *L'interaction*.

1994. La 'double articulation' de la conversation radiophonique. In C. Kerbrat-Orecchioni and C. Plantin (eds.) *Le trilogue*. Lyon: Presses Universitaires, pp. 201–224.

Quasthoff, U. 1981. Zuhöreraktivitäten beim konversationellen Erzählen. In P. Schröder and H. Steger (eds.) *Dialogforschung* (Jahrbuch 1980 des Instituts für Deutsche Sprache.) Düsseldorf: Schwann, pp. 287–313.

Sacks, H. 1971. Lectures (May 24, SS 158 Y). Mimeo, University of California at Irvine.

Sacks, H. and E. Schegloff 1979. Two preferences in the organization of reference to persons in conversation and their interaction. In G. Psathas (ed.) *Everyday Language. Studies in ethnomethodology*. New York: Irvington, pp. 15–21.

Schegloff, E. A. 1982. Discourse as an interactional achievement: some uses of 'uh huh' and other things that come between sentences. In D. Tannen (ed.) *Analyzing Discourse: Text and talk*. Georgetown University Round Table on Languages and Linguistics 1981. Washington, D.C.: Georgetown University Press, pp. 71–93.

Schegloff, E. A. and H. Sacks 1973. Opening up closings. *Semiotica*, 8: 289–327. Reprinted in R. Turner (ed.) 1974, *Ethnomethodology*. Harmondsworth: Penguin, pp. 233–264.

Schmidt, H. 1982. *Mhm. Der Anteil der Suprasegmentalia am Austausch von Rezipientensignalen in der gesprochenen französischen und deutschen Sprache.* Diss., University of Konstanz.

1982. Mhm. Intonation und kommunikative Funktion von Rezipientensignalen im Französischen und Deutschen. *Zeitschrift für Literaturwissenschaft und Linguistik,* 49: 101–123.

Schwitalla, J. 1993. Uber einige Weisen des gemeinsamen Sprechens. Ein Beitrag zur Theorie der Beteiligungsrollen im Gespräch. *Zeitschrift für Sprachwissenschaft,* 11 (1): 68–98.

Selting, M. 1993. Emphatic speech style – with special focus on the prosodic signalling of heightened emotive involvement in conversation. In C. Caffi and R. Janney (eds.) *Involvement in Language.* Special issue of *Journal of Pragmatics,* 22: 375–408.

1995. *Prosodie im Gespräch. Aspekte einer interaktionalen Phonologie der Konversation.* Tübingen: Niemeyer.

Smith, B. H. 1968. *Poetic Closure: A study of how poems end.* University of Chicago Press.

West, C. and D. Zimmerman 1982. Conversation analysis. In K. Scherer and P. Ekman (eds.) *Handbook of Methods in Nonverbal Behavior Research.* New York: Cambridge University Press, pp. 506–541.

Yngve, V. 1970. On getting a word in edgewise. *Papers from the Sixth Regional Meeting of the Chicago Linguistic Society,* pp. 567–578.

5

Conversational phonetics: some aspects of news receipts in everyday talk

JOHN LOCAL

1 Introduction

Phonological theory is in a mess. The mess is of two kinds – the 'theory' isn't really theory, and there is an almost total lack of genuine interest in relating the so-called phonological analysis to a serious and sensible phonetics. These days phonology often seems to be more concerned with pictures on paper (pick up any book on autosegmental or metrical phonology) and specious universality than with the abstraction of categories from speech, the specification of their contrastivity-domains and the explication of their exponency or phonetic interpretation.

In the recent past, along with colleagues at the University of York, I have been engaged in an attempt to sort this mess out somewhat. This attempt has two distinct strands. One is work on phonological theory (Kelly and Local 1989), computational phonology and high-quality natural-sounding speech synthesis (Coleman 1990, Coleman and Local 1992, Local 1992b, Local and Coleman 1991). The other centres around work on phonetic detail in everyday conversation (French and Local 1983, Local 1992a, Local, Wells and Sebba 1985, Local and Kelly 1985, 1986, Local, Kelly and Wells 1986).

The second aspect of our work, on the phonetics of interaction, has been concerned with showing that close attention to phonetic detail combined with conversation analytic techniques can reveal interesting and important regularities in the organization of everyday talk. We have employed a particular kind of detailed impressionistic parametric phonetic observation to describe and understand the ways in which speakers deploy phonetic resources to undertake interactional work of various kinds. Although this work focusses on conversational interaction, it is conducted with the same theoretical assumptions as our general and computational phonological research. Its initial thrust came from a concern to construct rigorous, data-respecting theories of the organization of the sound systems in languages. As such it represents what we take to be a serious attempt to get to grips with phonetic detail and, in a Firthian manner, 'renew the connection' of the analysis with the behaviour of everyday speakers.

In this chapter I will discuss some analytic observations arising from this second strand of our work on the phonetics of everyday conversation. I will focus on prosodic and other phonetic characteristics of the interactional particle *oh* and demonstrate that there are a number of phonetic details which can serve to discriminate this particle as it appears in various sequential positions and with various interactional functions. The statements I make are intentionally restricted in scope, for it is clear that only by conducting tightly organized micro-analyses of talk can we hope to come to a proper understanding of the general architecture and functioning of speech in interaction.

2 Preliminaries

The particle *oh* turns up in a wide variety of forms and locations in everyday conversation. It may be employed as a way of displaying 'sudden remembering' (Jefferson 1978:221–222) and it is one of the many ways of displaying affiliation or interactional alignment with co-participants.

The impetus for the work undertaken here comes from the extraordinarily interesting paper by John Heritage (1984a). In that paper he discusses in detail the functioning and sequential placement of 'the particle "oh"' which is 'used to propose that its producer has undergone some kind of change in his or her locally current state of knowledge, information, orientation or awareness' (1984a:299). What I present here is an attempt to build on Heritage's analysis and to try and unpick some of the phonetic aspects of *oh* in its function as a 'change-of-state token'. In particular, I shall try to highlight the extent to which phonetic parameters are intertwined with lexis and syntax in the interactional functioning of *oh*. In doing this I shall point up the need to be very careful in assigning 'meaning' to pitch contours. In order to make sense of the phonetic details we observe, the analysis must be situated in an interactional framework where the categories of the analysis are carefully warranted, or justified, by the interactional behaviour of the participants themselves and not simply by the armchair intuitions of the analyst. This requirement is one of the central tenets of conversation analytic (CA) research. At the heart of CA is an attempt to come to an understanding of the skills which ordinary speakers deploy in constructing and participating in socially organized interaction. This involves the recognition that contributions to interaction are 'contextually oriented' (Heritage 1984b:242). Heritage goes on to observe that: 'This contextualization of utterances is a major, and unavoidable, procedure which hearers use and rely on to interpret conversational contributions and it is also something which speakers pervasively attend to in the design of what they say.'

On the whole, linguists have been singularly reluctant to address this aspect of everyday language behaviour. It is salutary that even in the hey-day of sociolinguistic studies little attention was paid to the formal linguistic correlates of *interactional* behaviour. One British linguist, however, was notable for his interest in such matters. In 1935 J. R. Firth called for a form of enquiry that treated speech forms as contextualised productions. In making his appeal Firth was careful to warn against developing nothing more than 'a loose linguistic sociology without formal accuracy' (1935:36). The conversation analytic strategy of research is one way of answering this type of warning. Conversation analysis requires that any analytic claims about social interaction be warranted by means of 'participant orientations'. That is, the analysis proposed must be tied to, and grounded in, the observable behaviour of participants in the interaction. This stringent requirement reflects an endeavour to make analytic claims commensurate with a participant's analysis. CA thus has important implications for all studies of spoken language in that it provides a formal method which can free analysts from traditional reliance on their own intuitions. In particular CA should have much to say to practitioners of 'intonational analysis'. In 1986 Local, Kelly and Wells argued that traditional intonational studies dealing with 'discourse phonology' had been 'less than satisfactory' (1986:411). They proposed that the first reason for this was to be found in the way certain phonic events were routinely excluded *a priori* from consideration with pitch given a functional primacy. Secondly, they drew attention to the widespread reliance on analysts' intuitions in establishing and explicating functional categories. Thirdly, they suggested that there was a tendency to make 'simplistic, monosystemic statements about the relationship of functional categories to phonetic exponents' (1986:412). It should be clear that the kinds of analytic imperatives in CA should provide the impetus to look closely at phonetic and functional detail and offer to analysts a means of avoiding the problems identified by Local, Kelly and Wells.

The work I report on here is still in a preliminary state, although, as I will show, there are interesting systematicities to be elicited from this data and provisional analysis. Consequently, this chapter will concentrate on the description of a representative selection of data fragments with a minimum of theorising.[1]

2.1 *Phonetic characteristics of freestanding* Oh *as a display of* 'news-receipt'

In order to give some preliminary indication of the focus of this paper consider data fragments 1–6. (The representation of the data fragments retains Gail Jefferson's original transcription conventions. For an explanation of these conventions, which are those routinely adopted in the Conversation Analysis literature, see Atkinson and Heritage 1984:ix–xvi.)[2]

(1) **NB I.6: 2**
    EMMA: Yeah. I thought maybe Carl wz out albacore fishin.
    LOTTIE: He went out marlin fishing last night.
→ EMMA: ↓Oh:
                            (.)
    EMMA: Cz ther: gittin s'm albaco:re,
    LOTTIE: YeOh: I know it. °Jesus°

(2) **NB II.1: 2**
    EMMA: Bud's gon'play go:lf now up Riverside he's js
            leavin'
                          (0.2)
→ LOTTIE: Oh:
                          (0.5)
    EMMA: So: Kathern' Harry were spoze tuh come down

las'night pbt there wz a <u>dea</u>th'n the fam'ly <u>so</u> they
couldn'come so Bud's as'd Bill tuh play wih the
comp'ny deal so I guess he c'n play with im ↓so

LOTTIE: <u>Oh</u>:: goo::d.

EMMA: <u>WHAT A MISERBLE WEEKE:ND.</u>

(3) **Rah II: 1**

JENNY: =Hello there I rangy'earlier b'tchu w'r ou:t,

IDA: [↑<u>Oh</u>: I musta been at <u>Dez</u>'s mu:m's=

→ JENNY: [↓a<u>Oh</u>::. h=

IDA: =b't <u>mi</u>:nd <u>you</u> wiv been in a <u>good</u> <u>hour</u>r enna <u>hahlf</u> tuh <u>two</u>::

(4) **Rah B. IDJ(12): 1**

IDA- Ye:h °h <u>uh</u>:m (0.2) I've jis' rung tih teh- eh tell
you (0.3) uh the <u>things</u> 'av arrived from <u>Bar</u>ker'n
<u>Stone</u>'ou [:se,
                       [
                       [

→ JENNY: [<u>Oh</u>:::::
                   (.)

JENNY: Oh c'n I <u>c'm</u> rou:nd, hh

(5) **HG II: 25**

     =[[   ]
                              ]

HYLA: So <u>I</u> don'know'f ah'll g'char]ged the seventy
fi'c(hh)<u>ents</u>(h)'r not

NANCY: =No I <u>don't</u> think you <u>will</u> but- (.) <u>might</u> git charged
something=
                   (0.3)

→ HYLA: <u>Oh</u>:.=

NANCY: =<u>Unle</u>: - you <u>know</u> w't you shoulda do:;ne?=

HYLA: =<u>Call</u>'the operator en said I gotta wrong [number,]
                                  [   ]

HYLA: [u-<u>Ye</u>:a:]h,=

(6) **Trip to Syracuse**

C: She decided to go away this weekend.=

E: =Yeah

C: °hhh (.) So that (.) y'know I really don' have a place
ti'stay

→ E: °h<u>O</u>:::h. (0.2) So you're not gonna go up this weekend?

The fragments characterize the common features of the freestanding
news-receipt *oh*s in the current data:

(i) They may or may not have an initial glottal stop but they never occur with a final glottal stop (cf. the Question-Answer-*oh* sequences discussed below).

(ii) They have utterance prominence (they are stressed). They are all done with falling pitch movement (which ends low in the speaker's range), although the range and starting pitch height varies from token to token (fragments (1) and (5) have mid starts; fragments (3), (4) and (6) have mid-high starts; fragment (2) starts low).[3]

(iii) They are variably extended in time and done with tense articulatory setting.

(iv) They may be accompanied by creaky voice quality but not by breathy voice quality.

(v) They are typically diphthongal – and close back (either throughout or in the closing part of the diphthong).

(vi) They are often produced in the environment of pauses (usually following pauses: fragments (1), (2), (4) and (6)).

(vii) As Heritage (1984a) indicates they routinely terminate news-telling or informing sequences (subsequent talk is often done by the *oh*-producer: fragments (1), (4) and (6)). That is, when speakers deploy such *oh*-tokens, they are typically placed at points in the talk where the informing in progress is possibly complete or they may be strategically deployed to signal that as far as the *oh*-producer is concerned the news-informing is for practical purposes complete.

Evidence for the sequence-terminating potential of these *oh*-tokens can be found in both sequential and phonetic aspects of the talk. We can observe that we routinely find new topics (or reversions to previously curtailed topics) being started after such *oh*-productions (e.g. fragments (1) and (2)). These topic changes are frequently lexically marked with disjunctions such as *but* (e.g. fragment (3)) and with marked upgradings in pitch and loudness features of the utterances (e.g. fragments (1) and (3)). Another possibility is that the *oh*-producer performs a subsequent turn-soliciting question (e.g. fragments (4) and (6)) – in itself a nice piece of evidence that the producers of these *oh*-tokens are sensitive to the sequential implications in that by employing one of these tokens they have effectively

terminated the telling sequence. This gives them the opportunity/
right/necessity to do the next turn at talk.

From these fragments it will be seen that the pitch characteristics
are very constrained; only *falling* pitch movement is illustrated. One
account for this pitch choice might be that a falling pitch contour
here strongly projects finality/completeness (a common assertion in
the intonational literature but see Local 1986 and Local, Kelly and
Wells 1986 for a detailed refutation of this claim), and that co-
participants orient to this in not continuing with their talk or in
proposing topic changes. But what happens if *oh* is not produced
with falling pitch? What if it were to be produced with rising pitch?
Does this get the informer to progress the informing? Somewhat
unexpectedly, when I searched through the data I had difficulty in
finding news-receipt *ohs* done with anything but falling pitch. There
are, however, two exceptions. These are shown in the fragments
following, where the *oh*-tokens are done on both occasions with
rising pitch. Both are somewhat more complex examples than we
have seen to this point, but, significantly, neither straightforwardly
supports the notion that the pitch contour is central to determining
the terminating potential of freestanding *oh*.

(7)   **NB II.1: 1**
       EMMA: Well Bud hadtuh play go:lf uh Thursdee. (.) So'e
       EMMA: [didn'take] Sa-uh f-] Fridee o:ff s[o
              [   ]   [
       LOTTIE: [Oh : : :   ] : : : : .]   [Yeh rode
       LOTTIE: down muh my bi:cycle th[ere en:nu:h h] uh=
                                      [   ]
  →   EMMA: [O h : : : ; ?]
       LOTTIE: =wz nobuddy wa(h)s the ↑: :re.
       EMMA: On ↑Fridee hu[:h?
                           [
       LOTTIE: [Ye:ah.
       EMMA: O[h (that's] °a se:h°)
               [   ]
       LOTTIE: [I thought]
       LOTTIE: Ye:h.

(8)   **NB II.2: 2**
       EMMA: [°hhhhh]Budjs lef']t'play go:lf he's gotta go tuh
              [   ]
       NANCY: [(0.4)] °Y e h ah°]
       EMMA: Riverside=

```
NANCY:   [↓ O h : .   ]
         =[            ]
EMMA:    ['nna comp'n]y dea:l so, °t°h[hhhhh
                                      [
→  NANCY:                              [Oh::?
EMMA:    ↑GOD[it's bih-  ]
            [            ]
NANCY:      [Tuh River]side tihda:y?
EMMA:    °hhh Yeah they: theh gun'tee off et twelve<it's a
         comp'ny dea:l so (.) th'couple wz spozetih come do:wn
         tuh (.) la:s'ni:ght'n yuhknow k-Harry en Kath'rn ther
         uh keh cz Harry wz gunnuh play k-
NANCY:   Oh[:.
           [
EMMA:      ['n comp'ny en then °hhh there wz a death in their
         fa:m'ly so: (.) [hhh
                         [
NANCY:                   [Aww:::.
```

In fragment (7), the rising pitched *oh* is done in overlap with Lottie's turn *Yeh rode down muh my bi:cycle there en:nu:h huh*. Lottie does then indeed appear to continue but the continuation =*wz nobuddy wa(h)s the↑::re.* does not amount to very much of a development of the telling and it falls to Emma to pursue the informing with her turn: *On ↑Fridee hu:h?*. One thing to notice here is that, standardly, news-receipt *ohs* are achieved in the clear. (This is, of course, partly a product of their being produced where tellings/informings are complete or potentially complete.) Here Emma's rising pitched *oh* is placed at a point in Lottie's turn which is potentially complete; so the 'continuing' in Lottie's talk might be apparent rather than real. Moreover, Emma's *oh*-token is, in terms of its phonetic constitution, rather different from the freestanding news-receipt *ohs*. It is not produced as a diphthong or as a close back (rounded) vocoid. Instead we have a monophthong of a back open somewhat unrounded quality (see below for further discussion of such phonetic characteristics in the discussion of freestanding *oh*-tokens in question-elicited informings).

In fragment (8) the rising pitched *oh*-token is produced at the end of Emma's turn, which begins with an out-of-the-blue announcement: *Budjs lef' t'play go:lf he's gotta go tuh Riverside=*. It is preceded by a falling pitched *oh*-token which is placed at a possible telling-completion point (after *go tuh Riverside=*). However, this first *oh*-token (which is phonetically like those described earlier) gets overlapped by Emma continuing *'nna comp'ny dea:l so* (a turn-yielding construction with a trail-off conjunctional (Local and Kelly 1986)), perhaps displaying that, although the *oh*-token was placed at a possible completion point, she had more to say. Notice though that, although Nancy produces a rising pitch *oh*-token, Emma does not orient to it as being a news-receipt which provides for the possibility that the telling is not yet complete. That is, rising pitch in itself does not cue incompleteness. Although Emma is the person to produce the sequentially next talk, instead of expatiating on Bud's golfing trip, she begins an exclamation which prospectively opens up a new topic: *↑GOD it's bih-*. This utterance has the phonetic characteristics of new topic starts: specifically, it is louder and higher in pitch than preceding talk. It is not until Nancy produces the question-framed solicit *Tuh Riverside tihda:y?* that Emma provides an extended version of her news announcement which in turn gets a high-to-low falling pitched *oh*-token from Nancy, again placed at a possible completion point in the telling. However, this too gets overlapped with Emma doing a continuation which ends, similarly to her first, with a trail-off *so:*. This utterance is then followed by a sequence-terminating monophthongal *oh*-token, *aww:::.*, of a somewhat advanced and unrounded, back half-open quality which is different phonetically from the qualities observed in *oh*-tokens considered to this point (for details see question-elicited informings below).

   In summary then, on the basis of the data under consideration, freestanding *oh*-tokens which display news-receivership have a number of recurrent phonetic characteristics and are designed, and oriented to by other participants, as relevantly telling-final or topic-curtailing. They are typically produced with falling pitch, but, on the basis of the two 'exceptions' discussed above, pitch would not, on its own, appear to be a determining feature of their interactional function. If one of the functions of *oh* in these sequences (no matter what its pitch characteristics) is to propose that its producer was previously uninformed but is now informed, we can see that an entirely appropriate thing for the news-teller to do is to terminate the telling on the basis that speakers avoid telling recipients what they already know (Grice's maxims). To pursue a telling after the production of *oh* then might reasonably be seen as 'interactional overkill' unless, of course, talk from the 'now-informed recipient' could be taken to indicate that their 'informedness' was incomplete.

2.2 Oh *with additional turn components*

As John Heritage indicates (1984a:302), freestanding *oh*-receipts of prior informings are comparatively rare. Indeed the examples I have presented represent the entirety of those I could find in the current data. It is far more common to find *oh*-initiated turns with additional structure. Typically this is of two kinds: (i) some sort of assessment formulation which displays that the producer is dealing with particular aspects or implications of the informing – treating it as carrying good or bad news (e.g. *Oh no, Oh wow, Oh good*) or (ii) *oh* plus some kind of next-utterance-soliciting component – typically a partial repeat or reworking of the verbal element of the prior informing utterance (e.g. *Oh you did did you, Oh have you, Oh they're not*). Fragments (9)–(17) illustrate the first of these types.

(9)   **NB IV.7: 6**

    EMMA: I:'ve quit s:mokin ↓yihknow en evryth*ing hh
                            (0.7)
    BARBARA: Well wenjih stop tha*t
    EMMA: THE DAY YOU LE:FT.h
                            (0.6)
    BARBARA: Left whe:re.
    EMMA: From here in September=
    BARBARA: =e-How m'ny cigarettes yih had.
                            (0.5)
    EMMA: ↑↑NOgh:ne.
→   BARBARA: Oh rea↑lly?
    EMMA: NO:.
                            (.)
    BARBARA: ↑Very ↑goo↓*:d.
    EMMA: VERY good.= = °hhh ↑WILL YOU ↓AH'LL k- uhAh'll CALL
               [YIH D U H]MORROW 't=

(10) **NB II.2: 1**
    EMMA: °hh How you ↑doin.
    NANCY: °t hhh Pretty go͟od I gutta ra͟i:se . h °hh[hh
                                                                                    [
    EMMA: [Kuu:u[d.
                                                                                         [
    NANCY: [↑Yeh
            two dollars a week.h
                                        (.)
→   EMMA: Oh[w o͟ : w.]
                 [͟   ]
    NANCY: [↑↑uh:::h]uh hu[:h hu:h↑   ]
                                    [   ]
    EMMA: [Wudee gun:]do with it a:↓ll.
    NANCY: Gol' I ri͟lly I ji͟s don't know how ah'm gunnuh spe͟nd all
            tha͟t money.

(11) **NB II.2: 4**
    EMMA: =°hh ↑Jackie lo͟oked u͟:p↑ °h Hey that wz the s͟ame sp͟ot we͟
            too off fer Ho͟:nuhlu͟lu
                                (0.3͞)
    EMMA: Where they pu͟ut him o͟:n, (0.6) et that chartered
            pla:[ce,
                  [
→   NANCY: [Oh: ri͟↑ll[y?
                            [
    EMMA: [y:::Ye::ah,
    NANCY: ↑Oh: fer heave͟n ↓sa:[kes,
                                           [
    EMMA: [ExA͟:Ctly

(12) **NBII.1: 2**
    EMMA: Bu͟d's gon'play go͟:lf no͟w up R͟iverside he's js leavin'
                                (0.2͞)
    LOTTIE: Oh͟:.
                                (0.5)
    EMMA: So: Kathern' Harry were spoze tuh come down las'night
            pbt there wz a de͞ath'n the fam'ly so they couldn'come
            so Bud's as'd Bil͞l tuh play wih the͟ co͟mp'ny deal so I
            gue͞ss he c'n pla͟y with im ↓so
→   LOTTIE: Oh:: goo::d.
    EMMA: WHA͞T A͞ MI͟SERBLE WEEKE͟:ND.

(13) **HG II: 16**
    HYLA: Getting my hair cut tihmorrow,=
→   NANCY: =Oh ri͟ll͟y?
                                (.)

HYLA: Yea:[:::h,
            [
NANCY: [Oh so soo:n?

(14) **Rah B.1.VMJ(10): 2**
VERA: °hh Uhr:m, uh Val u-ih it's uhr birthday tihday so she's
        gon do:wn fer a: (0.2) eh: birthday present off Freddy.
→ JENNY: °h Oh l[ovely.
                 [
VERA: [Eh: b't the'll be up any ti:me now en ah
        thought oh well ah'll jis give yih a remindih [yih know

(15) **Rah B.2.JV(14): 8**
JENNY: I'm'nna do s'm spaghetti'n: ( ) n-eh::meatballs
        f'teafuh this lot now,
→ VERA: Oh lovely.
JENNY: Cz they didn't have u they only had fish
        fingihs'n chips fih dinnuh,
VERA: °eeYes.°
JENNY: B't thez no↑thing in to:wn.=
JENNY: =Mahrks'n S[pencihs shelves w'↑c l e a : u h.]
                   [   ]
VERA: [Well they wouldn'stay fer a meal.]

(16) **NB II.3: 5**
LOTTIE: En Ru:th uh: this friend a 'mi:ne oh: °hhh well it (.)
         e-eh sh- I let 'er stay et the 'waiian hou:se: >over the
         week<. So we're goin uh: (.) e:-eh t'morruh morning ou:t.
→ EMMA: Oh:: goo::d. Gunnuh rent a boa:[t? er]
                                         [   ]
LOTTIE: [Ye:::]ah=
EMMA: =Ah[hah?]
           [   ]
LOTTIE: [Ye:]ah.

(17) **Frankel TC1.1: 2**
GERI: hhuh[heh .
             [
SHIRLEY: [°hh So 'e tried tih jump in th'car.
( ): hh
→ GERI: Oh: boy,h=
SHIRLEY: =cz I wz Js' getting ou:t.=
GERI: =S[o didju]interdu:ce 'er?
           [   ]
SHIRLEY: [(   )]
SHIRLEY: Of COU: rse.

Like the freestanding *oh*-tokens discussed above, these *oh* + assessment turns routinely occur/are placed at the termination of a topic/news-informing. In fragment (10) Emma's <u>Oh</u> *wo:w.*, which is produced in response to Nancy's news about being given a pay-rise, simply gets a kind of laughter response from Nancy. It is not until the in-overlap question from Emma: *Wudee gun:* <u>do</u> *with it a:⌡ll.* that Nancy produces further on-topic talk: *Gol' I <u>rilly</u> I <u>jis</u> don't know how ah'm gunnuh <u>spend</u> all <u>that</u> money.*

In fragment (12), Lottie's <u>Oh::</u> *goo::d.* receipt of Emma's news about Bud's golf trip and the cancellation of Katherine and Harry's visit because of a death in the family, is delicately placed after the turn-yielding trail-off production of *so*. It is immediately followed by a topic-changing exclamatory turn from Emma (the news-producer) which is produced with increased loudness and overall higher pitch than the preceding turn. Fragments (15) and (17) also evidence the disjunctive phonetics associated with topic starts or restarts (Local 1992a) produced after an *oh*+assessment turn. In (15), for instance, Vera produces *Oh <u>lovely</u>* in response to Jenny detailing what she is cooking for tea. After this turn Jenny does a brief account which serves to motivate her news. Notice here that Vera's minimal response to this, *°eeYes.°*, after which she offers no further talk or pursuit of topic, can be taken to indicate that her *Oh <u>lovely</u>* was indeed designed not to be a larger topic-extending turn. What we then get is Jenny producing *B't thez no⌡thing in to:wn.=*, which restarts a topic (minimally begun much earlier in the conversation) and is explicitly marked with the lexically disjunctive *but*. This utterance is characterized by an increase in loudness, in overall pitch height and pitch at its beginning which contrasts with her previous (accounting) utterance.

Although we can observe some similarities with freestanding *oh*, from a phonetic point of view these *oh*-tokens + assessments are rather different. While all the freestanding *oh*-tokens were produced with dynamic pitch movement, the pitch associated with these *oh*+assessment tokens may or may not be dynamic. However, they are to some extent similar to the freestanding tokens in that they are produced with initial glottal stops and have utterance prominence (are stressed). In the present case however, all tokens begin with glottal closure; this contrasts with freestanding tokens where initial glottal closure is variable. Moreover, if the *oh*-producer is a speaker of an English accent where the phonologically mid back long item in the V-system has diphthongal exponents, these *oh*-tokens, like those of freestanding news-receipt *oh*, will be produced as closing diphthongs.

With the exceptions of fragments (9), (11) and (13) all the *oh* + assessments in the fragments illustrated (and this is the general pattern) are done with terminal falling pitch movement. Like the falling pitch movements discussed earlier we always find these utterances ending low in the speaker's pitch-range.

The *oh*-tokens in these terminal-falling utterances may themselves have falling pitch movement associated with them. I can find no generalization which would determine *when* they have or do not have such dynamic pitch movement. Significantly, the three fragments where the *oh* + assessment has final rising pitch movement are all cases of *oh really*. On no occasion do we find utterances such as *oh good*, *oh lovely*, or *oh wow* produced with dynamic rising pitch. In retrospect this may seem obvious, given the lexical content of the turns and the kinds of pragmatic work which these *oh* + assessments can be seen to be doing. However, its obviousness trades on a naive and unexplicated sense of the 'meaning' of rising pitch. As I have already suggested, such an issue may not be nearly so transparent or well understood as the literature on intonational meaning might lead us to believe. Notice, in this context, that the productions of *oh really* with a rising pitch contour function in a very similar fashion to all the other *oh* + assessment tokens and are similarly placed and treated in the course of the interaction – they occur at telling-termination points and they do not appear to engender more on-telling talk from the other participant despite the occurrence of rising pitch. So, for instance, in (9) Barbara's *Oh rea↑lly?*, which responds to the prior informing (concerning Emma having given up smoking), is followed by a reconfirmation of the prior information: *NO:.* from Emma, which in turn is followed by assessments from both participants. After this there is a reversion to a prior topic concerning Barbara's visit. (As Jefferson 1981 notes, these turns having the sequential structure: (1) news announcement, (2) *oh really?*, (3) reconfirmation and (4) assessment, represent a regular way in which *oh really* news-receipts run off.)

Similarly, the *Oh rilly?* produced by Nancy with rising pitch movement in fragment (13) simply gets a reconfirmation from Hyla: *Yea::::h,*. Further talk is not done by Hyla, who made the news announcement: *Getting my hair cut tihmorrow,=* until Nancy's *oh*-prefaced clarification utterance: *Oh so soo:n?*. Again then, we can observe that it is the constituency of the *oh*-utterance as a whole (its lexico-syntactic and phonetic shape) rather than any single aspect (e.g. pitch) which creates its interactional meaning and function.

2.3 Oh *plus partial repeats of prior turn*

When we come to examine turns with the second class of *oh* + additional components we find a quite different sequential organization operating. These turns, rather than being placed at points of completeness in the news-telling or being deployed to curtail tellings, are typically found where an informing is produced as a 'hearably incomplete' news announcement. They can be seen to be engaged in work to get the news-informant to continue. They are certainly treated in this way. Fragments (18)–(26) exemplify this state of affairs:

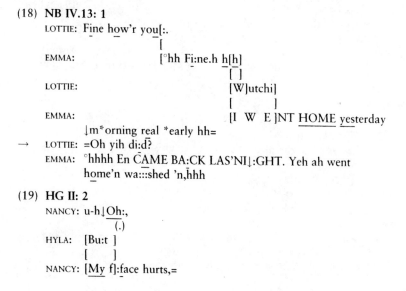

(18) **NB IV.13: 1**

    LOTTIE: Fine how'r you[:.
                        [
    EMMA: [°hh Fi:ne.h h[h]
                             [ ]
    LOTTIE: [W]utchi]
                     [   ]
    EMMA: [I W E]NT HOME yesterday
    ↓m*orning real *early hh=
→   LOTTIE: =Oh yih di:d?
    EMMA: °hhhh En CAME BA:CK LAS'NI↓:GHT. Yeh ah went home'n wa:::shed 'n,hhh

(19) **HG II: 2**

    NANCY: u-h↓Oh:,
              (.)
    HYLA: [Bu:t]
          [   ]
    NANCY: [My f]:face hurts,=

```
        HYLA:  =°W't-°
                    (.)
→       HYLA:  Oh what'd'e do tih you.
                    (.)
        NANCY: ↑GOD'e dis (.) prac'ly killed my dumb fa:ce,=
```

(20) **Rah. B. IDJ(12):**
```
        JENNY: I[saw Jano this mohrning=
                [
        IDA:    [Yes
        JENNY: =in in: uh Marks'n Sp[encers]
                                     [      ]
→       IDA:                         [Oh you did di[dju  [y e s, ]
                                                   [      [        ]
        JENNY:                                     [Mm:[:. °hh ]She wz
               buyin a ↑whole load of stuff she siz she's getting
               hhh ↑huh[huh]
                       [   ]
        IDA:    [hnh]heh-ha-ha-ha
```

(21) **Rah I: 8**
```
        VERA:  uRight yeh °hh Oh I met Jano:, eh:::m yestihday en she'd
               hahdda foh:rm from the Age Concehrn about thaht jo:b.h=
→       JENNY: =Oh=she=hahs?
        VERA:  So: eh she wz sending the foh:rm bahck[the:n you ] know ]
                                                     [      [        ]        ]
→       JENNY:                                       [Oh she di-]aOH:w]'l
               thaht's goo:d ah'm s- ↓pleased she applie:[d,
                                                         [
        VERA:                                            [Ye:s, yes she
               appl- eh she: rahng up on th'Mondee moh:rning. yih[know
                                                                 [
        JENNY:                                                   [M:mm Oh
               goo:d,=
```

(22) **WPC 1. MJ(I): 38**
```
        JENNY: It's- the u-roo:ms see:m bigguh:,
                          (0.7)
        MARIAN: Ye::s[::
                     [
        JENNY:  [do:wnst[eh:s,
                        [
→       MARIAN:         [↑Oh do the↑:h,
                          (0.2)
        JENNY:  eh: (0.3) But thev unly got the two bedroo[:ms,
                                                          [
        MARIAN:                                           [°hh
```

MARIAN: Ye::s[::

             [

JENNY: [ahnd the: uh:m (0.4) kitchen: um

(23) **NB I.1: 7**

                                       [°hhh   Hey
GUY: ↑how'bout sh:'ow bout She:rcliffs.c'n yih git on nere?
                      (0.7)
JOHNNY: °khh I think so They ↑cha:rge too much Gu:[y

                                         [

→   GUY: [Oh doh they?
JOHNNY: Yeh ↑I ↓think so:,

(24) **Rah B.1.JMA(13):**

         [
JENNY: [°hhheh u-hOh: deah °hhh I [went round lahs'=

                                 [

ANN: [(Ho:peless.)
JENNY: =night cuz Ida'd got huhr fuhr::niture so she'd rung me up
       t'[say

          [

→   ANN: [Oh hahs she.
JENNY: Mm [::

           [

ANN: [Dz it look. ni:ce.
JENNY: °hhhh Well it's ↓beautiful fuhrnitchuh. °hh But eh:m (0.2)
       the table is gohr:geous'n the che:z. [It's- it's rou:nd.

                                          [

(25) **Rah II: 17**

IDA: Uh I went last Wednesdih yih know °hh Oh ↑by the wa:y=
→   JENNY: =Oh didche ↑keep fi:t,
IDA: eeYhhe: [:s,

               [

JENNY: [Didju:=

(26) **NB IV.13: 4**

EMMA: Yih like tih see'er ali:ve
           (0.4)

194   John Local

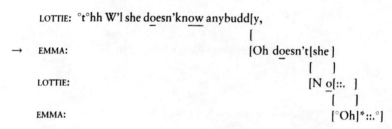

LOTTIE: °t°hh W'l she doesn'know anybudd[y,

                                              [
→ EMMA: [Oh doesn't[she]
                                      [   ]
   LOTTIE: [N o[::.]
                                      [   ]
   EMMA: [°Oh]*::.°]

In each of these fragments we find a news-announcement which is
receipted by an *oh*-prefaced utterance. The additional components
in these *oh*-turns typically build on the verb phrase of the prior turn
or involve some re-doing of the auxiliary of that turn. Fragments
(19) and (25) are somewhat different in this respect and represent an
alternative pattern. In (19) the additional components do not
rework the verb phrase of the prior utterance. Rather they are
couched in the form of a wh-question which builds on the
knowledge, just acquired, that Nancy has been to a dermatologist
for treatment for a skin condition. Similarly, the additional
components of the *oh*-prefaced turn in fragment (25) address the
implications of what has been said: *I went last Wednesdih.*

Jefferson (1981) discusses these '*oh*-plus-partial repeat'
'newsmarks' and suggests that such a structure typically occurs in
an environment 'in which a telling is obviously forthcoming, or [it]
is overlapped by a telling, or gets a telling, or is followed by a
request for a telling'. Importantly, she points up the fact that in
such cases talk is 'either volunteered by recipient . . . or solicited
by newsmarker' (1981:79). Thus they are rather different interactional objects from the kinds of *oh*-news-receipts discussed up to
this point.

Within this class of turns there are two principal syntactically
different types. The first type is exemplified by the instances in
fragments (18), (20) and (21). In this type of turn we find the *oh*-
token immediately followed by a pronoun + auxiliary verb (there
may be additional components as in fragment (20)). In the second
type, exemplified by fragments (22)–(26), the organization of the
turn is such that the *oh*-token is immediately followed by a verbal
element + pronoun (again there may be additional components as in
fragment (25)). (Fragment (19) is somewhat different again in being
a wh-construction but its phonetic properties group it with the

pronoun–auxiliary fragments.) In contrast to the behaviour of the *oh*-tokens discussed so far there is a systematic distribution of whether or not the *oh* particles in these turns are initiated with glottal stops. In the case of the turns with the structure *oh* + verbal element the *oh*-particle is regularly produced with an initial glottal stop, whereas in the *oh* + pronoun types the opposite is the case (on occasion lax breathy phonation can be observed in this type).

In terms of pitch configurations these two types are similar in that both can be done with falling or rising pitch either throughout the utterance or as a final dynamic on-syllable rise or fall. In (19) and (20), for example, there is a dynamic pitch fall associated with the first verbal or auxiliary element, which continues over any remaining material in the turn. So, for instance (with the syllable bearing the prominent, dynamic pitch fall underlined): Oh what'd'e do tih you, oh you did didju yes. In the other case, rather than dynamic pitch fall we find a step down from the stressed verbal element to the pronoun (e.g. fragments (24) and (26)). Notice that in contradistinction to other *oh*-turns with falling pitch this whole class regularly get treated as requiring the co-participant to pursue the news-telling.

The two types are similar also in respect of their possibility of co-occurrence with rising or upstepping pitch. Again, however, the precise details differ. In some of these utterances (e.g. in fragment (18)) we observe a dynamic rising pitch movement associated with the verb *did*. In others we find a pitch step up from stressed verbal element to pronoun (fragments (23), (25) and (26)). A regular and systematic distinction in terms of pitch between the two types is found in the relationships between the pitch of the *oh*-particle and other items in the turn. In the first type where the structure is *oh* + pronoun + verbal element, the *oh* + pronoun part (or in the case of fragment (19) – Oh what'd'e do tih you. – all the material before *do*) is produced on a level pitch. In the second type there is always a pitch discontinuity between the *oh*-particle and the following material. So, for instance, we find a pitch step down from *oh* to the next word in fragment (22) and a pitch step up from *oh* to the next word in fragments (23), (24) and (26).

There are a number of phonetic features which distinguish this class of *oh* + partial repeats from the other *oh*-turns that I have considered so far. A first observation is that they are not typically produced in the environment of preceding pauses as are some other kinds of *oh*-receipts. In the cases I have found in the present conversational materials, these *oh* + partial-repeat turns are either 'latched' (that is, produced very quickly after the completion of a prior turn, e.g. fragments (18), first instance in (21) and (25)) or produced in overlap towards the end of the news/information-giving turn (fragments (20), second instance in (21), (22), (23), (24) and (26)).

In none of the cases I have found of *oh* + partial repeat (whether of the form *oh* + pronoun + verbal element or *oh* + verbal element + pronoun) is the *oh*-particle accented. All the cases I have exhibit *oh* produced rhythmically short (usually diphthongal or a close back vocoid) and unstressed. In all the *oh* + pronoun + further material cases, moreover, there is an interesting rhythmic relation obtaining between the first two elements of the turn in that the *oh* element and the following pronoun are produced, unstressed, with the same rhythmic quantity (an observably 'equal–equal' relation to borrow Abercrombie's (1965a) terminology).

2.4 Freestanding oh-*tokens in question-elicited informings*

To this point I have dealt only with *oh*-tokens which are produced in response to informings which are initiated by the news-bearer themselves. I want now to turn to a quite different kind of *oh*-news-receipt which is produced as a response to informings which are elicited by means of questions. The data fragments below illustrate the phenomenon.

(27) **Rah A. 1. IMJ(2): 2**

```
                        [
IDA:         [Ah thi- et-y-ah: think there wz only about three
             things ordered was it ohr fouhr.
JENNY:  eh-u-Foh ah think theh wz two: fuh Kim'n two fer I:van.
→  IDA:       Oh:.
JENNY:  B't I(c) I don't know what quite.
IDA:          nNoh:. No[h. A'rright thez about three things theahr.=
```

(28) **NB I.6: 7**

```
                     [
LOTTIE:        [Whenyuh go:- thah (.)[yesti-]
                                     [     ]
```

EMMA:					[Uh F̲]ri:dee.
						(0. 3)
→	LOTTIE: O̲h̲:.
							(.)
	LOTTIE: Uh[(huh?)
			[

(29) **WPC 1. MJ(I):1**
				[
JENNY:				[When dz S̲us̲'n g[o bahck.=
						[
MARIAN:					[°hhhh
JENNY:		[(			)
		=[
MARIAN:		[u-She: goes bahck on S̲ahtihda:y̲=
→	JENNY:		=O[h̲:.
			[
MARIAN:		[Ah:n: Stev'n wz heuh (.) all l̲ahs'week'e only went
		bah'yestihd̲a:y.
JENNY:		O̲h̲:.
MARIAN:		°hh̄hhh So: uh 's been qui'u-he[ctic.hh e̲h h̲uh h̲]uh
		°hhhh
						[			]

(30) **Rah B. 2. JV(14): 1**
		[	]				]
VERA:	[A h̲ :]I thought ah'd a'caught]yuh ah thought you
	coul̲da called up fuh coffee.
JENNY: O̲h̲:::. Hahv t̲h̲ey̲'av yih v̲isitiz g[one t̲hen,]
					[		]
VERA:					[Theh'v ↓g̲o̲]:ne. Yes,
→	JENNY: O̲h̲[:ah.]
		[	]
VERA:		[E::n]:- theh'v g̲un tuh J̲ea̲:n's m̲othuh's

(31) **NB II.2: 5**
				[ ]
EMMA:		[Oh]h̲o:w'd[j̲íh d̲o with yer final[s.
			[			[
NANCY:			[°u		[°t I̲: don'kno:w I
		aven'g̲ott'n they'll mai̲:l my g̲ra̲:des yuhkn̲ow bu[t̲
→	EMMA:						[O̲h̲:::.
				(0.2)

(32) **NB II.2: 21**
				[
EMMA:				[Yih kn̲o̲w wher'e is i̲s

                 the:n,
                                          (0.8)
      NANCY: I have never had any of it retu:rned Emma, h
→   EMMA: Oh::.
      NANCY: At a:ll, so: [I jist assoom thet the notice the e.: the=
                           [
      EMMA: [°(   )°
      NANCY: =telegram thet went fr'm th'bank w'ss return' becuz he
              didn't w:ant to accept it.
                                          (0.4)
      EMMA: OH:.h

(33) **HG II: 25**
      N: =°hhh Dz he 'av'iz own apa:rt [mint?   ]
                                        [   ]
      H: [°hhhh]Yea:h,=
→   N: =Oh:,
                          (1.0)
      N: How didju git 'iz number,
                          (.)
      H: I(h) (.) c(h)alled infermation'n San Fr'ncissc(h)[uh!
                                                            [
→   N: [Oh::::
          .. (.) Very cleve:r, hh=
      H: =Thank you[: I- °hh- °hhhhhhhh=
                    [
      N: [W'ts 'iz last name,
      H: =Uh:: Freedla:nd. °hh[hh
                               [
→   N: [Oh [:,
                                   [
      H: [('r)Freedlind.=
      N: =Nice Jewish bo:y?
                          (.)
      H: O:f cou:rse,=
      N: ='v [cou:rse,]
              [   ]
      H: [hh-hh-hh] hnh °hhhhh=
      N: =Nice Jewish boy who doesn'like tih write letters?

Heritage (1984a) remarks of such sequences:

. . . in proposing a change of state, the oh receipt is once more nicely fitted
to the Q–A sequence in which it participates. For the producer of a question
proposes, with the production of a question, to assume the status of pre-
sently uninformed about its substance and thereby proposes as well that the
respondent, in answering the question, assume the status of informed. Here

then the production of 'oh' . . . confirms an answer as an action that has involved the transmission of information from an informed to an uninformed party. (309–310)

Notice, in the light of these observations, that the onus for displaying the satisfactoriness of the information may be seen to fall more on the questioning news/information-recipient than in other cases where the news is proffered rather than solicited. In interactional sequences then, where we have question-elicited information, recipients, by deploying an *oh*-token, propose that a possibly complete answer is acceptably complete for the present purposes. Or, in contrast, by the withholding of *oh* or by the building of the *oh* turn in a particular way, the questioner can display that they are proposing that the answer is, for instance, inadequate in some way, is not complete or is uninformative. This provides for the possibility that doing or not doing an *oh*-token in such sequences can have an effect on the production of further news/information from a co-participant. Not surprisingly then, it is fairly common to find question-elicited informings being dealt with, in the first instance, by non-*oh*-receipts (e.g. *yeah*, or *mm*):

(34) **WPC 1. MJ(1): 2**
```
        MARIAN:   °hhhh (.) °Um::° 'Ow is yih mothih by: th'we:y.h
                                      (.)
        JENNY:    We:ll she's a:,h bit bettuh:,
  →     MARIAN:   Mm [::,
                    [
        JENNY:     [eh- She came: do:wn on: Sahtidee:eveni[ng
                                                          [
  →     MARIAN:                                           [↑Oh: did
                  [s h e a e ,h ]
                  [             ]
        JENNY:    [fih the fuhr]:s'ti:me.
        MARIAN:   Ye:s,
        JENNY:    Ye[s.(   )- ah d]on't know whethuh she came ah: didn't=
                    [             ]
        MARIAN:   [O h ↑: : . ]
        JENNY:    =ring them yestuhday,
        MARIAN:   No-o.h
        JENNY:    Eh:' (0.2) yihknuh ah don't n'whethuh she came down:
                  lahs:t ni:ght,
        MARIAN:   °hh No:.=
        JENNY:    =Jus depends on 'ow she fee- °hh She's no:t just
                  ri:ght thou:gh,
```

In this fragment we see that a first response to a question-elicited informing is a 'continuation' token *Mm::*, from Marian. When Jenny provides a more specific detailing of her mother's improvement out of illness: *She came: do:wn on: Sahtidee:evening*, this gets a strong news-receipt ↑*Oh: did sheae,h.*⁴ Compare also the information receipt produced by Nancy following her eliciting utterance, *Nice Jewish bo:y?*, in fragment (33), for which Heritage gives the following description:

> In this case, the respondent (H) confirms the inference with an utterance 'O:f cou:rse,' which treats the inference as self-evident rather than merely likely. In turn, this confirmation is receipted by N with a repetition of the confirmation . . . which preserves this treatment and asserts it on her own behalf. In effect, the recipient withholds a change-of-state proposal and thus retrospectively proposes that her previous, question-intoned inference is to be heard as having been a comment on something self-evident rather than an inference concerning something still in doubt. (1984a:310–311)

Thus, sequences in which we find *oh*-responses to question-elicited informings have rather different properties and potentials with respect to the subsequent development of the interaction. They also typically have a very different phonetic shape from other *oh*-tokens considered so far. Although all the cases I have been able to track down in the current data are done with terminal falling pitch and, like many other *oh*-tokens, are systematically produced with initial glottal stops and may be variably extended in time, they may, unlike the other tokens considered so far, be done with *rising–falling* pitch (e.g. fragments (29), (31) and the first two instances in (33)). They may also (unlike other *oh*-tokens) terminate with complete glottal closure (e.g. fragments (27), (30), (32) and the first instance in (33)), and they can be noticeably nasalized. Moreover, their vocalic quality is quite distinct from any of the *oh*-tokens considered so far. Most frequently, *oh*-responses to these question-elicited informings are realized as monophthongs. Typically, these monophthongs are back vocoids, usually open or half open. Qualities vary around cardinal vowels 5 and 6; if in the region of cardinal 6, the vocoid is routinely slightly unrounded.

A nice example of the distinction between freestanding *oh*-tokens in question-elicited informing sequences and in proffered informings can be seen in fragment (29). Here we find the question-elicited informing being responded to with a freestanding *oh* which has a falling pitch movement and a vocoid somewhat advanced from cardinal 7, and slightly unrounded. This *oh*-token is overlapped by talk from Marian: *Ah:n: Stev'n wz heuh (.) all lahs'week'e only went bah'yestihda:y.*, which is designed to be a continuation of her preceding response to the question. Following this Jenny produces a canonical freestanding *oh* news-receipt which is done with falling pitch movement, has clear (non-glottalised) phonation and which is diphthongal (beginning in the region of back, advanced, lip-spread, half open and closing towards a slightly advanced and open close back rounded vocoid).

One interesting aspect of the organization of these *oh*-tokens is that they are frequently overlapped by further talk from the questioned party. Routinely, this overlapping talk is configured to propose that it is a continuation of the response to the question. In such places we frequently find continuation items such as *and* (e.g. fragments (29) and (30)). In fragment (32) we find the post-*oh* turn starting with *at a:ll*, which can be construed as a retrospective syntactic addition/repair to the response-to-question utterance: *I have never had any of it retu:rned Emma, h.* These post-/overlapped-*oh* utterances warrant more investigation than I can give them here. They never occur with the phonetic characteristics of topic starts. Rather they have the pitch, loudness and rhythmic features (including tempo acceleration 'rush-throughs') which typically characterize continued utterances. They may well provide evidence for the delicate task of negotiating the extent to which a response to a question is satisfactorily complete. Despite the production of further, overlapping talk from co-participants the production of *oh*-tokens in question-elicited informings regularly curtails the flow of talk, as the fragments illustrate.

2.5 Oh *and 'surprise'*

In discussing these *oh*-receipts of question-elicited informings Heritage (1984a:309) points out that the production of an *oh*-receipt 'is not necessarily associated with the degree to which an answer is unexpected'. Certainly, for the fragments I have presented to this point, it would be difficult to locate any interactional behaviour which could be used to warrant any of the *oh*-tokens as being designed to signal the extent of expectedness of the 'news'.

Nonetheless, this is a matter of some linguistic and interactional interest, for it is quite common to read in books which deal with English 'intonation' that certain 'tones' or 'tunes' have 'meanings' which could be employed for just such a purpose. For example, O'Connor and Arnold (1961) gloss rising–falling tone when used with 'interjections' as *greatly impressed by something not entirely expected* (1961:48); similarly, Roach (1983) writes of the rise–fall that it 'is used to convey rather strong feelings of approval, disapproval or *surprise*' (1983:119 – my emphasis). Notice, however, that, although we may get rising–falling or rising–falling–rising pitch co-occurring with the *oh*-tokens in fragment (33), they do not seem to function to signal 'surprise' or unexpectedness of the news being imparted. There is certainly no interactional evidence for such an analysis (see the quote from Heritage above). The complex rising–falling(–rising) contoured *oh*-tokens in fragment (33) (where the second instance is higher in overall pitch than the first, and the third higher overall than the second) are perhaps employed in some kind of desultory humour-engaged work (this is a jokey sequence with laughter particles occurring throughout). So, for instance, Nancy's turn following her first *oh*-token is simply formulated as a follow-up question. Nancy says nothing that would suggest that Hyla's response to *Dz he 'av'iz own apa:rtmint?* is in any way surprising. Nor is there any interactional evidence in (34) that the rising–falling contour with which Marian's *oh*-token is produced is accomplishing such work. The important point here is that if we want to propose that rising–falling pitch is 'doing surprise' it is essential to show that this is indeed how the participants themselves take it and to identify the appropriate interactional evidence. These last remarks are offered as a caveat, if one were required, against a simplistic assigning of meaning to pitch contours independently of the interactional, lexical and grammatical environments in which they occur (see Cruttenden 1986). However, if we examine some of the *oh*-tokens in the present corpus, it *is* possible to find instances where particular pitch configurations do go around with what we might wish to recognize as 'surprised' receipts.[5] Consider the following data fragments:

(35) **Rah B. 1. IDJ(12): 2**

JENNY: ᶜh Av you <u>seen</u> uhr,

```
IDA:      Ye- °h Well she's gon to m: eh: eh: Chestuh:.
                             (0.9)
IDA:      Ja[no:,
            [
JENNY:    [↑Jano hahs.
IDA:      ↑Ey?
JENNY:    No she hasn't?
                             (0.8)
IDA:      Ye:s. She's go::ne,
          (0.7)
IDA:      She went Just before dinner.
                             (0.2)
→  JENNY: Oh↑:::. Oh[I ( thought ),        ]
                    [                       ]
IDA:                [She wz in suuch a ]ruush,
```

(36) **Frankel TC 1.1: 15–16**

```
                    [
SHIRLEY:            [°hhh So if you guys want a place tuh sta:y.
                             (0.3)
GERI:     °t °hhh Oh well thank you but you we ha- yihknow
          Victor,
→  SHIRLEY: ↑OH that's ↑RI:GHT.=
GERI:     =That's why we were going [(we)
SHIRLEY:                            [I FER↑GO:T. Completely.
```

(37) **WPC 1. MJ(1): 7–8**

```
MARIAN:       N[o : ,
               [   ]
JENNY:        [it's a ]s:safe seat fer everythin:g [°ehhr,
                                                   [
MARIAN:                                            [°hh
                             (0.2)
JENNY:    Reahlly,
MARIAN:   i-Thaht's ra[h ih tis relly ye:s:, yes,=
                      [
JENNY:                [So:.
JENNY:    =End eh,
                             (0.3)
→  MARIAN: ↑Oh:: ad didn't realahz it wz so neah coorss it's Ma:y
          next week °hh
JENNY:    Ye:[s
```

(38) **NB: II.4: 8–9**

```
EMMA:     God I can't go inna boat fer a long time'e siz ↑no
          boating er no::,
                             (0.2)
```

```
        EMMA:    [[GO:LF,  ]
                 [[        ]
        NANCY:   [[Bud was ]n't playing go:lf?
                                    (0.7)
        EMMA:    No:
  →     NANCY:   ↑Oh:↓:.
                           (.)
        EMMA:    [[°hhhh< ]
                 [[       ]
        NANCY:   [[I js:<  ]
                           (0.2)
        EMMA:    [[N  O  : , ]
                 [[          ]
        NANCY:   [[thought they ] prob[ably] would be] playing ] ah ]
                                      [    ]        ]          ]    ]
        EMMA:                         [No: ] BILL'S  ]↓GAH:N] NE]X'
                 [DOOR]
                 [       ]=
        NANCY:   [°khh  ]
  →     NANCY:   [[Oh::: tha  ]t's r[* i g h t   ] y * e a : h, ]
                 =[[         ] [              ]             ]
        EMMA:    [[yih ↓kno*w]   [THEY'VE ch]ecked ou:t. ]So=
        NANCY:   =°ee [Ya:h°
                     [
        EMMA:        [°hhheeahhoo IT'S JIS KAHNA DU:LL, Ghod whatta
                 m::iser'ble miser'ble:
        NANCY:   °tch °hhah
        EMMA:    w[eeke:n'.
```

(39) NB: III:1: 3
```
        FRAN:    °hhhhhh Oh: come o:n. [I could]n' j's come down the:re,
                 hn=
                              [       ]
        TED:                  [H m : ? ]
        FRAN:    =°t°hh I got two other kids. remember?
  →     TED:     Oh:: that's ri[:ght,
```

(40) NB: III:1: 2
```
        FRAN:    ((f)) Wul when didju guys go:::.
        SHARON:  Ah: Saturday? hh
  →     FRAN:    ((f)) Oh: fer, cryin out loud. I thought it wz the
                 e:nd'v th'mo:nth you were go:::i:[n.
                                                  [
        SHARON:                                   [Mm-mm,hh
```

In all these fragments the *oh*-tokens are done with high, wide-range rising–falling pitch. There would indeed seem to be grounds to claim that this pitch contour was contributing to a display of 'having been misinformed (rather than uninformed) but now being informed' in fragments (35), (37) and (40), and of 'recollection' *post* a wrongly assumed state of affairs in fragments (36), (38) and (39). In fragment (35), Jenny's *oh*-receipt turn has a lexical formulation of her previous assumption: *Oh I (thought)* which is followed shortly by what might constitute the grounds for her misinformedness *she sid she wz getting visito:rs*. In fragment (36) Shirley's ↑*OH that's* ↑*RI:GHT* (where *oh* is done with wide rising–falling pitch) is followed in her next turn by an explicit lexical formulation which, in proposing her forgetfulness, offers an account of her previous talk and also proposes that she has now undergone a change-of-state in terms of realization (cf. also (38)). Fragment (38) provides two further instances of *oh* + rising–falling pitch contour functioning as displays of revisions of understanding. In this sequence Nancy seeks clarification about whether or not Bud (Emma's husband) was playing golf. On being told *No* by Emma, Nancy produces an *oh*-token realized with rising–falling pitch. Emma makes no lexical response to this, and Nancy produces a display of the assumption underlying her prior question: *I js:* [=just] *thought they probably would be playing* which is overlapped by an emphatic negative from Emma. Emma then provides an account of Bud's movement which is in turn receipted by Nancy with a rising–falling pitched *oh*-prefaced turn which acknowledges Emma's account and her previous misassumption.

   Oh-particles accompanied by rising–falling pitch contours, then, may accomplish displays of having been misinformed and displays of forgetfulness. There are insufficient instances in the present corpus to say whether there are systematic phonetic differences between these two types of utterance. However, one property which they have in common is worth noting. The *oh*-particle prefaces more talk from the same speaker, which has an explicit display of the previous misinformedness or forgetfulness. This distinguishes them from other *oh*-particles with rising–falling contours, such as those in fragments (33) and (34). We should note too that, while some of the *oh*-tokens where 'surprise' can be warranted may begin with glottal closure, none end in such closure. The first of the *oh*-tokens with rising–falling pitch illustrated in fragment (33) indicates that other kinds of *oh*-token with such pitch movement may allow a final glottal closure. On the basis of the present data it would seem likely that, irrespective of the intuitions of linguists, rising–falling pitch contours with *oh* do not *by themselves* accomplish 'surprise' of previous misinformedness. Rather they do so precisely when they have such explicit formulations accompanying them.

3 Summary

In this chapter I have attempted to outline some of the phonetic characteristics of *oh*-tokens in everyday conversation. I have concentrated on four types of *oh*-token:

(i) freestanding *oh*-tokens;
(ii) *oh*-tokens with additional components in the same turn:
    (a) with assessment formulations
    (b) with partial repeat or reworking of the verbal element of the prior informing utterance;
(iii) freestanding *oh*-tokens in question-elicited informings;
(iv) *oh*-tokens functioning as indicators of 'surprise'.

The following summarises the main phonetic characteristics of each group:

(i) In the present corpus these typically display falling pitch ending low in the speaker's range. The starting pitch may vary in height. They may have initial glottal stop but never a final one. They often have creaky phonation, are variably extended in time and typically diphthongal.

(ii) (a) These may or may not have on-syllable dynamic pitch movement. The pitch contour of the turn may be overall rising or falling. However, if the assessment form is *oh wow, oh boy, oh good,* or *oh lovely,* the pitch falls. They begin with glottal closure and are typically diphthongal.

    (b) These may be done with falling or rising pitch either throughout the turn or as final dynamic on-syllable movement. The *oh*-token is never stressed. There are two main syntactic forms and some phonetic characteristics vary between these forms: (1) the *oh*-token + verbal-element form has regular production with initial glottal closure. There is a pitch discontinuity between *oh*-token and next word of turn; (2) the *oh* + pronoun form is typically not produced with initial glottal stop. Sometimes these *oh* + pronoun tokens have lax breathy phonation. There is a noticeable 'equal–equal' rhythm which characterizes the *oh*-token and the following pronoun.

(iii) These are usually produced with final falling pitch but may be produced with *rising*-falling pitch. They may be variably extended in time. They are done with initial glottal closure, may have final glottal closure and are often noticeably nasalized. They are typically monophthongal.

(iv) These are produced with dynamic on-syllable rising–falling pitch. They may begin with glottal closure but never terminate with such closure. They may be either monophthongal or diphthongal.

4 Conclusion

As I suggested at the beginning of this chapter, remarkably little is known in detail about the phonetics and phonology of naturally occurring talk. Virtually nothing of interest is known of the *interactional* implications of particular kinds of phonetic events in everyday talk. As long ago as 1959, David Abercrombie drew attention to this gap in knowledge. In a paper addressed to language teachers, entitled 'Conversation and spoken prose' he suggests that one reason for this is that what 'linguistics has concerned itself with, up to now, has almost exclusively been – spoken prose' (1965b:4). He concludes that '(g)enuine spoken language or "conversation" . . . has hardly been described at all in any language, whether from the phonetic, phonological, or grammatical point of view' (1965b:9). This chapter, along with others in this book, is an attempt to redress the balance somewhat and to demonstrate the resources offered by CA in yielding insightful, warranted analysis of the phonetic organization to be found in the everyday talk of ordinary people.

Appendix A: impressionistic phonetic records of *oh*-tokens

	'articulatory'	pitch contour
1. Emma:	↓O̱h̠:	
	Λ̞̰₊ U̠̰̞	
2. Lottie:	Oh̠:	
	ʔᴧ̈ə̠O̞̰₊	
3. Jenny:	↓aOh::. h=	
	ʔə̠̰ṵ:ˈ	
4. Jenny:	↓aOh::. h=	
	ʔə̠ṵ̰₊ ::ɦ	
5. Hyla:	O̱h:.=	
	ʔᴧÖˈ	
6. E:	°hO:::h.	
	(inbreath) ʔə̠ṵ̰ ::ˈ	

7. Lottie: [Oh : : :]ːِ : : .]
_____

Ɔ̟ꞔ 𝆺𝅥𝆺

_____

8. Nancy: [Oh:ِ?
_____

ʔʌ̝ö:

_____

9. Barbara: Oh rea↑lly?
_____

ʔʌ̞₊ ʊ

_____

10. Emma: Oh[w o̲ : w.]
_____

ʔŏ̰₊ ʊ

_____

11. Nancy: [Oh: r̠i↑ll[y?
_____

ʔʌ̞̌ʊ

_____

12. Lottie: Oh:ِ: goo̲:d.
_____

ʔʌ̰̞ ö:

_____

13. Nancy: =Oh r̠illy?
_____

ʔo̲₊ ʊ̞

_____

210   John Local

14. Jenny: °h Oh l[ovely.

                  (inbreath) ʔöʉ

15. Vera: Oh̲ lovely.

                  ʔə̣ü

16. Emma: Oh̲:: goo̲::d.

                  ʔö̞ʊ̣

17. Geri: Oh̲: boy,

                  ʔʌ₊, ʉ₊

18. Lottie: =Oh yih di̲d?

                  öʊ̌

19. Hyla: Oh̲ what'd'e do̲ tih
                  you.

                  ɔ̝ö

20. Ida: [O̲ h you d̲i d
                  d̲i[dju[ye s̲]

                  ọʊ̣

21. (a) Jenny: =O̱h=s̠he=ha̱hs?

               əu̯

21. (b) Jenny: [Oh s̠he di-]

               ə̣u

22. Marian: [↑O̱h do the↑:h,

               ʔʌ̰̃ ṵ̃

23. Guy: [Oh do̱h they?

               ʔo̟ṷ̆

24. Ann: [Oh ha̱hs she.

               ʔöu̯

25. Jenny: =O̱h didche ↑ke̱e̱p̱
              fi̱:t,

               ʔöṷ̟

26. Emma: [Oh do̱esn't[she]

               ʔo̟ṷ

27. Ida: O<u>h</u>:.

     ʔo̠ˑ‿   ⌒

28. Lottie: O<u>h</u>: .

     ʔo̰ˑ‿   ⌒

29. Jenny: =O[<u>h</u>:.

     ʔɑ̟ˌ:ʔ   ⌃

30. Jenny: O<u>h</u>[:ah.]

     ʔæ̆ɑ̟̰:ʔ   ⌒

31. Emma: [O<u>h</u>:::.

     ʔɑ̤ˑæ̆   ⌃

32. Emma: O<u>h</u>::.

     ʔö:ʔ   ⌃

33. (a) N: =O<u>h</u>:,

     ʔɑ̟ˑʔ   ⌃

33. (b) N: [Oh::::

                          ʔɑ̰ ::   ~

33. (c) N: [Oh[:,   =Oh:,

                          ʔɑ̰̃ˑ   ___

34. Marian: [↑Oh: did

                          ʔɔ̰ˑ   ___

35. Jenny: Oh↑::::.
                          Oh[I(thought),]
                          O̰ :Ṵ:   ___

36. Shirley: ↑ O H   that's
                          ↑RI:GHT.=
                          ʔɑ̰ 'ə   ~-~

37. Marian: ↑Oh:: ad didn't
                          realahz
                          ʔoṵ   ~

38. Nancy: [[Oh::::   tha]t's
                          r[*igh t]
                          ʌ'ṵ:.   ~

39. Ted: Oh:: that's ri[:ght,

                            ?ɔ̃˙ʊ̆˙   ∧ – ∧

40. Fran: ((f)) Oh: fer, cryin
                            out loud.

                            ?ə̃ɒ˙   ∧ – – ﹨

Appendix B: extracted F0 tracks for *oh* fragments

F0 tracks are given with frequency in Hertz displayed logarithmically on
the vertical axis and time in seconds displayed on the horizontal axis. In a
number of cases the quality of the original recordings, the presence of
overlapping talk, or particular voice quality of an individual speaker prohibited the successful extraction of an F0 track. Fragments are numbered
and the corresponding CA transcription given. Transcribed material
enclosed in curly brackets -{ }- is not represented in the F0 tracks.

Fragment 1. Emma: ↓Oh:

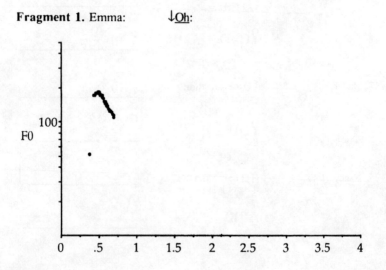

Fragment 2. Lottie: O<u>h</u>:

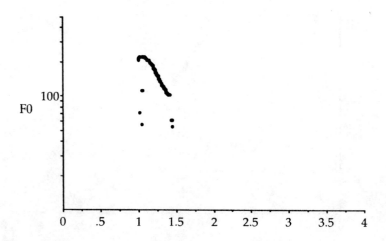

Fragment 3. Jenny: ↓aOh::. h=

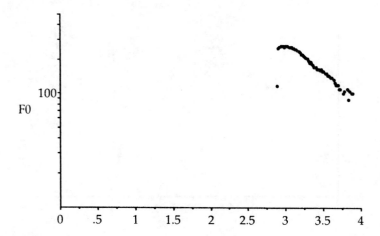

Fragment 4. Jenny: [O<u>h</u>:::::

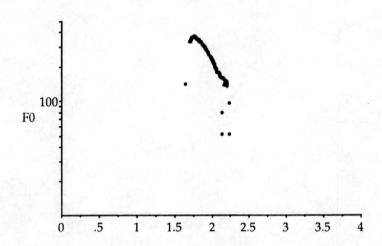

Fragment 6. E: °hO:::h.

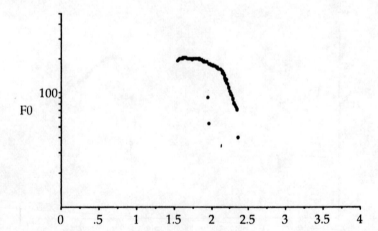

Fragment 9. Barbara: Oh rea↑lly?

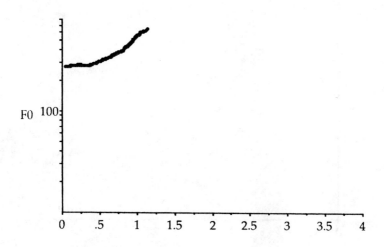

Fragment 11. Nancy: [Oh: ri↑ll[y?

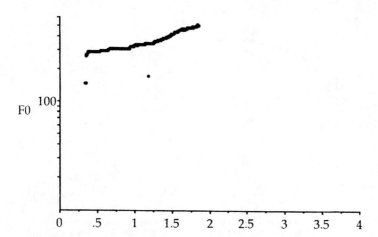

Fragment 12. Lottie: <u>Oh:</u>: go<u>o:</u>:d.

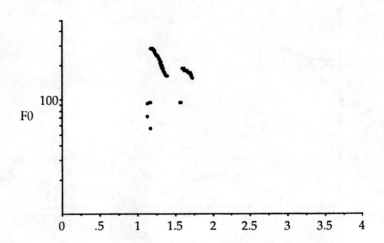

Fragment 13. Nancy: =Oh <u>ril</u><u>l</u><u>y</u>?

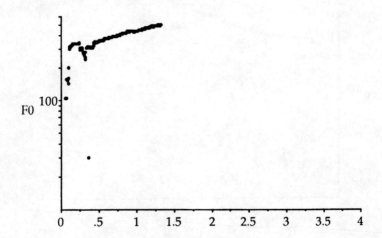

Fragment 15. Vera: O<u>h</u> <u>l</u>ovely.

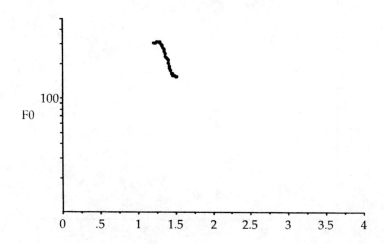

Fragment 16. Emma: <u>Oh::</u> go<u>o:</u>:d.

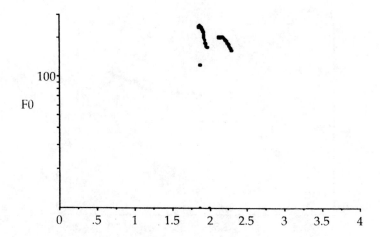

Fragment 17. Geri: <u>Oh</u>: boy,h=

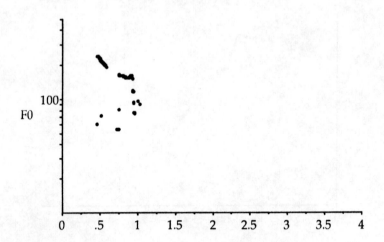

Fragment 18. Lottie: =Oh yih di:d?

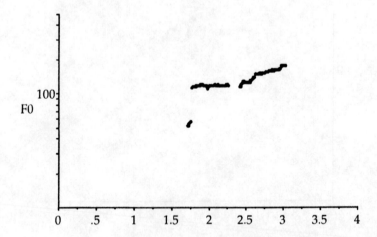

Fragment 19. Hyla: <u>O</u>h what'd'e <u>do</u> tih you.

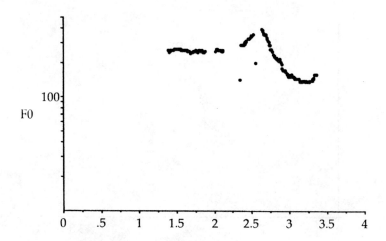

Fragment 22. Marian: [↑<u>O</u>h do the↑:h,

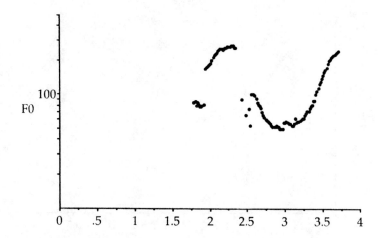

Fragment 23. Guy: [Oh d<u>o</u>h they?

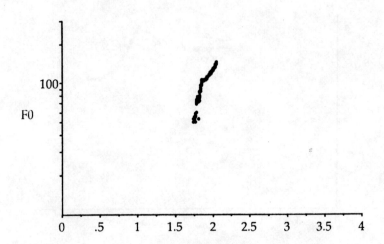

Fragment 27. Ida: O<u>h</u>:.

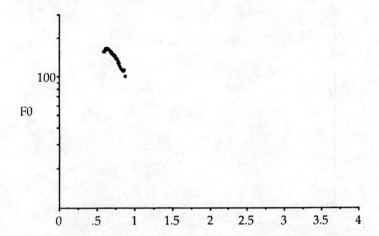

Fragment 28. Lottie: <u>Oh</u>: .

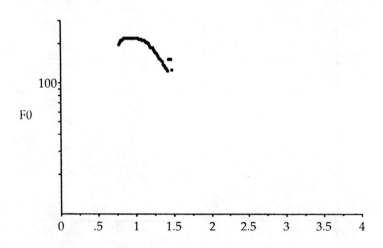

Fragment 30. Jenny: O<u>h</u>[:ah.]

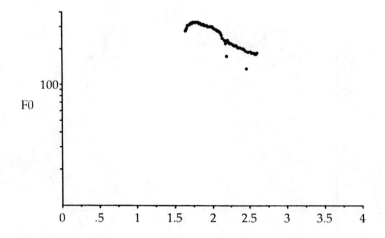

Fragment 32. Emma: O<u>h</u>::.

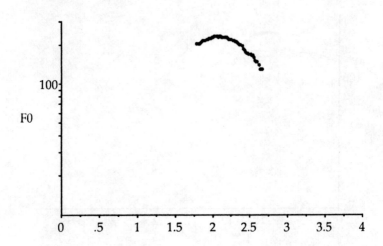

Fragment 33a. N: =<u>Oh</u>:,

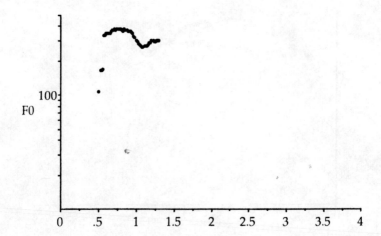

Fragment 33b. N: [Oh::::

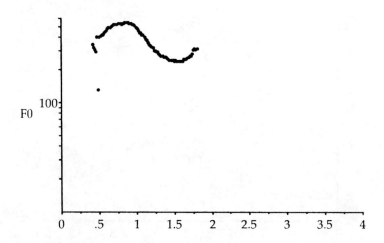

Fragment 33c. N: [Oh[:,

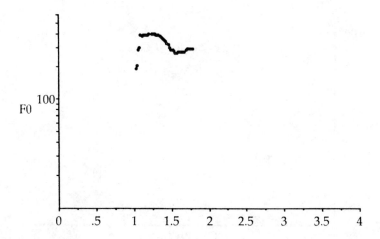

Fragment 34. Marian: [↑<u>Oh:</u> {did [s h e a e̠ ,h]}]

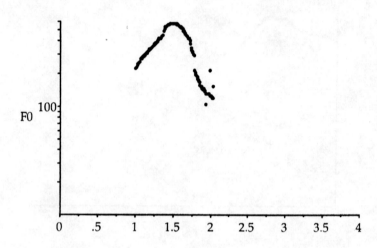

Fragment 35. Jenny: Oh↑:::. {Oh[<u>I</u> (thought),]}

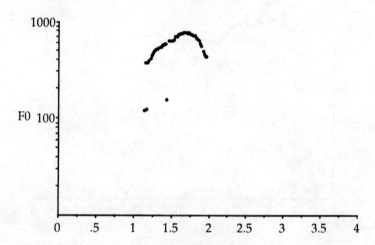

Fragment 36. Shirley: ↑<u>OH</u> that's ↑<u>RI</u>:GHT.=

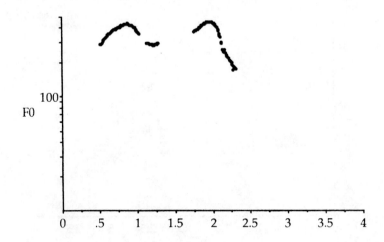

Fragment 37. Marian: ↑<u>O</u>h:: (ad didn't <u>re</u>alahz it wz so <u>n</u>eah)

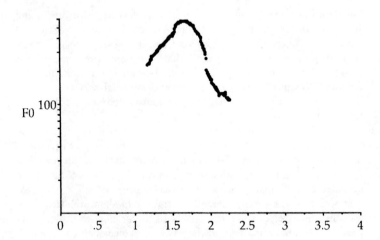

228   John Local

Fragment 38. Nancy: ↑Oh:↓ :.

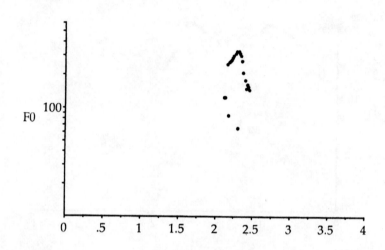

Notes

1 The data fragments are drawn from some twenty hours of British and
American English tape-recorded telephone conversations. Although I
have been selective in the fragments I present, in order to give some
range of possibilities, I do not think that I have misrepresented what is
going on. The turn of interest is indicated by an arrow in the margin.

2 Although I employ conventional Conversation Analysis transcriptions
throughout, I have provided impressionistic parametric phonetic
records of relevant parts.

3 The notation employed in CA transcriptions for articulatory phonetic
and pitch characteristics is not straightforward to interpret in impressionistic phonetic terms. To facilitate interpretation I include two
appendices. The first provides impressionistic phonetic records of the
articulatory and pitch features for particular pieces of talk considered.
The second gives computationally extracted fundamental frequency
(F0). In a number of cases the quality of the original recordings, the
presence of overlapping talk, or the particular voice quality of an individual speaker prohibited the successful extraction of an F0 parameter.

4 See Heritage (1984a:306) for further discussion of this fragment.
Compare also fragment 6 (though it is not question-elicited) where E
responds to C's reformulation of his informing *She decided to go away
this weekend.=* with a continuation-oriented *=Yeah* which prompts
further talk from C formulated as an 'upshot': *So that (.) y'know I
really don' have a place ti'stay.* Her subsequent *oh*-token, however,
displays news-receipt, as can be seen in part by her formulation of the

consequences of C not making the trip: *So you're not gonna go up this weekend.*

5 One means of expressing surprise available to speakers is to use versions of what Heritage (1984a) refers to as 'assertions of ritualized disbelief, e.g. "yer kidding," "really?", "did you?" etc.' (1984a:339).

References

Abercrombie, D. 1965a. Syllable quantity and enclitics in English. In D. Abercrombie *Studies in Phonetics and Linguistics*. Oxford University Press, pp. 26–34.

   1965b. Conversation and spoken prose. In D. Abercrombie *Studies in Phonetics and Linguistics*. Oxford University Press, pp. 1–9.

Atkinson, J. M. and J. Heritage (eds.) 1984. *Structures of Social Action. Studies in conversation analysis*. Cambridge University Press.

Coleman, J. S. 1990. Unification phonology: another look at 'synthesis-by-rule'. *Proceedings of the Thirteenth International Conference on Computational Linguistics. COLING 90*, Vol. III. Helsinki: Association for Computational Linguistics, 75–84.

Coleman, J. S. and J. K. Local 1992. Monostratal phonology and speech synthesis. In P. Tench (ed.) *Studies in Systemic Phonology*. London: Pinter Publishers, pp. 183–193.

Cruttenden, A. 1986. *Intonation*. Cambridge University Press.

Firth, J. R. 1935. The technique of semantics. *Transactions of the Philological Society*, pp. 36–72.

French, P. and J. K. Local 1983. Turn-competitive incomings. *Journal of Pragmatics*, 7: 17–38.

Heritage, J. 1984a. A change-of-state token and aspects of its sequential placement. In Atkinson and Heritage (1984), pp. 299–345.

   1984b. *Garfinkel and Ethnomethodology*. Cambridge: Polity Press.

Jefferson, G. 1978. Sequential aspects of storytelling in conversation. In J. N. Schenkein (ed.) *Studies in the Organization of Conversational Interaction*. New York: Academic Press, pp. 219–248.

   1981. The abominable 'Ne?': a working paper exploring the phenomenon of post-response pursuit of response. Occasional Paper No. 6. University of Manchester, Department of Sociology. Abridged version in P. Schröder and H. Steger (eds.) 1981, *Dialogforschung. Jahrbuch 1980 des Instituts für deutsche Sprache*, Düsseldorf: Schwann, pp. 53–88.

Kelly, J. and J. K. Local 1989. *Doing Phonology: Observing, recording, interpreting*. Manchester University Press.

Local, J. K. 1986. Patterns and problems in a study of Tyneside intonation. In C. Johns-Lewis (ed.) *Intonation and Discourse*. London: Croom Helm, pp. 181–198.

1992a. Continuing and restarting. In P. Auer and A. di Luzio (eds.) *The Contextualization of Language*. Amsterdam: Benjamins, pp. 272–296.

1992b. Modelling assimilation in a nonsegmental, rule-free phonology. In G. Docherty and R. Ladd (eds.) *Papers in Laboratory Phonology II*. Cambridge University Press, pp. 190–223.

Local, J. K. and J. Coleman 1991. Artificial intelligence for speech synthesis. *Proceedings of the Conference of the Digital Equipment Computer Users Society UK, Ireland and Middle East*. University of Warwick, pp. 397–406.

Local, J. K. and J. Kelly 1985. Notes on phonetic detail and conversational structure. In *Belfast Papers in Linguistics*, VII. Jordanstown: University of Belfast, pp. 1–15.

1986. Projection and silences: notes on phonetic and conversational structure. *Human Studies*, 9: 185–204.

Local, J. K., J. Kelly and W. H. G. Wells 1986. Towards a phonology of conversation: turn-taking in Tyneside English. *Journal of Linguistics*, 22: 411–437.

Local, J. K., W. H. G. Wells and M. Sebba 1985. Phonology for conversation: phonetic aspects of turn delimitation in London Jamaican. *Journal of Pragmatics*, 9: 309–330.

O'Connor, J. D. and G. F. Arnold 1961. *Intonation of Colloquial English: A practical handbook*. London: Longmans.

Roach, P. 1983. *English Phonetics and Phonology: A practical course*. Cambridge University Press.

6

Prosody as an activity-type distinctive cue in conversation: the case of so-called 'astonished' questions in repair initiation

MARGRET SELTING

In this chapter, I shall show that specific prosodic marking cues are used by participants in German conversation to distinguish between 'normal' and so-called 'surprised' or 'astonished' questions in the initiation of repair. This distinction appears to be indicated by prosodic means only. Prosodically unmarked initiations of repair and their marked counterparts are shown to construct different subtypes within repair sequences, in that they make different sequential implications relevant for the next turn. Unlike a prosodically *unmarked* configuration in repair initiation, which is used to signal 'normal' problems of hearing and understanding, a prosodically *marked* configuration is used as an 'astonished' or 'surprised' signalling of a problem of expectation which requires special treatment. Via prosodic marking, any question and/or repair-initiation form can be made into an 'astonished' question. The use of 'astonished' questions, however, is restricted to the initiation of repair sequences.

In section 1 of the chapter, I shall give an introduction to my terminology and the premises underlying my analysis. In section 2, I shall present a first illustrative example of the particular contrast under analysis in this paper, before explicating the goals of my analysis in more detail in section 3. In section 4, further data extracts are presented in which the contrast between marked versus unmarked prosody is shown to be relevant for a variety of different repair-initiation types in conversation. These data will be used to argue that in order to explicate the basis of participants' differential interpretation of repair-initiation types – initiation types which are similar in linguistic structure and wording – prosody must necessarily be taken into account. Conclusions are drawn in section 5.

The chapter makes clear that prosody is not merely an additional and therefore dispensable signalling cue; in the cases under analysis, it distinguishes between activity types which would otherwise appear identical, yet which yield different recipient reactions.

1 Introduction

In previous work (Selting 1992, 1993, 1995), I have argued that intonation, in particular a unit's terminal pitch movement, cannot be explained with reference to the syntactic category of sentence type. In grammars and linguistic research, intonation is commonly thought of as being closely related to syntactic sentence-structure types such as declarative, interrogative, imperative and exclamatory. The general assumption is that a particular syntactic sentence type, in unmarked cases, calls for a particular unmarked intonation; other intonations are said to constitute marked cases. So, for instance, in German, declarative sentences are said to have falling terminal pitch; rising terminal pitch is said to turn them into questions. Interrogative sentences using a question word (*w-Fragen*, i.e. those which correspond to wh-questions in English) are commonly said to call for falling terminal pitch in unmarked ('neutral') cases, whereas rising terminal pitch in these interrogatives is claimed to be a marked choice and interpreted as 'polite', 'interpersonally marked', or the like. On the other hand, interrogative sentences using subject–verb inversion, often called yes/no questions (*Entscheidungsfragen*), are said to reverse this picture by calling for rising terminal pitch in unmarked cases, and falling terminal pitch in marked cases (Pheby 1981:875).[1] Yet, for instance, in the case of question-word questions in German, to explain the difference between falling and rising final pitch movements with reference to categories like 'neutral' versus 'polite', or 'interpersonally marked', or the like, can hardly explain the use of both question types one after the other in successive question–answer sequences in conversation, without any other indication of changed relationship between the interlocutors. I have tried to show that intonation is not systematically related to syntactic sentence types, but to activity types in conversation. These are constituted and contextualized by the use of activity-type distinctive bundles of cues. Beside syntactic and semantic cues which indicate the semantic relation to the prior turn, prosodic cues, above all the terminal pitch movement in conversational questions, are used as distinctive signalling cues in different types of questions, each of which requires a different type of response. In particular, terminal pitch movement is used as a resource to distinguish between non-restricting 'open' conversational questions and more restricting 'narrower' ones; or between an acoustic problem with rising *was* (English *what*), and a referential problem with falling *was* (Selting 1992). Analysis shows that intonation must be conceptualized as an autonomous signalling system (see Bolinger, most recently 1989, and Gibbon 1984), from which speakers choose cues, used in co-occurrence with cues from other autonomous signalling systems, for the constitution and contextualization (Gumperz 1982, Auer 1992) of interactively relevant activity types in conversation.

In this chapter, I shall concentrate on repair sequences, more specifically on so-called other-initiated repair sequences in which speakers indicate problems of understanding (Schegloff, Jefferson and Sacks 1977). For such problem signalling, the speaker resumes or echoes a problematical item from the prior turn. Within this type of activity, the precise form of the resumption and the prosodic structure differentiate between various problem types (see also Selting 1987a, 1987b). In the following, I shall deal with a particular type of contrast that is constituted by prosodic means only: the contrast between 'normal' and 'astonished' initiations of repair. I will show that these are treated by the recipient in the next turn in different ways, which I will reconstruct as being the result of the following kinds of recipient interpretation: prosodically unmarked initiations of repair are interpreted by the recipient of the trouble-source turn as 'normal' – i.e. non-astonished – initiations of repair, which signal problems of hearing and understanding and which make subsequent self-repair by the producer of the trouble-source turn conditionally relevant. If certain prosodic marking cues are used, though, the same kinds of initiation format are interpreted as so-called 'surprised' or 'astonished' initiations of repair, ones which signal problems of expectation and which have quite different sequential implications from their unmarked counterparts.[2] The terms 'normal' and 'astonished'/'surprised' are used as labels to subsume the recipients' context-sensitive interpretations of prosodically unmarked and marked initiations of repair, interpretations which in turn are reconstructed from the observable treatment of these utterances in next turns.

I shall take for granted that, for the constitution of conversational activities, speakers use bundles of prosodic cues as a resource. These bundles can be broken down into separate distinctive features, each of which adds a separate meaning component to the conversational activity. The bundles of prosodic cues that are mostly used as prosodic marking devices are *marked* global and/or local *pitch* and/or *loudness* variations in relation to surrounding turns. 'Global' refers to the use of a prosodic parameter like pitch or loudness for a stretch of talk or an entire turn-constructional unit; it usually entails more than one accent. 'Global pitch' encompasses both pitch register (high, mid, low) and pitch direction (falling, rising). It is global pitch register and pitch direction that make a prosodic unit sound cohesive and that speakers can resume after a break in order to constitute continuation of a yet unfinished unit (Local 1992). In order to specify pitch register for short turn-constructional units where relevant, the global parameter is also occasionally used for units with only one accent. 'Local' refers to the use of a prosodic parameter in smaller segments of speech, like for instance the pitch movement in and shortly after an accented syllable or the use of increased loudness in an accented syllable to constitute an extra-prominent accent.

2 A starter

Extracts (1) and (2), in which different versions of the problem-signalling word *bitte* (the equivalent of the English *pardon*) are used by the same speaker, Ron, stand as a first example of the contrast under analysis here. (The transcription symbols used in these and the following extracts are given in the appendix. The conventions which are most important for my analysis will be mentioned in the running text as well.)

(1)   K1: 1056–1061

```
    1 RON: ┌ denk ich SCHON daß das auch (.) AUSschlaggebmd ist
           │       M(  \                      \                    )
           │                                  ⟨f                 f⟩
           │        I do think that that is also        decisive
    2 NAT: │                            ich war SIEbm JAHre mit ihm zuSAMM
           │                                F(  /    \                \    )
           │                                ⟨ f                           f⟩
           └                            we were together for seven years
              (.)
→   3 RON: BIDde=
           (/   )
           ⟨all⟩
           pardon
    4 NAT: ┌ =ich war SIEbm JAHre mit ihm zusamm̩=also da is
           │      F( \     \                    )
           │      we were together for seven years    so there
    5 RON: │                                          =AHja
           │                                          (\   )
           └                                          oh yeah
    6 NAT: SCHON (0.6) ne GRUNDlage oder ne BA(h)sis dageWESN̩
           M(  \            \                \         \   )
           was          a base         or  a   basis    there
```

In line 3, the speaker Ron uses *BIDde* to signal a problem of acoustic decoding with respect to the prior turn. The token *bidde* is a
colloquial variant of *bitte*. It is realized here with fast speech rate,
with a rising pitch movement in a mid pitch register (and range) on
and after the accented syllable. The expected way to treat this problem is for the recipient to repeat the trouble-source turn. This is
done in line 4, though with an altered intonation contour and followed by a further elaboration.

   In contrast to this, in extract (2) line 4, the problem-signalling
word is realized in its standard segmental form *bitte*, with normal
speech rate and a rising pitch movement, but this time the speaker's
pitch rises much higher and he uses extra loudness in comparison to
surrounding turns.

(2)   K2: 127–135

```
    1 IDA:    aber ich KANN mir das äh:m nochmal opeRIERN lassen
                  F( \                              \         )
              but I can have that        ehm  operated on some time
              (1.3)
```

```
   2 IDA:  ┌ ich hab ṇ ZAHNarzt=der MACHT das
          │      F [( \      )    ( \      )]
          │  I know a dentist who's willing to do that
   3 RON: │            woZU:
          │             ( \ )
          └            what for
              (.)
→  4 RON:  BITte
           (/↑  )
           ⟨f   f⟩
           pardon
           (0.8)
   5 IDA:     *JA(h) ich weiß AU nich
             M( \              \
             well I don't know either
   6 IDA:  ┌ ich hab immer PECH mit ÄR(h)Ztn
          │              \        \      )
          │  I always have bad luck with doctors
   7 NAT: └                           ((laughs))
             (1.0)
   8 IDA:  da bin ich dann mal nach ewigem warten
           once after having waited for ages I went
   9       zum zahnarzt gegangn (1.0)
           to a dentist
  10       un sitz im stuhl und hatte: arge zahnschmerzen
           and I was sitting in the chair and had a bad toothache
```

This time, the recipient Ida does not treat the token *BITte* as the signalling of an acoustic problem. She does not repeat the trouble-source turn, but starts telling Ron about how her dentist offered to operate on her tattoos. The repetition of *zahnarzt* in line 9 is an 'embedded repetition' (Jefferson 1978) to focus on the main character of her story, i.e. her dentist, first introduced in her story announcement in line 2. However, before telling her story in detail, Ida suggests with **JA(h) ich weiß AU nich* (line 5) that the event she has offered to tell a story about, i.e. her dentist offering to operate on her tattoos, is quite unusual. This shows that Ida interprets Ron's realization of his token *BITte* as signalling something which in lay, everyday categorization could be called 'astonishment' or 'surprise', and that she, in agreeing that there is reason for Ron's being 'astonished', orients to his having indicated this reaction to her story announcement. Thus, Ida treats Ron's version of *BITte* as a so-called 'astonished' initiation of repair, as the signalling of a problem of expectation: Ron has indicated that it runs counter to his expectations that a dentist would be willing to operate on a patient's tattoos. This unexpected event is what Ida gives more information about in her response.

In sum, both versions of the repair initiation *bitte* in (1) and (2) are realized with rising pitch; this is the expectable pitch movement when this item is used as a repair initiation and does not count as a prosodically marked cue. In contrast to the mid pitch register and range, moderate loudness and, less importantly here, fast speech rate in version (1), version (2) exhibits, beside normal speech rate, pitch movements moving to a very high peak and extra loudness in comparison to surrounding units. I shall call the version used in (1) 'prosodically unmarked', and the version used in (2) 'prosodically marked'. 'Unmarked' refers to an inconspicuous realization of cues which does not trigger any particular inferences, 'marked' refers to a conspicuous, noticeable realization of parameters which may trigger special inferences. The difference between the prosodically unmarked and the prosodically marked versions of *bitte* can be seen in the acoustic analyses given in Figure 6.1:[3] the prosodically marked version shows up as clearly longer in duration (= the acoustic correlate of length) and it rises higher in fundamental frequency (= the acoustic correlate of perceived pitch). In addition, it is realized with greater perceived loudness. As both versions are produced by the same speaker, they are directly comparable; for technical reasons they can only be presented in isolation here. The prosodically

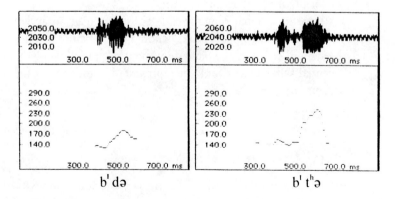

Figure 6.1 Two versions of *bitte*

unmarked version is treated as signalling an acoustic problem, the
prosodically marked version, a more 'marked' meaning. In the cases
analysed in this paper, recipients' reactions to the marked versions
suggest that they interpret them as signalling what could be
described in lay, everyday language as 'astonishment' or 'surprise'.

3 Aims of the analysis

In the following, I shall present more data extracts, now concen-
trating on prosodically unmarked versus marked versions of different types of repair initiation. The parameters needed for the
description of prosodic marking are:

(i) for global pitch and loudness variations:
(a) global pitch that is high or higher than in surrounding
units, denoted by 'H( )' in the prosodic line of transcripts; if
the parallel lines below represent a speaker's 'normal' pitch
range, two accented syllables with H( ) could be represented
as follows:

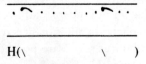

H(\   \   )

(b) increased global loudness in relation to surrounding
units, denoted by '⟨f f⟩';

(ii) for locally marked accent variants:
(a) large local pitch range for the constitution of an accent
with an extra high pitch peak, denoted by '↑' before or after
the symbol denoting the pitch movement in and following the
accented syllable; this could be represented as follows for the
accents shown:

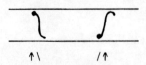

↑\   /↑

(b) local increase of loudness for the constitution of an extra
loud and strong accent, denoted by '⟨f⟩' beneath the accented
syllable.

The following combinations are used as a resource for the signalling of so-called 'astonished' initiations of repair: either the combination of the two global parameters, high global pitch and greater loudness (with possibly further local marking), or the combination of at least one of the global parameters, high pitch or increased loudness, with at least one locally marked accent constituted by a larger pitch range or markedly greater loudness in an accented syllable.

The simple rationale behind prosodic marking seems to be that by the use of these parameters the speaker intends to make the respective utterance clearly noticeable, extra-prominent prosody being deployed as a cue to point the recipient to some kind of inference. Parameters other than marked realizations of pitch and loudness, for instance marked sound-elongations or markedly faster or slower tempo, may occasionally be used, but in my data they do not occur systematically as a cue to 'astonishment' or 'surprise'. 'Astonishment' or 'surprise' is used as a label for a context-sensitive interpretation of bundles of prosodically marked cues in certain types of repair initiation, either explicit problem signalling or securing of understanding. The same cues may trigger quite different inferences in other sequences and contexts, inferences such as 'emphasis', 'indignation', etc. This chapter will be restricted to cases in which the inferences can be reconstructed to be such things as 'astonishment' or 'surprise'.

The goal of my analysis is to show the following:

(i) There is a systematic difference between initiations of repair constituted with and without prosodic marking, which can be reconstructed from recipient reactions or other subsequent activities: in the utterance types under analysis here, prosodic marking is used as an activity-type distinctive signalling cue which makes differential reactions relevant in the next turn.

(ii) The bundles of constitutive prosodic cues that speakers use in constructing the initiation of repair can be broken down into their single parts. The bundles are used in co-occurrence with other linguistic cues in the unit, and in a specific sequential environment, to constitute the particular activity type. Prosodic marking is used as an additional cue, as it were 'on top of' the unmarked cues. I shall give examples in which both the syntactic structure and the (unmarked) final pitch movement are kept constant, but, in the marked versions, particular prosodic marking cues are used in addition to the unmarked cues.

(iii) Prosodic marking can seemingly be used in all repair-initiation techniques and formats, but these are then heard as different in type categorization from their unmarked versions. If we try to reconstruct participants' interpretations of initiations of repair, prosodically unmarked ones can be said to be interpreted as 'normal', whereas prosodically marked ones can be shown to be interpreted as the 'astonished' signalling of a problem of expectation, or an 'astonished' understanding check, depending on whether they resume a specific item from the prior talk or merely infer a possibly problematic issue (Selting 1992). Prosodically marked initiations of repair in which a problematic item is explicitly resumed are reconstructed as an 'astonished' indication of a problem of expectation whose treatment by the recipient is now relevant, whereas prosodically marked initiations of repair in which a problematic inference is drawn from the prior talk and proffered to the recipient for acceptance or rejection, are analysed as 'astonished' understanding checks. Prosodically marked initiations of repair have two aspects: the 'content' which is referred to via a repair-initiation technique with particular wording, and the 'astonishment overtone', which is cued via prosodic marking. Both must be dealt with by recipients. In addition to doing the self-repair, participants orient to the use of prosodic marking: preferably, they either agree and align with the initiator's 'astonishment', or they account for why they are not astonished like the interlocutor; and they either treat, or try to ignore, the particular activity type indicated by the use of prosodic marking. If recipients try to ignore the 'astonishment' component and treat the marked version as if it were the unmarked version, initiators may accept this or invest extra interactional work to insist on some orientation to their 'astonishment'.

My methodology is adopted from Conversation Analysis: I shall present data in which similar initiations of repair in an unmarked and a marked version are treated as different activity types by recipients. This differential treatment of utterances which, aside from prosodic marking, are otherwise alike will warrant my analysis and serve as evidence for the interactive relevance of prosodic marking.

Cues are used as a resource; i.e. the constitution and signalling of 'astonishment' can be actively used and displayed, e.g. for strategic purposes; this does not necessarily mean that the speaker is really astonished. The question whether the speaker in fact feels 'astonished' or 'surprised', or only displays this to the recipient for one reason or another, cannot be handled with the methodology used in this analysis.

4 More data

4.1 Further examples of prosodically unmarked versus marked initiations of repair and their treatment

The above extracts (1) and (2) showed cases in which an unmarked and a marked version of the repair initiation *bitte* were used to indicate different problem types. In the following examples (3) and (4), problem types similar to these are signalled by different versions of the single question word *was* (English *what*) as a repair initiation:

(3)   BB12/1B: 42–47
  1 SOC: dann müssn se inne **SE**nnestadt gehn (.)
                     (\   )
     then you must go to Sennestadt
  2   äh dort zum dort wo sie sich auch **AN**gemeldet habm
                              (\   )
     eh there to there to where you also registered
  3 KLI: ja die **KIN**dergeld s ge**KOMM**
         F(\   \ )
     yes the child allowance has arrived
→ 4 SOC:

     was
     (/)
     what

```
  5 KLI:   ds KINdergeld is geKOMM̩
            F(\                    \   )
                     ⟨all⟩
            the child allowance has arrived
            (.)
  6 SOC:   jaa
            \
            yes
```

In extract (3) line 4, the question word *was* refers back to the prior turn. It is realized here with a rather non-salient rising pitch. Like *bidde* in (1), this question word is interpreted as the signalling of an acoustic problem, and the recipient reacts with a repetition of the problematical turn.

The same word is realized quite differently in extract (4) line 9:

```
(4)   BB9/2B: 6–21
       6 SOC:   das KOStet allerDINGS
                it costs something though
       7 SOC:   sag ich Ihn ma gleich vorher
                ⟨all                    all⟩
                I'll tell you beforehand
       8 SOC:   PRO seite drei MARK
                F( \               \   )
                per page three marks
  →    9 KLI1:


                  ✔
                _____
                WAS
                H(/ )
                <f  >
                what


      10 SOC:   ich MUSS also jetz
                    ( \
                I have to now
      11 SOC:   JEde beglaubichte SEIte nehm ich ihn̩ drei MARK
                F( \               \                \   )
                for every notarized page I take three marks
                (.)
      12 KLI2:  wieSO kostet das denn GE:L:D:
                R(\                       \   )
                but why does it cost money
```

13 KLI2: der **BRAUCHT** das doch für ne (.) be**WER**bung
          R(\   \   )
          he   needs   it for an   application
          (1.5)
14 SOC: spielt **KEI**ne **ROL**le
         doesn't matter
         (.)
15 KLI2: ⌈also in **GÜ**tersloh kostets über**HAUPT** nichts
          │ H(/   \   )
          │ *but in Gütersloh it doesn't cost anything*
16 SOC: │   das   **EIN**zige was
         └   *the   only thing which*
17 SOC: das **EIN**zige was **KOS**tenlos is sind ä:hm:
         the only thing which is free is   ehm
18 SOC: äh be**GLAU**bigungņ für **REN**tņ (.) **SACH**ņ (.)
         eh notarizations for old age pensions

In this case, the question word *WAS* (line 9) has high pitch and
increased loudness. Here, the following turns suggest that the client
Kli1 has understood Soc's words and the lexical meaning of these
words perfectly well, but he has not expected that notarizations of
school reports cost money at all (on the interrelation between the
referential and affective use of linguistic items, see also Haviland
1989, Ochs and Schieffelin 1989). The recipient Soc's treatment of
this signal is not a straightforward repetition. She first starts by
referring to the regulations which she must follow, but cuts this
off; then she reformulates her original statement. She thus treats
the problem as if it were a problem of understanding, without
treating the clients' problem of expectation.

However, the client Kli2, Kli1's partner, is not satisfied with this.
In lines 12, 13 and 15, she insists on a treatment of the problem of
expectation by asking another question, and by stating more explicitly the clients' own expectations. This insistence on the problem
confirms the interpretation that the first repair initiation was
intended to indicate a problem of expectation via the use of the
prosodic marking, even though the speaker Soc did not treat it in
the way expected by the clients.[4] The fact that this conversation
takes place between an official and clients in an institutional context, may have consequences for the handling of the 'astonishment'
component of this problem: Soc can refer to official regulations and
does not have to account further for her own lack of alignment with
the clients' astonishment.

In the prior two extracts, in which both prosodically unmarked and marked versions of otherwise identical repair-initiation formats were used, it was only the prosodic marking which distinguished between an acoustic problem and a problem of expectation. For the constitution of an 'astonished' initiation of repair to indicate a problem of expectation, it is above all the prosodic marking which is used as a resource: prosodic marking distinguishes this activity type from the corresponding unmarked version. In contrast to the unmarked version, the marked version is used to construct another category type, initiating a different repair sequence in which the problem signalled as well as the initiator's astonishment must be dealt with.

The following extracts (5) and (6) present an unmarked and a marked version of a technique for initiation of repair which Schegloff, Jefferson and Sacks (1977:368) call 'partial repeat of the trouble-source turn':

(5)   S-34-3: 228–233
    1 KLI: na der hat (? AUCH ?) FIEber gehabt
              well he also had a fever
    2   aber is WEgn die ZÄHne nur
                F(\   \   )
              but that's because he's teething
              (..)
→   3 SOC:

               ——————————————
               •   •   •   •   ✔   •
               ——————————————

               wegn die wegn der ZÄHne
                        (/   )
               <p   p>
               because of because of teething

               (..)
    4 KLI: ja: da KRIEgn die ja meist n bisken FIEber (.)
                L,F(\   /   )
              well   they   normally get a fever then
    5   aber DAŞ nich so SCHLIMM
                L,F(\   \   )
              but it doesn't matter

In line 3, Soc repeats and grammatically corrects the problematical part of the prior turn, which he arguably does not understand. Yet, it is not the correction of grammatical case marking which is focussed on (*wegen der* (Dat.) instead of *wegen die* (Acc.)), but the entire phrase *wegn der ZÄHne*. The utterance has rising terminal pitch in a mid pitch range and is produced with decreased loudness. Kli has told Soc about his (Kli's) baby son, who has been ill; Soc does not seem to know that babies often get a fever when teething. In response to Soc's initiation of repair, Kli formulates his knowledge that babies normally get a fever under these circumstances as a generalization. With this, the sequence is closed.

In extract (6), Nat produces a repetition of the problematic item from the preceding turn, in a prosodically marked form:

(6)   K2: 38–47 ((Topic: Ida's scars on her arm))
       1 NAT: was **WIE** has dich da geSCHNITTN
                 H,F(\   /   )
                 what how did you cut yourself there
       2 IDA: ((brief groan)) na mit na SCHERbe ((laughs quietly))
                                      M(\   )
                                oh with a piece of broken glass
→   3 NAT:

       mit   na   **SCHERbe**
                     H(↑\   /)
       with a piece of broken glass

       ((Nat chortles))
       (1.5)
       4 IDA: JA: ich WEIß au nich
                 M(/   \   )
                   〈all   all〉
                 yeah I don't know either
       5 IDA: ⌈ ähm: (.) irgnwie: (..) is da mit eimmal n schnitt
              │ *ehm   somehow   there suddenly was a*
       6 NAT: ⌊ t(h)
       7 IDA: ⌈ gewesn: un:d (approx. 3 secs.) un denn is mir dabei
              │ *cut   and   and then I*
       8 NAT: ⌊ ((laughs))
       9 NAT: ⌈ **WIE** machs **DAS** denn wo **LIECHT** denn die **SCHER**be
              │ F(/   \   )   F(\   \   )
              │ *how do you do that where do you find a piece of broken glass*
      10 IDA: ⌊   ((laughs))

11 NAT: aufm   BOden ((laughs))
          M(\   )
     on the ground

In line 3, the problematic item from line 2, *mit na SCHERbe*, is
repeated with high global pitch and with an extra high pitch peak
on the accented syllable. Nat is astonished that Ida could have hurt
her arm with a piece of broken glass. Ida admits with *JA: ich WEIß
au nich* that this is unusual (line 4), but she starts telling the story
from the point when the cut was 'suddenly' there, whereupon Nat
interrupts and asks more explicitly how this is possible, since she
assumes that pieces of broken glass are usually found on the ground
(lines 9 and 11). Presumably Nat thinks that something more extra-
ordinary must have happened, like an awkward fall, which would
have left Ida with such scars on her arm. Nat thus insists that Ida
further treat the content component of her initiation of repair.

In contrast to prosodically unmarked initiations of repair, prosodically marked initiations of repair are used to point out a contradiction between the items echoed from the prior turn and the
speaker's own expectations. While the cited resumption (echo) is
constitutive of certain types of repair initiation and problem signalling more generally (Selting 1992), it is the prosodic marking that
indicates 'astonishment' or 'surprise'. The examples show that the
analysis of the difference between prosodically unmarked and
marked initiations in otherwise identical repair-initiation formats
cannot be reduced to a purely sequential analysis. In the cases presented above, the preceding context is similar, but initiations of
repair that differ only in prosodic marking yield different recipient
reactions; the contrast thus differentiates sub-types *within* repair
sequences.

With respect to problem treatment, two components can be distinguished, which I shall label the astonishment component and the
content component. While in extract (2) the recipient attended to
both the astonishment and the content component of the problem,
in (4) the recipient attended to neither component, and in (6) the
recipient attended to the astonishment component but did not
attend to the content component in her immediate reaction. Soc's
lack of alignment with her clients' astonishment in (4) was
explained with reference to the institutional context of the interaction. Nevertheless, in this case, as in (6), the recipients' non-treat-

ment of the content component of the problem resulted in insistence
on problem treatment by the problem initiators. Thus, the initiators' insistence exhibited an orientation to their having indicated a
problem of expectation before, which their interlocutors' next-turn
treatment did not address satisfactorily.

Recipient responses show that prosodically *marked* initiations of
repair are interpreted by recipients as involving two aspects of a
problem: (i) on the level of astonishment, the signalling of an emotional overtone which needs to be attended to by the recipient, with
agreement and alignment being the preferred reactions,[5] and (ii) on
the level of content, the problem of contrasting and incompatible
expectations as the basis of speaker's non-understanding, which
requires clarification and repair. The recipients of prosodically
marked questions are routinely expected to orient to both components.

The following extracts show more examples of prosodically
marked repair initiations, in which yet a further initiation technique
is used: full sentences, which in lay, participant categorizations
would presumably be called 'astonished questions'. Extract (7)
shows a case in which the recipient orients to both the content
and the astonishment overtone of the repair initiation:

(7)   K5: 210–221
    1 ELI: HAS du denn an deiner diss
            M,R(/
            so have you worked on
    2   geARbeitet in letzter zeit
            /   .   )
            your dissertation recently
    3 LEA: NEE   NUR als ich wußte dann is der doktoRANdntermin
            (\ ) R(/   \   /)
            no   only when I knew there was this meeting for postgraduates
    4 LEA: (0.6) hab ich mich mal   KURZ n abend HINgesez
                       M(\   \   )
            then I sat down briefly for an evening
    5 LEA: ((laughs for *c*. 1.5 secs))
    6 LEA: JA un dann hab ich erst n SPÖkes gemacht ne
            L,R(\   /   /)
            ⟨   all   ⟩
            well and then I first did some silly things you know

```
  7 LEA:  ┌((laughs))
  8 ELI:  │ mhm (.)
         └   \ /

  9 ELI:  ┌ m geNAU ja
         │      ( \ ) \
         └ m exactly yes
 10 LEA:    ((laughs))
→11 CIS:
```

```
            ✔   ·   ·   ·   ˙

         WAS has du gemacht
         H( /                    )
          <f  >
         what  did  you  do
```

```
 12 LEA:  ┌ irgendwie so ZETtelchen geSCHRIEBM
         │        F( \                /   )
         │  I made some little notes
 13 ELI:  │ sie hat ne ganz nette EINladung geschriebm
         │               (\                  )
         └ she wrote a very nice invitation
 14 LEA:  ┌((laughs for c. 2 secs))
 15 CIS:  │      (1.0)            hmhm
         └                        \ /
            (1.1)
 16 ELI:  mit BILDchen und ziTAT
            F( \                \ )
          with a little picture and a quotation
```

Lea has just told the others that she has not worked on her disserta-
tion much recently, and that, on one occasion, instead of sitting
down to work on it, she first did some silly things (see line 6).
The problem-signalling question in line 11 is a resumption of the
problematic expression *n SPÖkes gemacht* from line 6, which was
formulated there as a funny and self-mocking statement. Yet, here
too, the analysis cannot be left at the sequential level. This question
is not the signalling of an acoustic problem: if it were, Lea would
presumably recycle and repeat verbatim. It is also more than just the
indication of an ordinary meaning problem with respect to the
lexical item *spökes*: if it were merely that Cis did not know the
word, Lea or Eli could be expected to give a neutral paraphrase.
Instead, the answer is paraphrased in a self-mocking way as well.

Lea and Eli both respond to this question by giving some background information about the activity Lea has referred to with the expression *n SPÖkes gemacht*. The whole repair-initiation turn is spoken with high and rising global pitch, and the accent on the question word *WAS* is stronger and louder than the surrounding accents. These two features, louder local accent and higher global pitch than the surrounding stretches of talk, make the question prosodically marked.

Recipient treatment of Cis' question seems to be a result of her use of prosodic marking. In lay, participant categorizations, the speaker Cis signals 'surprise' or 'astonishment' as a kind of overtone to her question. Cis is obviously amazed at Lea's description of her avoiding work as *n spökes machen*; presumably she did not expect such a disrespectful characterization, and is now curious to know what activity this characterization is actually referring to.

In answering, however, Lea does not take the problem seriously. She retains the self-mocking and playful modality which she initiated before, and answers that she wrote some 'little notes', before bursting into laughter again and displaying enjoyment at Cis' astonishment. This mocking treatment implies that Lea is acknowledging and reacting to Cis' display of astonishment. Speaker Eli, however, preserves a more serious modality and answers Cis' question in a straightforward fashion by telling her the real activity which Lea engaged in. Although initially aligning with Cis' serious and astonished enquiry, Eli's subsequent choice of the diminutive *bildchen* (line 16), however, shows ultimate alignment with Lea's playful modality.

Thus, neither Lea nor Eli treat the problem signalled as an acoustic one or as a meaning problem with respect to the lexical item *spökes*. They both take it that a problem of expectation with respect to the activity which Lea calls *n spökes machen* is being indicated. In responding to Cis' question, they orient to both the content and the overtone of her question.

In contrast, the repair initiation in (8) below is not treated as such, at least not immediately. This is an example of a prosodically marked verb-initial question resuming a trouble source from the prior turn. Here, however, the treatment is more complex than in the cases discussed so far.

(8) KO:37: 7ff.

```
  2 DOR:  wie HATtese denn nich SCHISS von wegn mit deiner
          F ( \                              \
          how so weren't you afraid about x-raying your
  3 DOR:  LUNge röntchen daß de da: (.) dein RAUchen feststelln
          \                           /                    )
          lungs          that they'd find out about your smoking
  4 MAR:  DO:CH:
          ( - )
          ⟨tense⟩
          oh I was
          (.)
  5 DOR: ⌐ bo DA hätt ich ja total e (.)
        │  F( \
        │  I would be totally e
  6 MAR: │ aber das hab ich doch IMmer
        │  M(                    \   )
        └  but I always feel like that
  7 DOR: ⌐ DA hätt ich ja total SCHISS vor
        │  F( \                       \    )
        │  I would be totally afraid of that
  8 MAR: │ hab ich doch IMmer (.) NEI:N:
        │  M(          \    )  L(-   )
        │  I always feel like that    no
  9 ELI: │ hat se was geSACHT
        │           ( /   )
        └  did she say anything
 10 MAR:  die hat die hat
          L(
          she     she
 11 MAR:  ich bin ni ma geFRAGT wordņ ob ich (.) RAUche=
          L,F( \                              \    )
          I wasn't even              asked if I  smoke
→ 12 DOR:
```

```
          =HAM se no NIMmals geFRACHT
          H,F(\          \       /    )
          <f                        f>
          didn't    they   even   ask
```

13 MAR: **NEEE**
    (\   )
    no

14 DOR: <u>**EHR**</u>lich nich
    H(/   )
    ⟨ f ⟩
    really not
    (1.4)

15 DOR: **OH**
    H(\ )
    oh

16 MAR: ┌ das **RAU**chen **KÖN**ŋ die da nich **FEST**stelln
     │ F (↓/   ↑ \   \   )
     │ ⟨*a bit tense*   *a bit tense*⟩
     │ *the smoking   they   cannot find out about*

17 ELI: │   **DO:CH** =
     └   L(-   )
                                   oh yes they can

18 ELI: ┌ =das (?**SEHN** die?)
     │   L(\   )
     │ *they see it*

19 DOR: │ =ja **WENN** die dich **AB**hö:rn (.)
     │   F(\   /   )
     │ ⟨   *a bit tense*   ⟩
     └ *well if they listen to you(r lungs)*

In line 12, the speaker Dor asks a prosodically marked question
with the finite verb in initial position: *HAM se no NIMmals
geFRACHT.* As this 'cites' a part of the prior turn, it would be
called an echo question in linguistic sentence-type classification. Its
prosodic format has high global pitch and increased global loudness, starting with an extra loud accent on the verb. The background is as follows: Mar has had an official health examination
the same morning. Dor thinks that a person's smoking would be
an issue to be commented on in an official health certificate (lines
2–3). Yet, Mar has just said in lines 10–11 that she was not even
asked whether she smokes. This is cited as the problematic issue
by Dor in her question. Yet, with the marked prosody, Dor's
question is not a simple 'echo' to secure understanding. The analysis of the following turns suggests that Dor is 'astonished' and
that she is pointing to a contradiction between her own expectations and the state of affairs Mar has just described. This can be
seen from the fact that after Mar has answered Dor's astonished

question with *no* only, Dor now signals her problem a second time in line 14: *EHRlich nich.*

The turn in line 14 also has high global pitch and a loud accent. Dor insists on the point and implies that Mar's response so far has not been sufficient. In fact, Dor does not seem to doubt the truth of Mar's statement, but expresses her 'astonishment' a second time. When no verbal correction from Mar is forthcoming (cf. the 1.4 second pause between lines 14 and 15), Dor now produces a 'change-of-state token' (Heritage 1984) *OH*, again with high global pitch. In using this token, she presents a further piece of retrospective evidence that she has had a problem of expectation. By presenting her expectation now as changed, she implies that she indeed had another expectation before, which was contrary to the events as Mar presented them, but at this point she refrains from further treatment of her astonishment.

In giving her general view of the issue in line 16, Mar explains why she herself is not astonished, namely because doctors cannot tell whether their patients smoke or not. This explanation is in direct contradiction to the expectation implicit in Dor's question in lines 2–3, and thus implies a correction of Dor's beliefs. Mar focusses on the expectations underlying Dor's problem and initiates a clarifying discussion.

Thus, instead of accepting that Dor has a reason to be astonished and addressing the astonishment in her question, which would presumably be the preferred treatment for Dor, Mar only responds minimally and then rejects the reasons for Dor's astonishment, at the same time accounting for why she does not agree or align with it. In addition, Mar's explanation (account) is postponed: it is thus presented in a turn-shape characteristic of dispreferred responses (see Schegloff, Jefferson and Sacks 1977; Pomerantz 1984).

We may conclude that, in cases in which recipients do not address a speaker's astonishment immediately and simply react with, for example, confirmations as in (8), they may later give reasons for not being astonished, thereby providing postponed accounts and/or corrections of a co-participant's expectations. This seems to be a dispreferred way of dealing with a speaker's display of astonishment.

So far, the analysis has reconstructed the treatment of the two components of prosodically marked initiations of repair as follows.

In response to the astonishment overtone, recipients either orient to the astonishment, as in (2) and (6), or they later account for lack of alignment, as in (8); an exception is (4) where, due to the institutional context, an account is arguably not necessary. In response to the content component, recipients treat the problem of expectation, as in (2) and (7), or speakers initiating repair indicate whether they are satisfied with problem treatment by insisting on further problem treatment, as in (4), (6), and (8) (line 14), or by refraining from doing so as in (8) (line 15) and (10) below.

4.2 'Astonished' proffers

In the following extracts, repair is not initiated by repeating or resuming a trouble source verbatim or almost verbatim. Instead of formulating direct resumptions of problematic items or turns, speakers formulate inferences from prior talk, with which they want to check their understanding. The inference is proffered to the recipient for acceptance or rejection; recipients are meant to confirm or correct the speakers' understanding and possibly to contribute to problem solving. If speakers formulate these proffers in prosodically marked form, they present them as being in contrast to their own expectations.

In extract (9), the speaker Nat constructs a prosodically marked explicit understanding check in a verb-second sentence structure. The initiation of repair is treated as expected, in that the recipient orients both to the astonishment and to the content component.

```
(9)   K2: 291–312 ((Topic: Ron's musical instruments))
      1 RON:  unDANN muß ich noch: (.) klaVIER machen
             F( \                    /              )
             and then I have to         play the piano
             (.)
      2 NAT:  SCHÖN
               ( \ )
             ⟨  p  ⟩
             nice
      3 RON:  JA: ((laughs)) also für  MICH is es mehr (1.0) quäleREI
             (-)                    L,F( \                        \ )
             well          well for me it's rather a          torture
```

```
 4 NAT: ┌ WArum:
        │ L( \    )
        │      why
 5 RON: │       und ZWANG
        │            L ( - )
        │            and compulsion
 6 IDA: │                     has du das in deiner JUgend nicht geLERNT
        │                     ⟨all  ⟩            F(\         /    )
        └                     didn't you learn it when you were young
 7 RON:  NEIN
         H( - )
         ⟨extra high pitch⟩
         no
 8 RON: ┌((laughs))
 9 IDA: │ na(hh)
        └  \
10 NAT: ((laughs briefly))
        (1.2)
11 RON:  UND giTARre is noch dabei
         F(\        \              )
         and there's still the guitar
         (1.0)
12 NAT:
```

```
         klaVIER FINDS du nich SCHÖN
         H ( \    ↑\              /  )
         piano   you   don't   like

         (0.7)
13 NAT: ┌  ICH hätts gern geLERNT
        │ M,F(/               \   )
        │    I would have liked to learn it
14 RON: │         ich  MAG (.) ich  MAG das instrument
        │              M( \        R( \
        └          ⟨f        f⟩
                   I do like I do like the instrument
15 RON:  SCHON gerne=
              \        )
         all right
```

```
16 NAT:  ⎡ = JAA
         ⎢   M( \ )
         ⎢     yeah
17 IDA:  ⎢     ja wemman das so SPÄT (.) anfangen MUSS zu lern̩:
         ⎢                   R( \                    \           )
         ⎢           ⟨all            all⟩          ⟨  f  ⟩
         ⎢           well if you have to start with it that late
18 RON:  ⎢                            bloß:                   also mir
         ⎣                            but                     just  I
19 RON:  ⎡  FÄLLT das sehr SCHWER (1.1) das spieln
         ⎢  F( \                   \            \  )
         ⎢                                   ⟨p        p⟩
         ⎢     find it    very hard          to play
20 NAT:  ⎣                            ähn
                                       \/
```

Ron, who is a music student, has been talking about his instruments, and in particular about his struggle to learn to play the piano. In line 12, *klaVIER FINDS du nich SCHÖN*, Nat checks her inference that Ron does not like the piano. This is done with high global pitch and a locally marked accent with an extra high pitch peak. Nat's utterance clearly jumps up in pitch in comparison to the surrounding utterances.

With this marked prosody, Nat presents the proffered negative assessment as being in contrast to her own expectations; it implies her own positive assessment of the piano. This interpretation is reinforced when, after Ron does not respond immediately to Nat's utterance, Nat provides the background for her expectation in line 13, namely, her own wish to have had the opportunity to learn to play the pinao. With this in mind, she finds it hard to believe that Ron should not like the instrument. Ron then takes his turn in overlap, restricting the scope of his prior statement of dislike: he does like the instrument but he finds it hard to play.

The fact that Ron now starts in overlap and aligns quickly with Nat's positive assessment of piano playing (line 14), is evidence that agreement with an assessment is the preferred response, even if the speaker has to restrict it. Furthermore, it is evidence that Nat's inferential check indeed implied the expression of astonishment at the contrast between her own positive and Ron's inferred negative assessment. Ron's self-repair, restricting his statement of dislike,

orients to Nat's display of astonishment and clarifies his own attitude for her.

An 'astonished' verb-initial proffer is also made by Eli in extract
(10) line 4:

(10) KO: 18:2ff. ((Topic: whether Mar may have been secretly tested for
       AIDS))

    1 MAR: nee **HAM** se nich ge**MACHT** **HAM** se nich ge**MACHT**
        \ F(\   \   ) F(\   \ )
        no they didn't do that   they didn't do that
    2 MAR: ((clears her throat))
    3 MAR: **DA**für müssn se **BLUT** abnehm
        M(/   \   )
        for that they must take blood
→   4 ELI:

        ham se <u>**KEIN**</u> **BLUT** abgenomm
        H(\   \   /   )
                <f f>
        didn't they take any blood at all

    5 MAR: **NEE**e
        M(↑\ /)
        no
    6 ELI: **HA GOTT** se(h)i **DA**(h)**NK**
        M(\) M(\   \   )
        ah   thank   God
    7 ELI: ⌈ ((laughs))
    8 MAR: | (.)   also was die ge**MACHT** habm is ((etc.))
        | ⟨all   all⟩ R(/   )
        ⌊ *well what they did   is*
    ((After this, Mar describes in detail what her health examina-
    tion consisted of.))

Eli, who must undergo the following day the same kind of health
examination that Mar has just gone through, has obviously
expected (fearfully) that in the official examination an applicant's
blood is tested. When Mar asserts that she could not have been
secretly tested for AIDS because they did not take blood, Eli is
reminded of her worry. Beside her extra loud accent on the lexical
item *KEIN*, the entire utterance, except for the last syllable, is
realized with high global pitch to constitute this 'astonished ques-

tion'. Here, too, in her first reaction Mar only responds with *NEEe*; after this, Eli signals her relief and refrains from insisting on further treatment.

So far, the analysis suggests that a speaker's initiation of repair in prosodically marked form makes relevant the recipient's (i) orientation and attention to the astonishment overtone, and (ii) treatment of the problem of expectation on the level of content. With respect to (i), there seems to be a preference for recipient's agreement and alignment with the repair initiator's displayed astonishment, as reconstructed from extracts (2), (7) and (9). With respect to (ii), recipient's potential treatment of the problem of conflicting or contrasting expectations is relevant, as extracts (2), (7) and (9) have shown.

Looking back at extracts (4), (6), (8) and (10), in which the 'astonished' initiation of repair is not immediately treated as such, we can now see that in these cases the recipients in their first reactions have tried to treat the prosodically marked initiations as if they were their unmarked counterparts, i.e. ignoring the astonishment overtone. In cases like these, however, initiators now indicate whether they are satisfied with this treatment. Either they ask a second question and thus insist on the treatment of their problem (see extracts (4) and (8) (line 14)) or they signal a 'change-of-state' and that the problem need not be treated further (see (8) (line 15) and (10)).

In such cases, in which recipients do not align with the speaker in astonishment by, for example, recognizing that the speaker's astonishment is justified, an account for recipient's lack of astonishment, like in (8), is appropriate in everyday conversation between equals whereas, in institutional contexts, cases like (4) suggest that officials need not account for their lack of astonishment or alignment when following regulations.

The fact that speakers may try to ignore the prosodic marking of such utterances and treat them as unmarked implies, however, that the prosodic cues are indeed used additionally, as it were 'on top of' the other signalling cues constitutive of unmarked activities. In cases where recipients do not want to treat the problem-signalling astonishment overtone of a question straight away (or at all), they can first attempt to respond as if it were a prosodically unmarked repair initiation. If questioners' problems are solved by this, they refrain from further problem treatment. If questioners are not satisfied, they can invest extra interactional work and insist on problem treatment. This shows that, even in cases where prosodically marked questions are not treated as such immediately, participants nevertheless orient to the prosodic marking. As a result, the treatment of prosodically marked 'astonished' initiations of repair is an interactive achievement, which in many cases can be reconstructed as overtly negotiated.

As the foregoing and the following examples show, prosodic marking appears to be usable with all types of initiation of repair, which are then heard as 'astonished' initiations of repair to check understanding or to indicate problems of expectation, depending on their semantic relation to the prior turn. Prosodic marking is always used in addition to the other activity-type distinctive cues, with the prosodic marking literally 'overtoning' the other cues.

The constitution of dispreferred responses is not just a deviant case. Extract (11) shows how a recipient's display of lack of alignment with interlocutor's astonishment can be deployed as a resource. In line 8, high global pitch and increased global loudness are used in an inferential check following the change-of-state token *ACH so*, whereas a similar combination of cues is used in line 4 to contextualize overlapping talk as 'interruption':

```
(11)  K1: 555–568 ((Topic: the bistro in which Ida works))
       1 IDA:   also ss in der GÖkerstra:ße=
                     F[ ( \           )
                 well it's in Gökerstreet
       2 IDA:   =das heißt EINfach nur BIStro:
                     F(\              \  / )]
                 the name is simply only bistro
       3 IDA:  ┌   (.) das ist das EINzige
              │              (\
              │        it is the only one
       4 RON: │ ((inbreath)) ach  DAS bistro ┌ mhm
              │               H( \        )  │  \ /
              │           (f             f)  │
              └          oh that bistro      │
       5 IDA:                                │ KENNST du DA:S=
                                             │ F( \        / )
                                             └ do you know that
```

6 RON: =JAja ich **WO:HN** da um die ECke
       (\ )   F(\   \   )
       indeed I live around the corner from there

7 NAT: ((laughs))

→   8 IDA:

       ↖   ↘   •   •   ↖   •   •   •   ↘   •

        ACH so du wohns **AUCH** in willemshaven
        H(\   )   H(\   )
        <all   all>
        <f   f>
        oh   you   also   live   in   willemshaven

9 NAT: ((giggling briefly))
10 IDA: ⌈   IS das WITzich ((whispery laugh))
        │   M(\   \   )
        │   ⟨p   p⟩
        │   *how amusing*
11 NAT: │ ((still giggling   ))
12 RON: ⌊ ((laughing quietly   ))
13 RON: HAB ich dir glaub ich LETZTmal schon geSA:GT=
        M(\   \   \   )
        I think I in fact told you that last time

In this extract, Ida, Nat and Ron are talking about the bistro in which Ida works in the evenings. Ron has asked Ida which bistro this is. After Ida has located and named it (lines 1 and 2), Ron interrupts further identificatory talk since he has now recognized the bistro; interruption here cuts off 'overtalk'. The interrupting *ach DAS bistro* has high global pitch and increased loudness. However, it is produced in overlap; here these cues are equally as interpretable as cues contextualizing the talk as turn-competitive (French and Local 1983, Selting 1995).

The turn in line 8, however, is non-overlapping. Ida gives the change-of-state token *ACH so* and the formulation of her inference that if Ron lives around the corner from where she works, he must live in the same town that she lives in. The entire turn is realized with high global pitch, with increased loudness and with speech rate which is faster than surrounding turns. Ida is arguably signalling her 'surprise' or 'astonishment' here; she intends to check her new discovery by proffering it to Ron as an inference which he should accept or reject. Yet Ron and Nat react with laughter: they do not align with Ida, for example, by accepting the news as a mutual discovery, or by admitting that Ida has reason to be astonished, or by giving reasons for lack of alignment. Instead, they treat Ida's discovery as conveying her late awakening to a fact that they have known all along. Apparently, Ida thought that Ron lived in another town. Furthermore, Ron did not comment on the coincidence that he and Ida live in the same town, when shortly before he himself discovered that Ida works near his place. As Ida's sarcastic comment in line 10 suggests, she now feels that she is being made fun of. In the following, Ron explains his own lack of reaction earlier, i.e. his own non-astonishment and non-alignment with Ida, by stating that he has told her before where he lives but she must have failed to hear it. Thus, even though Ida's astonished inferential check is not treated in the preferred way, both recipients do orient to her display of astonishment: their non-alignment is deployed here to make fun of the problem signaller.

4.3 A final contrast pair: prosodically unmarked versus marked use of a recipient token

The examples presented so far have shown that, regardless of differing syntactic structure and differing semantic relations to the prior turn, prosodic marking in understanding checks or problem-signalling turns can always be analysed as the added expression of 'surprise' or 'astonishment', the expression of a contradiction deriving from a statement or inference from prior talk with respect to the speaker's own expectations. Extracts (12) and (13), finally, present evidence that the same kind of contrast also operates between prosodically marked and unmarked versions of the recipient token *ja*:

```
(12)  K4: 326–331
  1 CIS:    MAL wieder BERge ja(h)
            F( \           /   ) /
            some mountains again you mean
  2 LEA:    ja ECHT ich w   MUSS auch WANdern ne
            ( \    )        M( \         \       /)
            yeah right I have to do some hiking you know
```

→ 3 CIS:

    ✔

    JA
    (/)
    yeah

  4 LEA: JA ich b öh ich **KANN** hier nich laufen
         (\ )   H,F(\   )
         yeah I   eh I can't hike around here
         (.)
  5 LEA: ⌐ dat **LANG**weilt mich ne
               F(\   /)
         ⟨all⟩
         it's boring here you know
  6 CIS: ja **DAS** STIMMT das is hier
                      F(\   \   ) -
         ⌐   *yeah that's true here it is*

In line 3, Cis uses the recipient token *JA* with a rising pitch movement in a mid pitch register. Its use appears to exhibit interest in the ongoing talk and to yield the turn again to the prior speaker. It can thus be used as a technique to avoid taking the turn for a contribution of one's own.[6] In line 4, Lea continues by elaborating on the previous topic, followed by Cis' display of agreement.

This combination of interest display and floor pass is also conveyed by the use of the prosodically marked version of *ja* in extract (13). This time, however, the prosodic marking can be reconstructed as producing the same additional interactive meaning as in the above cases, namely, the expression of 'astonishment' vis-à-vis a contradiction deriving from prior talk with respect to speaker's own expectations.

(13) K4: 154–175
    1 CIS: wenn ich morgens **AUF**stehe
                    M(/
        when I get up in the morning
    2 CIS: beziehungsweise be**VOR** ich aufstehe (0.6)
                       \   )
        ⟨all   all⟩
        or   rather   before   I get up

3 CIS: dann: (.) TRINK ich eiṇ: TEE im bett
             M(\   \   )
        then   I have a cup of tea in bed
((lines 4–6 omitted))
7 CIS: un DANN ess ich ersma irgnwie:
             F(\
        and then first of all I eat
8 CIS: irgnwas SÜßes dazu=
                 \   )
        something sweet with it

→   9 ELI:

                ∪
                ‾‾‾
                JA
                H(/)
                <f>
                yeah

10 CIS: mhm
          \ /
         ⟨ h ⟩
11 ELI: ((clears her throat))
12 LEA: ⌈ NEE das KANN ich nich
        │ L(\ ) L,F(\   )
        │ *no   that I can't do*
13 ELI: │   äNEE
        │   F(\ )
        │   ⟨   f⟩
        └   *no*
        (1.0)
14 CIS: ⌈ ((laughs))
15 ELI: │ RAUCH ich ne zigaRETte dazu
        │ R(/   \   )
        └   *I smoke a cigarette*
16 ELI: ⌈ ((laughs))
17 LEA: │ JA   DAS ma ich AUCH
        │ (\) F(/   \   )
        │ ⟨f   f⟩
        │ *yes that's what I do too*
18 CIS: │ ((laughs)) j(h)a das kenn ich
        │   ⟨f   f⟩
        └   *yes that's what*
        (..)

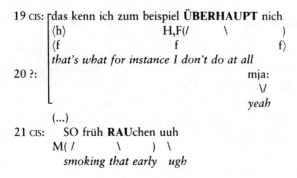

19 CIS: ⌈das kenn ich zum beispiel **ÜBERHAUPT** nich
          ⟨h⟩   H,F(/   \   )
          ⟨f   f   f⟩
          that's what for instance I don't do at all
20 ?:   mja:
                                                          \/
                                                         yeah
        ⌊
        (...)
21 CIS: SO früh **RAU**chen uuh
             M(/   \   )   \
             smoking that early   ugh

In line 9, *JA* is used again with a rising pitch movement, but now in
a high pitch register and with increased loudness. Just before this
extract starts, the speakers have discovered that they all like sweets
differently. Eli is astonished that Cis eats sweets early in the morning. The prosodic marking of her *JA*, apart from yielding the turn
back to Cis for further talk, as the *JA* in extract (12) did, adds an
astonishment component and thus implies that there is a contradiction derived from prior talk in relation to Eli's own expectations.
In this context, the prosodically marked *JA* is a first manifestation
of the speakers' differing behaviour towards sweets. It is used as a
pre-disagreement before the actual launching of the disagreement.
Yet in line 10, Cis merely confirms her prior statement without
addressing Eli's display of astonishment. After this, participants
deal with the now apparent conflict of expectations by making
explicit their early morning habits. That Eli's own habit, which is
the basis of her expectations, is the opposite of Cis' is made explicit
in lines 13 and 15: she smokes a cigarette in the morning. This is
Lea's habit, too, who shows agreement with Eli's expectations in
lines 12 and 17. After Eli and Lea have voiced their views, Cis in
turn gives her view on the fact that they smoke in the morning (lines
19–21): she never smokes early in the morning. In this case then,
when recipient Cis does not align with Eli's display of astonishment
right away, Eli and Lea give accounts for being astonished, thereby
producing retrospective evidence for the analysis that Eli's prosodically marked *JA* in line 9 indeed displayed a contradiction of expectations which required dealing with.

5 Conclusions

My analysis has shown that the use of particular clusters of prosodic signalling cues are systematically and methodically used to
distinguish between different activity types, which have differing
sequential implications for their recipients. The clusters of prosodic
cues constitutive of 'prosodic marking' are combinations of
increased global and/or local pitch and/or loudness, in particular

either   high global pitch plus increased global loudness,
or   high global pitch or loudness plus a locally marked accent
           with an extra high pitch peak or locally increased loudness.

Initiations of repair with and without prosodic marking have been
shown to have different sequential implications for the next turn.
The use of prosodic marking in initiations of repair is routinely
oriented to by recipients. Their treatment of these utterances suggests that they interpret them as activities in which speakers are
manifesting a contrast or a contradiction derived from their own
expectations with respect to an interlocutor's prior talk, as displays
of an overtone which in lay, participant terms could be labelled
'surprise' or 'astonishment' with respect to the content referred
to. Depending on the semantic relation to the prior turn, i.e.
whether they explicitly resume or cite a problematic item or infer
a problematic issue from the prior talk, prosodically marked initiations of repair will be heard as 'astonished' initiations of repair to
signal that there is a problem of expectation whose treatment by the
recipient is now relevant, or to check understanding by proffering
an inference to the recipient for acceptance or rejection.[7]

Prosodic marking is used in addition to other contextualization
cues but seemingly overrides them all. It constitutes an 'overtone'
which adds an expression of astonishment and thereby changes the
activity type from a 'normal' to an 'astonished' initiation of repair
in which a problem of expectation is indicated. In subsequent turns,
both the astonishment overtone as well as the content of the repair
initiation must be dealt with by the recipients. The sequential implications of prosodically marked repair initiations are thus that (i)
with respect to the astonishment overtone: 'attention should be
given to the justification of and possible reasons for speaker's astonishment', and (ii) with respect to the problem content: 'potential

treatment and clarification of the problem of expectation may be required'.

With respect to (i), there seems to be a preference for 'agreement' and 'alignment' by recipient with the speaker in the establishment and assessment of the unexpectedness of the trouble source, and its possible justification. If recipients do not agree with the speaker's astonishment, they may later account for their lack of alignment, thereby exhibiting an orientation both to the interpretation of astonishment as well as to the preference for alignment. As non-alignment implies a dispreferred correction of the speaker's beliefs, it is often postponed.

With respect to (ii), recipients of the problem-signalling may react as follows: either they start problem-solving activities such as giving more information or making explicit their own expectations, or they first treat the prosodically marked initiation of repair as if it were an unmarked one. The problem signaller may then invest more interactional work and indicate what kind of further problem treatment is expected. The latter may involve the problem being signalled as now irrelevant if, for instance, speakers have changed their expectations, or it may involve speakers insisting on problem treatment by asking another question on the issue, often now stating their problem in a more explicit way (see also Selting 1987a, 1987b).

This treatment of prosodically unmarked versus marked initiations of repair shows that participants do indeed orient to the absence or presence of prosodic marking cues. Unlike prosodically unmarked initiations of repair, which normally indicate problems of hearing or understanding, prosodically marked initiations of repair are interpreted by recipients as indicating 'astonishment' due to a problem of expectation; they make treatment of both the content and the overtone component of the problem-signalling sequentially relevant. Recipient reactions to prosodically unmarked and marked versions of initiations of repair differ with, and are made conditionally relevant by, the initiator's differential use of bundles of prosodic cues. Prosody thus differentiates between types of problem handling *within* repair sequences.

My analysis has shown that recipients' and analysts' interpretations of 'astonishment', or 'surprise', are not merely unanalysable or holistic interpretative judgements. Rather, speakers use cues to contextualize particular activity types via the triggering of interpretative frames associated with these cues. Prosodic cues are used as a resource and oriented to by participants in the construction and interpretation of activity types in conversational interaction. The labels of 'astonishment' or 'surprise' derive from the reconstructed context-sensitive interpretations of these cues by recipients in repair sequences.

Yet, the signalling cues of high global pitch plus increased global loudness do not work independently of sequential position. As French and Local (1983) have shown (and as is verified by many examples in my own data), they also contextualize 'interruption' in the sequential position of overlapping speech. In contrast, the 'astonished' initiations of repair analysed in this paper are non-overlapping. In activities other than initiation of repair and interruption, the prosodic cues high pitch plus locally marked accents can be used, for instance, to indicate 'emphasis' (Selting 1994) or 'indignation' (Günthner, this volume). Labels like 'astonishment'/'surprise', 'indignation', 'emphasis', etc., are thus context-sensitive interpretations of particular bundles of prosodic cues in particular kinds of utterances in particular sequential positions in conversation. On the other hand, high global pitch by itself is not enough to signal these contextualizations. High global pitch by itself, for instance, is common in topic-initiating turns and questions.

As the difference between activity types may be indicated and constituted by prosodic marking alone, prosodic cues require systematic analysis when explicating participants' construction and interpretation of activity types. Prosody provides in some cases the *only* distinctive signalling cue, distinguishing between otherwise seemingly identical activity types in conversation. Without differentiating between prosodically unmarked and marked versions of, e.g. *bitte*, *was*, *ja*, etc., the different participant reactions to these items could not be accounted for.

Appendix: transcription conventions

Transcription symbols in the text line of transcripts

aber **DA** kam	primary accented syllable of a unit
aber DA kam	secondary accented syllable of a unit
S<u>I</u>cher	extra strong/loud accent
si̅ːcher	lengthening of a sound
sːiːchːerː	lengthening of an entire word
(ʔer kommt ?)	dubious transcription
a(l)so	dubious sound within a word
*	glottal stop
ŋ, m̩	syllabic sounds, based on sonority and length
=	latching
(.)	brief pause of up to approx. 0.5 sec.
(..)	each dot approx. 0.5 sec. pause (here 1 sec.)
(0.8)	pause timed in tenths of a second
⌈ich gehe	simultaneous talk, overlapping utterances
⌊ jaha	
((laughs))	para- and/or non-linguistic events

Transcription symbols in the prosody line of transcripts

Global pitch (noted before the left parenthesis)

F,R,H,M,L( )	notation of the global pitch direction and register throughout the accent sequence delimited by parentheses: F = falling, R = rising, H = high, M = mid, L = low. (Parentheses are usually noted before the first accent and at the end of the cohesive unit.)
H,F( )	combination of global characterizations: here falling within the high register
[( )( )]	combined contours with only weak or no boundaries between units with different global pitch direction (e.g. 'paratones')

Prototypical accents or unaccented local pitch movements, on and after accented and/or unaccented syllables

\	falling
/	rising
-	level
\/	falling–rising
/\	rising–falling

Accent modifications

↑\, ↓/, ↑-, /↑	locally larger pitch movements than in surrounding accents, higher or lower pitch peaks or valleys than usual

(Outside the parentheses, local pitch movements function as 'pre-head' or as 'tail' after the accent sequence.)

Prosodic parameters (used with local or global extension; the extension is indicated by the position of the angled brackets)

⟨f⟩	*forte*, loud
⟨p⟩	*piano*, soft
⟨l⟩	*lento*, slow
⟨all⟩	*allegro*, fast
⟨dim⟩	*diminuendo*, decreasing loudness
⟨tense⟩	tense articulation

Notes

For helpful discussion and criticism of a previous version of this paper I am grateful to the participants of the Sociolinguistic Colloquium at the University of Konstanz: Elizabeth Couper-Kuhlen, Aldo di Luzio, Manfred Faust, Susanne Günthner, Hubert Knoblauch and Frank Müller. Further special thanks are due to Elizabeth Couper-Kuhlen for extensive help with both the details of the analysis and the language of this chapter.

1 See also von Essen (1964); for more recent research using the same kind of basic assumption, see Wunderlich (1988) and Altmann, Batliner and Oppenrieder (1989); for a description of a similar situation in English see Halliday (1967) and the more recent summary in Arndt and Janney (1987: Ch. 6).

2 In the literature, interpretations like 'astonished question' are made very unsystematically and mostly without an attempt to reconstruct their sequential and prosodic basis. An early exception is Bolinger (1957) who, in his discursive typology of questions, notes with his 'original questions' that there are cases in which the question word is produced on higher pitch or with larger pitch range and 'we note irritation, insistence, etc.' or 'keyed up interest' (1957:137).

3 The upper part of the diagram shows the waveform, the lower part fundamental frequency (f_0), both analysed with the program Signalyze running on a Macintosh computer. I am grateful to Peter Auer for allowing me access to this equipment.

4 Soc's treatment of Kli1's problem can be systematically accounted for by a preference organization among problem types in this kind of institutional context (see Selting 1987a, 1987b).

5 To align with the astonishment component of these activities, something like 'I know! Isn't that amazing!' is required.

6 In this respect, *ja* is similar to recipient tokens such as *mhm, uh huh,* etc., which are analysed by Schegloff (1982), but it seems to display more 'interest'.

7 It remains an open question whether the difference between prosodically unmarked and prosodically marked initiations is a gradual or a categorial one. I tend to think it is a gradual one, which, especially in cases of unclear contrasts, calls for conversational negotiation.

References

Altmann, H., A. Batliner and W. Oppenrieder (eds.) 1989. *Zur Intonation von Modus und Fokus im Deutschen.* Tübingen: Niemeyer.

Arndt, H. and R. W. Janney 1987. *InterGrammar.* Berlin and New York: Mouton de Gruyter.

Auer, P. 1992. Introduction: John Gumperz' approach to contextualization. In P. Auer and A. di Luzio (eds.) *The Contextualization of Language.* Amsterdam and Philadelphia: Benjamins, pp. 1–38.

Bolinger, D. 1957. *Interrogative Structures of American English.* Publication of the American Dialect Society, No. 28. Alabama University Press.

1989. *Intonation and its Uses. Melody in grammar and discourse.* London: Edward Arnold.

French, P. and J. K. Local 1983. Turn-competitive incomings. *Journal of Pragmatics,* 7: 17–38.

Gibbon, D. 1984. Intonation as an adaptive process. In D. Gibbon and H. Richter (eds.) *Intonation, Accent and Rhythm: Studies in discourse phonology.* Berlin: de Gruyter, pp. 165–192.

Gumperz, J. J. 1982. *Discourse Strategies.* Cambridge University Press.

Halliday, M. A. K. 1967. *Intonation and Grammar in British English.* The Hague: Mouton.

Haviland, J. 1989. 'Sure, sure': evidence and affect. *Text,* 9: 27–68.

Heritage, J. 1984. A change-of-state token and aspects of its sequential placement. In J. M. Atkinson and J. Heritage (eds.) *Structures of Social Action. Studies in conversation analysis.* Cambridge University Press, pp. 299–345.

Jefferson, G. 1978. Sequential aspects of storytelling in conversation. In J. N. Schenkein (ed.) *Studies in the Organization of Conversational Interaction.* New York: Academic Press, pp. 219–248.

Local, J. K. 1992. Continuing and restarting. In P. Auer and A. di Luzio (eds.) *The Contextualization of Language.* Amsterdam and Philadelphia: Benjamins, pp. 233–258.

Ochs, E. and B. Schieffelin 1989. Language has a heart. *Text,* 9: 7–25.

270   Margret Selting

Pheby, J. 1981. Intonation. In K. E. Heidolph, W. Fläming and W. Motsch, *Grundzüge einer deutschen Grammatik*. Berlin: Akademie-Verlag, pp. 839–897.

Pomerantz, A. 1984. Agreeing and disagreeing with assessments: some features of preferred/dispreferred turn shapes. In J. M. Atkinson and J. Heritage (eds.) 1984. *Structures of Social Action. Studies in conversation analysis*. Cambridge University Press, pp. 57–101.

Schegloff, E. A. 1982. Discourse as an interactional achievement: some uses of 'uh huh' and other things that come between sentences. In D. Tannen (ed.) *Analyzing Discourse: Text and talk*. Georgetown University Round Table on Languages and Linguistics 1981. Washington, D.C.: Georgetown University Press, pp. 71–93.

Schegloff, E. A., G. Jefferson and H. Sacks 1977. The preference for self-correction in the organization of repair in conversation. *Language*, 53: 361–382.

Selting, M. 1987a. *Verständigungsprobleme. Eine empirische Analyse am Beispiel der Bürger-Verwaltungs-Kommunikation*. Tübingen: Niemeyer.

1987b. Reparaturen und lokale Verstehensprobleme – oder: zur Binnenstruktur von Reparatursequenzen. *Linguistische Berichte*, 108: 128–149.

1992. Prosody in conversational questions. *Journal of Pragmatics*, 17: 315–345.

1993. Phonologie der Intonation. Probleme bisheriger Modelle und Konsequenzen einer neuen interpretativ-phonologischen Analyse. *Zeitschrift für Sprachwissenschaft*, 11(1): 99–138.

1994. Emphatic speech style – with special focus on the prosodic signalling of heightened emotive involvement in conversation. In C. Caffi and R. W. Janney (eds.) *Involvement in Language*. Special issue. *Journal of Pragmatics*, 22: 375–408.

1995. *Prosodie im Gespräch. Aspekte einer interaktionalen Phonologie der Konversation*. Tübingen: Niemeyer.

von Essen, O. 1964. *Grundzüge der hochdeutschen Satzintonation*. Ratingen: Henn.

Wunderlich, D. 1988. Der Ton macht die Melodie – zur Phonologie der Intonation des Deutschen. In H. Altmann (ed.) *Intonationsforschungen*. Tübingen: Niemeyer, pp. 1–40.

7

The prosodic contextualization of moral work: an analysis of reproaches in 'why'-formats

SUSANNE GÜNTHNER

1 Introduction

This chapter will analyse the prosodic devices used in everyday moralizing. The focus will be on reproach activities in 'why'-formats, as encountered in a data collection of informal talk (dinner conversations in the family, breakfast interactions, coffee chats, telephone calls between friends) and media conversation (talk-shows on TV and radio phone-ins). An analysis of my data reveals that a great number of reproaches in German are packaged in *warum-* or *wieso-* ('why'-) formats. This applies to reproaches which are produced *in situ*, that is, in the ongoing communication:[1]

(1) warum lä:sch se au immer rei:.
   why do you always let her in

as well as to those which appear as reconstructions of past reproaches:

(2) ich hab der Katharina jetzt auch gesagt warum steht das ni:cht im
   and so I told Katharina why isn't it in the
   Kulturanzeiger.
   Kulturanzeiger

Even self-reproaches may be constructed with 'why'-formats:

(3) ich hab mir da Vorwürfe gemacht. warum hab ich ihr das gesacht.
   I reproached myself. why did I tell her about it

This chapter, however, will concentrate primarily on *in situ* reproaches constructed in ongoing interaction.

   'Why'-constructions are of great interest for linguistic analysis because they can represent 'real' questions asking for a reason:

(4)   warum magst du Stuttgart nich?
      why don't you like Stuttgart?

as well as reproaches focussing on another's misdeeds and demanding a 'remedial reply':

(5)   warum zum Teufel fra:gsch se dann net direkt
      why the hell don't you ask her directly then

The analytic questions then are: how do participants differentiate
between a 'why'-question and a 'why'-reproach? What role does
prosody play in cases where there are no verbal signals (such as
lexical items) that clearly indicate the specific activity type? Is there
a distinctive 'prosody of reproach'? Or do prosodic features function as contextualization cues (Gumperz 1982) which interlocutors
orientate to in their interpretation of the ongoing activity? In addition, I shall address the issue of why reproaches in everyday interaction are often packaged in 'why'-formats.

   On the basis of the analysis it will be argued that prosody is one
of the constitutive components that distinguish between different
activity types ('why'-utterances as reproaches versus 'real' questions) and is sequentially implicative for the kind of reaction
expected from the co-participant. The analysis will show that prosody functions – in co-occurrence with syntactic, lexico-semantic
and rhetorical features – as a signalling system used by participants
in conversation in order to contextualize and interpret interactive
meaning and communicative activities (Couper-Kuhlen and Selting:
chapter 1 of this volume).

2 Reproaches as communicative forms of moralizing

Modern societies – as Luckmann (1993) points out – no longer
possess a generally obligatory moral order and a dogmatized hierarchy of values with canonic ideas of what a 'good' life should be.
Instead of traditional concepts of morality, we find a tendency
towards a 'privatization' of morality. However, even if there are
no longer specific moral institutions which proclaim a canonized
moral code, and even if sub-systems in our society (such as science,
economy, law) have disassociated themselves to a great extent from
morality, this does not mean that morality has disappeared from
everyday interaction.

Moral norms and values, which function as interpretative mechanisms for the evaluation of the 'rightness' or 'wrongness' of people's behaviour and attitudes, are continually constructed and reconfirmed in social interactions (Bergmann and Luckmann 1993). Everyday communication represents a central focus for our orientation to moral norms and values, and everyday talk can be shown to be heavily interspersed with moral elements. For instance, when we gossip, we tend to demonstrate our moral indignation about the behaviour of the 'object of gossip' (Bergmann 1987). When we evaluate the behaviour or character of a third person, we often provide evidence for our evaluation by telling exemplary stories which are loaded with moral judgements and values (Günthner 1995).

Reproach activities can be considered as communicative forms of everyday 'moralizing'. In these activities interlocutors focus on an infringement of expectations concerning situatively appropriate behaviour and, in doing so, demonstrate their own orientation to moral rules and values. In reproaching, a speaker provides a verbal sanction for the infraction of a social norm (Goffman 1971:95). Thus, moral norms and values form the basis on which certain ways of behaving may become situatively expectable and others may be judged as inappropriate.

The communicative category 'reproach' is more than an analytic, 'second order construct' (Schütz 1971): it is also an ethnotheoretic term which interlocutors refer to in everyday communication. This is evident from the following transcript segment. The family – consisting of the father (V), the mother (M), the daughter (T) and the son (S) – is playing cards (*Doppelkopf*), when V reproaches M for not having played a higher card. (Transcription conventions for this and the following examples are listed in the appendix.)

(6) 'Doppelkopf' (*Doppelkopf*)
    25 s: man muß ihn (richtig austrinken sonst . . . .)
        you have to (finish the drink properly otherwise . . . .)
    26   (-)
→ 27 v: warum hast denn nischts reingetan.
        why didn't you throw in a high card
    28   haste nischt.
        didn't you have anything

```
    46 T: [naja] aber das war jetzt kein kein Argument.
           [yeah] but that's not the point
    47     da hamse dich jetzt nur geärgert.
           they were just teasing you
    48     des war jetzt nicht gerechtfertigt,
           it was not right
→   49     der Mami en Vorwurf zu machen.=
           to reproach Mum like that
→   50 V: =nei:n warum hat se's dann  [nisch rein]getan.=
           well why didn't she throw one in
    51 T:                             [(..hihi . .)]
    52 T: =na weil se in dem Augenblick gedacht hat
           well because at that moment she thought
    53     daß de's nisch kriegst.
           you wouldn't get it
    54     oder was weiß ich kann doch des is doch Spielfreiheit.
           or whatever one can there is such a thing as freedom of play
```

S has introduced a side-sequence about spilling one's drink, when V in line 27 returns to the card game with his question to M about not having thrown in a high card. His question is not answered by the addressee (M) herself, however, but by the daughter T, who rejects V's criticism as unjustified. In her return of criticism (lines 46–49) T metapragmatically labels V's activity as a 'reproach' (line 49); that is, by the use of 'explicit reflexive language' (Lucy 1993) she verbalizes the inference she has drawn from V's utterance.

In most cases, however, participants produce and reproduce reproaches without any explicit metapragmatic reference to the ongoing speech activity. In these cases the interpretation of the 'why'-format as a reproach (rather than a 'real' question) may be discoverable by examining how the respective utterance is treated in following talk. For instance, in the following segment S has called telephone information and asked for the number of 'a family called Weißer in Konstanz'. After checking her computer, the information operator responds:

```
(7)  Telefonauskunft (Telephone information)
     12 A: ich hab keine Familie Weißer in Konstanz.
            I don't have a Weißer family in Konstanz
     13     nur eine Familie Weiß.
            only a Weiß family
     14 S: ja die wohnen glaub ich auf der Reichenau.
            I think they live on the Reichenau
```

15   und gar nicht direkt in Konstanz.
        and actually not directly in Konstanz
→   16 A: warum sa:gen Sie dann Konstanz.
        then why did you say Konstanz
     17 s: tut mir leid ich dachte die Reichenau fällt unter Konstanz.
        I am sorry I thought the Reichenau belonged to Konstanz
     18   (2.5)
     19 A: also die Nummer ist
        okay the number is

S's correction of where the family lives (lines 14–15) is responded to by the operator in a 'why'-format: *warum sa:gen Sie dann Konstanz* (line 16). This 'why'-utterance is constructed as the second part of a *wenn. . .dann* ('if. . .then') sequence.[2] By using such a construction, A forms a 'quasi-logical argument' (Perelman 1982): she indicates that if S's present statement (*die wohnen. . .auf der Reichenau und gar nicht direkt in Konstanz* (lines 14–15)) is correct, S's behaviour ('saying Konstanz') stands in contrast to it. Thus, A confronts S with an apparent contradiction in her behaviour and asks for a clarification. This method of putting one's partner in a situation of incompatibility, where a present statement or thesis is shown to be in conflict with a previous statement or thesis, is often employed in argumentation to ridicule one's opponent and make him or her lose credibility (Perelman 1982:54ff.). This kind of 'questioning' adds an invasive and aggressive character to the 'why'-format.

Although the activity is not metapragmatically named here, the sequential organization demonstrates that it is interpreted by S as a reproach: she does 'remedial work' (Goffman 1971) by producing an apology,[3] *tut mir leid* (line 17), and an excuse, in which she rejects full responsibility and appeals to her ignorance: *ich dachte die Reichenau fällt unter Konstanz.* (line 17). Thus, S's response to the 'why'-utterance not only indicates her interpretation of it, but also makes the reproach interactively relevant: by providing an apology and an excuse, she sequentially co-produces the remedial interchange.

After this short introduction we can now turn our attention to the structural features of reproach activities. The participation framework of a reproach activity consists of:

   (i) the producer of the reproach (e.g. A in (7));

(ii) the moral addressee of the reproach; that is, the person whose behaviour or action is being criticized (e.g. S in (7));[4]

(iii) the communicative addressee of a reproach. In most cases the communicative addressee is identical to the 'moral addressee', but this is not necessarily so: in (6) above the communicative addressee is the daughter and the moral addressee is the mother: *warum hat se's dann nisch reingetan* (line 50).

Reproach sequences can be treated as 'remedial interchanges': the producer of a reproach and thus the person who calls attention to the misconduct assumes that the addressee is 'morally responsible' for the inappropriate behaviour or action. That is, it is assumed that 'he who fails to guide himself by a particular rule has done so at best because of momentary lapse, at worst because of faulty character, and that although he has not conformed, he is capable of doing so, should have desired to conform, and, in any case, ought now to conform' (Goffman 1971:99). The addressee of the reproach, whose behaviour or attitude is judged as 'inadequate', 'bad' or 'wrong', is expected to do 'remedial work' by providing an account[5] or an apology and thereby demonstrating that s/he 'had a right relationship to the rules' (108). As remedial interchanges are face-threatening activities and thus endanger the 'ritual order', the initiation of a remedial interchange inevitably opens up the possibility that instead of performing remedial work the co-participant may challenge the initiator's legitimacy and a quarrel may ensue.

We can now describe some characteristics of reproaches.

In reproaching, the speaker articulates the violation of rules: an act, a type of behaviour or a character trait of a present co-participant is negatively evaluated. The reproach does not necessarily have to focus on the addressee's inadequate or inappropriate act:

(8)   und worum läsch du dir des au[6] immer gfa:lln
       and why do you always accept all this

but can also focus on the addressee's refraining from doing an appropriate act:

(9)   warum ma:chsch du eigentlich nie en Kühlschrank richtig zu.
       why don't you ever close the fridge properly

The behaviour of the moral addressee is displayed as 'deviant' (McHugh 1970), i.e. the speaker assumes that there were alternative ways of acting and that the addressee knew about these alternatives.

These alternatives are sometimes made explicit (i.e. in constructions such as 'why do you never . . . ', 'why didn't you do . . . ') and are presented as the expected, adequate pattern of behaviour, whereas the course of action chosen is treated as not reasonably explainable.

Thus, reproaching shows an orientation to social norms which are assumed to be valid for the participants. These moral norms and values are part of the sociocultural repertoire of knowledge and form the basis on which certain acts or types of behaviour can be judged as in/appropriate. In this respect, reproaching can be seen as 'doing moral work' and performing social control.

Reproaches generally refer to a preceding action (often including indexical expressions, such as 'this', 'that', or in German modal particles such as 'denn') and rely on shared situational knowledge.

If 'why'-utterances are used both to ask 'real' questions and to do moral work by criticizing another's inappropriate behaviour, what are the linguistic cues participants use to differentiate these activities? Can we identify lexico-semantic devices which interactants employ to signal and interpret the 'why'-utterances as reproach activities? And what signals do participants orientate to in their interpretation if there are no lexico-semantic cues indicating which activity type is being performed?

3 Prosody and 'why'-reproaches

In order to answer these questions, we shall now examine 'why'-formats in more detail.

The following transcript is taken from a TV talk-show on celibacy. Professor Ranke-Heinemann (R), a woman theologian, is attacking Bishop Krenn (K), the representative of the Catholic church, who has just stated that celibacy was propagated by Jesus:

(10) Zölibat (*Celibacy*)
```
      157 R:  wenn Paulus sacht
               if Paul says
      158      ein Wort Jesu zur Ehelosigkeit kenne ich nich,
               I do not know of any teaching by Jesus on celibacy
      159      hh' dann müssen Sie sich doch sagn
               hh' then you must admit
      160      das ham wir wohl später erfunden.
               that we invented it all later on
→     161      warum geben Sie das nich mal zu.
               why don't you just admit that
```

162 к: Frau Professor lesen Sie doch des siebte Kapitel im ersten
        Korintherbrief
        Professor Ranke read the seventh chapter in the first
        epistle to the Corinthians

R uses direct reported speech to quote Paul and to support her
argument. The reported speech is embedded in a *wenn. . .dann*
construction, with which she implies that if the 'if' part (Paul's
quote) is true, the following 'then'-sequence (that the Catholic
church invented celibacy; lines 159–160) is its 'quasi-logical' consequence. This confrontational move is followed by asking K why
he does not acknowledge the fact. K counters by referring R to
another biblical source ('the seventh chapter in the first epistle to
the Corinthians'); in doing so, he not only displays that he has
interpreted R's question as a reproach which is unjustified, but he
also indirectly formulates a counter-reproach (implying that R has
not read the Bible properly). In this example negatively loaded
lexico-semantic devices referring to K's behaviour (*erfunden*
'invent', *zugeben* 'admit', *nich mal* 'not. . .just') seem to trigger
the interpretation of R's 'why'-utterance as a reproach and not a
'real' question.

   Yet excerpt (11) below demonstrates that negatively loaded lexico-semantic features do not always provide a sufficient basis for the
interpretation of a reproach. Sara is telling her friend Eva about her
recent depression and how upset she is whenever she hears about
her ex-husband (Jürgen) and his new lover. Eva advises her to stop
this kind of information flow, because it does not do her any good.
Sara then explains her ambivalence:

(11) Rache (*Revenge*)
    1 SARA: ich wills hören in ne' b'
             I want to hear it you know b'
    2   und das was ich hören will,
             and what I hear
    3   soll in ne bestimmte Richtung gehn.
             I want to go in a particular way
    4   [näm]lich daß es zwischen Jürgen und der knallt.
             namely that she and Jürgen are breaking up
    5 EVA: [aber]
             but
    6 SARA: hh' und des hör ich nich [sondern]
             hh' and this is not what I'm hearing but

→   7 EVA: [aber wa]rum warum
                                    but why why
→   8 EVA: hör' möch' möchtest du des hören.
                 do you hea' wan' want to hear all this
    9   we' aus Rache?
                 be' out of revenge
    10   g' gegen gegen Gefühlen gegenüber dem Jürgen?
                 for for for your feelings about Jürgen
    11   (0.5)
    12 SARA: ja:hh. ich glaub einfach damit er des sieht des geht so nich.
                 yes. I believe it is because I want him to see that it won't
                 work that way

While Sara explains why she is eager to have information about her
ex-husband, Eva tries to interrupt her (line 5) and finally succeeds in
doing so (line 7), producing a 'why'-format (lines 7–10). Sara's
reaction to this 'why'-utterance (line 12) clearly demonstrates her
interpretation of the turn: the inference drawn is that Eva is asking a
'real' question, which makes an answer giving reasons conditionally
relevant. With what kind of cues does Eva provide Sara which lead
her to infer that the 'why'-utterance is to be treated as a 'real'
question? The sequential features (the attempted and then successful
interruption) and the semantic devices, the pre-element *aber* 'but'
indicating an upcoming disagreement and the morally loaded term
Rache 'revenge' actually suggest a reproach; yet the 'why'-construc-
tion is treated as a 'real' question. These devices are thus not always
sufficient in accounting for how participants differentiate between
reproach activities and 'why'-questions. We need a more refined
linguistic analysis that takes prosody into account.

A comparison of prosody in the 'why'-utterances of (10) and
(11) reveals significant differences in their realization. (The transcriptions from now on will take prosodic parameters into account.)

(10) Zölibat (*Celibacy*)
    157R: WENN *PAULUS SACHT
           if Paul says
    158   ↑ ⟨EIN WORT *JESU ZUR EHELOSIGKEIT KENNE ICH
           NICH,⟩
           I do not know of any teaching by Jesus on celibacy
    159   hh' DANN MÜSSEN SIE SICH DOCH SAGN
           hh' then you must admit
    160   DAS HAM WIR WOHL SPÄTER ER*↑FUNDEN↓.
           that we invented it all later on

→   161   ↑ ⟨WARUM *GE↑↓BEN SIE DAS NICH MAL ZU.⟩
             why don't you just admit that
    162ᴋ: Frau Professor lesen Sie doch des siebte Kapitel im ersten
          KO*RINTHERBRIEF
          Professor Ranke read the seventh chapter in the first epistle
          to the Corinthians

(11) Rache (*Revenge*)
       6 SARA: hh' und des *hör ich nich [sondern]
                 hh' and this is not what I'm hearing but
→   7 EVA: [ABER WA]RUM WARUM
                                        but why why
→   8 EVA: hör' möch' möchtest du des *HÖREN.
                 do you hea' wan' want to hear all this
       9   we' aus *Rache?
                 be' out of revenge
      10   g' gegen gegen Gefühlen gegenüber dem *Jürgen?
                 for for for your feelings about Jürgen
      11   (0.5)
      12 SARA: ja:hh. ich glaub einfach damit er des sieht des. *geht. so.
                 nich.
                 yes. I believe it is because I want him to see that it won't
                 work that way

Both 'why'-utterances have falling terminal pitch; however, whereas
↑ ⟨WARUM *GE↑↓BEN SIE DAS NICH MAL ZU.⟩ in (10)
(l.161) shows prosodic affect[7] marking, in (11), *ABER WARUM
WARUM hör' möch' möchtest du des *HÖREN.* (lines 7–8), prosodic cues marking an affective stance are missing. ↑ ⟨WARUM
*GE↑↓BEN SIE DAS NICH MAL ZU.⟩ carries high global[8]
pitch, a global increase of loudness and a rise–fall on the accentuated syllable of the verb *GE↑↓BEN*. Furthermore, because the
main accent is placed on the finite verb (and not on the affix *zu*)
the utterance has so-called 'verum-focus' (Höhle 1991–1992).[9]
According to Höhle, by placing the main accent on the finite verb
in German, the speaker of a declarative sentence is not presenting
the action or event referred to by the finite verb as new information
but instead is asserting 'it is true that . . . '. Thus, the accentuated
verb receives a semantic 'verum' element. In 'why'-sentences, the
utterance sounds more insisting and slightly impatient when the
finite verb is accentuated.[10] By contrast, in the 'why'-utterance
*ABER WARUM WARUM hör' möch' möchtest du des
HÖREN., there is neither high global pitch nor a rise–fall. The

increase of loudness lasts only through the overlap and reformulation, and the main accent is not on the finite verb.[11]
    As the reactions to these 'why'-utterances indicate, co-partici-
pants seem to orientate to the prosodic cues by responding in activ-
ity-specific ways: whereas a prosodically unmarked 'why'-utterance
with no particular affective display is not interpreted as a reproach
but is treated as a 'real' question (11), a prosodically marked[12]
'why'-utterance is responded to with justifications and counter-
reproaches (10). This comparison indicates that prosody may override other cues, such as negatively loaded lexico-semantic constructions. Prosodic features can thus function as important devices to
distinguish between different types of 'why'-utterances and thereby
signal different communicative activities (see also Selting 1995 and
chapter 6 of this volume).
    We shall now examine further reproaches to find out if the
observed prosodic features – global increase of loudness, high
global pitch, a rise–fall on the accentuated syllable and verum-
focus – reappear.
    The following two fragments stem from a TV discussion just
before the state elections in Baden-Württemberg (Germany).
Representatives of the different political parties are discussing the
economic and social situation in Baden-Württemberg. This is a very
antagonistic debate, dominated by argumentative sequences, confrontational moves and accusations.
    T, the representative of the CDU (Christian Democrats) is
demanding that legal proceedings for political asylum be speeded
up. D (the representative of the Liberal Democrats, FDP) responds
by asking why T and his party did not take such measures earlier.

(12) Vor der Wahl (*Before the election*) 1
        361 D: deswegen ham Sie schon ne *zei:tlang [des Thema tatsächlich]
                therefore for some time you ((avoided)) the topic actually
        362 T: [(mir sins erschte *Land)]
                                                        (we are the first state)
            Herr Döring
            Mr Döring
  →   363 D: JA WARUM HÄNDT SIE'S DENN V[OR ↓*JAH:↑↓]
            REN NET GMACHT.
                why didn't you do it years ago
        364 T: [ehrlich.]
                                                        honestly

365 T: ha' wir sen doch=s *einzige Land des des gmacht hat,
         ha' we are the only state that did it

In line 363 D asks a question which T manifestly interprets as a
'reproach', since he responds with a justification (line 365).[13] How
does D contextualize this 'why'-utterance as a reproach? For one,
the lexico-semantic and rhetorical devices used produce an affective
stance: the modal particle *denn* typically appears in questions asking for reasons, justifications or accounts (König 1977:120). In
order to legitimize this reproach, D also employs linguistic hyperbole,[14] upgrading and intensifying the putative offence: *vor ↓*JAH:
↑↓REN*. Phonetic lengthening in this phrase iconically indicates an
extremely long duration. Furthermore, these verbal features co-
occur with affectively marked prosody: the whole turn is spoken
with increased loudness and a rising–falling glide (with low onset)
on an elongated vowel in *↓*JAH:↑↓REN*. However, instead of
verum-focus, the main accent is on *↓*JAH:↑↓*.

Thus, the prosodic features common to reproaching 'why'-
utterances so far seem to be high falling and/or extreme rising–falling pitch movements on accentuated syllables and a global increase
of loudness. The next excerpt, however, demonstrates that for a
'why'-format to be interpreted as a reproach, global loudness
need not necessarily be involved.

T (a Christian Democrat) claims that S and his party (the Social
Democrats, SPD) have not been able to 'contribute to the problem
of the increasing number of people requesting political asylum'. S
reacts by stating that several members of his party have already
declared that this problem must be solved by amending the constitution:

(13) Vor der Wahl (*Before the election*) 2
      895 S: .hh daß zum Beispiel in dieser Asyldebatte die Frau Däubler-
               Gmelin GANZ *KLAR
               .hh that for example in this debate on asylum Ms Däubler-
               Gmelin very clearly
      896   ich hab das in den baden-württembergischen Ga*zetten,
               I read about it in the Baden-Württemberg journals
      897   in den *Zeitungen nachlesen können,
               in the newspapers
      898   .hh aus dieser Asyldebatte *klar gesagt hat,
               .hh concerning this debate on asylum she clearly said

899   .hh daß eine euro*PÄ:ische Flüchtlingslösung,
      .hh that a European solution to the refugee problem
900   auf der Basis der *<u>Gen</u>fer Konvention Vorrang <u>hat</u>.
      on the basis of the <u>Geneva</u> convention is preferred
901   vor nationalen Flüchtlings*<u>regelung</u>,
      to national conventions for <u>dealing</u> with refugees
902   und daß die:ses ↑*<u>auch</u>↓ im Wege einer Verfassungsan-
      passung. (-)
      and that this problem should be solved
903   ge*<u>regelt</u> werden=müsse,
      by amending the constitution
904   Herr ↑*<u>Klo:</u>↓se hat als Fraktionsvorsitzender mehrmals mit
      mir am <u>Sam</u>schtag
      Mr Klose in his function as head of the party explained
      several times to me on Saturday
905   *hier in Baden-Württemberg er [klärt],
      here in Baden-Württemberg
→ 906 T: [wa]rum *<u>TU::N</u>↑↓ Sie's
      dann nicht.=
                              why don't you do it then
907 s: =JA WEIL WIR *<u>NICHT</u> (-)
      well because we (-)
908   WIR KÖNN'N DOCH *NICHT (-)
      of course we
909   DIE VERFASSUNG. ALS. S.P.*D. ÄNDERN.
      the SPD cannot change the constitution

T's question in line 906 is responded to by S with a highly affect-
loaded justification (lines 907–909). Although the 'why'-utterance
*warum *TU::N↑↓ Sie's dann nicht.* (l. 906) does not show global
loudness, its prosodic packaging still gives rise to the impression of
a 'reproachful tone': it has terminal falling pitch with an extra
strong main accent on the verb *TU:N↑↓*, thereby drawing attention to the action that S is being accused of having failed to carry
out. With its main emphasis on the finite verb, the utterance carries
verum-focus. Moreover, the 'why'-format shows affect-marked
intonation: *TU:N↑↓* has a rise–fall in the form of a glide on a
lengthened syllable. With his reaction displaying prosodically
marked irritation (global increase of loudness, marked accentuation), S orientates to the preceding utterance in two ways (lines
907ff.): by providing an account in the form of a 'because' response,
and by returning the high level of affect with signals of his own
irritation.

Yet these examples of reproaches in 'why'-formats (10, 12 and 13) stem from conflict-laden media interactions where, due to the affective loading of the situation and the antagonistic framing of the debate, 'why'-utterances may easily be taken as reproach activities. What cues do participants provide in settings which are not contextually framed as antagonistic media events?

Let us return to the reproaches in transcripts (7) and (6):

(7) Telefonauskunft (*Telephone information*)
        14 s: ja. die wohnen glaub ich auf der *Reichenau.
                I think they live on the Reichenau
        15   und gar nicht direkt *in Konstanz.
                and actually not directly in Konstanz
→   16 A: WARUM=*SA:↑↓GEN=SIE=DANN=KONSTANZ.
                then why did you say Konstanz
        17 s: tut mir leid. ich dachte die Reichenau fällt unter *Konstanz.
                I am sorry I thought the Reichenau belonged to Konstanz
        18   (2.5)
        19 A: also die *Nummer ist
                okay the number is

What cues does S orientate to in interpreting the 'why'-format as a reproach? The embedding context is not conflict-laden, nor are there negatively loaded lexico-semantic features that might trigger the interpretation of a reproach. One cue might be that a telephone information operator is presumably not interested in the 'real' reason for S's 'saying Konstanz'. Aside from this background assumption, however, the reproach activity is primarily contextualized prosodically. The operator's 'why'-utterance has a 'reproachful tone', which S reacts to by doing remedial work. It not only has falling terminal pitch but also shows a combination of prosodically marked features: the turn as a whole is spoken with increased loudness and tempo, and the 'why'-utterance has an extra strong and loud accent on the verb *SA:↑↓GEN (verum-focus) with an extreme rising–falling glide on a lengthened syllable *SA:↑↓. The latter cue serves to foreground the action and thus the 'problematic and inadequate' behaviour of 'saying Konstanz'.

(6) 'Doppelkopf' (*Doppelkopf*)
    25 s: man muß ihn (*richtig austrinken sonst . . . .)
        you have to (finish the drink properly otherwise . . . .)
    26 (-)
→ 27 v: WARUM *HAST↑↓ DENN NISCHTS REI:NGETAN.
        why didn't you throw in a high card
    28 *haste nischt.
        didn't you have anything
    . . .
    46 t: [NAJA] ABER DAS WAR JETZT *KEIN KEIN ARGUMENT.
        [yeah] but that was not the point
    47 DA HAMSE DICH JETZT *NUR ge↑Ä:RGERT↓ .
        they were just teasing you
    48 DES WAR JETZT *NICHT GERECHTFERTIGT
        it was not right
→ 49 DER MAMI EN VORWURF ZU MACHEN.=
        to reproach Mum like that
→ 50 v: =nei:n warum *HAT↑↓ se's dann [nisch REIN]getan.=
        well why didn't she throw one in
    51 t: [(..hihi . . .)]
    52 t: =NA WEIL SE IN *DEM AUGENBLICK GEDACHT HAT
        well because at that moment she thought
    53 DASS DE'S NISCH KRIEGST.
        you wouldn't get it

Both of V's 'why'-constructions (lines 27 and 50) have falling terminal pitch and are prosodically marked by rise–falls. In addition, the first one (line 27) is spoken with increased loudness. Furthermore, both 'why'-constructions have their primary accent on the finite verbs *HAST↑↓ and *HAT↑↓ and thus carry verum-focus. This kind of accent placement is especially marked when, as in these cases, the accentuated finite verbs have no lexical content. What the speaker emphasizes is not the temporal function of the verb but his problem of expectation: the action of the moral addressee is highlighted as inappropriate. The speaker can thus be heard to imply that he is not primarily interested in the reasons for the other's action but in constructing the action in question as problematic.

To summarize, so far, among the prosodic features used in these 'why'-formats signalling reproach, the combination of global increase of loudness and verum-focus seems to predominate. However, there are cases which show only one feature, i.e. either a global increase of loudness (12) or verum-focus (13). One might

be tempted to conclude that a reproachful voice must employ at
least one of these devices. However, as the next transcript segment
indicates, this is not necessarily the case: even when both features
are missing, a 'why'-utterance may still be interpreted as a
reproach.[15]
Marianne has suggested to her friend Ina that she put in an
application for a job with the GFA company. Marianne has worked
for this company before and was quite pleased with her job. After
going for an interview, Ina calls Marianne and complains about the
interview situation. She states that she is not going to apply for jobs
'at this kind of company any more'. Marianne now responds:

(14) Idioten (*Idiots*)
      39 MARIANNE: du hasch jetzt ne *völlig andre Erfahrung gmacht bei
                    der GFA als ich.
                    you just had a totally different experience from mine
                    at GFA
      40   i mein' (-) des hängt einfach zsamme *wer in diesem
                    Interview [sitzt]
                    I mean' (-) h' it depends on who is doing the
                    interviewing
      41 INA: [ja. ja.]
                                yeah yeah
      42 MARIANNE: und du HATTESCHT da wohl ziemliche IDI*O↑↓TEN.
                    and you must have had some real idiots
      43   hh' oder aber=was=natürlich=e'=
                    hh' or of course what e'
      44   es kann schon sein daß die al*lergisch reagieren
                    it might be that they reacted allergically
      45   wenn sie merken da *kommt jemand
                    when they noticed that this is someone
      46   die will eigentlich eher ↑*wiss↓enschaftlich [(arbeiten)]
                    who would rather do scientific work
      47 INA: [ja aber]
                                                               yes but
  →   48 INA: warum lassen se mich dann [*KO:MM↑↓]EN
                    Marianne.=
                    why did they ask me to come then Marianne
      49 MARIANNE: [ja]
                                               yes
      50 MARIANNE: =ja. ja.=
                    yes yes
      51 INA: ich mein die ham doch hundertzwanzig *Leut
                    I mean they have a hundred and twenty people

After Marianne's attempt to find possible reasons for the negative outcome of the job-interview (lines 42–46), Ina counters, signalling an upcoming disagreement (*ja aber* (l.47)) and then produces a 'why'-utterance *warum lassen se mich dann* *KO:MM↑↓EN *Marianne*. (l.48). The verb *KO:MM↑↓EN carries the main accent and is marked with extra loudness. The first syllable has an elongated vowel with a slowly rising–falling glide: Ina's voice sounds highly irritated and has a whiny quality to it. This affective loading is increased even more when she calls her interlocutor by name and thus employs a re-alignment technique. Although the description of behaviour in question, *kommen lassen*, is not evaluative by itself, Ina's 'lamenting voice' portrays it as negatively evaluated. The combination of vowel elongation and rising–falling glide is a prosodically marked feature in German phonology and can be treated as a form of prosodic hyperbole based on *amplificatio*. *Amplificatio* as a rhetorical device involves affective intensification or even exaggeration in order to highlight the negative or positive aspects of a topic (Quintilian 1972/1975:8, 4, 28) and to persuade the listener of the legitimacy of a claim. In this context the expressive tone signals an affectively loaded negative evaluation of the action in question and renders it a 'reproachable'.[16]

The 'why'-reproach (lines 47–48) has an interesting sequential embedding: Marianne reacts to Ina's complaint about GFA with a possible interpretation of the event (lines 39ff.). Ina takes this account as a potential excuse for the company's procedure and utters a reproach. This puts Marianne in the interactive position of representing the moral addressee. By now providing agreement tokens (*ja. ja.*, line 50), Marianne not only demonstrates her interpretation of the prior turn as a justified reproach but also signals her co-alignment with Ina's disapproval, thus distancing herself from the moral addressee. This documents how the interactive roles of producer and moral addressee in reproaches are locally constructed.

The analysis so far indicates that, if certain prosodic features such as increase of loudness, expressive pitch movement, lengthening and glide accompany the 'why'-format, they tend to function as prosodic hyperboles, affectively amplifying and highlighting the behaviour at issue. Such affectively loaded 'why'-utterances are then interpreted as reproach activities with specific sequential implications: in cases where the moral addressee is present, they initiate a remedial interchange, making accounts or apologies conditionally relevant. When the moral addressee is not present, a signalling of co-alignment towards the negative assessment of the behaviour at issue is expectable.

The next segment demonstrates that, in addition to the features of marked prosody observed in reproach activities so far (increase of loudness, verum-focus, rising–falling glide, increase of tempo), staccato accentuation with clear-cut, abrupt syllables may also occur.

In this conversation between Dora and her friend Leo, Dora calls their common acquaintance Pia 'impertinent'. She uses irony to express her disapproval of Pia's behaviour ('how very considerate', line 11). Leo now defends Pia and questions Dora about her negative assessment:

(15) Verdammt nochmal (*Damn it*)
       11 DORA: des's *RÜCK.sichtsvoll.
                  how very considerate
       12   (0.8)
→   13 LEO: h' wie' wieso: (.) verDAMMT↑↓. NOCH.MAL. eh'
                  *HASCH↑↓ jetzt da einfach'
                  h' why damn it do you just have to'
       14   du' du *WEISCH↑↓ wie das' wie das in diesem Kaff dort
                  dort au läuft. und [und]
                  *you you know how it' how things work in that godfor-
                  saken town. and and*
       15 DORA: [ja.]
                                      yes.
       16 DORA: aber=daß=es=dort=IDI*O:↑↓TEN=gibt=und=solche=die's=
                  nicht=sind.
                  *but that some of the people there are idiots and others
                  aren't*
       17   DES=WEISS-I=*↑AU.
                  that I know too

After Dora's ironic evaluation of Pia's behaviour, Leo produces an utterance with a 'why'-format (line 13). Although he breaks the construction off, the accent placement shows verum-focus on the finite verb *HASCH↑↓*. This 'why'-utterance carries high affective colouring: it has a local increase of loudness, high falls on DAMMT↑↓, *HASCH↑↓ and *WEISCH↑↓ and a staccato articulation of DAMMT↑↓.NOCH.MAL. These prosodic features co-occur

with the swearwords _verDAMMT↑↓.NOCH.MAL_ (l.13) and imply
a negative judgement of Dora's actions. Here too the recipient of
the affectively loaded 'why'-utterance reacts by returning the high
level of affect (lines 15–17): Dora not only produces a turn with a
dissenting format, neatly tied to the prior turn by taking up some of
its lexical items (_du *WEISCH↑↓. . .WEISS=I_), but she also uses
prosodic affect marking (increase of loudness, increase of tempo,
rise–falls) to signal her own irritation.

As this excerpt illustrates, a communicative intent – such as
reproaching – is frequently signalled on different levels simultaneously: syntactic, lexico-semantic, rhetorical and prosodic. Such
redundancy of coding facilitates the process of inferencing: the
cues have a mutually intensifying effect which results in the enact-
ment of, for example, a reproach context (Auer 1992). The more
cues that come together, the less ambiguous is the interpretation of
the activity as a reproach.

Concerning the verbal level, the cues that may indicate reproach
activities include:

(i) lexico-semantic devices such as negatively loaded terminology
(_gefallen lassen_ 'accept all this', _zugeben_ 'admit', _warum zum Teufel_
'why the hell', _verdammt nochmal_ 'damn it') and certain modal
particles (_denn, auch_). These features signal a negative evaluation
of the action focussed on;

(ii) rhetorical devices such as linguistic hyperboles and extreme
case formulations (such as _immer_ 'always'; _vor Jahren_ 'years ago').
These function as upgrading devices to stress the seriousness and
repeatedness of the offence reported. Furthermore, _wenn. . .dann_
constructions are employed as 'quasi-logical arguments', placing
the moral addressee in a situation of incompatibility.

When these verbal cues co-occur with the prosodic devices identified here, they not only distinguish different communicative meanings (such as reproaching versus 'real' questions) but are also
sequentially constitutive, as they implicate specific types of participant reaction.

4 Is there a 'reproachful voice'?

Now, if prosodic cues are related to the process of inferencing and
help to enact the context in which the interpretation of a reproach

takes place, then one might ask: are there any reproach-specific prosodic cues? Can one find empirical evidence for what in ethnotheoretic terms is called a 'reproachful voice'?

When we consider the reproaches analysed here, prosodic displays of affect turn out to be their common characteristic. In fact, the interrelationship between 'moral work' and the activation of affective frames (signalling anger, indignation, astonishment, etc.) has been mentioned in empirical studies on other moralizing activities, e.g. gossiping,[17] moral indignation[18] and complaints.[19] Studies within moral psychology argue that we tend to react with feelings of shame or guilt when we ourselves violate moral norms which we take as being valid. When our moral expectations are disappointed by the actions of another person, we react by displaying emotions such as indignation or anger.[20] If affective involvement seems to be at stake in communicative situations where speakers moralize, one might ask if specific prosodic devices exist that indicate particular (moralizing activities and) affective stances.

So far, there have been very few detailed empirical analyses of affective talk in naturally situated everyday interaction, although the relationship between prosody and affect display has been emphasized again and again.[21] In their work on language and affect, Ochs and Schieffelin (1989) describe some of the linguistic resources available to speakers across languages and communities for displaying dispositions, moods, attitudes and feelings. Among these linguistic features, which include particles, affixes, pronominal systems, qualifiers, emphatics, hedges, adverbs, verb voice, tense/aspect systems, modals, word order and repetitions, they also list 'phonological features' such as intonation, voice quality, sound repetition and sound symbolism. However, they do not show how these parameters work in detail.[22]

In her survey of the relationship between prosody and affect, Couper-Kuhlen (1986:173) points out that most of the previous studies on prosody and the signalling of affect have been unsatisfactory: the heterogeneity and the inadequacy of many experiments make a comparison of the results extremely difficult. Furthermore, these experimental studies try to examine the prosody of affect in a context-free way, ignoring the fact that affect display in everyday interaction is part of larger communicative activities or genres, and that prosodic cues do not appear in isolation but always occur concurrently with lexico-semantic and syntactic structures, with rhetorical elements and paralinguistic features such as 'tone of voice'.[23]

Looking once more at the 'why'-formats which appear in the *in situ* reproaches examined here, we obtain the following picture:

(1) ↑ ⟨warum *LÄ:SCH↑↓ se au immer rei:. . .⟩
(5) WARUM ZUM TEUFEL *FRA:GSCH↑↓ SE DANN NET DIREKT.
(6a) WARUM *HAST↑↓ DENN NISCHTS REI:NGETAN.
(6b) =nei:n warum *HAT↑↓ se's dann [nisch REIN]getan.=
(7) WARUM=*SA:↑↓GEN=SIE=DANN=KONSTANZ.
(8) und wo ↑rum↓ läsch du dir des au IMMER g*FA:LL↑↓N.
(9) ↑ ⟨warum=*MA:CHSCH↑↓=du=eigentlich=NIE=en=Kühlschrank= richtig=zu.⟩
(10) ↑ ⟨WARUM *GE↑↓BEN SIE DAS NICH MAL ZU.⟩
(12) JA WARUM HÄNDT SIE'S DENN V[OR ↓*JAH:↑↓] REN NET GMACHT.
(13) [wa]rum *TU::N↑↓ Sie's dann nicht.=
(14) warum lassen se mich dann [*KO:MM↑↓]EN Marianne.=
(15) h'wie' wieso: (.) verDAMMT↑↓. NOCH.MAL. eh' *HASCH↑↓ jetzt da einfach'

These utterances can be divided into two groups with respect to primary accent placement:

(i) 'why'-utterances showing narrow focus: a contrastive interpretation is intended in (12); the problematic item is refocussed in (8) and (14);

(ii) 'why'-utterances showing a verum-focus: (1), (5), (6a,b), (7), (9), (10), (13) and (15). Accent placement is marked, due to the fact that the main accent is shifted to the left and placed on the finite verb. (6a), (6b) and (15) are the most striking cases, as the accentuated finite verb has no lexical content. The accent shift to the farthermost verb in a non-contrastive German utterance is used to indicate emphasis: the utterance sounds more insisting and slightly impatient.

In eleven out of the twelve cases, the verb carries the primary accent, and in all these cases there is a rise–fall. The speaker is thus signalling expectation problems concerning some inadequate action or behaviour by the moral addressee.

Concerning the prosodic parameters of reproach activities, there appear to be:

(i) certain prosodic features that are activated in all 'why'-reproaches: falling terminal pitch, rising–falling (falling–rising) pitch movements, narrow or verum-focus;

(ii) prosodic features that appear in most 'why'-reproaches: global increase of loudness, lengthening and glide on the verb, primary accent placement on the verb;

(iii) prosodic features that show up occasionally: increase of tempo, staccato accentuation.

As terminal falling pitch and rising–falling/falling–rising pitch movement, as well as narrow or verum-focus are also used in other activities, this compilation indicates that it is impossible to detect a single prosodic parameter which – in a context-free manner – is always and exclusively distinctive for a 'reproachful voice'. Instead there appears to be an interplay of various prosodic cues that – in combination with other linguistic, rhetorical and contextual features – constitutes a context in which 'why'-formats are interpretable as reproaches. Generally the prosodic marking we find in 'why'-formats comes close to what Selting (1994) calls 'emphasis'. However, as 'emphasis' can be used to signal a great variety of affective stances (such as interest, relevance, importance, unexpectedness and high positive as well as high negative emotional load), this category seems to be too broad for our analysis: it cannot explain what enables participants to differentiate between 'why'-formats signalling great interest or positive surprise from reproaches. Thus, the contextualization cues for reproaching must be more specific. A closer look at the 'why'-utterances that signal reproach demonstrates that prosodically signalled 'emphasis' co-occurs with falling terminal pitch and a narrow or verum-focus.

This observation is in agreement with Selting's (1992) analysis of German prosody in conversational questions. Contrary to Pheby (1981), who states that German *w-Fragen* 'wh-questions' call for falling terminal pitch in unmarked cases, and that if they show rising terminal pitch, they are to be interpreted as 'polite', 'interested' and 'interpersonally marked', Selting (1992) maintains that prosodic devices such as terminal pitch are used to distinguish between different types of conversational questions, e.g. non-restricted and restricted questions: *wieso-* and *warum-* ('why'-) questions with rising terminal pitch are treated as non-restricted 'open' questions, whereas falling terminal pitch signals a contradiction between the speaker's and the interlocutor's expectations and invites the interlocutor to deal with this problem of expectation in the subsequent turn. The difference between these 'why'-utterances and the 'why'-formats in my data is that the former tend to be prosodically unmarked. A further distinction lies in the fact that problems of expectation can also be signalled just by uttering the question words *warum* or *wieso* ('why'), whereas in reproaches the offensive or neglected behaviour is (explicitly) mentioned. In spite of this, reproach activities seem to be related to 'why'-questions signalling a problem of expectation because, in reproaches, the violation of expectations concerning appropriate behaviour is focussed on. What distinguishes them from general expectation problems, however, is that they are not value-neutral, but contain a negative evaluation. Thus, the combination of emphatic prosody (such as increase of loudness, expressive pitch movement, lengthening, glide, etc.) with falling terminal pitch and narrow or verum-focus restricts the number of possible interpretations. Moreover, in many of the cases examined here, the speaker's voice has a 'lamenting' tone, which clearly indexes a negative evaluation. The impression of 'lamenting' is signalled by a rising–falling glide on an elongated vowel: *LÄ:SCH↑↓, *FRA:GSCH↑↓, *SA:↑↓GEN, g*FA:LL↑↓N, *MA:CHSCH↑↓, *TU::N↑↓, *KO:MM↑↓EN.

Instead of there being one specific reproach parameter, a combination of prosodic features seems to be responsible for the fact that 'why'-utterances in moralizing contexts take on the interpretative value of a reproach. The ethnotheoretic term 'reproachful voice' can thus be seen as a folk-label used for the context-sensitive interpretation of these cues in particular kinds of sequential environments.

5 The non-accountability of prosodic cues

The question I want to address now is why so many reproaches are packaged in 'why'-formats.

As my data show, there are many cases where a bundle of cues co-occur and where this 'co-occurrence in configuration' (Silverstein 1993:48) gives a specific 'prototypical reading' to the utterance. However, participants also construct 'why'-formats that do not show co-occurring, redundant contextualization cues and do not unambiguously allow a process of inferencing which clearly signals a reproach. Instead, these formats are uttered with an opaquely 'reproachful tone' – and show no other verbal indications of reproach, as the following fragment illustrates.

This transcript is taken from a family dinner conversation, during which the children R and G are serving punch. They are talking about the fruits they have added to the punch, when the father (V) asks the children why they bought the peaches (line 18):

```
(16)  Cocktail
      15  V:  was *Bo:le? (ä) (fer/tische scho/n). (fertig Mischun)
              what punch (er) (ready-made) (ready made)
      16  R:                      nehm=wer noch [ma:l (.)] *Pfirische mit;
                                  you take peaches
      17  G:                      [jaa::.]
                                  yeah
  →   18  V:  worum habt Ihr *DIE↑↓ gekauft. (-)*l(h)OHNT sisch [das].
              why did you buy those (-) was it worth it
      19  G:                                              [isch]
                                                          I

      20      wollte das ma pro*biern;
              wanted to give it a try
      21      ne *Ma:rk neununneunzisch
              one mark ninety-nine
```

V produces a 'why'-utterance (line 18), adding a potential reason for the behaviour in question. Based on the discussion so far, the inference to be drawn from the prosodic realization of this utterance is that of a reproach. The utterance has falling terminal pitch, contrastive focus and a rise–fall on *DIE↑↓. The second phrase is separated from the 'why'-utterance by a short pause (-). *l(h)OHNT carries the primary accent and is articulated with increased loudness and falling intonation, indicating that the utterance is not intended as a 'real' question. Instead, V seems to assume that it is *not* worthwhile. G's reaction, however – she first states her reason for buying the peaches and then mentions the price, thus answering the second part of the 'why'-turn – is prosodically unmarked and could actually be an answer to a 'real' question.

This example demonstrates that 'why'-formats with prosodic contextualization appropriate for reproaching actually leave a certain amount of interpretative 'room' which co-participants may orientate to: the syntactic structure of a 'why'-utterance – even if it is realized with a reproachful tone – means that the recipient can always decide to interpret the utterance as a genuine question.

Instead of maintaining a clearly polarized distinction between (i) 'why'-formats which imply reproach and lead to apologies or accounts, and (ii) 'why'-formats which signal 'real' questions, speakers may produce 'why'-utterances which do not show such unambiguity, but rather 'play' with ambiguity and interpretative vagueness. We thus have an example of what Silverstein (1976:47) calls the 'pragmatic indeterminacy of utterances that can be manipulated by the individuals in an interaction'. The formats at hand enable interlocutors to negotiate a kind of buffer zone in which the expression of a negatively loaded evaluation of the other's behaviour is hinted at without this necessarily having serious interpersonal consequences. I would argue that this structural ambiguity is one of the reasons why so many reproaches are packaged in 'why'-formats. With a 'why'-utterance the speaker first of all asks for reasons and explanations for the behaviour in question, presenting the focussed action as not understandable in itself. This leaves the addressee the possibility to treat the 'why'-utterance as a 'real' question and provide reasons. Consequently, 'why'-formats can be seen as conversational 'pre-sequences' (Levinson 1983), which are used to check out whether there is any reason which might have led, or even 'forced', the addressee to do the seemingly inappropriate act. If the recipient provides such reasons or initiates remedial work right away, the speaker can avoid the dispreferred activity of producing a direct reproach. Thus, 'why'-utterances represent 'off record' strategies: they are often realized in such a way 'that it is not possible to attribute only a clear communicative intention to the act' (Brown and Levinson 1978:216). Speakers leave themselves an 'out' by providing several defensible interpretations and cannot be held to have committed themselves to just one particular interpretation of the utterance. Off-record strategies are – as Brown and Levinson (1978:216) show – important devices which speakers use when they want to perform a face-threatening activity but wish to avoid the responsibility for doing so.

This kind of conversational indirectness is an important device in everyday moralizing: if a generally obligatory moral code can no longer be taken for granted in modern societies, and one cannot be reasonably certain about one's interlocutor's moral attitudes and views, explicit moralizing becomes a risky intersubjective undertaking. Thus, forms of moral indirectness and obliqueness become important devices in everyday moral interactions. As, in reproaches, not only a general action or type of behaviour is judged according to someone's moral norms, but the behaviour of the co-participant is negatively evaluated, this activity bears a face-threatening potential and can provoke teasing, counter-reproaches, and may even end up in quarrelling. Goffman (1971:156) refers to the interactive risk of 'priming moves', as he calls the initiating step of a remedial interchange, and remarks that – due to this risk – they tend to be uttered 'in various disguises'. Instead of an 'outright challenge, we are likely to find devices such as a "set-up question": should the asker receive the expected answer, he will be in a clear position to challenge or to negatively sanction the respondent, but at the same time he leaves a little room open for an unanticipated answer that might adequately account for the apparent infraction'.

Due to their structural ambivalence and their 'disguise' as potential questions, 'why'-formats provide for what Silverstein (1976: 47–48) calls 'diplomatic nonindexicality'. Speakers have the opportunity to retreat by disputing the reproach frame, claiming that they meant their question literally. They may thus take the 'semantico-referential function of speech' as the officially or overtly recognized one, to which they 'may retreat with full social approval' and thereby avoid any possible offence to the recipient. Common formulas for this kind of opting out are: *Ich hab ja bloß gefragt. Reg dich doch nicht so auf*, 'I was just asking a question. Don't get so jumpy about it', or *man wird ja nochmal fragen dürfen*, 'there is nothing wrong with asking, is there'. Hearers – on the other hand – may also manipulate the pragmatic indeterminacy of the 'why'-format, as it allows them to respond to the utterance 'as though it constituted a semantico-referential event, all the while understanding completely the distinct function of the indexes which overlap in surface form' (Silverstein 1976:48). This playing with pragmatic indeterminacy is possible when the producer of the potential reproach uses primarily prosodic cues, because prosody is less accountable than, for example, syntactic, lexico-semantic and rhetorical features are. Due to its great 'sensitivity, elasticity, and freedom', prosody 'always lies on the border of the verbal and nonverbal, the said and the unsaid', as Vološinov (1976:102) maintains. It neither carries referential meaning nor is it – due to individual voice differences – easily reproduced. When prosodic means are referred to at all it is usually metapragmatically ('Your tone was so reproachful', 'It was the way you said it that implied that you were angry').

6 Conclusion

This chapter has concentrated on one communicative activity of everyday moralizing – reproaching in 'why'-formats – and has studied the prosodic means which participants use to carry out this moral work.

The analysis has demonstrated that in 'why'-formats prosodic marking functions as a contextualization cue to differentiate between 'real' questions and reproach activities and thus has important sequential implications. However, rather than being able to isolate a single unambiguous cue that only and always contextualizes a 'reproachful voice', we are confronted with an interplay of prosodic features which – in co-occurrence with lexico-semantic, rhetorical and sequential cues – guide participants' inferences concerning the activity in question. The prosodic features that are used to signal a reproach include: falling terminal pitch, global increase of loudness, extreme rising–falling (or falling–rising) pitch movements, falling glides on lengthened syllables, narrow or verum-focus, staccato accentuation and increase of tempo. Combinations of these prosodic features, which trigger the impression of affective irritation and thus a negative evaluation of the topic at hand, are regularly accompanied by lexico-semantic devices (such as negative-affect terminology or modal particles) as well as rhetorical devices (*amplificatio* figures or *wenn. . .dann* structures).

The analysis thus indicates that prosodic cues – in co-occurrence with syntactic, lexico-semantic and rhetorical ones – function as part of a signalling system used by participants to index and interpret meaning in everyday communication and, in our special case, to distinguish between 'real questions' and moralizing reproaches.

Appendix: transcription conventions

[ja das] finde ich	conversational overlap
[du ab]	
(-)	short pauses of less than 0.5 sec.
(0.5)	pauses of 0.5 sec. and longer
(??)	unintelligible text
(gestern)	uncertain transcription
=	continuous utterances
=und=dann=ging=	fast tempo
÷	slow tempo
?	intonation phrase-final: rising
′	intonation phrase-final: slightly rising
.	intonation phrase-final: falling
,	intonation phrase-final: slightly falling
↑ ⟨word word⟩	global high pitch
↓ ⟨word word⟩	global low pitch
↑like↓	high fall
↓like↑	low rise
like↑↓	rise–fall
*WO:HR	primary accent of the intonational phrase
a:	lengthening
°no°	soft voice
°°no°°	very soft voice
NEIN	loud voice
<u>no</u>	strong accent, emphasized
to.tal.ge.nervt.	staccato-like rhythm
mo((hi))mentan	laugh particles within the utterance
hihi	giggling
hahaha	laughter
((hustet))	non-lexical phenomena (e.g. coughing)

Notes

I would like to thank Peter Auer, Jörg Bergmann, Thomas Luckmann, Margret Selting, Ruth Ayaß and Gabi Christmann for their helpful comments on this chapter. Many thanks also to Kajo Koch, Rainer Rothenhäusler and Allison Wetterlin, who listened to the tapes and checked the prosodic features. I am extremely grateful to Elizabeth Couper-Kuhlen not only for her valuable suggestions but also her support all through the different versions of this paper.

1 All examples quoted in the text are taken from authentic conversations.
2 *Wenn. . .dann* formulations are commonly found in reproaches. See Günthner (1993).

3 For a discussion of apologies see Goffman (1971) and Owen (1983).
4 In the special case of self-reproaches, the producer and moral addressee of the reproach are identical. Cf. the following transcript, in which Zora reconstructs a self-reproach:

Gottfroh (*Very happy*)
48 Maya: HH: ch' Zora (-) ja. ich bin so hh' gottfro:h
   HH ch' Zora (-) yeah I am so hh' very happy
49 Zora: ich hab mir da Vorwürfe gemacht. warum hab ich ihr das gesacht.
   I reproached myself again and again   why did I tell her about it.
50 Maya: n' nein. des war schon richtig. daß du mirs gesagt hast.
   n' no. it was good that you told me about it

5 According to Scott and Lyman (1968) 'accounts', which are likely to be invoked when a person is accused of having done something 'bad', 'wrong', 'inept', etc., consist of 'excuses' and 'justifications'. Whereas with a justification, the speaker accepts responsibility for the act in question but at the same time denies the pejorative quality associated with it, an excuse – on the other hand – is used to admit that the action in question is wrong, inappropriate or bad, but the speaker denies full responsibility (for example, by appeal to accident or misfortune).
6 The modal particle *au*, which is the Swabian version of *auch*, tends to signal a negative evaluation of an event. See Engel (1988:232).
7 As I am not concerned with speakers' sincere dispositions but rather with conventional displays of emotion, I shall use the term 'affect' as proposed by Ochs and Schieffelin (1989:7) taking it to be 'a broader term than emotion, to include feelings, moods, dispositions and attitudes associated with persons and/or situations'.
8 'Global' refers to the use of pitch or loudness for an entire turn-constructional unit. See Selting (in this volume).
9 I am grateful to Susanne Uhmann and Margret Selting for suggesting the concept of 'verum-focus' in this context.
10 The effect thus seems to be similar to that of 'verum-focus' in imperatives, which gives utterances an emphatic and insisting tone (Höhle 1991–1992:119).
11 A further difference lies in the candidate answer given in this sequence. Candidate answers may help to decrease the possibility of interpreting the 'why'-utterance as a reproach.
12 In accordance with Selting (this volume), 'marked prosody' refers to 'a conspicuous, noticeable realization of parameters which may trigger special inferences'.
13 Reactions to reproaches in 'why'-formats may also be ambiguous: providing a reason can be seen as a reaction to a 'why'-question as well as a justification to a reproach. See Bergmann (1992) on utterance sequences which on the surface seem to be 'innocent, helpful and affiliate utterances', yet have a hidden 'veiled morality' structurally built in.

14 Lexico-semantic forms of *amplificatio*, which are used as a means of intensification and exaggeration, come close to what Pomerantz (1986) calls 'extreme case formulations'.

15 This excerpt differs from the ones analysed so far because the reproach is uttered *in absentia* and makes somewhat different recipient reactions expectable. However, prosodic cues are also used in this case to signal the reproach activity.

16 Extreme rising–falling (or falling–rising) pitch movements or 'sing-song-intonation' (Retzinger 1991, Christmann 1993) have also been referred to as signalling 'indignation'. Yet this kind of expressive pitch cannot be considered a sufficient cue for signalling indignation, as it also occurs in other contexts where in co-occurrence with linguistic cues it signals other affects (e.g. lamenting). However, it does seem to enact an affectively loaded context. See Günthner (1995) and Christmann (1993) for prosody in indignation stories.

17 See Bergmann (1987).

18 See Günthner (1995) and Christmann (1993).

19 See Drew (1992).

20 See Tugendhat (1993).

21 For a discussion of prosody and affect see Ochs and Schieffelin (1989) and Selting (1994).

22 See Besnier (1990) for a survey of findings on affect and language behaviour.

23 See Crystal (1969:282–308).

References

Auer, P. 1992. Introduction: John Gumperz' approach to contextualization. In P. Auer and A. Di Luzio (eds.) *The Contextualization of Language*. Amsterdam and Philadelphia: Benjamins, pp. 1–38.

Bergmann, J. 1987. *Klatsch. Zur Sozialform der diskreten Indiskretion*. Berlin: de Gruyter.

1992. Veiled morality: notes on discretion in psychiatry. In P. Drew and J. Heritage (eds.) *Talk at Work*. Cambridge University Press, pp. 137–162.

Bergmann, J. and T. Luckmann 1993. *Formen der kommunikativen Konstruktion von Moral: Gattungsfamilien der moralischen Kommunikation in informellen, institutionellen und massenmedialen Kontexten*. MORAL-Projekt: Arbeitspapier 1. University of Konstanz.

Besnier, N. 1990. Language and affect. *Annual Review of Anthropology*, 19: 419–451.

Brown, P. and S. Levinson 1978. Universals in language usage: politeness phenomena. In E. M. Goody (ed.) *Questions and Politeness*. Cambridge University Press, pp. 56–324.

Christmann, G. B. 1993. 'Und da hab ich wirklich so einen Zornesausbruch gekriegt. . .'. Moral mit Affekt: die moralische Entrüstung am Beispiel von Ökologie-Gruppen. MORAL-Projekt: 6. University of Konstanz.

Couper-Kuhlen, E. 1986. An Introduction to English Prosody. London: Edward Arnold and Tübingen: Niemeyer.

Crystal, D. 1969. Prosodic Systems and Intonation in English. Cambridge University Press.

Drew, P. 1992. On morality and conduct: complaints about transgressions and misconduct. Paper presented at the Werner Reimers Stiftung Conference on Moral Dimensions of Dialogue, Bad Homburg, Nov. 1992.

Engel, U. 1988. Deutsche Grammatik. Heidelberg: Julius Groos.

Goffman, E. 1971. Relations in Public. Microstudies of the public order. New York: Basic Books.

Gumperz, J. J. 1982. Discourse Strategies. Cambridge University Press.

Günthner, S. 1993. 'Kannst du auch über andere Leute lästern.' Vorwürfe als Formen moralischer Kommunikation. MORAL-Projekt: Arbeitspapier 9. University of Konstanz.

    1995. Exemplary stories. The cooperative construction of moral indignation. In Examples. Special issue of VERSUS: 70: 145–173.

Höhle, T. N. 1991–1992. Über Verum-Fokus im Deutschen. In J. Jacobs (ed.) Informationsstruktur und Grammatik. Linguistische Berichte, Special issue 4, pp. 112–142.

König, E. 1977. Modalpartikeln in Fragesätzen. In H. Weydt (ed.) Aspekte der Modalpartikeln. Tübingen: Niemeyer, pp. 115–130.

Levinson, S. C. 1983. Pragmatics. Cambridge University Press.

Luckmann, T. 1993. Moralizing communication: observations on some modern procedures. Paper presented at the Centre for the Study of Cultural Values' conference on De-Traditionalization: Authority and Self in an Age of Cultural Uncertainty. Lancaster. July 1993.

Lucy, J. 1993. Metapragmatic presentationals: reporting speech with quotatives in Yucatec Maya. In J. Lucy (ed.) Reflexive Language. Cambridge University Press, pp. 91–126.

McHugh, P. 1970. A common-sense conception of deviance. In J. D. Douglas (ed.) Deviance and Respectability. New York: Basic Books, pp. 61–88.

Müller, F. E. 1991. Metrical emphasis: Rhythmic scansions in Italian conversation. KontRI Working Paper 14. University of Konstanz.

Ochs, E. and B. Schieffelin 1989. Language has a heart. Text, 9: 7–25.

Owen, M. 1983. Apologies and Remedial Interchanges. A study of language use in social interaction. Berlin, New York, Amsterdam: Mouton.

Perelman, C. 1982. The Realm of Rhetoric. London: University of Notre Dame Press.

Pheby, J. 1981. Intonation. In K. E. Heidolph, W. Flämig and W. Motsch, *Grundzüge einer deutschen Grammatik*. Berlin: Akademie-Verlag, pp. 839–897.

Pomerantz, A. 1986. Extreme case formulations: a way of legitimizing claims. *Human Studies*, 9: 219–229.

Quintilian, M. F. 1972/1975. *Ausbildung des Redners*. Darmstadt: Wissenschaftliche Buchgesellschaft.

Retzinger, S. M. 1991. Shame, anger, and conflict: case study of emotional violence. *Journal of Family Violence*, 6(1): 37–59.

Schütz, A. 1971. *Gesammelte Aufsätze. Bd. I: Das Problem der sozialen Wirklichkeit*. The Hague: Martinus Nijhoff.

Scott, M. and S. Lyman 1968. Accounts. *American Sociological Review*, 33: 46–62.

Selting, M. 1992. Prosody in conversational questions. *Journal of Pragmatics*, 17: 315–345.

1994. Emphatic speech style – with special focus on the prosodic signalling of heightened emotive involvement in conversation. In C. Caffi and R. W. Janney (eds.) *Involvement in Language*. Special issue of *Journal of Pragmatics*, 22: 375–408.

1995. *Prosodie im Gespräch. Aspekte einer interaktionalen Phonologie der Konversation*. Tübingen: Niemeyer.

Silverstein, M. 1976. Shifters, linguistic categories, and cultural description. In K. H. Basso and H. A. Selby (eds.) *Meaning in Anthropology*. Albuquerque: University of New Mexico Press, pp. 11–55.

1993. Metapragmatic discourse and metapragmatic function. In J. Lucy (ed.) *Reflexive Language. Reported speech and metapragmatics*. Cambridge University Press, pp. 33–58.

Tugendhat, E. 1993. Die Rolle der Identität in der Konstitution der Moral. In W. Edelstein, G. Nunner-Winkler and G. Noam (eds) *Moral und Person*. Frankfurt: Suhrkamp, pp. 33–47.

Vološinov, V. N. 1976. *Freudianism. A marxist critique*, trans. by I. R. Titunik. New York: Academic Press.

8

On rhythm in everyday German conversation: beat clashes in assessment utterances

SUSANNE UHMANN

1 Introduction

This chapter deals with a rhythmical phenomenon that has been described as *beat clash* in metrical phonology. Beat clashes are highly marked rhythmical structures in which the phonologically unmarked alternation between prominent and non-prominent syllables is cancelled in favour of a succession of prominent syllables. It will be shown that participants in natural German conversation not only let beat clashes happen, but that beat clashes are actively constructed by turning non-prominent syllables into prominent ones. These achieved beat clashes regularly occur within assessment utterances, but seem to be restrained by sequential constraints: beat clashes occur in extended first assessments like stories, news or informings and in seconds to these conversational objects, but they are absent in first and second assessments of assessment pairs. This absence is claimed to be not accidental but systematic and it is accounted for by regarding the operative preference structure of assessments.

I will thus start the chapter by discussing the organization of assessment pairs and stress some differences between German and English data. In section 3 a phonological account of beat clashes will be presented. Section 4 deals with the analysis of beat clashes in assessment utterances and section 5 with the absence of beat clashes in assessment pairs.

2 Assessments

Assessments represent a good choice as an object of research since collecting instances in everyday conversation quickly leads to a large corpus. Whatever the subject of the conversation seems to be, the participants routinely make assessments. Talking about a person, an event or an experience and assessing that person, that event and that experience seem to be tightly linked and sometimes even inseparably intertwined. Following Goodwin and Goodwin (1992:154f.), I distinguish between (i) the phenomenon or referent being assessed, i.e. the *assessable*, (ii) the linguistic means for assessing, i.e. the *assessment signals: lexical assessment terms* like *toll* ('great'), *irrsinnig* ('terrific'), *Bilderbuchstrand* ('storybook beach'), etc. or *non-lexical assessment sounds* like *ahhh* or *haaa* 'whose main function seems to be the carrying of an appropriate intonation contour' (Goodwin 1986:214); (iii) the turn or utterance containing an assessment signal, i.e. the *assessment turn* or *assessment utterance*, and (iv) the person using an assessment signal, i.e. the *assessor*.

Assessment terms occur at different loci in conversation. One place, which was described in the seminal work of Pomerantz (1975, 1984) and adopted for German data in Auer and Uhmann (1982), is in turns just subsequent to an initial assessment term. The production of a first or initial assessment by speaker A and a second assessment by speaker B, the recipient of the first assessment, is called an *assessment sequence* or *assessment pair* if the referent in the second assessment is the same as in the first. As the use of an assessment term does not necessarily imply the speaker's intention to open up an assessment sequence, Pomerantz – following a major claim of ethnomethodological conversation analysis – put her emphasis on the reaction of the recipient as the main resource of interpretation. As a result second assessments turn out to be the most important cue for the interpretation of an assessment sequence. From the sequential point of view first and second assessments are closely connected. Although Pomerantz avoids the term *adjacency pair*, she claims that 'the initial assessment provides the relevance of the recipient's second assessment' (Pomerantz 1984:61). However, as assessors can be held responsible for the positions they state, the occurrence of a second assessment depends

on the recipient's knowledge of what is being assessed. Yet knowing
the assessable doesn't necessarily mean that speaker and recipient
share its evaluation. With respect to the initial assessment a recipient has two options: he or she may decide to *agree* with a prior
assessment or may alternatively decide to *disagree*. Detailed analysis
of the sequential organization of assessment sequences has shown
that these options are not equivalent, but constrained by multiple
layers of preferences for second assessments, which depend on the
activity type initiated by the first assessment.[1] Yet in the majority of
assessment pairs the operative preference structure is: agreement
preferred, disagreement dispreferred and 'across different situations, conversants orient to agreeing with one another as comfor-
table, supportive, reinforcing, perhaps as being sociable and as
showing that they are like-minded' (Pomerantz 1984:77).[2]

The following transcripts provide evidence that interlocutors do
indeed show a formal preference for agreement – irrespective of
whether they are talking about men, antique shops, sailors or
professors. The first assessment is marked by one asterisk (*) the
second by two (**), transcription conventions employed are listed
in the appendix:

```
(1)   Hundertfünfzig 14
        1 H: wie alt,
        2 X: ja:: so:: sechsenzwanzig glaub=ich
 *      3 H: "schö::nes Alter
 **     4 X: ja ne hehe (0.8) 'best(h)en 'Jah(h)re

        1 H: how old
        2 X: oh about twenty-six I think
 *      3 H: nice age
 **     4 X: yeah huh hehe (0.8) prime years


(2)   Antiquitäten 1
        1 N: also (.) mmh (.) dieser Antiquitätenladen da euch gegenüber,
 *      2    also der hat ja schon nen mords Verhau in sein Laden=
        3 X: =wie, wo? ah=so
 **     4    ja da siehts schon oft ganz grauenvoll aus;

        1 N: well (.) mmh (.) that antique dealer across from you
 *      2:   well he's got a frightful lot of junk in his shop
        3 X: who, where oh
 **     4:   yeah it looks pretty dreadful in there at times
```

(3)   Seglerinnen 3
*   1 A: all die 'Segler sin da 'glücklich draußen. ne,
* *   2 B: haja die sin ganz (.) 'happy.

*   1 A: *all the yachtsmen are happy out there aren't they*
* *   2 B: *oh yeah they're having a fine time*

(4)   Roro 410
*   1 S: 'h der isch eine trübe Tasse 'meine G(h)üt(h)e
       2 X: warum?
       3 S: hhe wenn der da unten reinkommt (0.5) hehe (.(h)..) (dann) gehts
       4 SO: (dann) wenn=er=scho anfängt zu redn
       5 S: aoah! I also i weiß °(net)°   I
* *   6 X: I naja der hat so ne gewisse (Art) I

*   1 S: *'h he's a sad sack my goodness*
       2 X: *why that*
       3 S: *hhe when he comes in down there (0.5) hehe (.(h)..) then there's*
       4 SO: *when he just starts to talk*
       5 S: *aoah I I don't know*   I
* *   6 X: *I well he's got this way about him* I

In Pomerantz's terms, example (1) shows an instance of agreement
with an 'upgraded' assessment term, and (4) a 'downgraded' assessment. Examples (2) and (3) are neither upgraded nor downgraded,
nor strictly speaking are they same assessments since, according to
Pomerantz, only those second assessment terms count as 'same
assessments' which repeat the term of the first assessment with an
added *too* (*schön* 'pretty'- *auch schön* 'pretty too') or those which
include proterms. It was argued, however, in Auer and Uhmann
(1982) that the concept of 'same assessment' has to be broad-
ened – at least for German data – so that semantically same evaluations like *mords Verhau* and *ganz grauenvoll* in example (2) or
translation equivalents, like *glücklich* and *happy* in (3), can be
taken into account and do not have to be arbitrarily classified as
either semantically upgraded or downgraded. From a sequential
point of view this three-dimensional distinction is reduced to a
two-dimensional distinction: same evaluations are either used as
sequence terminators (like upgrades and some downgrades) or
they preface disagreements and the sequence is expanded until
agreement is achieved (like some downgrading evaluations). Due
to this ambiguity of sames and downgraders only upgraded second

assessments can be considered *clear agreements* and should thus be the most preferred recipient reaction.[3]

However, although it can be shown that agreeing is conversationally preferred, proffering a first assessment has to be done on uncertain grounds. The first assessor can only assume – for example due to joint cultural norms – that the recipient will share his or her evaluation, but if the topic is being discussed for the first time, the first assessor has only limited knowledge about the opinion of the recipient. Even if he or she knows the recipient and his or her evaluation of the assessed referent due to a shared interactional history, the latter may have recently changed his or her mind. First assessors therefore always take the risk that their recipient will not share their point of view:

(5)   Hundertfünfzig 15
```
        1 H:  ...
        2 X:  ja
        3 H:  und eh: (.)
  *     4 X:  e(h)r''fahre(h)n (.) 'sehr erfahren
        5 H:  woher weißt du das,
        6               (2.0)
        7 X:  ja wir ham uns mal drüber unterhalten
        8               (1.0)
        9 X:  w(h)oher wei(h)sse d(h)as
       10     | hehe
       11 H:  | he | he
       12 X:        | hehe i(h)s das nich e(h)n biß(h)chen un(h)ver(h)schämt?
       13     | hehe
       14 H:  | nö:(h):(h) find(h) ich ni(h)ch 'hh
       15     ken(h)n d(h)ich d(h)och
       16 X:  ach s | o;
       17 H:         | he | hehehehe |
       18 X:              | hehehehe | nun ja (.)
       19 H:  (ja) sowas mag ich ja;
 (*)   20 X:  cir(h)ca hundert(h)fünfzig Frau(h)en w(h)enn er sich r(h)echt
              ent(h)sinnt
       21               (1.0)
       22 H:  mehr nich?
       23 X:  nein hehehe
       24 H:  Heini kam auf über tausend
       25 X:  ja ja d(h)u sag(h)test es hehe
       26 H:  hehehe
       27 X:  h(h)ä ich mein s:- soviel könn natürlich nich alle bieten
```

```
      28       das is klar hehe | he
      29  H:                    | he | he
*     30  x:                         | aber ich fand die hundertfünfzig
               auch schon nich schlecht;
**    31  H: och ja is schon ganz gut


       1  H:  ...
       2  x:  yeah
       3  H:  and uh
*      4  x:  experienced (.) very experienced
       5  H:  how do you know
       6               (2.0)
       7  x:  oh we talked about it once
       8               (1.0)
       9  x:  how do you know
      10       |hehe
      11  H:   | he | he
      12  x:      | .hehe. isn't that a bit cheeky
      13       | hehe
      14  H:   | naw (h) (h) I don't think so 'hh
      15       I know you
      16       oh
      17         he | hehehehe|
      18  x:        | hehehehe| oh well (.)
      19  H:  (yeah) I like that
(*)   20  x:  approximately a hundred and fifty women if he remembers
               correctly
      21               (1.0)
      22  H:  is that all
      23  x:  yeah hehehe
      24  H:  Heini got up to more than a thousand
      25  x:  yeah that's what you said hehe
      26  H:  hehehe
      27  x:  course I mean not everyone has that much to offer
      28       that's for sure he | he
      29  H:                      | he | he
*     30  x:                           | but I thought the hundred and fifty
               wasn't so bad either
**    31  H: oh yeah it's pretty good
```

In line 4 X assesses a referent; X claims that this referent (a fellow student of X) is not only *experienced* but *very experienced*. Assessing a referent depends on a certain amount of knowledge, so the recipient is entitled to enquire about the basis of the assessor's knowledge. This is of course not always done; in most cases it is just silently taken for granted that the assessment is founded on solid facts. However, in this excerpt (line 5), H asks the question: *how do you know? As X cannot claim personal knowledge, she gives an explanation of the evaluation (*) in line 20: approximately a hundred and fifty women if he remembers correctly.* X's assessment and her explanation clearly invite agreement, because her evaluation is in agreement with the cultural values. Yet instead of proffering a congruent assessment (something like *ja das ist wirklich ausgesprochen erfahren* 'oh yes that is really quite experienced') or a non-lexical assessment sound (something like *ahh* or *ohh*) and thereby showing that she shares this value system, H displays disagreement with X's explanation in line 22: *Is that all?* H also gives an explanation in line 24; she claims that she knows somebody else (*Heini*) whose sexual experience is grounded on more than 1,000 different partners. After X and H have agreed that *Heini* is an exceptional case, X proffers again a positive assessment stated with double negation (*schon nich schlecht*) and H (line 31) performs a semantically downgraded second assessment (*schon ganz gut*) which is treated as agreement and terminates the sequence.

The position of the second assessor, by contrast, is much safer than the position of the first assessor. Because the estimation of the first assessor is already known, a second assessor who wants to agree can do this as strongly as he wishes and as soon as possible. Starting in overlap with the first assessment allows the second assessor to display that he has only 'accidentally' not taken the risky position of first assessor and that he has seen the situation as early and as clearly as the first assessor:

```
(6)   Diffpsych 648
      1 TA:  ich muß no=mal schnell kuckn was ich da hab
      2      ich hab da so viel ((Ta blättert in ihren Mitschriften))
      3 ?:   °°hh°°
      4 ?:   |°mm;°
      5 TA:  |wißt=er | das hat überhaupt | ke*inen Zweck
      6 B:            | (. . . . . . . . . . . . .) |
      7 TA:  des hat überhaupt | kein S-
*     8 X:                     | des is wirklich blöd
      9      daß=du=des nich vorher mal |durchgelesn hast
**   10 CL:                             |ds find=i auch blöd; wirklich;
```

```
    1 TA:  I'll have to take a look again at what I've put down
    2      I've got so much ((Ta thumbs through her notes))
    3 ?:   °°hh°°
    4 ?:   |°mm;°
    5 TA:  |you know |there's absolutely |no sense
    6 B:            |(. . . . . . . . . . ) |
    7 TA:  there's absolutely |no s-
*   8 X:                     |that's really a pity
    9      that you didn't read it through |beforehand
**  10 CL:                                |I think it's a shame too really
```

Due to this bias between first and second assessments it is not
surprising that conversants have options to avoid the risky position
of first assessor. This position can be systematically avoided by
asking (Q) the recipient about his or her point of view. By asking
co-conversants about their evaluation, speakers can put themselves
in a very strong position. Upon completion of the elicited initial
assessment, a second assessment is still conditionally relevant but
the evaluation of the fellow conversant is now available:

```
(7)  Kanaldeckel
Q   1 O:  hast as Zeugnis scho gsehn Franz; (.)
    2 F:  mmei °(. . .grad am Josef scho gsagt hab)°
*   3      sehr gutes Zeugnis (.)
**  4 O:  SECOND ASSESSMENT

Q   1 O:  have you seen the report yet Franz (.)
    2 F:  mmei (. . .was just telling Joseph)
*   3      a very good report
**  4 O:  SECOND ASSESSMENT
```

Concerning the temporal organization of assessment pairs, it has
been shown that when a speaker produces an initial assessment, a
second assessment is relevant upon completion, if the assessed referent is accessible to the recipient. In the case of agreement, congruent
second assessments are performed without delay as, for example, in
extracts (1)–(3) or with overlap (ex. 6).

However, although recipients might be invited to agree with an
initial assessment, they may nonetheless find themselves in a position where expressing their point of view would lead to disagreement. If agreeing with one another is indeed a formal preference
within assessment pairs and if agreement is done without delay,
then disagreement should be oriented to by the participants as

something dispreferred and as something to be held off or to be produced with delay, i.e. various ways of leaving the dispreferred disagreement unstated are expectable. Instead of producing disagreements upon completion of the initial assessments, invited second assessors regularly delay their assessment with a gap followed by a request for clarification (RCl) or with a gap followed by a repair-initiating repeat (RIR)[4] of the assessment term. In both cases first assessors are provided with a slot for explaining or restating their first assessment:

```
(4)    Roro 410
*       1  s:  h der isch eine trübe Tasse 'meine G(h)üt(h)e
RCl    2  x:  warum?
        3  s:  CLARIFICATION/MODIFIED FIRST ASSESSMENT

*       1  s:  h he's a sad sack my goodness
RCl    2  x:  why that
        3  s:  CLARIFICATION/MODIFIED FIRST ASSESSMENT


(7)    Kanaldeckel
        1  o:  hast as Zeugnis scho gsehn Franz; (.)
        2  F:  mmei °(. . .grad am Josef scho gsagt hab)°
*       3      sehr gutes Zeugnis (.)
RIR    4  o:  naja sehr gut;
              . . .
        7  F:  MODIFIED FIRST ASSESSMENT

        1  o:  have you seen the report yet Franz (.)
        2  F:  mmei (. . .was just telling Joseph)
*       3      a very good report
RIR    4  o:  well very good
              . . .
        7  F:  MODIFIED FIRST ASSESSMENT
```

Participants sometimes even show their orientation to the absence of second assessments upon completion of their initial assessments by expanding their turns (E). In the next example, this is done twice, because Sol also modifies his first assessment in line 3 (M*). After a direct question, like the second expansion in line 4, the relevance of a second assessment is actually strengthened, so that further delay is not possible:

```
(8)    RoRo 550
*       1  SOL: der Müller der isch a ''nur positiv
E1     2       (find=i)
```

M*   3   der isch so 'nnett der Mensch du (.)
E2   4   'h findsch net?
**   5 x: aja "doch=i=find den a unheimlich nett.

*   1 SOL: *that Müller he's A-okay*
E1   2   *(if you ask me)*
M*   3   *he's such a nice guy you know*
E2   4   *don't you think*
**   5 x: *oh yeah sure I think he's awfully nice too*

The delaying or withholding of a disagreeing second assessment with the help of gaps followed by requests for clarification or repair-initiating repeats does not remove their conditional relevance. However, in the emerging gap or in the sequential next position to requests for clarification and repair-initiating repeats, the first assessors are given an opportunity to orient to an upcoming disagreement and to modify their first assessment in such a way that the recipient's agreement becomes more expectable. These modifications are frequently done by means of downgraded assessments so that the differences between the speaker's position and the presumed position of the recipient are lessened. Speakers very rarely use upgraded or even same evaluations in these contexts. This can only be explained if we suppose that the interpretation of an upcoming and as yet unstated disagreement is available to the first assessor and that the achievement of agreement is being prepared.

In example (7) F successfully modifies his assessment in line 7, the modification coming after a relatively long silence (line 5) and in partial overlap with the delayed disagreement. Although very late, F achieves agreement from O in line 9:

(7)   Kanaldeckel
      1 o: hast as Zeugnis scho gsehn Franz; (.)
      2 F: mmei °(. . .grad am Josef scho gsagt hab)°
*   3   sehr gutes Zeugnis (.)
      4 o: naja sehr gut;
      5   (1.0)
**   6   sehr gut | kann mas doch a net heißn |
M*   7 F: | 'relativ sehr gutes Zeugnis |
      8   °in bezug auf ihre Leistungen°
**   9 o: ja:! ja (.) do do hot er recht.

      1 o: *have you seen the report yet Franz (.)*
      2 F: *mmei (. . .was just telling Joseph)*

```
*   3      a very good report
    4 O:   well very good
    5         (1.0)
**  6      very good | is not exactly the right word
M*  7 F:              | relatively very good report
    8      in relation to her effort
**  9 O:   yes yes (.) he's right on that
```

In example (4) the requested clarification is given by the first assessor and by one of his recipients in lines 3–5 and it also leads to the conditionally relevant second assessment by X in line 6:

```
(4)   Roro 410
*    1 S:   he der isch eine trübe Tasse 'meine G(h)üt(h)e
RCl  2 X:   warum?
     3 S:   hhe wenn der da unten reinkommt (0.5) hehe (.(h)..) (dann) gehts
     4 SO:  (dann) wenn=er=scho anfängt zu redn
     5 S:   aoah! | also i weiß °(net)°                |
**   6 X:          | naja der hat so ne gewisse (Art) |

*    1 S:   h he's a sad sack my goodness
RCl  2 X:   why that
     3 S:   hhe when he comes in down there (0.5) hehe (.(h)..) then there's
     4 SO:  when he just starts to talk
     5 S:   aoah | I don't know              |
**   6 X:         | well he's got this way about him |
```

It will be noted that in both examples (7) line 9 and (4) the second assessors start their second assessment with a pre-turn particle (ja:! ja and naja). This is not an accidental feature of these second assessment turns; instead, overwhelmingly,[5] German second assessments consist of two components and exhibit the following structure: pre-turn particle + assessment utterance. In (9) what looks like a counter-example turns out to corroborate this analysis, because what at first sight appears to be a first assessment prefaced by a particle and followed by a second assessment without particle:

```
(9)   China 8f
*    I:   'ja, ist natürlich 'unheimlich 'blöd.
**   T:   °und das natürlich ne 'irre Be'lastung°.

*    I:   yeah, it's really awfully stupid
**   T:   and that's of course a terrible amount of work
```

turns out to be an assessment second to an extended informing, which stretches from line 1 to line 12:

(9)   China 8f
    1 T: also=die=ham irgendwie en 'Vorschlag 'ein:gerei:cht,
    2   man 'könnte jetzt weiterhin 'Gräzistik 'Staatsexamen
        stul'dieren, |
    3 I: |hmhm |
    4   (0.5)
    5 T: 'aber 'nur als 'zweites 'Hauptfach,
    6   (0.4)
    7 |wo'bei| ma=noch=n 'Zusatzfach 'braucht,
    8 I: | hm |
    9 T: also 'zwei 'Hauptfächer hast dann:=
    10   =zum Beispiel 'Deutsch, 'Griechisch
    11   (0.3)
    12 |'und| brauchst=dann noch nen 'Zusatzfach.
    13 I: |hm |
    14   (0.6)
** 15 I: 'ja, ist natürlich 'unheimlich 'blöd.
    16 T: °und das natürlich ne 'irre Be'lastung°.
    17 I: ja
    18   (1.8)
    19 I: °°ach=du 'je'mi'ne:°°((Lat: Jesu domine))
    20   (1.4)
    21 T: °°hm°°

    1 T: *well somehow they turned in a proposal*
    2   *that you could still take Greek studies for your state*
      examilnation |
    3 I: *|hmhm |*
    4   (0.5)
    5 T: *but only as a second major*
    6   (0.4)
    7   *|and you | would need an additional subject*
    8 I: *|hm |*
    9 T: *so you'd have two majors*
    10   *for example German Greek*
    11   (0.3)
    12   *|and| you still need an additional subject*
    13 I: *|hm |*
    14   (0.6)
** 15 I: *yeah, it's really awfully stupid*
    16 T: *and of course a terrible amount of work*
    17 I: *yes*
    18   (1.8)
    19 I: *oh good lord*
    20   (1.4)
    21 T: *°°hm°°*

The analysis of the putative second assessment of T, the deliverer of the informing, in line 16 cannot proceed without caution either. A strictly sequential analysis would see line 16 as a typical instance of a 'confirming assessment', which news deliverers can and routinely do perform subsequent to the assessment of the recipient (see Pomerantz 1975:59). By this analysis, line 16 would be the third turn of a triple sequence: informing/news – recipient's assessment – confirming assessment. However, in producing her assessment in line 16, T displays orientation to her news delivery by strongly attaching it to her prior talk: prefaced by the coordinative conjunction *und* ('and') and referring to her news with the reference term *das* ('that'), T's assessment is a prototypical display of a 'concluding assessment' (see Pomerantz 1975:40), which summarizes T's position and performs the completion of the news in such a way that it is recognizable to the recipient. Although I has already displayed her recognition in line 15, she again displays her agreement and understanding in lines 17 to 19. The turn again exhibits the format of a second assessment: pre-turn particle (line 17) + assessment (line 19).

Before I proceed to a closer examination of the complex structure of second assessments, it is necessary to stress another difference between the American data analysed by Pomerantz (1975, 1984) and the German data. Unlike the American second assessments, German second assessments show pre-turn particles (*ja, aja, naja,* etc.) not only in disagreeing (cf. the particle *well*) but in agreeing seconds as well. However, the particles used for clear agreement are not the same as those used for potential disagreement: clear agreeing is done with an unmodified *ja*, as the examples (1), (2), and (7) line 9 show. This particle co-occurs with upgraded – ex. (1) – and same-assessment terms – ex. (2) and ex. (7) line 9. The particles used in the other examples show instances of a modified *ja: haja* in example (3) line 2 and *aja* in example (8) line 5 which are prefacing same assessments, and *och ja* in example (5) line 30 which prefaces a downgraded assessment. In excerpt (4) line 6 the particle *naja* also precedes a downgraded assessment and the same particle is used in the repair-initiating repeat – ex. (7) line 4 – where it announces an upcoming but unstated disagreement. That a second assessment prefaced with *naja* is indeed systematically used and

interpreted as a yet unstated but forthcoming disagreement can be
corroborated by the further sequential development of example (4):

(4)   Roro 410
*   1 s: he der isch eine trübe Tasse 'meine G(h)üt(h)e
RCl   2 x: warum?
         3 s: hhe wenn der da unten reinkommt (0.5) hehe (.(h)..) (dann)
                  gehts
         4 so: (dann) wenn=er=scho anfängt zu redn
         5 s: aoah! | also i weiß °(net)° |
* *   6 x: | naja der hat so ne gewisse (Art) |
         7 so: °h|m°
M*   8 s: | was langweiligeres als den gibts net du (0.5)
         9   also a pri'ori sag=i halt ne
(* *) 10 x: aja d:es is halt (.) irgendwie i=glaub da (wieder) stark mit
                  rein
         11   daß sich der halt aus (.) ner ganz anderen Gegend kommt
         12   also die Leute da oben tendieren eher dazu (.)
         13   °(also)° ganz sich | aufzuführn
M*   14 s: | aah! des is son richtig verstreuter
                  Professor in spe du (.)
         15   fürchterlich. (.)

*   1 s: *h he's a sad sack my goodness*
RCl   2 x: *why that*
         3 s: *hhe when he comes in down there (0.5) hehe (.(h)..) then*
                  there's
         4 so: *when he just starts to talk*
         5 s: *aoah | I don't know*
* *   6 x: *| well he's got this way about him*
         7 so: *°h|m°*
M*   8 s: *| he's as dreary as they come I tell you (0.5)*
         9   *I mean he's more than I can bear offhand you know*
(* *) 10 x: *well it's just (.) somehow I think (again) a big role*
         11   *that he just comes from (.) a completely different part of the*
                  country
         12   *I mean the people up there are more likely to (.)*
         13   *(I mean) to behave | like that*
M*   14 s: *| ooh he's a real absent-minded*
                  professor-to-be you know (.)
         15   *horrid*

In example (4) the pre-turn particle *naja* in line 6 precedes a downgraded assessment, which only So is willing to interpret as a congruent assessment (cf. the minimal token of agreement in line 7),

whereas S's interpretation of disagreement is displayed in line 8, where S restarts the assessment sequence with another first assessment. However, instead of modifying his assessment by a downgraded assessment term to achieve agreement, S uses an upgraded assessment: the assessed referent is not only 'a sad sack' but he is an 'extreme case' (see Pomerantz 1986) because he is 'as dreary as they come'. By means of this extreme case formulation S legitimizes his negative assessment and displays that he is oriented to an 'unsympathetic hearing', i.e. a hearing in which X 'reconstructs a circumstance that could be referenced by the description offered but that supports a position contrary to the original one' (Pomerantz 1986:221). X's turn in line 10 is an explanation of his second assessment which indeed claims that the assessed referent might not be legitimately assessed as a bore, but that he might be a victim of intercultural miscommunication. X has not started the explanation of his second assessment with the disagreeing pre-turn particle *naja* but with *aja*, which is combined with same-assessment terms frequently used in agreeing second assessments (see ex. (8)). Still, this combination is ambiguous and it can also be interpreted as upcoming, but not yet stated, disagreement. For a third time S renews his negative assessment in line 14 without taking X's argument into account. As X's and S's positions concerning the assessed referent are highly divergent no explicit agreement is achieved, because upon completion of the third first assessment, X doesn't proffer a second assessment. Further insight into the systematic interpretation of *naja* may be gained by examining the sequential structure of example (10):

(10) Schreibtischmäßig
*   1 T: ich find ja auch er hat=wieder - wesentlich schöneres
                 glänzenderes Fell gekricht; (.)
Cl   2 x: seit er hier is?
M*   3 T: also ich fan er- war sah ziemlich so rupfig und stumpf aus; h (.)
        4 x: noja;
        5   (3.0)
(**)   6 T: naja es kann aber auch sein
        7   daß ich diese ganzen (.) halb ausgefallenen Haare rausgebürstet
                 habe
        8   I daß I des jetz was ausmacht,
        9 x: I mm I

```
*     1 T:  I think so too he's got much prettier shinier fur again (.)
Cl    2 X:  since he's been here
M*    3 T:  I thought he was- looked rather ragged and worn h. (.)
      4 X:  well
      5         (3.0)
(**)  6 T:  well but then it could just be
      7     that I brushed out all this (.) half-loose hair
      8     | that | that makes a difference
      9 X:  | mm |
```

The first three turns of this extract exhibit the structure of assessment sequences with delayed disagreement: first assessment – gap – request for clarification – clarification/modification of the first assessment, which was not agreed with. However, after T's downgraded modification of her first assessment (cf. the repair marker *also* in line 3), X doesn't produce the conditionally relevant second assessment completely, but only its first component, i.e. the particle *noja*. This particle is followed by a developing 'intra-turn pause' of 3 seconds. In the course of this emerging pause T elects to resume talk in line 6, converting the pause into an 'inter-turn gap' (see Sacks, Schegloff and Jefferson 1974; Bergmann 1982). T does so, orienting to her fellow conversant's withholding and delaying of a disagreement, which is announced by the pre-turn particle *naja*. Yet T's turn in line 6 does not show the format of a modified first assessment (no repair marker as in the first modification in line 3); she instead herself formulates a counter-argument to her prior assessment (*aber*). Looking again at T's turn it can be noted that it shows the format of a second assessment: it is prefaced with a pre-turn particle – the disagreeing particle *naja*. That T's reversal is indeed interpreted as the conditionally relevant second assessment can perhaps be corroborated by the fact that the sequence is closed by X giving only a minimal response in line 9.

Pre-turn particles are a constitutive element of German second assessments in assessment pairs; they have turned out to be an important cue for a *scalar* interpretation of second assessments. The pre-turn particle *naja* especially has an unambiguous function which makes it work even without any assessment term. Owing to the ambiguity of sames and downgraders, upgraded second assessments prefaced with the particle *ja* can be considered *clear agreements* and are thus the most preferred recipient reaction:

(11) Second assessments in assessment pairs

agreement/potential disagreement
clear agreement <- > *unstated disagreement*

ja	ja	modified *ja*	modified *ja*	*naja*
+ upgrade	+ same	+ same	+ downgrade	(+ downgrade)

It has been further shown in this section that assessment pairs are organized in such a way that stated agreements are maximized and stated disagreements are minimized. The latter is achieved by the prospective second assessor's delaying or withholding their assessment, which is interpreted by the first assessor as forthcoming disagreement and oriented to with a modification of the first assessment. Yet although agreement is preferred, there is a systematic bias between the position of first and second assessor. Proffering a first assessment has to be done on insecure grounds; without an already stated point of view towards the assessable, first assessors always face the risk that their recipients will not share their evaluation.

3 Metrical rhythm: on the phonology of beat clashes in German

Up to this point in the analysis, rhythm has not been considered in any systematic or analytically relevant way. In congruence with the tradition of ethnomethodological conversation analysis, the sequential organization of assessments has been the focus of interest. Before I can turn to the description of beat clashes in assessment utterances and show their interactional relevance, I will briefly outline some theoretical aspects of rhythmical organization.

In doing so we will enter the field of metrical phonology, which I presume to be relevant for the analysis of beat clashes in conversational data, for it provides a basis for the systematic description of the phenomena encountered. Metrical phonology deals on the one hand with *prominence relations* (stress), either within morphological and syntactic domains or within hierarchically organized prosodic–phonological domains[6] (syllables, feet, prosodic words, prosodic phrases, intonational phrases, intonational utterances). Prominence relations can be represented in branching tree structures with nodes labelled *s* (strong) or *w* (weak). On the other hand metrical phonology deals with *rhythmic structure* (accent), which more or less linearizes a succession of syllables to achieve *rhythmic alternation*. Partly in response to these two different types of problem, two different models of description, *metrical trees* and *metrical grids*, have been developed and controversially discussed.[7] For the purpose of this chapter, I will concentrate on the construction of the metrical grid. Yet, even with this limitation, I cannot claim that the following remarks are exhaustive.

Metrical grids are sets of layers built up horizontally above beat positions (x). The smallest unit for the description of rhythmic structure is the syllable (σ). The building up of the grid starts with the identification of syllables and the lowest layer of the grid therefore corresponds in a one-to-one relation to the number of syllables. In the framework of non-linear phonology this layer is responsible for text-to-grid and text-to-tune (pitch accent) alignment. Depending on theoretical considerations the higher layers correspond to morpho-syntactic or prosodic phrasing. Vertically the height of the columns represents the degree of prominence placed on each beat position. For a German intonational phrase (IP) with two accent domains (AD) a metrical grid could look like (12):[8]

(12)

			x		Level 5:	Nuclear Stress Rule	
x			x		Level 4:	pitch accent assignment	
x		x	x		Level 3:	word stress	
x	x	x	x	x	Level 2:	all syllables without reduced vowel	
x	x	x	x	x	x	Level 1:	all syllables
σ	σ	σ	σ	σ	σ		

[IP [AD1su si] [AD2ißt ba na nen]]
    Susie   eats bananas

While talking, speakers organize their utterances in patterns of more or less prominent syllables. The phonological generalization, expressed by Selkirk's (1984:52) Principle of Rhythmic Alternation, claims that the overall rhythmic patterns of natural speech tend to achieve an alternation between prominent, i.e. stressed (strong), and non-prominent, i.e. unstressed (weak) syllables. By means of this alternation languages are said to avoid strings of consecutive unstressed syllables as well as strings of consecutive stressed syllables:

(13) Principle of Rhythmic Alternation
  (a) Every strong position on a metrical level n should be followed by at least one weak position on that level.
  (b) Any weak position on a metrical level n may be preceded by at most one weak position on that level.

With respect to (13) the metrical grid of (12) is well-formed. However, this is not always the case. The two ways in which metrical grids can be ill-formed are by violations of (13a) or (13b) and they are discussed in the literature under the headings *beat clash* and *beat lapse*. Since Liberman and Prince (1977), it is especially beat clashes and their resolution via the Rhythm Rule or Iambic Reversal, Beat Movement or Beat Deletion and Beat Addition that have been at the centre of attention.[9] Following Nespor and Vogel (1989:98) the definition of stress clash in a *stress-timed*[10] language like English or German crucially depends on the definition of adjacency:

(14) Minimal stress clash

x		x	word
x		x	foot
x	(x)	x	syllable
σ	(σ)	σ	

Nespor and Vogel define as clashing those configurations with no more than one intervening unstressed syllable between two syllables with minimally level 3 stress. They also claim that there is no rule that moves a beat from one grid position to another. What happens instead according to Nespor and Vogel (1989:77) is 'that a beat is merely deleted by a rule of Beat Deletion (BD)'. As the physical correlate of BD is destressing, the affected syllable is perceived as weaker and the perception of beat clash is eliminated. However, Beat Deletion reduces stress only when it is at the minimal level that constitutes clash, which is level 3 in English. The remedy that Nespor and Vogel (1989:100ff.) suggest for level 4 and higher accents is Beat Insertion (BI). BI (X) is used to create a distance between two accents. The extra beat can be inserted in one of two positions if there is an unstressed syllable between the two accents. If the beat is inserted before the unstressed syllable the acoustic correlate is lengthening of the accented syllable, and if it is introduced after the unstressed syllable its physical correlate is a pause. If Beat Insertion is applied to create a distance between a level 3 and a level 4 beat instead of Beat Deletion on level 3, there is a slight difference in meaning, i.e. a change in focus. According to Nespor and Vogel the following grids show remedies of stress clash in English:

(15) (a) stress clash   (b) BD   (c) BI (lengthening)

```
            x                       x                       x
        x       x                   x                   x       x
        x       x               x       x               x       x
        x       x               x       x               x       x
        three books             three books             three X books
```

(16) (a) stress clash   (b) BI (pause)   (c) BI (lengthening)

```
                x                       x                           x
          x         x               x       x               x           x
          x         x               x       x               x           x
          x         x               x       x               x           x
          x    x    x               x   x   x               x       x   x
        Mississippi won         Mississippi X won       Mississi X pi won
```

Nespor and Vogel (1989:77) also claim that 'in certain cases, another strong stress may appear elsewhere in the string but . . ., this is the result of a more general phenomenon of Beat Addition (BA), a rule that eliminates lapses, whether they are inherently present or whether they arise as the result of BD'.

(17) (a) stress clash   (b) BD   (c) BA

```
                x                       x                       x
            x       x                   x               x       x
        x   x       x           x   x   x       x       x   x   x   x
        x   x x x   x           x   x x x       x       x   x x x   x
        achromatic lens         achromatic lens         achromatic lens
```

Beat Deletion and Beat Insertion seem to be more frequent remedies for beat clashes in German than Beat Movement (i.e. Beat Deletion plus Beat Addition). This might be due to the higher number of secondary accents but also to the fact that at the phrase level inflectional endings, which all contain a schwa as syllable nucleus, and accent-neutral suffixes provide intervening unstressed syllables. Configurations with the strongest pressure for change, i.e. no intervening unstressed syllable, cannot be found in German *adjective + noun* phrases. In *noun + noun* phrases such a beat clash can occur in cases like (18a), but Beat Deletion alone (18b) is more likely to apply than Beat Deletion plus Beat Addition (18c). In fact, (18c) sounds rather odd:

(18) (a)   (b)   (c) ?

```
        x                    x                      x
    ┌───────┐                x          x           x
    │ x   x │                x          x           x
 x  │ x   x │ x        x   x   x   x    x    x   x   x
 x x x  x  x x        x  x x   x   x x  x  x x  x   x x
```
Präsident Weizsäcker   Präsident Weizsäcker   Präsident Weizsäcker

As in English, only Beat Deletion (19b) instead of Beat Deletion plus Beat Addition (19c) applies in left-headed constructions:

(19) (a)   (b)   (c)*

```
        x                    x                      x
    ┌───────┐                x                      x
    │ x   x │                x          x   x       x      x
    │ x   x │ x              x   x x    x      x   x x
    x  x  x  x               x   x x x        x   x x  x
```
einen Rock anziehen   einen Rock anziehen   einen Rock anziehen
to wear a skirt

Compounds are especially interesting objects in prosodic phonology. German compounds like *Oberlandesgericht* 'Higher Regional Court of Appeal', *Nachmittag* 'afternoon' or *Generalfeldmarschall* 'field marshal' are composed of more than one lexeme. Although each of them retains its own stress pattern, only one syllable is singled out to carry the primary stress (i.e. the pitch accent) of the whole unit. The rules which identify this syllable crucially depend on the internal structure of the compound – but details are not relevant for the purpose of this chapter – and secondary stresses are assigned to the main stresses of the other lexemes:

(20)

```
        x
 x      x      x
 x      x      x
 x x x  x  x   x
```
[Ober[landes[gericht]]]

In the case of beat clashes derived from configurations with the strongest pressure for change, i.e. no intervening syllable with a level-1 beat, Beat Deletion only (21b and 22b), instead of Beat

Deletion plus Beat Addition (21c and 22c), applies both to the right and to the left of the most prominent syllable:

(21) (a)   (b) BD   (c)* BD + BA

```
  x                            x                   x
 ┌─────┐
 │x   x│                       x                   x      x
 │x   x│x                      x   x x             x      x x
 └─────┘
  x   x x                      x   x x             x      x x
 [Nach[mittag]]               [Nach[mittag]]      [Nach[mittag]]
```

(22) (a)   (b) BD

```
       x                                    x
    ┌─────┐
    │x  x│ x                                x
 x  │x  x│ x   x                   x  x  x     x     x
    └─────┘
 x x x  x    x   x                 x  xx x     x     x
 [General[feld[marschall]]]        [General[feld[marschall]]]
```

The stress pattern of (22c) sounds as odd as (18c) and if it is heard at all, it will be on a barracks square. (22d) is probably the most natural realization:

(22) (c)² BD + BA   (d) BI

```
        x                                  x
   x       x                          x    x
   x   x  x    x     x                x  x    x    x    x
 x x x x    x     x                   x x x   x    x    x
 [General[feld[marschall]]]          [General X [feld[marschall]]]
```

The compounds discussed so far all belong to a group called *determinative compounds* (Determinativkomposita). There are two other semantically different groups, *coordinative compounds* (Koordinativkomposita) and *augmentive* or *elative* *compounds* (Augmentiv- or Elativkomposita). Determinative compounds [XY] denote a special type of Y-entity and its sister-constituents are related in such a way that X specifies Y (23a). In coordinative compounds the sister-constituents are in a relation of addition (23b), whereas in elative compounds X intensifies Y (23c). The three types of compound also show differences in their accentual patterns. Unlike the determinative compounds, which designate by rule only one syllable to bear the primary stress, coordinative compounds and elative compounds have no internal hierarchy and treat their sister-constituents with equal rights: under appropriate circumstances, for example if the constituent is focussed, every element receives a pitch accent (PA) and a level-4 beat. If there is more than one level-4 beat, the last beat on this level receives a level-5 beat if it also bears the last pitch accent of the intonational phrase (IP):

(23) (a) determinative compound	(b) coordinative compound	(c) elative compound
	x	x
x	x x	x x
x	x x	x x
x x	x x	x x
x x	x x	x x
[IP Fischmarkt]	[IP schwarzweiß]	[IP stinkreich]
fish-market	*black-and-white*	*stinking rich*

Coordinative compounds are quite rare in German and in most cases they fuse with other elements to form determinative compounds: *rotgrünblind* 'red-green-blind', *Schwarzweißfilm* 'black-and-white film', etc. Elative compounds, however, are morphologically very productive. Most of them are lexicalized, which means especially in the case of monosyllabics that beat clash is not an ill-formed metrical structure.[11] Well-known minimal pairs like: (syllable boundaries are marked by dots (.) and ambi-syllabicity by a tilde (~)) *'blut.'arm/'blut.arm* 'very poor'/ 'anaemic', *'stein.'reich/'stein.reich* 'very rich'/'stony', *'Höl~len. 'lärm/'Höl~len.lärm* 'infernal noise'/'noise in hell' show that Beat Deletion cannot apply, because this would transform the elative compound into a determinative compound:

(24) (a) elative compound	(b) determinative compound
x	x
x x x	x x
x x x	x x
x x x	x x x
x x x x x	x x x x x
ein blutarmes Mädchen	ein blutarmes Mädchen
a very poor girl	*an anaemic girl*

In these cases of intensifying elative compounds the Principle of Rhythmic Alternation seems to be abandoned and beat clash is systematically lexicalized. Yet this fact does not prove the Principle of Rhythmic Alternation to be wrong. On the contrary: elative compounds – though frequent and well-formed lexicalisations in German – are highly marked cases with respect to their rhythmical properties (see Uhmann 1994). It is only on the basis of the description of beat clash as a marked (but not always ill-formed) structure by metrical phonologists that the aim of this chapter, i.e. to describe the avoidance of remedies for clashes or even the systematic production of clashes in everyday conversation, can be accounted for.

4 Beat clashes in assessment utterances

Speaking is a rhythmic process. In this respect human language and especially verbal interaction are in no way different from other recurrences of events in time which determine the way we experience ourselves (heartbeat, breathing, etc.) and the world we live in (alternation of day and night, the phases of the moon, etc.).[12] Yet although all human beings experience the rhythm of their bodies, their languages are said to differ with respect to their underlying rhythmic pattern. Languages such as German or English are classified as belonging to a group called *stress-timed* languages, whereas languages like Spanish, Standard Italian or Turkish are examples of *syllable-timed* languages. Although both English and German are said to be stress-timed, the unmarked degree of rhythmically integrated speech, i.e. *isochrony*, seems to be higher in British and American colloquial English than in German.[13] This might be due to certain structural–phonological characteristics of German, namely the large number of secondary accents. Analysis of conversational data has shown the impressive amount of interactional work rhythm does in everyday conversation, because it is especially the prosodic make-up of speakers' turns that plays a crucial role as a *contextualization cue*. Cook-Gumperz and Gumperz (1978) as well as Gumperz (1982, 1992) have introduced the notion of contextualization in order to subsume under a common heading procedures and techniques available to participants for the task of not only conveying meanings or propositions, but, at the same time, constructing contexts in which their utterances become interpretable.

The analysis of beat clashes as a contextualization device naturally leads back to the analysis of conversational data. It is not abstract lexical features of words or phrases, i.e. stress, but accentuation patterns of spoken discourse[14] that become the centre of attention. The accent notation in the transcripts will be a relational and not an absolute one, which means that accent notation is restricted to the domain of intonational phrase. If intonational phrases are not too complex, each line in the transcript belongs to an intonational phrase. Within an intonational phrase a syllable notated with a *primary accent* (') is phonetically realized with a pitch accent which corresponds in grid notation to a beat of at least level 4. If an intonational phrase contains more than one pitch accented syllable, syllables perceived as equally strong are also notated with primary accents. Prominences perceived as weaker, but still above the level of lexical stress (cf. note 14) are noted as *secondary accent* ('). Again an intonational phrase can contain more than one secondary accent. Sometimes speakers provide accented syllables with extra prominence (phonetically realized by means of increased pitch range which can also be accompanied by extra intensity and duration of the accented syllable). These extra strong syllables are notated as *emphatic accents* ('). The relational character of accent notation implies that, for example, the actual phonetic prominence of a secondary accent in one intonational phrase can be the same as the prominence of a primary accent – even uttered by the same speaker – in another intonational phrase, because in this environment it might be the strongest accent. Relational accent notation orients to the fact that participants in natural conversation do not calculate Hertz, decibels and centiseconds, but perceive successions of alternating prominences or successions of prominences with more-or-less equal strength.

Examples (25) and (26) are instances of beat clashes on the elative compounds 'haut.'nah '(lit.) as close as skin', 'vivid' and 'eis.'kalt 'icy cold' which seem to 'infect' their environment in such a way that they occur in intonational phrases with higher *density of accented syllables* (see Uhmann 1989, 1992) than surrounding intonational phrases by the same speaker:

(25) China 52
    1 I: für 'mich wär das ja auch ne 'irre 'Chance
    2   gleich dann (0.9) in das 'volle 'Leben da ei(h)nzustei(h)gen hehehe
    3 T: jaja jaja (.)
→ 4 I: s(h)o 'a(h)lles 'ganz 'haut'nah (0.5) 'mit'zu'kriegen,

    1 I: *for me it would also be a terrific opportunity*
    2   *to (0.9) plunge right into the full of life hehehe*
    3 T: *yeah yeah*
→ 4 I: *to experience it all very vividly (0.5)*

(26) Hundertfünfzig 10
    1 H: (. . .) schon richtig 'Frühlings(stimmung)?
    2 X: jaja (.) wie es: wa-
    3   also=es blüht alles: (.) und: (0.5) (sehr) 'warm
    4   (1.0)
    5   es war 'schön
    6   und jetzt stehn wir hier wieder in diesem häßlichen 'Kiel
→ 7   es is 'eis'ka:lt 'regnerisch (.) 'miese 'Stadt;

    1 H: *(. . .) already real spring (atmosphere)*
    2 X: *oh yes (.) it was-*
    3   *well everything was in blossom (.) and (0.5) (quite) warm*
    4   *(1.0)*
    5   *it was beautiful*
    6   *and here we are again in hideous Kiel*
→ 7   *and it's icy cold rainy (.) miserable city*

These excerpts show instances of remedies of beat clashes as well as
the avoidance of remedies, because in example (25) Beat Insertion
(X), which corresponds to a pause, creates a distance after three
clashing accents:

(25)′   (26)′

```
    x   x   x   x                      x   x   x
   ┌──────────┐                       ┌──────────┐
   │x   x   x │  x   x                 │x   x   x │
   │x   x   x │  x  x  x               │x   x   x │   x
   └──────────┘                       └──────────┘
    x   x   x   x  x  x  x             x   x   x   x   x
 ganz haut.nah X mit.zu.krie.gen      eis.kalt reg.ne.risch
```

The speech waveform and the fundamental frequency (f_O) of example (25) (Fig. 8.1)[15] show that the duration of the syllables that were
perceived with beat-clashing accents have a remarkably high correspondence in duration and they are also set off prosodically by
changes in the f_O contour that can be phonologically analysed as
pitch accents. Yet beat clashes do not need elative compounds as a

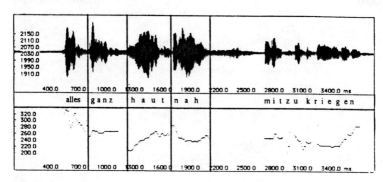

Figure 8.1

starting point. In natural conversation speakers not only let beat clashes happen (as in examples (25) and (26)), but they are also deliberately produced on words which lexically have only one primary stressed syllable:

(27) China 52f.
```
    1 T:  aha (0.3) dann ists auch viel 'spannender;
    2 I:  hm
    3 T:  weil man dann so die Struk'turen gut mitkriegt=
    4     =vor allem das to- intere'ssante ist halt das sind 'Leute.
→   5     die 'alle "jah're'lang in 'England stu'diert ham;
```

```
    1 T:  oh (0.3) it's also much more exciting then
    2 I:  hm
    3 T:  because you get to know the structures
    4     especially the to- most interesting part is the people
→   5     who've all studied for years in England
```

(28) China 56
```
    5 I:  ist es 'schön da?
    6 T:  in Kuala'lumpur?
    7 I:  mhm 'lohnts sich da zwei Tage zu 'bleiben
    8 T:  aah lohnts sich 'schon weil die hm Stadtzentrum ist noch so in
          Kolonialstil
    9     ist eine der 'wenigen Städte wo nicht nach der (.) Be'freiung
   10     e:h die ganzen Kolo'nialgebäude 'niedergerissen wurden
   11 I:  mhm
   12 T:  von daher ises schon interessant
   13     so vom Stadt | bild  | her
   14 I:               | mhm |
→  15 T:  aber s=is halt "ir're: 'heiß °inner Großstadt°
```

 5 I: *is it pretty there*
 6 T: *in Kualalumpur*
 7 I: *mhm is it worth spending a couple of days there*
 8 T: *oh it's worth it because the hm city centre is still in colonial*
     style
 9   *it's one of the few cities where after the (.) liberation*
10   *uh all the colonial buildings didn't get torn down*
11 I: *mhm*
12 T: *and for that reason it's quite interesting*
13   *from the point of view of the townlscape*
14 I: lmhm
→ 15 T: *but it's frightfully hot in the big city*

Speakers achieve beat-clashing rhythms in these examples by Beat
Addition on syllables that would 'normally' receive only level-1
prominence (cf. the two schwa-syllables) and not more than level-
2 prominences in the 'ideal' metrical grids after Beat Deletion (x) to
eliminate the beat clashes between the first and the third syllable.
Let us suppose that each syllable is promoted to greater prominence
by adding two extra metrical beats; then the internal prominence
relations are kept constant but the conditions for beat clash are met.
In both cases we perceive three clashing accents:

(27)′ (a)		(b)		(28)′ (a)		(b)	
lexical pattern		beat clash		lexical pattern		beat clash	
		x				x	
		x				x	
x		x	x	x		x	x
x	(x)	x x x		x	(x)	x x x	
x	x	x x x		x	x	x x x	
x x x		x x x		x x x		x x x	
jah.re. lang		jah.re. lang		ir~re heiß		ir~re heiß	

Again the acoustic analysis of the beat clashes (fig. 8.2) shows their
similarity in duration and the increased pitch range on the empha-
tically accented syllable *ir-*. However, even more interesting is the
comparison between the beat-clashing accentuation on the adjective
irre in example (28) and another realization of this adjective (fig.
8.3) by the same speaker in example (29):

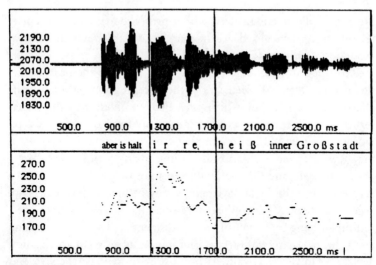

Figure 8.2

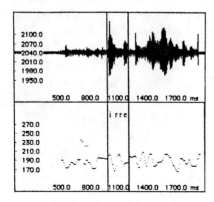

Figure 8.3

(29) China 15
1 ı: ja=die Ho'tels sind=sicher (0.6)
→ 2 т: ° 'irre | 'teuer °
3 ı: | ° 'relativ | ja (0.5) relativ | teuer.°
4 т: | °ja glaub ich auch° |

1 ı: *yes the hotels ar- of course* (0.6)
→ 2 т: *frightfully | expensive*
3 ı: | *relatively* | *yes* (0.5) *relatively* | *expensive*
4 т: | *yes I think so too* |

Here, the adjective is realized with a prosodic make-up that corresponds to its lexicalized accent pattern, which shows the schwa-syllable -*re* without any metrical strengthening.

Returning to function we have to ask, what do the beat clashes do in these turns? It seems as if the accentuation pattern of the elative compounds, in which one element intensifies the other, serves as a blueprint to contextualize 'intensity' or 'emphasis' on words which would be less emphatic or less strong assessments if they were realized without beat clashes. "*Ir're 'heiß* is much hotter than *'irre 'heiß* and "*jah're'lang* means not only a few years but a very long time. In the latter iconicity may be involved, too, because accenting every syllable takes more time than accenting only one.

Emphasizing and intensifying assessment terms are the starting point in the exploitation of beat clash as a contextualization device.[16] However, I want to propose a shift of perspective and look at the sequential organization of assessments realized with beat clashes and try to show that if assessments are packaged in such a way, they occur – compared to assessments which are not prosodically marked by a beat-clashing rhythm – in sequentially constrained contexts. As we have seen in section 2, assessments regularly occur at four different loci in conversation: (i) as first assessments in assessment pairs, (ii) as seconds in assessment pairs (cf. examples (1) to (8)), (iii) as firsts in stories, news or informings and (iv) as seconds to stories, news or informings (cf. example (9)).

4.1 Beat clashes in second assessments to informings

The placement of assessments as seconds to informings is motivated because news, stories or informings can be interpreted as kinds of 'extended first assessments'.[17] However, explicit assessment terms can be regularly absent (see example (9)) if the teller of the informing can be sure that interpretation and evaluation are recoverable from the content itself, so that the content of the talk, its connotations and the evaluative loading provide the relevance of the recipient's second assessment. The following examples show instances of second assessments to informings:

(30) China 34f
```
     1 T:  ehe=ansonsten von Kuala Lumpur bis Kota Bharu
     2      sinds=so (0.2) 'sechs 'acht 'Stunden;
     3      ° mim 'Bus; ° (0.6)
     4      geht 'schon 'auch. (0.9)
     5 I:  ja aber das is doch ehm der 'Witz schlecht | hin, |
     6 T:                                            | jaja |
     7 I:  | erst bis hier erst nach 'da: |
     8 T:  | jaja        hmhm       | hmhm
     9 I:  und dann | wieder zurück die ganze Strecke |
    10 T:           | das 'blöde ist halt hier inner    | Mitte
    11                (1.4)
*   12 T:  ist 'alles nur 'Dschungel.
    13      da komms halt kaum | durch  |
→**  14 I:                     | 'hhhha | "span | 'nend   |
    15 T:                                      | hehehehe |
    16                (0.8)
    17      u(h)nd 'da(h)rum gibt(h)s k(h)aum Querstraßen=
    18      =die 'bauen zur Zeit eine,
    19      von (0.3) Penang nach Kota Bharu 'die müßt jetzt fertig sein=
    20      =darum glaub ich daß es da 'Busverbindungen gibt
    21                (1.0)
    22      aber ansonsten 'hier gibts 'absolut 'keine Ver'bindungen °rüber°
```

```
     1 T:  uhuh otherwise from Kuala Lumpur to Kota Bharu
     2      it's about (0.2) six eight hours
     3      by bus (0.6)
     4      that's okay too (0.9)
     5 I:  yeah but this is the biggest joke of | all   |
     6 T:                                       | yeah  |
     7 I:  | first to here and to there |
     8 T:  |yeah        hmhm       | hmhm
     9 I:  and then | back again the whole way   |
    10 T            | the stupid part is here in the | middle
    11                (1.4)
*   12 T:  it's all just jungle
    13      you can hardly get | through
→**  14 I:                     | hhhha | how | exciting  |
    15 T:                                   | hehehehe |
    16                (0.8)
    17      and that's why there are hardly any roads across=
    18      =they're building one now
    19      from (0.3) Penang to Kota Bharu it should be finished by now=
    20      =that's why I think there are bus connections
    21                (0.1)
    22      but otherwise there are absolutely no connections across
```

In extract (30) T and I are sitting over a map and T is helping I to plan her trip to Malaysia. In lines 5–9, I complains about not being able to take a direct route and T informs her thereafter about the reason for the complicated detour. However, T's informing deserves a closer look. T starts her turn in line 6 in 'recognitional terminal overlap' (see Jefferson 1984) confirming I's complaint *der Witz schlechthin*, and in extended overlap with I's turn she co-participates in the complaint with *das blöde ist halt*. Only when simultaneous talk is brought to completion does T pause in the middle of a turn-constructional unit for 1.4 seconds and provide the necessary information: what may look like a short distance on the map is in fact unpassable jungle. Owing to the evaluative loading that accompanies the term *Dschungel* for Western Europeans, T's talk is not treated simply as an informing, but as an affect-displaying assessable that can be responded to. In line 14, I co-participates with a 'reciprocal affect display' (see Goodwin and Goodwin 1992:157): she responds with a non-lexical assessment signal, a deep and impressed inbreath *'hhhha*, followed by an assessment adjective *spannend* ('exciting'). Lexically, this adjective has only one main stress on the first syllable, but here it is produced with two clashing accents *''span'nend* to intensify the second assessment and to provide a strong display of the assessor's emotional involvement.

Second assessments are, as we have seen in section 2, relatively safe places, because the assessor already has access to the estimation of first assessor or teller of the informing. In a second assessment the recipient can indicate not only receipt of the informing, but also agreement or disagreement with the explicit or implicit first evaluation. However, unlike second assessments in assessment pairs, second assessments that agree with informings do not always close the sequence. Even agreeing assessments following informings are regularly followed by another assessment in third position, i.e., immediately subsequent to the second assessment of the recipient, deliverers of an informing provide a 'confirming assessment' (see example (9), line 16). In extract (30) the confirming is done in partial overlap with I's assessment not by an explicit assessment but by T's laughter (line 15) and her partly laughing resumption in lines 17 to 22. With their string of assessments and T's laughter the participants are able to display to each other that they share the evaluation of the information and their displaying of congruent understanding terminates the sequence.[18]

If it is indeed the case that deliverers of news or informings regularly use this place to confirm the evaluation of the recipient, then it would be expected that on some occasions they will use this slot to start the negotiation of agreement in cases where they do *not* share the evaluation of their recipient. This happens in example (31), where K is stressing the dangers pedestrians and users of public transportation face in the jungle of big cities:

```
(31)  Rheinuferbahn
         1  K: die: (.) ehm (.) Rheinuferbahn hat vorher die ehm (.) Kölner
         2      Hohenzollernbrücke mit dem 'h alten Kölner Hauptbahnhof
                verbunden=
  *      3      =aber: eh 'h um vom Kölner Hauptbahnhof zum Bonner
  *      4      Hauptbahnhof zu komn is also imma: schwierig gewesen
 (*)     5      weil dazwischen also noch 'hh zirka zweihundertfünfzig Meter
 (*)     6      'Fußweg waren und | he
 **      7  E:                   | 'wie:: 'ent'setz'lich! | hehe  | 'h he | 'hh
         8  K:                   | ja:,   |        | ja
                aber: eh
         9      wenn das eh ''grade wäre
        10      dann wäre das ja noch was gewesen
        11      aber da mußte man über mehrere Straßen | und eh
        12  E:                                         | hm (.) ''Slalom
                (0.5)
        13  K: richtich
```

```
         1  K: the (.) uhm (.) Rhine River Motorway used to uhm (.)
                connect the Cologne
         2      Hohenzollern Bridge with the 'h old Cologne Main Station=
  *      3      =but uh 'h um to get from the Cologne Main Station
  *      4      to the Bonn Main Station has always been difficult
 (*)     5      because inbetween there were approximately two hundred
                and fifty metres
 (*)     6      to walk and | he
 **      7  E:              | how awful | he he | 'h he | 'hh
         8  K:              | yes  |      | yes
                but uh
         9      if it had been uh straight
        10      it would have been all right
        11      but you had to cross several streets | and uh
        12  E:                                       | hm (.) slalom (0.5)
        13  K: right
```

K informs E about the connection between the main station in Cologne and the main station in Bonn and assesses it in line 4 as *schwierig* ('difficult'). What follows in lines 5 and 6 is an explanation which provides E, who has claimed that she is not familiar with public transportation between Cologne and Bonn, with the necessary knowledge to agree with K's assessment. K claims that the connection is difficult because of a walk of 250 metres. Semantically and sequentially, E's assessment in line 7 is an agreeing, upgraded, second assessment, because *entsetzlich* ('awful') is a much stronger assessment term than *schwierig* and it is also not delayed but produced in overlap with K's turn. Yet K does not treat E's assessment as an agreement. Prefaced with *ja aber* ('yes but') he produces another argument (lines 8 to 11) to explain his evaluation: not only the distance of 250 metres makes it difficult, but also the fact that several streets have to be crossed. E comments on this explanation in line 12; her comment *Slalom* is acknowledged by K (*richtig* 'right') and the sequence is closed after the negotiated agreement.

Why does K treat a semantically and sequentially perfect upgraded agreeing assessment as disagreeing? This can be explained by a closer look at the realization of E's assessment turn. First: the assessment term is followed by laughter. Second: the prosodic realization of the assessment term shows the rhythmically marked structure of beat clash instead of rhythmic alternation. Instead of the one main accent on the penultima (*ent'setzlich*) E produces three clashing accents, *'ent'setz'lich*, which (like in all the other examples of beat clash) intensifies the assessment adjective. By treating a very strong agreement as a disagreement, K displays that he treats E's assessment as the opposite of what she means, i.e. as irony. Exaggerated assessments can cue irony and in this case the exaggeration is done prosodically, so that the beat clashes – together with E's laughter – are the decisive cue to contextualize an ironical assessment.

Returning to the format of second assessments in German, it will be noticed that seconds to informings exhibit a different structure compared to seconds in assessment pairs. Pre-turn particles, which were analysed in section 2 as a constitutive part of second assessments in assessment pairs, are absent in second assessments to informings:

seconds in assessment pairs: pre-turn particle + assessment term
seconds to informings: non-lexical assessment signal +
                                assessment term *or* exclamatives

A different two-part structure is found and the position of the pre-turn particle is filled with a non-lexical assessment sound (see example (30)). Of course, non-lexical assessment sounds are not restricted to the position preceding a second assessment to an informing (see example (4), line 5), but pre-turn particles sound inappropriate in this position. Another format which is regularly produced in seconds to informings is represented in example (31) *wie entsetzlich!*. It is the format of exclamatives.[19] Syntactically, exclamatives roughly fall into two groups: exclamatives with an interrogative w-element like *wie* and exclamatives without such a w-element. In German, verb-second sentences especially possess ambiguity between an interrogative and a declarative interpretation. Although the phonetic details are not absolutely clear, it is indisputable that intonation plays a crucial role in disambiguation (*Wie groß ist er geworden?* 'How much taller has he become?'/*Wie groß ist er geworden!* 'How much taller he's become!'" *Das find ich ja interessant!* 'I find that interesting!'/*Das find ich ja interessant.* 'I find that interesting.') Intonationally marked exclamatives show a falling intonation contour and at least one pitch accent. This exclamative pitch accent is realized early in the intonational phrase, shows wide pitch range and amplitude, and duration of the accented syllables is increased, too. It has been noted in the literature that pitch accents in exclamatives show a certain independence from the focus-background structure of the sentence (cf. Altmann 1993:30ff.). If this is indeed so (further research will be necessary), exclamatives are highly suitable objects for beat-clashing accentuation patterns.

4.2 *Beat clashes in stories, informings or news deliveries*

Assessments with beat clashes are not restricted to the position of second assessment. They also occur as implicit or explicit first assessments in stories, informings or news deliveries. Excerpt (32) shows an instance of implicit assessment in line 3:

(32) China 25f
    1 T: ich hab | dir ne |
    2 I: | aber irgendwie | ja
→ * 3 T: ja. ne 'Karte von 'Ma''lay:'sja mal | mitgebracht |
            ((ehrfurchtsvoll))
** 4 I: | 'ts ahhh:: | to:ll:
                          ((click))
    | °ah-°
    5 T: | ° jetz paß auf.°
    6   und zwar ich hab
    7   son 'ganz 'tolles 'dickes 'Buch über Ma'laysia;
    . . .
   14   ehm (0.8) des is jetz (0.7) der 'Hauptteil
   15   da'zu gehört noch (0.3) der Teil von 'Borneo,
   16   der 'Norden von 'Bor | neo=da= | kannsse aber 'nich hin
   17 I: | hmhm |

    1 T: *I've brought | you a |*
    2 I: * | but somehow | yeah*
→ * 3 T: *yes I've brought along a map of | Malaysia*
            ((reverently))
** 4 I: *| 'ts ohhh great*
                          ((click))
    | oh
    5 T: *| now listen*
    6   *you see I have*
    7   *this wonderful great big book on Malaysia*
    . . .
   14   *uhm (0.8) that's the (0.7) main part now*
   15   *there's (0.3) a part of Borneo which belongs to it*
   16   *the northern part of Bor | neo but | you can't go there*
   17 I: *| hmhm |*

T informs I that she has brought a map of Malaysia. Instead of one main accent on the penult[20] T pronounces the name with three clashing accents and a prolongation of the main stressed syllable. By means of this prosodic realization T displays that she does not want I to focus exclusively on the naming and identification of a referent, but that she wants to draw I's attention to the evaluative loading of the term, i.e. reverence. I co-participates in T's affect display. Instead of simply acknowledging receipt of T's information by producing a 'continuer' hmhm (see Schegloff 1982), as she does later in line 17 where another country is introduced without beat-clashing accents,[21] she joins T's prosodically delivered evaluation in recognitional overlap by starting her assessment turn with a dental click followed by another non-lexical assessment sound *ahhh::* and the assessment adjective *toll* ('great'). Notice that I proffers her assessment in the format of second assessments to informings, namely the replacement of pre-turn particles by non-lexical assessment sounds.

Comparing the sequential placement of I's responses shows that the continuer occurs at the boundaries of two turn-constructional units and 'bridges' them (Goodwin 1986:207f.), whereas the assessment in line 4, which also starts in overlap with T's talk, is produced as a 'concurrent assessment' (see Goodwin 1986:213): it is placed within T's current turn-constructional unit and brought to completion by T's attention-focussing formulation *jetz paß auf* ('now listen') before she starts to talk about another referent, a book about Malaysia.

It seems to be the case that beat clashes are useful devices which provide for the speaker's affect display and which secure an immediate subsequent assessment. It also seems to be the case that in this position recipients regularly use assessment sounds, a combination of a non-lexical assessment sound plus an assessment adjective, or exclamatives. Example (33) shows another instance of such a response following the beat clashes in line 15:

```
(33)  China 19
         1 I:   ge'nau in 'der 'Zeit;
         2       gabs=en Ar'tikel in 'News'week,
         3 T:   hmhm
         4            (0.8)
         5 I:   ehm (.) da hatte en en son ameri'kanischer Journa'list,
         6            (1.0)
         7       ehm halt son paar 'schwarze Stu'denten da inter'viewt,
         8 T:   hmhm
         9            (1.0)
    *   10 I:   und (0.8) die: die ham also richtige 'Hor'ror,
        11       so 'Horrormeldungen (0.6) von sich gegeben; (0.3)
  (*)   12       der 'eine (0.5) war ma ver'droschen worden,
        13       vonner 'ganzen (0.3) 'Horde chi'nesischer Kommili'ton; (0.3)
        14       "weil 'er sich er'dreistet hatte,
   →   15       eine 'Chi'ne'sin 'zum "Tee einzuladen;=
   **  16 T:   ="n e i : : n : : ! ((entsetzt))
```

```
      1 I:   exactly at the same time
      2      there was an article in Newsweek
      3 T:   hmhm
      4            (0.8)
      5 I:   uhm (.) an American journalist
      6            (1.0)
      7      uhm had interviewed a few black students there
      8 T:   hmhm
      9            (1.0)
*     10 I:   and (0.8) they well they had real horror
     11      like horror stories (0.6) to tell (0.3)
(*)  12      one of them (0.5) had been beaten up
     13      by a whole horde of Chinese fellow students (0.3)
     14      because he had had the audacity
→    15      to invite a Chinese woman to tea;=
**   16      =no     ((horrified))
```

I is telling T about an article published in *Newsweek*: black students
studying in China have reported horrible news. One was beaten up
by a whole horde of Chinese fellow students because he dared to
invite a Chinese woman for tea. I's series of utterances is a tightly
sequenced story-telling which starts with a story preface (lines 10,
11) containing a strong first assessment (*Horrormeldungen*) which
prefigures the forthcoming story and serves as a blueprint for the
recipient to detect something horrible in I's talk. The story (or the
explanation of the first assessment) follows in lines 12 to 15; it
consists of one turn-constructional unit, but its content is divided
into two parts: first, a description of what Chinese students have
done (lines 12, 13) and, second, the providing of the reason for this
behaviour (line 14), which culminates in the climax of the story (line
15). I produces this last intonational phrase with five clashing
accents.[22] Immediately after this complex turn-constructional unit
is brought to completion, T performs an operation which is different from her actions in lines 3 and 8: she no longer simply acknowledges receipt of the information I is providing, but via extended
prolongation and exclamative intonation she assesses it as something really horrible and unbelievable and displays her indignation
and dismay. Again the beat clashes secure subsequent congruent
evaluation.

However, unlike the assessment in example (32) (line 4), T does not produce a concurrent assessment by starting her response directly after the beat clashes, which would look as follows:

```
1 A:  "weil 'er sich er'dreistet hatte,
2     eine 'Chi'ne'sin 'zum "Tee | einzuladen;   |
3 B:                             |"n e i : : n : : ! |
```

```
1 A:  because he had had the audacity
2     to invite a Chinese woman to | tea |
3 B:                               | no |
```

Owing to the fact that in extract (33) the recipient's response is not primarily aligned to beat clash on a single word, but to a whole proposition, she starts her evaluation immediately upon completion of the unit:

```
(33)  China 19
      14 I:  "weil 'er sich er'dreistet hatte
      15     eine 'Chi'ne'sin 'zum "Tee einzuladen;=
      16 T:  ="n e i : : n : : ! ((entsetzt))
```

```
      14 I:  because he had had the audacity
      15     to invite a Chinese woman to tea
      16 T:  no            ((horrified))
```

T is able to anticipate termination of this turn-constructional unit because I has signalled termination and thus a 'transition relevant place' (see Sacks, Schegloff and Jefferson 1974) on every parameter available: I produces a falling intonation contour on the infinitive *einzuladen*, which prosodically closes the current unit. On the semantico-pragmatic level, the climax of the story is reached, and as announced in the story-preface, I has told something horrible and she has also underlined her evaluation with the beat-clashing rhythm. Syntactically, I has started this part of her turn with the subordinate conjunction *weil*, which projects a verb-final sentence, in this case expanded with an extrapositioned infinitive complement. The latter is also a verb-final clause, so that the beginning of the infinitive signals the end of the turn-constructional unit, because the infinitive represents the right part of the *sentence brace (Satzklammer)*. The left brace, represented by a finite verb or a subordinate conjunction, and the right brace enclose the *middle field (Mittelfeld)*. The right verbal brace serves as an important syntactic cue for the completion of turn-constructional units in

German and recipients – like T in example (33) – regularly use this cue to start their turn.

Yet on some occasions speakers do not stop after the right brace is completed, because – at least in colloquial German – constituents which 'ought' to have been placed in the middle field can be, and are regularly, produced after the right brace and thus after the syntactic closure (see Uhmann 1993 and Auer, this volume). Although these constituents occur after the right brace they belong semantically and syntactically to the preceding turn-constructional unit:

(33) (a) ''weil 'er sich er'dreistet hatte, eine 'Chi'ne'sin 'zum ''Tee
        einzuladen;='nachmittags
        because he had had the audacity to invite a Chinese woman to
        tea=in the afternoon
      (b) ''weil 'er sich er'dreistet hatte, eine 'Chi'ne'sin [nachmittags]
        'zum ''Tee einzuladen;
        because he had had the audacity to invite a Chinese woman
        in the afternoon to tea

It follows from the interpretation of the right brace as a cue to syntactic closure that these expansions are vulnerable to overlap if they follow an intonational phrase with a falling contour and if they are latched (cf. the equal signs) onto the prior turn-constructional unit without any break or pause (see Uhmann 1993:349):

(33) China 19
    15 I: eine 'Chi'ne'sin 'zum ''Tee einzuladen;=
    16 T: =I''n e i : : n : : ! I
    17 I: =I 'nachmittags I

    15 I: *to invite a Chinese woman to tea*
    16 T: I *no*   I
    17 I: I *in the afternoon* I

Yet example (33) might be looked at from a different point of view. Goodwin (1986:213) and Goodwin and Goodwin (1992) have shown that speakers actively work to organize their talk in such a way that recipients' assessments can be placed as *concurrent* assessments within the current turn-constructional unit. If this is so, the concurrence achieved in this extract might not be accidental but systematically accomplished by I's expansion:

(33) China 19
    14 I: "weil 'er sich er'dreistet hatte,
    15   eine 'Chi'ne'sin 'zum "Tee einzuladen;= | 'nachmittags |
    16T: | "n e i : : n : : ! |
    14 I: *because he had had the audacity*
    15   *to invite a Chinese woman to tea=| in the afternoon |*
    16 T: | *no* |

The overlapped expansion here contains very important information, namely that the invitation was for the afternoon. However,
although T overlaps the climax of I's story, I doesn't treat T's display of indignation and dismay as an intrusion and thus problematic for her own turn (see Goodwin 1986:211); instead of
expectable repair she responds to T's *nein* in her next turn in line
18 by confirming the reported event. This absence of repair might
show that this is not an instance of an error in turn-taking but a
systematically achieved event:

(33) China 19
    15 I: eine 'Chi'ne'sin 'zum "Tee einzuladen;=
    16 T: =| "n e i : : n : : ! |=
    17 I: =| 'nachmittags |=
    18 I: =doch!
    19 T: °nein; das s 'ab'surd.°
    20   (1.0)
    21   °°hmhm°°
    22 I: °°das 'wirklich verrückt.°°
    23   (0.5)
    24 T: °°hmhm°°
    25   (1.8)
    26 T: °komisch,°
    27   also ich kenn das auch von Ma'laysia und 'Thailand her,

    15 I: *to invite a Chinese woman to tea*
    16 T: |*no* |
    17 I: | *in the afternoon* |
    18 I: *yes he had*
    19 T: °*no that's absurd*°
    20   (1.0)
    21   °°*hmhm*°°
    22 I: °°*that's really crazy*°°
    23   (0.5)
    24 T: °°*hmhm*°°
    25   (1.8)
    26 T: °*funny*°
    27   *well I've heard of that in Malaysia and Thailand too*

What follows in the next turns is a repetition of T's second assessment in line 19. However, the repetition is not an identical self-quotation. The evaluative force that was carried by the intonation contour in line 16 is given lexical 'gestalt' and it is transformed into an assessment adjective. T's second assessment in line (19) is also produced with low volume (°). With even more reduction in volume (°°) I produces a confirming assessment in line 22. Between these two assessments a pause of one second and a minimal token of appreciation display that no more topically coherent talk is coming and that instead topic closure[23] is proposed. The actual closing is accomplished by T in line 26. As the recipient of I's story, she herself begins to tell a story and displays the relationship between I's story and her upcoming story by reference to I's talk; i.e. the anaphoric term *das* presupposes prior establishment and recoverability of the antecedent within the discourse and the *auch* foreshadows a congruent experience.

The next example shows again an instance of an implicit first assessment occurring in an informing. It is responded to with a very elaborate second assessment that recipient and speaker also collaboratively manage to place in the midst of the speaker's talk.

```
(34)  China 9
          1 T:  °ich 'muß übrigens heut noch zum 'Michelsen,°
          2      °um 'drei,°
  *       3      weils 'Schwierigkeiten gibt,
  →       4      mit dem 'Pe'king'auf'ent'halt. (0.5)
          5      ich hab den jetz einfach ge'bu:cht,
  **      6 I:  ''das: find=ich ja interes'sant!
          7      also da (0.5)
          8 T:  hmhm
  **      9 I:  'das find ich ja (0.7) find ich ja 'wirklich en 'Hammer. (0.4)
 (**)    10      weil=ich weil ich 'glaube daß das so die 'Linie is, (0.6)
         11      die: die wir auch schon eh g- be | merkt | haben, (0.3)
         12 T:                                   |'hmhm |
         13 I:  daß nämlich die Chi'nesen 'anfangen,
         14      an 'allen 'Ecken,
         15      | zu redu    |'zieren und zu kür'zen und zu 'sparen,
         16 T:  | ° zu kürzen° |
  →      17 I:  'wo |'sie 'nur | 'kön'nen;
         18 T:      | hmhm |
         19 T:  hmhm
         20          (0.5)
         21 T:  'hh weil d 'des: war ja 'so,=
```

```
     1 T:  by the way I'm going to see Michelsen today
     2      at three
*    3      cause there're problems
→    4      with the trip to Peking
     5      I've just gone ahead and booked it
**   6 I:  that's interesting
     7      so (0.5)
     8 T:  hmhm
**   9 I:  that's you know (0.7) that really beats everything (0.4)
(**) 10     cause I think that that's like the line (0.6)
     11     that we've | noticed | before (0.3)
     12 T:          | hmhm  |
     13 I:  that the Chinese are beginning
     14     everywhere
     15     | to reduce | and cut and save
     16 T: | to cut    |
→    17 I:  wher | ever they | can
     18 T:      | hmhm     |
     19 T:  hmhm
     20          (0.5)
     21 T:  'hh cause what happened was
```

The second assessment stretches from line 6 to 17, and it is second to T's informing that she is facing difficulties concerning a stay in Peking. Although T has rather intricately built up suspense by starting her turn in a low, confidential voice and reaching the climax of her informing in line 4 with a beat-clashing rhythm, it is notable against the background of the analysis developed so far that I does not start her extended evaluation immediately subsequent to the beat clashes in line 4. Although T has produced a semantically complete utterance and reached the end of the turn-constructional unit with a falling intonational contour, which is regularly used to cue a 'transition relevant place', the recipient's talk does not begin even after a silence of 0.5 seconds. T resumes talk and starts to elaborate her information. At the end of the intonational phrase in line 5 T's current turn has recognizably not reached completion – either prosodically or semantico-pragmatically. Yet, before T proceeds to give further details, I starts her assessment, which also culminates in a beat-clashing intonational phrase. Despite the long distance between the beginning of T's turn in line 5 and the continuation in line 21 the absence of repetition is evidence of the continuation of the turn-constructional unit:

(34) China 9f
    5 T: ich hab den jetz einfach ge'bu:cht,
         ((second assessment))
  21 T: 'hh weil d- 'des: war ja 'so,=
  22   =daß die Frau ''Matz:,
  23   'mich ge'fragt hat,
  24   ob=ich nich en paar Tage in 'Peking bleiben wollte,

    5 T: *I've just gone ahead and booked it*
         ((second assessment))
  21 T: *'hh cause what happened was*
  22   *that Ms Matz*
  23   *asked me*
  24   *if I wanted to stay in Peking for a few days*

This positioning of the extended assessment might be the only way to provide a strong display of the assessor's emotional involvement, a positioning which is both as close as possible to the beat-clashing accentuation and in the middle of the co-participant's talk.

In brief the present data suggest that beat clashes in assessment utterances are very useful devices. The phonologically highly marked beat clashes take the accentuation pattern of the elative compounds as a blueprint and contextualize emphasis and display emotional involvement. The expressiveness of the beat-clashing rhythm in second assessments is further strengthened by the frequent use of non-lexical assessment sounds and the packaging of the assessment turns in exclamatives. All these cues combine in the contextualization of intensifying the assessment term and the speaker's affect display. Due to this interpretation it is quite natural that these cues can be turned into the contextualization of irony. In first assessments in stories or news, beat clashes seem to be the ideal form of packaging, one which not only provides for the speaker's affect display but also secures an immediate subsequent or concurrent second assessment.

In the following section I will analyse some problems that speakers can face using beat-clashing accentuation patterns. I want to show that beat clashes can turn assessments into risky conversational objects. This analysis might shed further light on the absence of beat clashes in assessment pairs and thus corroborate the analysis presented so far.

4.3 Assessments with beat clashes as risky objects

What consequences does the fact that a speaker does not just perform an assessment, but also realizes it with a beat-clashing accentuation pattern, have for how the talk is heard and dealt with by the
recipients? One way to investigate this issue is to look at how
assessment terms and assessment utterances packaged in this way
are treated when they come to completion. It was argued in sections
4.1 and 4.2 that the beat-clashing accentuation pattern provides a
general strengthening: both assessment terms and the local relevance of recipients' responses are strengthened. Beat-clashing
assessments seem to be not at all risky but useful devices which
provide for recipients' and speakers' affect display and which – in
stories or news – secure an immediately subsequent second assessment.

However, looking at example (35) might shed further light on
why beat-clashing assessments can become risky objects:

```
(35)  China 17
 *        1 I:   die ham ganz 'irre Ge'schichten erzählt;
          2           (1.6)
          3 T:   °hmhm°
          4           (1.3)
(*)       5 I:   die hatten 'alle durch die Bank die 'Einschätzung daß
                 'China
 →        6      eh 'durch 'und 'durch 'ras'sis'tisch is.
          7           (1.0)
          8      und=daß=sie 'sie als Schwarze werden 'immer zu'letzt
                 bedient,
          9           (0.73)
         10      stehen immer zuletzt |       ehm        | in der Schlange,
         11 X:                         | ((Unterbrechung)) |
                 ((Unterbrechung))
          . . .
1st story 15 I:  °eh das an der 'Bar in° in diesem Dhing Dho | ng im |
                 Hotel erlebt,
         16T:                                          | hmhm |
         17 I:   da kam ein Afri'kaner an die 'Bar,=
         18      =also das ist ne ''Mini |bar, |
         19 T:                         |°hm° |
         20 I:   das da sitz könn pf- da gibt=es höchstens 'acht 'Sitzplätze
         21           (0.6)
         22      und ehm (0.8) da kam also dieser Afri'kaner,
         23           (0.5)
```

```
         24       'und so ne Mi'nute später kamen der Hans-'Gert und
                  'ich;=
         25 T:   =hmhm
         26 I:   und die Chi"nesin hat sich sofort an den Hans-'Gert
                  und an 'mich gewandt;
         27       und ge'fragt was wir 'trin Iken woll Iten.
         28 T:                            I hmhm  I
         29 I:   und 'wir ham dann gesacht ehm
         30       daß: doch der 'Herr: zu'erst I dagewesen  I sei=
         31 T:                              I hmhm hmhm I
→        32 I:   =und da hat=se uns ziemlich (.) 'komisch so
                  'kon'ster'niert (.) 'angeguckt,
         33       und dann hat sie 'ihn (.) be'dient.
         34               (1.7)
2nd story 35 I:  und I in=ner I 'Zug (0.6) inner=inner 'Bahnhofsschlange,
         36 T:       I °°hm°° I
         37 I:   hab ich das 'auch mal gesehn,
         38               (0.6)
         39 T:   hmhm
         40               (1.0)
         41 I:   'wie: da 'wurden 'Weiße nach 'vorne geschoben,
→        42       und (.) und zwar "vor 'ein 'Schwarzen.
         43               (1.4)
**       44 I:   "irrsinnich!
         45               (1.4)
         46 I:   und 'das ham 'die 'auch er'zählt,
         47               (1.0)
         48       ehm daß ihnen das in 'Schlangen 'dauernd (0.4) 'dau'ernd
                  passiert=
         49       =daß I die Chine I sen sich 'vordrängeln. (0.5)
         50 T:        I hmhm    I
         51 T:   °hmhm hmhm° (0.9)


*        1 I:    they told really incredible stories
         2               (1.6)
         3 T:    °hmhm°
         4               (1.3)
(*)      5       they were all without exception of the opinion that China
→        6       uh is thoroughly racist
         7               (1.0)
         8       and that they they as blacks are always served last
         9               (0.73)
         10      they always have to stand I uhm         I at the end of
                  the line
         11 x:                              I((interruption))I
                  ((interruption))
```

...

1st story 15 I: °uh this was my experience too in the bar° of the
| Dhing Dho | ng hotel
16 T: | hmhm
17 I: an African entered the bar
18 well it's a mini | bar |
19 T: | °hm° |
20 I: this there only pf-there are only eight seats
21   (0.6)
22 and uhm (0.8) well then this African came in
23   (0.5)
24 and about a minute later Hans-Gert and I came in
25 T: hmhm
26 I: and right away the Chinese woman turned towards Hans-
Gert and me
27 and asked what we wanted | to dri | nk
28 T: | hmhm |
29 I: and then we said uhm
30 that the other man was | there before | us
31 T: | hmhm hmhm |
→ 32 I: and then she looked at us rather (.) peculiarly full of
consternation (.)
33 and then she went to take his order
34   (1.7)
2nd story 35 I: and | in the | train (0.6) in the in the line at the railway
station
36 T: |°°hm°°|
37 I: I also once saw
38   (0.6)
39 T: hmhm
40   (1.0)
41 I: how whites were pushed in front
→ 42 yeah they were pushed in front of a black guy
43   (1.4)
** 44 I: crazy
45   (1.4)
46 I: and that's what they said too
47   (1.0)
48 uhm that this happens to them all the time (0.4) when
they stand in line
49 that | the Chin | ese push their way to the front (0.5)
50 T: | hmhm |
51 T: °hmhm hmhm° (0.9)

In extract (35) I is trying to receive a congruent assessment or a reciprocal affect display for her story. Yet three times she fails to receive any response at all. The first failure (line 7) occurs during I's very complex 'story preface' (see Jefferson 1978), which announces the reporting of *irre Geschichten* ('incredible stories') about racist behaviour in China such as black students being served last and standing at the end of queues. Although I proffers a 'superlative assessment' in line 6, she receives no 'newsmark' or 'solicit'. The second and the third failures occur after the main line of I's two stories (see lines 34 and 43), which she produces to underline her claim. This absence of recipient talk is dramatic, because neither appreciation nor understanding of the story is displayed. Jefferson (1978:234) has shown that 'storytellers do not explicitly challenge or complain of tangential recipient talk (as they do not complain of recipient silence)'. Storytellers instead resume talk to provide further instances to which recipients can respond. That recipient talk is indeed dramatically absent can be corroborated by the fact that I, instead of another resumption of talk, finally herself produces the conditionally relevant second assessment in line 44.

Does the analysis presented so far give any evidence that might account for I's failures? It will be noted that I's failures occur either immediately after a beat-clashing accentuation pattern (lines 6 and 42) or after the turn-constructional unit which contains the clashing pattern is completed (line 33). It was argued that beat clashes contextualize intensity such that assessment terms realized with a beat-clashing rhythm are semantically stronger than without this prosodic make-up. In excerpt (35) I proffers a very strong assessment *durch und durch rassistisch* and her claim that China is a racist country is formulated as a universal sentence (*Allaussage*). It was also argued (see section 2) that proffering a first assessment is a risky activity, because first assessors face the risk of stating an assessment which cannot be agreed with. It follows that the more strongly a first assessment is formulated, the greater the possibility that recipients will not share the evaluation. As open disagreement is dispreferred (see section 2), recipients delay or withhold their second assessment and first assessors are given the opportunity to orient to an upcoming disagreement by modifying their first assessment. First assessors have two options to deal with upcoming disagreement. They can either downgrade their assessment (see

example (8)) to achieve agreement on a less extreme position; or
they can alternatively try to convince their recipient by either proffering stronger or equally strong assessments concerning a different
aspect of the assessable or by providing further evidence that the
assessment has been made on solid grounds (see example (4), p.
306). The latter is done by I in excerpt (35). Immediately after
the passage presented in (35) she starts a third story, which is an
upgrade (see excerpt (33), pp. 339ff.) to underline her claim of
racism and this time she is successful: she achieves a reciprocal
affect display and her story also implicates subsequent talk.

Moreover, not only first assessments can become more risky
than they are due to sequential constraints; proffering a very strong
second assessment that is further intensified through beat clashes
can also turn the much safer position of second assessor into a risky
activity. Without the intention to contextualize irony second assessors can run into problems by producing their assessment terms
with a clashing accentuation pattern. The talk to be examined in
the next example occurred after a detailed discussion. For convenience T's introduction is presented again:

(36) China 15 (Continuation of (33))
  9/1 T: °Ich 'muß übrigens heut noch zum 'Michelsen,°
    2   °um 'drei,°
    3   weils 'Schwierigkeiten gibt,
    4   mit dem 'Pe'king'auf'ent'halt. (0.5)

  9/1 T: *by the way I'm going to see Michelsen today*
    2   *at three*
    3   *cause there're problems*
    4   *with the trip to Peking*

((Extended narrative by T about how her trip to Peking may not be
able to take place because there is no guarantee of a guide or
financial assistance. I makes suggestions about how T can organize
her trip by doing without a guide and by spending the night with
some of I's friends.))

  1 T: °°aha; aha;°° 'hh=ja,=
  2   =ich 'frag dich dann nochmal,
  3   weil: nachher treff ich mich mit dem 'Michelsen=
  4   =mal 'sehn was das er'gibt,
  5   das Ge'spräch.
  6   (2.5)

352   Susanne Uhmann

→** 7 I: ah: das is ja ne "Un'ver'schämt'heit
    8   (2.5)
    9 I: | ° find ich ° |
   10 T: | ° finds sel | tsam.° (0.5)

    1 T: *I see I see 'hh yes*
    2   *I'll get back to you again with questions*
    3   *because later I'm meeting Michelsen*
    4   *and I'll see what comes of that*
    5   *that talk*
    6   (2.5)
→** 7 I: *ah it's really an outrage*
    8   (2.5)
    9 I: | *°if you ask me°* |
   10 T: | *°it's odd°* (0.5) |

After a detailed discussion T produces a story exit device in lines
2–5 which refers back to the beginning of her story (see example 34:
China 9, lines 1–4). Although T and I have devoted a long stretch
of talk to working out T's stay in Peking, T has refrained from
formulating any accusations or strong negative evaluations.
Nevertheless, disappointment and anger can be presupposed. Yet
I's assessment in line 7 is obviously too strong, because T produces
a very weak confirming assessment only when I weakens her evaluation by stating it as her personal point of view.

5 Rhythm in assessment pairs

Although prosody was not regarded in any systematic way in section 2, it will be remembered that none of the extracts presented
there showed a beat-clashing rhythm – either with the first assessment or with the second assessment. For convenience, examples (1)
and (3) are presented again:

(1) Hundertfünfzig 4
     1 H: wie alt,
     2 X: ja:: so:: sechsenzwanzig glaub=ich
  * 3 H: "schö::nes Alter
 ** 4 X: ja ne hehe (0.8) 'best(h)en 'Jah(h)re

     1 H: *how old*
     2 X: *oh about twenty-six I think*
  * 3 H: *nice age*
 ** 4 X: *yeah huh hehe (0.8) prime years*

(3)   Seglerinnen 3
*   1 A: all die 'Segler sin da 'glücklich draußen. ne,
**   2 B: haja die sin ganz (.) 'happy.

*   1 A: *all the yachtsmen are happy out there aren't they*
**   2 B: *oh yeah they're having a fine time*

The issue now arises of whether this absence might be accidental and thus only due to a limited corpus, or systematic and attributable to the interplay between the sequential organization of assessment pairs and the contextualization function of beat clashes in assessment utterances. In order to answer the question why assessment with a beat-clashing accentuation pattern might be systematically absent in assessment pairs, it is important to recall the organization of such pairs.

It was stressed in section 2 that in everyday conversation a formal preference for agreement and a dispreference for disagreement can be assumed. However, it was also argued that not only agreeing is preferred, but unambiguous agreeing, i.e. agreeing with an upgraded second assessment. Further, both first and second assessors are held responsible for the positions they state, but a systematic bias between first assessors and second assessors turns the position of first assessors into a risky one. As agreeing by producing an upgraded or at least same assessment is preferred, interlocutors have to orient to this preference so that assessment pairs that show this formal preference can be achieved.

If a first assessor presents an assessment that is further strengthened by a beat-clashing rhythm, the second assessor faces the problem that proffering an unambiguous agreeing second assessment implies the production of an assessment that has to be at least as strong as, or even stronger than, the first. How can this be achieved? It can only be achieved by presenting a stronger or equally strong assessment term realized with a beat-clashing rhythm. This is of course not impossible, but as assessors are held responsible for the positions they state, first assessors systematically increase the possibility of stating a first assessment that cannot be agreed with if they produce an evaluation which is near the end of the evaluation scale. Moreover, first assessors presenting an assessment with a beat-clashing rhythm not only increase the possibility of disagreement, they also leave little room for recipients who actu-

ally share their point of view to perform the most preferred action,
i.e. the proffering of an upgraded second assessment.

   If the description of the interplay between the contextualization
function of beat-clashing rhythm and the organization of assessment pairs is indeed valid, we would expect that first assessors
who present an assessment with a beat-clashing rhythm, instead
of receiving a congruent second assessment, i.e. a same or upgraded
assessment term with a beat-clashing rhythm, have to cope with
recipients who do not perform the preferred next action. Extract
(25) might be such an instance:

```
(25)  China 52
  *      1 I:   für 'mich wär das ja auch ne 'irre 'Chance gleich dann (0.9)
 (*)     2      in das 'volle 'Leben da ei(h)nzustei(h)gen hehehe
         3 T:   jaja jaja (.)
→(*)     4 I:   s(h)o 'a(h)lles 'ganz 'haut'nah (0.5) 'mit'zu'kriegen,
         5                      (2.6)
 M*      6      ah das is find ich schon 'unheimlich 'gut.
         7                      (2.0)
 (*)     8      da 'seh ich dann auch mehr.
         9                      (2.2)
 (*)    10      dann: (.) renn ich da nicht so ver'loren tou'ristisch (0.8) in der
                'Gegend rum;
        11                      (1.7)
 **     12 T:   aja (0.3) dann ists auch viel 'spannender;
        13 I:   hm
(**)    14 T:   weil man dann so die Struk'turen gut mitkriegt=


  *      1 I:   *for me it would also be a terrific opportunity to (0.9)*
 (*)     2      *plunge right into the full of life hehehe*
         3 T:   *yeah yeah*
→(*)     4 I:   *to experience it all very vividly (0.5)*
         5                      *(2.6)*
 M*      6      *ah I think it's really quite good*
         7                      *(2.0)*
 (*)     8      *I can see more too*
         9                      *(2.2)*
 (*)    10      *then (.) I won't have to run around like a lost tourist (0.8)*
                *everywhere*
        11                      *(1.7)*
 **     12 T:   *oh yeah (0.3) it'll be much more exciting too*
        13 I:   *hm*
(**)    14 T:   *cause you get to know the structures*
```

I's turn starts with an already familiar structure: *first assessment* (line 1) + *explanation* (line 2). The fact that I will visit T's friends during her stay in Malaysia instead of staying in a hotel is assessed as an *irre Chance* ('terrific opportunity'), because it gives I the opportunity to experience local life. This sequence is not responded to with a second assessment displaying a congruent evaluation but simply confirmed. I resumes talk with a syntactically bound reformulated explanation in line 4 which contains the elative compound *'haut.'nah*, which is realized with a beat-clashing rhythm and underlined with laughter. In comparison to the explanation in line 2 the explanation in line 4 is semantically and prosodically strengthened. Yet this reformulated explanation is not responded to at all and recipient's talk remains dramatically absent for 2.6 seconds. I treats the non-appearing second assessment as an upcoming disagreement (cf. also examples 4 and 7) and displays this interpretation in a downgraded modification of her first assessment in line 6, which also fails to produce agreement. After another dramatic absence of recipient talk I starts to reformulate her explanation in lines 8 and 10. Here too, I states much weaker arguments, and line 10 especially shows a change of perspective, because the positive effect is formulated *ex negativo* as *nicht so verloren touristisch*. Neither explanation shows a beat-clashing rhythm. Although very late and after another silence, T performs a congruent second assessment, which on the basis of I's reformulations is the preferred upgraded second assessment. In order to produce this preferred action subsequent to I's strong assessment and her positive affect display contained in the beat-clashing explanation in line 4, T would have had to proffer a much stronger assessment.

That recipients are regularly not willing to do so can be demonstrated by the analysis of the next extract:

(26) Hundertfünfzig 10
     1 H: . . . schon richtig 'Frühlings(stimmung)?
     2 X: jaja (.) wie es: wa-
     3   also=es blüht alles: (.) und: (0.5) (sehr) 'warm
     4   (1.0)
     5   es war 'schön
  * 6   und jetzt stehn wir hier wieder in diesem häßlichen 'Kiel
→(*) 7   es is 'eis'ka:lt 'regnerisch (.) 'miese 'Stadt;

```
         8              (1.5)
(*)      9       E'xa(h)men.
  *     10       is(h)=a(h)lles sehr 'une(h)r | freu(h)lich he
        11  H:                                | hasse Rainer mitgenommen?
        12  x:  ja ja sicher, (.)
        13       ach sonst würd=ich das überhaupt nich aushalten
```

```
         1  H: . . . already real spring (atmosphere)
         2  x:  oh yes (.) it was-
         3       well everything was in blossom (.) and (0.5) (quite) warm
         4              (1.0)
         5       it was beautiful
  *      6       and here we are again in hideous Kiel
→(*)     7       and it's icy cold rainy (.) miserable city
         8              (1.5)
(*)      9       exams
  *     10       everything is very unplea | sant
        11  H:                             | did you bring Rainer with you
        12  x:  yes of course (.)
        13       oh otherwise I wouldn't be able to stand it
```

X's turn shows the same structure as I's turn in line 1 and 2 in
example (25): first assessment + explanation with beat-clashing
rhythm. The explanation is presented as a three-item list (see
Jefferson 1990). Yet, after list-completion, X's turn receives no second assessment. After silence from the recipient, X produces a
fourth item in the list, which underlines her negative attitude
towards Kiel. This fourth item, *Examen*, unambiguously carries
very negative connotations among students and is also underlined
with laughter, but X's turn is neither dealt with as an assessable nor
as something to be responded to with laughter. X receives neither a
second assessment nor a reciprocal affect display nor laughter. Her
turn is instead conversationally deleted by H's production of a
topically only slightly coherent question that is produced in overlap
with X's explicit assessment.

Of course, as shown in section 2, first assessors may also fail to
receive congruent second assessment without having underlined
their assessment with a beat-clashing rhythm. However, first assessments that are further strengthened through beat clashes increase
the risk of dispreferred next actions, because only recipients willing
to state an even stronger position than the first assessor will proffer
an upgraded second assessment.

It is not only first assessments in assessment pairs that are regularly produced without a beat-clashing rhythm; beat clashes are
also absent in second assessments. Could this absence also be systematic and accounted for on the basis of the analysis presented so
far? As upgrading second assessments are preferred, recipients
should make use of the opportunity to strengthen their assessment
through beat clashes. However, as shown in section 4.3 (see example 36), seconds to informings presented with beat clashes can
become too strong. In that case we would expect a semantically
congruent second assessment underlined with a beat clash not to
close the sequence but to lead to an expansion. Yet as not a single
instance of beat clash on a second assessment in an assessment pair
was found in the data, the recipients' avoidance might be another
instance that shows the formal preference for agreement.

6 Concluding remarks

Assessments with achieved beat clashes are rhythmically highly
marked structures. The unmarked alternation of prominent and
non-prominent syllables is cancelled in favour of a succession of
only prominent syllables. It has been shown that speakers not
only let beat clashes happen, but that beat clashes are achieved by
turning lexically non-prominent syllables into prominent ones.
These achieved beat clashes regularly occur within assessment
utterances. Assessment utterances occur at different loci in conversation: (i) within assessment pairs – as first and second assessments – and (ii) within stories, news or informings – also as first
and second assessments.

Although there is a sequential similarity of first assessments followed by second assessments upon completion in both conversational objects and a shared formal preference for agreement and
display of congruent evaluation, assessment pairs and stories,
news or informings also differ from each other. First, assessment
pairs consist of single turn-constructional units, whereas stories,
news or informings are realized as multi-unit turns. It follows that
what counts as 'upon completion' is different in these two conversational objects and has to be displayed in the case of stories.
Second, second assessments in assessment pairs exhibit a different
format compared to seconds to informings, i.e. seconds in assess-

ment pairs: *pre-turn particle + assessment term*; seconds to informings: *non-lexical assessment signal + assessment term* or *exclamatives*. Third, beat clashes regularly occur within stories or in news
but not in assessment pairs. This distribution in the rhythmical
make-up of assessments has been accounted for.

It was claimed that the absence of beat clashes in assessment
pairs is not accidental but systematic and accountable on the
basis of the analysis presented in this chapter. The emphasis and
intensification of assessments was identified as the basic cue provided by beat-clashing rhythm. It seems as if the accentuation pattern of elative compounds, in which one element intensifies the
other, serves as a blueprint to contextualize 'intensity' or
'emphasis' in utterances which would be less emphatic or less strong
if they were realized without beat clashes. Owing to this contextualization function, it is quite natural that these cues can be turned
into the contextualization of irony.

It has been shown in section 2 that assessment pairs are organized in such a way that stated agreements are maximized and
stated disagreements are minimized. This distribution does not
follow automatically from a shared evaluation system, but has to
be achieved by the participants. Yet although agreement is preferred, there is a systematic bias between the positions of first and
second assessor. Proffering a first assessment has to be done on
uncertain grounds. Without an already stated point of view towards
the assessable, first assessors always face the risk that their recipients will not share their evaluation. This risk of receiving an unpre-
ferred next action, i.e. no second assessment upon completion of the
first assessment or a second assessment interpretable as upcoming
disagreement, is systematically increased by strengthening a first
assessment with a beat-clashing rhythm, because only recipients
willing to state a position as strong as, or even stronger than, that
of the first assessor will proffer an upgraded second assessment,
which would have to be realized with a beat-clashing rhythm,
too. It seems to be an obvious conclusion to take the rare use of
beat clashes in first assessments of assessment pairs as an orientation of first assessors towards the formal preference for agreement.
However, it is not only first assessments in assessment pairs that are
regularly produced without a beat-clashing rhythm; beat clashes are
also absent in second assessments. As upgrading second assessments

are preferred, recipients should make use of the possibility of strengthening their assessment through beat clashes. Yet it was shown that seconds can also become too strong. In fact, not a single instance of beat clash on a second assessment in an assessment pair was found in the data: one conclusion may be that recipients' avoidance shows participant orientation towards a formal preference for agreement.

Although assessing a person, an event or an experience is also done in the course of story-telling, this aspect is not as focal as in assessment pairs. Stories, news and informings are also realized as multi-unit turns and tellers have to provide their recipients with information about the climax of the story and possible story completion points. First assessments in stories or news realized with a beat-clashing rhythm seem to be the ideal packaging: they provide not only for the prosodic identification of the climax of a story but also for the speaker's affect display. Both aspects are relevant information for the recipient, the first for the placement of the second assessment 'upon completion', the second for the recognition of the speaker's attitude towards the assessable and a reciprocal affect display. The risk of stating positions that cannot be agreed with is not totally abandoned in these conversational objects, but for storytellers or deliverers of news the balance of costs and rewards might lead to a different result. The aim of securing an immediate subsequent or concurrent second assessment might override the risk of stating an assessment which is difficult to agree with. Comparing the absence of beat clashes on seconds in assessment pairs and their use on seconds to informings, it is the expressiveness of the beat-clashing rhythm that might account for the different distribution. What might be 'too much' as a second in an assessment pair with its main function of displaying a congruent assessment might be well suited in an activity which beyond that has to display the understanding and appreciation of a story or informing. The beat-clashing rhythm is well suited to this reciprocal affect display and its expressiveness is further strengthened by the frequent use of non-lexical assessment sounds displaying emotional involvement and by the packaging of the assessment turns as exclamatives.

Appendix: transcription conventions

Each line of the transcript corresponds to an intonational phrase.

.;,?	strong falling, falling, rising, strong rising intonation at the end of an intonational phrase
!	exclamative intonation
I China I	onset and offset of simultaneous talk
I toll I	
=	linking without any intervening pause or gap
(1.5)	length of a silence
(.)	micro-pause of less than 0.2 sec.
'China	primary accent on the following syllable
′China	secondary accent on the following syllable
"China	extra strong accent on the following syllable
° China °	stretches of talk perceived as being spoken 'quietly' with low volume
°° China °°	very low volume
° China °°	low volume: decreasing
°° China °	low volume: increasing
Chi::na	sound stretching; the more colons the greater the degree of stretching
Chi-	cut-off of the prior sound or word
(. . . .)	talk occurred but could not be transcribed
(China)	unsure transcription
((Räuspern))	comments by the transcriber on non-verbal activities of the speaker
'hh	audible inbreath
'ts	dental click
hehe	laughter
Chi(h)na	a word spoken with laughter

Notes

I am grateful to Peter Auer and Elizabeth Couper-Kuhlen for their comments on an earlier version of this article and to C. John Foskett for correcting my English.

1 Preferred: agreement, acceptance of compliments; dispreferred: disagreement, agreement after self-denigration, self-praise in compliment responses.
2 '(. . .) the activity of performing assessments constitutes one of the key places where participants negotiate and display to each other a congruent view of the events that they encounter in their phenomenal world. It is thus a central locus for the study of the "shared under-

standings" that lie at the heart of the anthropological analysis of culture' (Goodwin and Goodwin 1992:182).

3 Cf. Pomerantz's (1984:66ff.) distinction between 'strong agreements' and 'weak agreements'.

4 In contrast to the repair-initiating repeats analysed by Jefferson (1972), the assessment term here is realized with a falling intonation contour.

5 Pre-turn particles seem to be systematically absent only when second assessments are produced in extended overlap with first assessments; cf. example (6).

6 There is no agreement on whether these domains are universal, whether they are all equally important, whether they are indeed organized by the 'Strict Layer Hypothesis' (see Selkirk 1984:26; Nespor and Vogel 1986) or whether prosodic structure, e.g. at the level of intonational phrasing, can show recursive organization (see Ladd 1986:322ff.).

7 There is an extensive literature on stress and rhythm in the framework of metrical phonology that cannot be taken into account here. For an introduction, see Goldsmith (1990:Ch. 4). An exhaustive treatment of the pros and cons of grid or tree models would also be out of place here. For German see, among others, Giegerich (1985) as a supporter of a tree-only theory, Uhmann (1991) for a grid-only theory, and Jacobs (1991) for a combination of grids and trees according to the notation of stress or rhythm. For German word stress a number of different approaches are under discussion, cf. Wiese (1988), Eisenberg (1991) or Vennemann (1991).

8 See Uhmann (1991:Ch. 4.2) for a more detailed account of metrical grid construction in German. Although much of this work is in the sense of Selkirk (1984), there are important differences, namely a more complex prosodical structure (cf. accent domains, AD) and the non-cyclic application of the Nuclear Stress Rule.

9 Liberman and Prince (1977:317) define the relation between the metrical elements (adjacency, alternancy, clash) as follows: 'Elements are metrically adjacent if they are on the same level and no other elements of that level intervene between them: adjacent elements are metrically alternating if, in the next lower level, the elements corresponding to them (if any) are not adjacent; adjacent elements are metrically clashing if their counterparts one level down are adjacent.' For critique, see Hayes (1984) and Selkirk (1984).

10 This distinction aims at identifying the smallest unit in which timing intervals are equal, i.e. *isochronous*: irrespective of the number or quality of intervening unstressed syllables, the duration from one stressed syllable to the next, i.e. the foot interval, is said to tend to remain stable in stressed-timed languages, whereas foot duration is said to vary depending on the intervening number of unstressed syllables in syllable-timed languages (see Pike 1945). For a critical discussion, see e.g. Auer and Uhmann (1988). Pike (1945:35f.) has already noticed beat clashing rhythms: 'in English, however, the [syllable-timed, S.U.] type

is used only rarely. In these particular rhythm units each unstressed syllable is likely to be sharp cut, with a measured beat on each one; . . . the general impression is that of *spoken chant*'.

11 For instance: *'stroh.'dumm*, *'stink.'faul*, *'stock.'steif*, *'haut.'nah*, *'stock.'kon.ser.va.tiv*, *'stock.'schwul*, *'kern.ge.'sund*, *'pu.del.'naß*, *'sau.'dumm*, *'sau.'kalt*, *'eis.'kalt*, *'blut.'jung*, *'blut.'arm*, *'scheiß.e.'gal*, *'tot.'schick*, *'Bom.ben.er.'folg*, *'Scheiß.'spiel*, *'Rie.sen.skan.'dal*, *'Bul~len.'hi.tze*, *'Höl~len.'lärm*, *'Pfunds.'kerl*, etc. For morphological details see Fleischer and Barz (1992:204f., 230ff.) and for the accent pattern see Kohler (1977:194) and Wurzel (1980).

12 Inseparably linked to rhythm is of course not only verbal interaction but movements of different complexity like walking, running, swimming and dancing and cultural achievements like music and poetry. Rhythm plays an important role even in painting: very young children produce so called 'Atembilder' simultaneously with both hands, the oldest ornaments which have been found exhibit rhythmic structure, and the rhythm of the brushstroke is an important device in impressionistic and expressionistic painting as well as in action painting.

13 See also note 10. If indeed speakers of German only quite rarely achieve rhythmically integrated speech, those instances in which isochrony is achieved must be of particular interactional interest. For a re-definition of isochrony as an interactionally relevant concept, see Auer (1990). For a detailed discussion and analysis of various levels of isochrony in conversational English, see Couper-Kuhlen (1993:Ch. 3) and the work by the research group at the University of Konstanz on 'Contextualization by rhythm and intonation': see Auer and di Luzio (1992).

14 Following Bolinger (1964:22f.) I want to distinguish between *stress* as an abstract lexical feature which can be assigned to any (but usually only one) syllable per word and *accent* as an actual prominence, which has to be phonetically realized. Even though a word of more than one syllable can be uttered without any pitch accent, i.e. with a completely flat intonation contour, one syllable carries the feature stress. Although the use of these terms is not totally consistent in Anglo-American literature, the ambiguity of 'Wortakzent' in German is especially problematic because it neglects important differences between the lexical feature and actual prominence. Cf. Uhmann (1991:21ff).

15 The acoustic measurements were obtained with the program 'Signalize[TM]'. I wish to thank P. Auer for helpful instructions and for making this program available to me.

16 See Selting (1994) for detailed analysis of emphatic speech style in story-telling, van Os (1989) for intensifying in German and Müller (1991) for metrical emphasis and rhythmic scansions in Italian.

17 See Pomerantz (1975:Ch. 2) and especially Jefferson (1978) for a detailed analysis of assessments in story-telling.

18 See Jefferson (1978:244) for the analysis of assessments as a 'prototypical telling-ending-device'.

19 The status of exclamatives in the system of sentence modes is under controversial discussion, cf. among others, Altmann (1993), Rosengren (1992).

20 Lexically, the word has the main stress on the antepenult *Ma.'lay.si.a*, but the last two syllables were fused by turning the syllable nucleus of the penult into a glide.

21 But notice that the naming is also embedded in a different activity.

22 This example shows the interplay between grammatical rules for accent placement and the use of beat clashes as a contextualization cue: there are no accents after the 'focus exponent' (see Uhmann 1991:Ch. 5), which is the argument in argument + predicate structures (see also (33) line 15) but the predicate in adjunct + predicate constructions as in example (25) line 4. A more detailed account is presented in Uhmann (1994).

23 See note 18 and Goodwin (1986), Goodwin and Goodwin (1992:169ff) for the reduction of volume as an important cue to this interpretation. Cf. also extract (9) lines 16 to 21.

References

Altmann, H. 1993. Fokus-Hintergrund-Gliederung und Satzmodus. In M. Reis (ed.) *Wortstellung und Informationsstruktur*. Tübingen: Niemeyer, pp. 1–37.

Auer, P. 1990. Rhythm in telephone closings. *Human Studies*, 13: 361–392.

Auer, P. and A. di Luzio (eds.) 1992. *The Contextualization of Language*. Amsterdam: Benjamins.

Auer, P. and S. Uhmann 1982. Aspekte der konversationellen Organisation von Bewertungen. *Deutsche Sprache*, 1:1–32.

1988. Silben- und akzentzählende Sprachen. Literaturüberblick und Diskussion. *Zeitschrift für Sprachwissenschaft*, 7:214–259.

Bergmann, J. 1982. Schweigephasen im Gespräch. Aspekte ihrer interaktiven Organisation. In H. G. Soeffner (ed.) *Beiträge zu einer empirischen Sprachsoziologie*. Tübingen: Narr, pp. 143–184.

Bolinger, D. 1964. Around the edge of language: intonation. *Harvard Educational Review*, 34 (2): 282–293. Also in D. Bolinger (ed.) 1972. *Intonation*. Harmondsworth: Penguin, pp. 19–29.

Cook-Gumperz, J. and J. Gumperz 1978. Context in children's speech. In N. Waterson and C. Snow (eds.) *The Development of Communication*. Chichester: Wiley, pp. 3–23.

Couper-Kuhlen, E. 1993. *English Speech Rhythm. Form and function in everyday verbal interaction*. Amsterdam: Benjamins.

Duranti, A. and C. Goodwin (eds.) 1992. *Rethinking Context*. Cambridge University Press.

Eisenberg, P. 1991. Syllabische Struktur und Wortakzent: Prinzipien der Prosodik deutscher Wörter. *Zeitschrift für Sprachwissenschaft*, 10: 37–64.

Fleischer, W. and I. Barz 1992. *Wortbildung der deutschen Gegenwartssprache*. Tübingen: Niemeyer.

Giegerich, H. J. 1985. *Metrical Phonology and Phonological Structure. German and English*. Cambridge University Press.

Goldsmith, J. 1990. *Autosegmental and Metrical Phonology*. Oxford: Blackwell.

Goodwin, C. 1986. Between and within: alternative sequential treatments of continuers and assessments. *Human Studies*, 9: 205–217.

Goodwin, C. and M. Goodwin 1992. Assessments and the construction of context. In A. Duranti and C. Goodwin (eds.), *Rethinking Context*, Cambridge University Press, pp. 147–189.

Gumperz, J. J. 1982. *Discourse Strategies*. Cambridge University Press.

1992. Contextualization and understanding. In A. Duranti and C. Goodwin (eds.), *Rethinking Context*. Cambridge University Press, pp. 229–252.

Hayes, B. 1984. The phonology of rhythm in English. *Linguistic Inquiry*, 15: 33–74.

Jacobs, J. 1991. Focus ambiguities. *Journal of Semantics*, 8: 1–36.

Jefferson, G. 1972. Side sequences. In D. Sudnow (ed.) *Studies in Social Interaction*. New York: Free Press, pp. 294–338.

1978. Sequential aspects of storytelling in conversation. In J. N. Schenkein (ed.) *Studies in the Organization of Conversational Interaction*. New York: Academic Press, pp. 219–248.

1984. Notes on some orderliness of overlap onset. In V. D'Urso and P. Leonardi (eds.) *Discourse Analysis and Natural Rhetorics*. Padova: Cleup Editore, pp. 11–38.

1990. List-construction as a task and resource. In G. Psathas (ed.) *Interaction Competence. Studies in Ethnomethodology and Conversation Analysis* 1. Lanham, Md.: University Press of America, pp. 63–92.

Kohler, K. J. 1977. *Einführung in die Phonetik des Deutschen*. Berlin: Erich Schmidt Verlag.

Ladd, D. R. 1986. Intonational phrasing: the case for recursive prosodic structure. *Phonology Yearbook*, 3: 311–340.

Liberman, M. and A. Prince 1977. On stress and linguistic rhythm. *Linguistic Inquiry*, 8: 249–336.

Müller, F. E. 1991. Metrical emphasis: rhythmic scansions in Italian conversation. KontRi Working Paper 14, University of Konstanz.

Nespor, M. and I. Vogel 1986. *Prosodic Phonology*. Dordrecht: Foris.

1989. On clashes and lapses. *Phonology*, 6: 69–116.

Pike, K. L. 1945. *The Intonation of American English*. Ann Arbor: University of Michigan Publications.

Pomerantz, A. 1975. Second assessments: studies of some features of agree-ments/disagreements. Ph.D. diss., University of California.

1984. Agreeing and disagreeing with assessments: some features of pre-ferred/dispreferred turn shapes. In J. M. Atkinson and J. Heritage (eds.) *Structures of Social Action. Studies in conversation analysis.* Cambridge University Press, pp. 57–101.

1986. Extreme case formulations: a way of legitimizing claims. *Human Studies*, 9: 219–229.

Rosengren, I. 1992. Zur Grammatik und Pragmatik der Exklamation. In I. Rosengren (ed.) *Satz und Illokution*, Vol. I. Tübingen: Niemeyer, pp. 263–306.

Sacks, H., E. A. Schegloff and G. Jefferson 1974. A simplest systematics for the organization of turn-taking for conversation. *Language*, 50: 696–735.

Schegloff, E. A. 1982. Discourse as an interactional achievement: Some uses of 'uh huh' and other things that come between sentences. In D. Tannen (ed.) *Analyzing Discourse: Text and talk.* Georgetown University Round Table on Languages and Linguistics 1981. Washington, D.C.: Georgetown University Press, pp. 71–93.

Selkirk, E. O. 1984. *Phonology and Syntax. The relation between sound and structure.* Cambridge, Mass.: MIT Press.

Selting, M. 1994. Emphatic speech style – with special focus on the proso-dic signalling of heightened emotive involvement in conversation. In C. Caffi and R. W. Janney (eds.) *Involvement in Language.* Special issue of *Journal of Pragmatics*, 22: 375–408.

Uhmann, S. 1989. On some forms and functions of speech rate changes in everyday conversation, KontRI Working Paper 7, University of Konstanz.

1991. *Fokusphonologie. Eine Analyse deutscher Intonationskonturen im Rahmen der nicht-linearen Phonologie.* Tübingen: Niemeyer.

1992. Contextualizing relevance: on some forms and functions of speech rate changes in everyday conversation. In P. Auer and A. di Luzio 1992, pp. 297–336.

1993. Das Mittelfeld im Gespräch. In M. Reis (ed.) *Wortstellung und Informationsstruktur.* Tübingen: Niemeyer, pp. 313–354.

1994. *Grammatische Regeln und konversationelle Strukturen. Fall-studien aus Syntax und Phonologie.* Habilitationsschrift, University of Wuppertal.

van Os, C. 1989. *Aspekte der Intensivierung.* Tübingen: Narr.

Vennemann, T. 1991. Skizze der deutschen Wortprosodie. *Zeitschrift für Sprachwissenschaft*, 10: 86–111.

Wiese, R. 1988. *Silbische und lexikalische Phonologie. Beiträge zum Chinesischen und zum Deutschen.* Tübingen: Niemeyer.

Wurzel, W. U. 1980. Der deutsche Wortakzent: Fakten – Regeln – Prinzipien. *Zeitschrift für Germanistik*, 1: 299–318.

9

The prosody of repetition: on quoting and mimicry

ELIZABETH COUPER-KUHLEN

1 Introduction

The research question which this chapter addresses is motivated by the growing awareness that speakers who are engaged in verbal interaction with one another employ adaptive strategies which entail 'matching' their speech behaviour in one way or another to that of their interlocutor. On the verbal level this matching may involve repetition of words, expressions or whole utterances, e.g. to contextualize affiliation or support (Tannen 1987, 1989). On the non-verbal level we may find rhythmic matching, as, for example, in English conversation, where adjusting one's rhythm and tempo to that of one's partner at turn transitions counts as a well-timed entry to the floor (Couper-Kuhlen 1993, Auer, Couper-Kuhlen and Müller (to appear)); or we may find melodic matching, as for instance in 'wheel-spinning' (Chafe 1988:7), where successive interlocutor turns are occupied with saying the same thing (albeit with different words) and intonationally echoing one another.

The general question with respect to verbal and non-verbal matching of this kind is: when does one speaker's repetition of the words and/or prosody of another become one speaker's mimicry of another? Under what conditions does matching speech behaviour switch from being something that interlocutors do together, to something that one interlocutor does *to* the other? Related to this is a question concerning the 'rules of mimicry' (Goffman 1974:537). Goffman has pointed out that, in quoting a person, we quite naturally 'quote' the overlay of accent and gesture as well. However, at some point – for instance, if a male speaker quotes a female speaker and 'too much' of the gender expression is taken over – the quoter becomes 'suspect', a mimic with presumably disaffiliatory intentions (1974:539). What counts as proper quoting of another's prosody? And what are the limits which determine how much copying is socially acceptable in a given culture or speech community? This chapter investigates such issues with special attention to pitch register. It will be shown that speakers have two ways of repeating the pitch register of another: relatively (using similar pitch levels but relative to their respective voice ranges) and absolutely (using exactly the same pitches). These different means are used by speakers as strategies for the accomplishment of interactional and social goals, the one contextualizing verbal repetition of a co-participant as quotation, the other contextualizing it as mimicry.

2 The relation between prosodic and verbal repetition

In order to address the research question properly, we must first of all clarify the relation between prosody, one aspect of the nonverbal part of speech behaviour comprising such features as melody, rhythm, pause, tempo, loudness, etc., and its verbal counterpart, the words, in communication. Prosody does not typically occur in discourse without some syllable-sized speech-like unit to carry it.[1] Yet the fact that prosody is carried by a lexico-syntactic structure does not mean that it is determined by that carrier. In fact, we should think of different prosodic configurations as being in principle interchangeable for one and the same lexico-syntactic string – and conversely, of different lexico-syntactic strings as being utterable with the same or similar prosodic configurations.

The nature of the relation between prosody and its obligatory, yet variable, verbal carrier holds for the field of repetition as well. On the one hand, prosodic repetition always involves the *presence*, in one degree or another, of verbal repetition – or its *absence*. We may find situations in which both words and prosody are repeated, as, for instance, when speaker A says 'With a flourish.' and speaker B repeats 'With a flourish.', using the same stressing, intonation, tempo, etc. Yet on the other hand, verbal and prosodic repetition are independent of one another. That is, lexico-syntactic or verbal repetition may occur with differing prosodic or non-verbal configuration, and prosodic repetition may occur with differing lexico-syntactic carriers. To cite an example of the former: A can ask

'What did they do in Chinatown.' and B can respond 'What did they do in Chinatown?', where the words remain constant but the intonation (speech melody) changes. To give an example of the latter: A can begin a list with, for example, 'Bread, butter' and B can continue with 'Marmalade, ice cream', where intonation remains constant but the words change. In sum, one speaker's prosody may or may not repeat another speaker's prosody and it is carried by some kind of verbal structure, which itself may or may not be repetitious of another speaker's words.

Verbal and prosodic repetition have at least two features in common. First, with respect to *form*: in both cases it is useful to conceptualize repetition not as a binary, plus-or-minus feature but as a cline, extending roughly from a 'perfect copy' at one extreme through a 'near copy' at some intermediate stage to a mere 'copy for all practical purposes' at the other extreme. On a verbal level, for instance, the exact reduplication of words can be distinguished from a modified replication, and the latter from a rough paraphrase.[2] The same sort of distinctions can be made on a prosodic level, as will be shown below.

Second, verbal and prosodic repetition are alike with respect to *function*, in that replication of form does not necessarily mean replication of function. As the writings of the Bakhtin circle have emphasized (primarily with respect to reported speech), the meaning of words is irrevocably tied to the context in which they are used (Vološinov 1926, Bakhtin 1934–1935). That is, however 'faithfully' an original bit of speech may be reported, its meaning is inevitably another because the reporting context is by definition different from the reported context (Vološinov 1926, 1930). From a formal point of view, much reported speech can be thought of as a kind of verbal repetition. Therefore, what holds for reported speech also holds for verbal repetition: repeated words can never have the same situated meaning as the original ones because the context is by definition a different one. The same applies to *prosodic* repetition, as we shall show below.

3 Types of prosodic repetition

If the notion of prosody, rather than being treated as an unanalysed whole, is broken down into specific dimensions, different kinds of prosodic repetition may be distinguished. The term *prosody* in its linguistic acceptation refers to those non-verbal dimensions of speech which have the syllable as their minimal domain and which can be related to the auditory parameters of loudness, duration and pitch. When we speak of prosodic *repetition* we can therefore distinguish a repetition or a copying of syllable loudness, of syllable duration and of syllable pitch. These features are, however, directly comparable only provided the utterances in question have identical syllables. When dealing with utterances of differing verbal make-up, more abstract patterns of relative length, loudness and pitch must be identified in order to compare the original with its copy. For instance, in languages where stress is a phonologically relevant category, the length, loudness and pitch of the first and/or last stressed syllables of two partially similar utterances or parts thereof may be compared.

In addition to these three dimensions with respect to the minimal domain of syllable, we may also distinguish prosodic features in a larger domain: a cohesive sequence of syllables, or an intonation phrase. Here too one can identify duration, loudness and pitch or pitch range for the whole sequence of syllables. Overall duration, when put in relation to the number of syllables articulated, gives an indication of speech rate (see Uhmann 1992). Overall pitch is sometimes referred to in the literature as 'key' (Sweet 1906:§169 cited in Crystal 1969:149). However, to avoid confusion with Brazil's notion of 'key' (Brazil, Coulthard and Johns 1980:60ff), which refers essentially to the relative pitch of the first stressed syllable of an intonation phrase, I shall speak here of *register* instead.[3] Thus, there are at least six ways – and undoubtedly more – in which it is meaningful to speak of prosodic repetition: repetition of length, loudness and pitch at the syllable level and repetition of speech rate, loudness and register at the phrasal level.[4]

The repetition cline is of course applicable to the single dimensions of prosody as well. For instance, repetition of syllable durations in an utterance can be more or less exact. The copied syllable may correspond to the length of the original in absolute terms – or it may correspond only relatively, e.g. in ranking (the same syllable in both utterances being the longest). With respect to syllable loudness, we can also distinguish absolute identity, e.g. in terms of decibels, or only relative similarity: a syllable may be loud with respect to some speaker-dependent norm in both original and copy. As far as pitch is concerned, the possibilities for repetition are more complex, due to the interaction of stress and pitch. It is customary to identify simple or complex pitch movements on or initiating on stressed syllables, which I shall refer to as *tones*. The stressed syllables of two utterances may have the same or a similar tone, with the same or similar amount of pitch excursion. Moreover, the pitch of unstressed syllables in a copy may have varying degrees of resemblance to those of the original. Finally, with respect to phrasal register, the global pitch of an intonation phrase may be identical on an *absolute* scale, e.g. in terms of Hertz values, or only similar on a *relative* scale to that of the original: e.g. it may be high (or low) in the speaker's voice range in both original and copy.

If we now combine the various types of prosodic repetition – and the differing degrees of identity which they may hold to the original – with the varying degrees of verbal replication conceivable, the number of ways in which an utterance or part of an utterance may be said to resemble another is rather mind-boggling. This chapter will focus on a subset of the possible combinations, viz. on cases of *pitch register repetition* accompanying verbally highly repetitive utterances or parts thereof.

4 Dynamics of register repetition

Register is one of the most challenging aspects of prosody to describe, partly because it has been largely ignored in intonational research, where attention has tended to focus on tones in isolated intonation phrases. Register differences do not make themselves apparent until sequences of intonation phrases are considered. The challenge in describing register becomes even greater when more than one speaker is involved. Speakers, as we all intuitively know, may have radically different natural voice ranges. The voice of a typical adult male, for instance, may cover a range from approximately 80–200 Hz. A typical female voice, on the other hand, may range from 180–400 Hz (see 't Hart, Collier and Cohen 1990:12).[5] Therefore, what is low or moderate pitch for a female may be high pitch for an adult male in absolute Hz terms. Conversely, what is high pitch for an adult male may be low or moderate for a female on an absolute scale. The challenge then is to determine under what conditions it is meaningful to speak of register repetition at all when speakers with different natural voice ranges are involved.

The following discussion will attempt to illuminate this issue empirically. The material on which the study is based comes from a Radio Picadilly phone-in programme entitled *Brain Teaser*, broadcast daily in Manchester several years ago.[6] In this programme listeners call in to the studio and try to guess the answer to a riddle which is announced on the air. The first caller with a winning answer receives a free T-shirt. Thereafter, a new riddle is introduced. My analysis covers cases of prosodic and verbal repetition in approximately two hours of recording from this programme. The data involve two different studio anchormen talking to a wide variety of male and female callers.

4.1 Register matching on a relative scale

The classical answer to the question of how to judge pitch register with respect to different natural voice ranges is to state that it must be done on a *relative* scale.[7] Absolute pitch values,[8] so prosodic theory goes, are meaningless unless they are put in relation to a speaker's individual voice range; see Crystal: 'what is important for the linguist is the relative aspect of the pitch change' (1969:111), or, somewhat more categorically, Chatman: 'Absolute frequency levels are of no significance in speech; low voices and high voices pronounce the same phrase octaves apart without introducing differences in form or meaning' (1965:189). According to received opinion then, two pitches or pitch registers in speech can only be meaningfully compared with respect to their relative location in different speakers' voice ranges.

In the *Brain Teaser* data, cases of lexical repetition are indeed often accompanied by *relative* register repetition, or matching.[9] For example:

```
(1)   MI:   it is complete
            though it seems it isn't
            what do you reckon
      CI:   well I think I've got this one
            and I got it as you were reading it ou:t
 →          is the answer hole
```

        (0.6)
→   M1: is the answer hole
     C1: yes
     M1: er: no
     C1: oh
     M1: mm why did you think that
     C1: well complete as whole w-h-o-l-e
     M1: mm
     C1: and h-o-l-e as a hole
     M1: yeah
     C1: and a hole (.) is complete
        although it seems it isn't
        ((he he he hm))

In this call the moderator (M1) repeats the caller's utterance *is the answer hole* but in doing so he does not match her pitch register in absolute terms. This can be seen from Figure 9.1, which shows an acoustic analysis of the two utterances.[10] Displayed are the unanalysed sound wave (in the middle of the display), amplitude (dotted-line peaks below but approaching the sound wave), fundamental frequency (horizontal dash-like marks above and/or below the sound wave), and zero crossings (typically the lowest trace in the display) over time for the two utterances. The fundamental frequency, calibrated in Hertz (50 Hz per interval starting from 40), corresponds roughly to pitch (see, however, below). From this display it can be seen that the caller's register is higher than that of the moderator in absolute terms. The caller's pitch contour begins at 301 Hz and ends at 144 Hz (cursor readings), whereas the moderator's repetition begins at 167 Hz and ends at 83 Hz. (Note that, aside from register, the contours themselves look rather similar.)

The acoustic analysis of fundamental frequency as we have it here, however, is not a wholly satisfactory representation of the way these contours are perceived (see also 't Hart, Collier and Cohen 1990). For one, the Hz scale is linear but we hear pitch logarithmically. That is, we need larger intervals at higher frequencies than at lower frequencies in order to hear equivalent pitch steps (Fry 1979:8f). The Hz values must therefore be converted to a logarithmic scale if the fundamental frequency curve is to correspond more closely to human perception of pitch. This has been done in Figure 9.2, where the initial, intermediate and final values

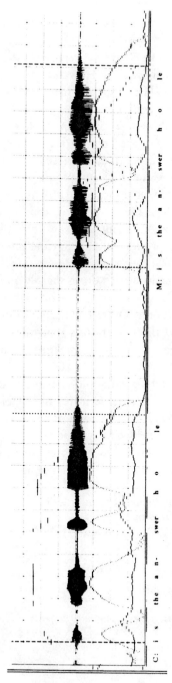

Figure 9.1 Combination display of "is the answer hole" (Ex. 1)

of the contours are expressed logarithmically in musical semitones
(ST).[11]

The upper diagram in Figure 9.2 represents the utterances on a
single *common* musical scale: all Hz values are expressed as semitone intervals from 50 Hz. From this diagram it can be seen that,
even when pitch is expressed in semitones, the two utterances do
not have matching absolute register. In the lower diagram, however, the Hz values have been put on a semitone scale relative to
each *individual* voice range (i.e. expressed as semitone intervals
from the lowest Hz value a given speaker is inclined to use).[12]
This representation makes it clear that the moderator's repetition
is a very good match of the caller's utterance in terms of relative
register. The caller begins about 8 ST above her lowest pitch (or
base) and rises to approximately 16 ST; the moderator does the
same in relation to his lowest pitch or base. Likewise, at the end
of the utterance, the caller's pitch drops sharply on *hole* from 15 ST
to her base: the moderator begins just a bit higher and also drops
sharply to his base on *hole*. Overall, the caller's utterance is high in
her voice range, and the moderator's repetition achieves a good
degree of relative register matching by virtue of its being equally
high in his.

In addition to matching phrase-level register, the repetition in
example (1) also has a fairly good match of syllable-level prosody.
That is, the length, loudness and pitch of single syllables are comparable in original and copy. The syllable-level match in other cases
of verbal repetition is often less close, although relative register
matching can still be identified. For instance, in:

(2) M2: it is complete though it seems it isn't (.)
           what d'you reckon
→   C2: the heart
           (0.5)
→   M2: the heart
     C2: yeah
     M2: straight from the heart: from Janet Burton (.)
           °h in Moston (.)
           and the heart is the wrong answer Janet
     C2: oh dear
     M2: it isn't the answer I'm looking for
     C2: never mind
     M2: never mind

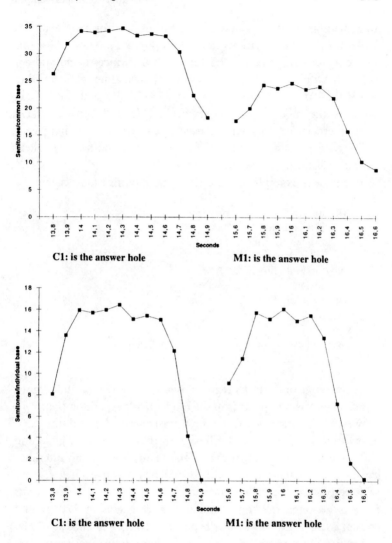

Figure 9.2 Relative register matching in "is the answer hole" (Ex. 1)

In repeating this caller's utterance, the moderator uses a higher, wider tone on *heart* than his caller does (Fig. 9.3). Notice, however, in the lower half of Figure 9.3 that both utterances begin and end similarly with respect to their individual bases, although in absolute terms the caller's contour begins at 278 Hz and ends at 193 Hz, whereas the moderator's begins at 137 Hz and ends at 88 Hz. Thus there is indeed some relative pitch register matching here, although the moderator has in effect partially modified the caller's overall register by extending its upper line.

In the next example, a more dramatic modification occurs:

```
(3)   M1:   anyway we have a new one
            it is complete (.)
            though it seems it isn't
            what do you reckon
 →    C3:   the Holy Bible
            (0.5)
 →    M3:   the Holy Bible: (.) is wro:ng
      C3:   oh::
      M1:   oh::
      C3:        never mind |°h°
      M1:                   |never mind never mind
```

Here the range of the pitch register used by the caller has undergone a radical extension upwards in the moderator's repetition (Fig. 9.4). However, the pitches of the first unstressed *the* and the final unstressed *-ble* are within 1 ST of each other in both original and copy (see the lower half of Fig. 9.4).[13] Thus, the second utterance can be said to achieve a modified match of relative pitch register with respect to the caller's utterance, although in absolute terms there is no pitch overlap at all: the caller begins at 270 Hz and ends at 213 Hz, the moderator begins at 110 Hz and ends at 89 Hz.

Let us now turn to the question of what relative register matching achieves when it accompanies a strongly repetitive utterance as in these examples. A speaker's pitch in relative register matching is rather Janus-faced. On the one hand, with its own individual base it is clearly marked as belonging to this particular individual; in other words, it indexes this speaker personally. On the other hand, its location in the speaker's voice range is not a 'free choice', because it is determined by the (relative) location of another speaker's pitch.[14] In other words, the pitch register is imposed from without. By

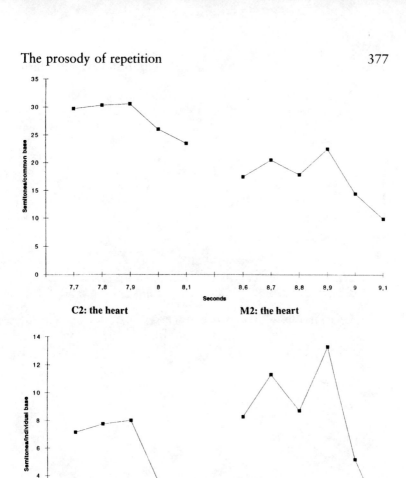

C2: the heart   M2: the heart

C2: the heart   M2: the heart

Figure 9.3 Relative register matching in "the heart" (Ex. 2)

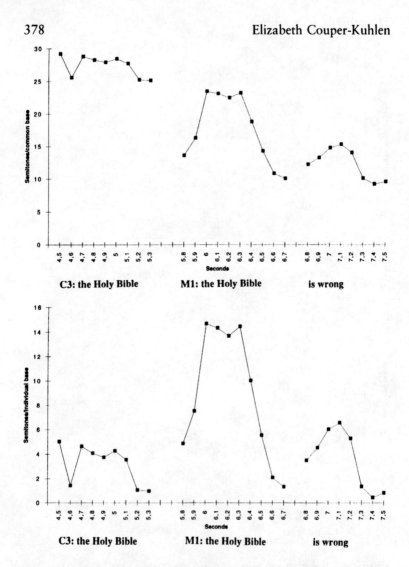

Figure 9.4 Relative register matching in "the Holy Bible" (Ex. 3)

analogy with the semantic distinction between words which are
'used' vs word which are 'mentioned',[15] the pitch register here is
'mentioned'.[16] Together with a repetition of caller's words, the
mentioned prosody can be heard as tagging the moderator's utterance as a *quotation* of caller's utterance. Its effect could be represented orthographically as follows:

(1') c1:   is the answer hole
            (0.6)
      m1: "is the answer hole"

(2') c2:   the heart
            (0.5)
      m2: "the heart"

(3') c3:   the Holy Bible
            (0.5)
      m1: "the Holy Bible:" (.) is wro:ng

Notice now that not every verbal repetition is marked with prosodic repetition. When the moderator says *and the heart is the*
wrong answer Janet, this repeat of *the heart* is not a quotation
because its prosody does not match that of the original in any
way. Only the moderator's voice (and prosody) are in play here,
whereas with the repeats in (1')– (3') both the caller's and the
moderator's voices can be heard. (To make this distinction clear,
we shall henceforth enclose verbal repeats with mentioned prosody
in quotation marks.) Examples (1')– (3') are thus quite literal examples of what Vološinov and Bakhtin described as one voice over-
laying another (Vološinov 1930, Bakhtin 1934–1935). The overlay
is all the more subtle, the higher the degree of matching. Where a
modification of syllable-level prosody accompanies register repetition, the modified syllables are in effect foregrounded. In Bakhtin's
framework, they evidence a 'contamination' by the reporting voice
of the reported voice. Their prosodic differences from the original
(e.g. greater syllable length, higher/wider tone, etc.) are attributed to
the reporter's voice, who is understood to be making some expressive comment on the words quoted.[17]

In the *Brain Teaser* data, cases of relative register matching with
verbal repetition like those above are similar in a number of ways.
On a sequential level, they have in common that it is routinely the
moderator who repeats an immediately prior turn or part thereof by

the caller. The caller's turn is typically one that has been prompted
by the moderator. For instance, in the examples give above, it is the
moderator who elicits a proposed solution to the riddle with *what
do you reckon* or the equivalent, and the caller who then offers a
candidate solution in the next turn. It is the caller's proffered guess
which the moderator then repeats. The proffering of a candidate
solution to the riddle by callers has strong sequential implications: it
makes some pronouncement by the moderator on the adequacy of
the solution with respect to the riddle conditionally relevant.[18] In
the data at hand, the task of signalling to the caller how adequate
the solution is, is often accomplished mechanically: for instance, a
jingle is blended in with the sound effects of a spluttering brass
instrument and a synthetic voice saying *oh dear! you blew it kid.*
Other times, however, the pronouncement of adequacy is accomplished personally by the moderator, typically following some kind
of verbal repetition.

A second way in which these sequences with relative register
repetition are alike is that they develop interactionally in constrained ways. In one group of examples, for instance, the moderator's quotation is treated by callers as an initiation of repair. Next
turns are addressed to the task of confirming or disconfirming the
moderator's assumption of what the proffered answer is. Thus in
(1), when the moderator repeats *is the answer hole*, the caller
responds with *yes*. The moderator's repetition together with the
caller's response creates an insertion sequence (Schegloff 1972),
embedded within the larger guessing sequence, itself formatted as
a question sequence. Once the moderator has a confirmation of
what the caller's proferred guess is, he pronounces on its correctness
by answering the caller's first question: *is the answer hole – no.*
Example (2) patterns similarly.

Example (3) illustrates another possible development: here the
moderator uses a quotation of the caller's proffered answer to construct a turn designed to pronounce on the adequacy of that answer.
In this case the floor does not pass back to caller until the moderator has completed the more extensive turn. This kind of turn construction accomplishes two tasks at once: via a quotation of the
caller's answer, the moderator displays his 'understanding' of it,
and at the same time via a pronouncement on adequacy (*is
wrong, is not the answer I'm looking for*, etc.) he announces

whether or not callers have 'won'. This second type of interactive development in sequences with relative register matching can be thought of as a telescoped version of the first, where the two steps (confirmation of guess and pronouncement on adequacy) are accomplished in separate turns.

Although displayed and treated as eliciting confirmation of or confirming the caller's guess, the moderator's verbal and prosodic repetition in (1)–(3) can also be seen to fulfil a staging function. Given the strong sequential implication which the proffering of a candidate solution creates for an immediate pronouncement concerning its adequacy, and given callers' expectable anticipation about whether or not they have won the game, the moderator's repetition – often with syllable lengthening, pausing and slow tempo/speech rate – can be heard to *delay* the pronouncement. This dramatic technique gives listeners in the radio audience time to examine the proffered solution and to wager a guess themselves on its appropriateness. Thus, it increases interest and heightens suspense not only for the caller but also (and especially) for the radio audience.

4.2 Register matching on an absolute scale

Yet significantly enough, there are numerous examples in the *Brain Teaser* data which belie the classical tenet that only relative pitch or register is meaningful in speech. These are cases of lexical repetition in which there is clear matching of register on an *absolute* scale. Extract (4) is a good example (⇒ signals absolute register repetition):

```
(4)    M1:  h you can find reference in any Latin dictionary to a briga:de
  →    C4:   °.h- .h troops
             (0.5)
  ⇒    M1:  "troops"(0.1)
             erm (0.1)
  ⇒         "troops" is wrong
       C4:  oh:
```

Here the moderator repeats the caller's proffered answer *troops* twice. The first repetition is not only a good approximation in terms of tone; it is also a perfect match of the upper level of the caller's register in absolute terms, as the combination display in

Figure 9.5 makes clear. Both the caller's utterance and the moderator's first rendition of it begin at 379 Hz (cursor readings) and fall steeply downwards.[19] The second repetition comes close to being an absolute match, being pitched at 353 Hz (cursor reading). Note that this absolute matching is not the result of accidental similarity between the caller's and the moderator's voice ranges. In fact, the normal voice range of this moderator is much lower than that of the caller: his natural base is approx. 83 Hz, hers is 129 Hz. The difference between the moderator's absolute pitch repetition and his own normal register is visible when we compare the pitch of his *"troops"* to that of his *erm*, which has a cursor reading of 126 Hz in Figure 9.5, or *is wrong* (see the upper half of Fig. 9.6). Because of the difference in natural pitch range between moderator and caller, his pitch on *"troops"* is higher, relatively speaking, in his voice range than her (identical) pitch on *troops*: this can be appreciated from the lower half of Figure 9.6. In order for the moderator to reach the same absolute pitch level as the caller, he must shift into falsetto. In this sense his absolute register matching can be seen as an achieved effect; we might say that it is part of the 'recipient design' of his turn.

Nor is this case of absolute register matching an isolated phenomenon. In fact, M1 is quite fond of using it, in particular when his caller has a naturally high voice. Compare:

```
(5)   M1:  it is complete though it seems it isn't
           what d'you reckon
 →    C5:  is it a spring
           (0.2)
 ⇒    M1:  "is it a spring" (0.1)
           no it isn't |s-
      C5:              |oh
      M1:  it's not a spring it's not a ring my pal (.)
           and it's certainly not a spring

(6)   M1:  you can find reference in any Latin dictionary to a brigade
           (1.0)
      C6:  is it rabble
           (0.6)
      M1:  is it-
           (0.2)
 →    C6:  "rabble"
           (0.3)
```

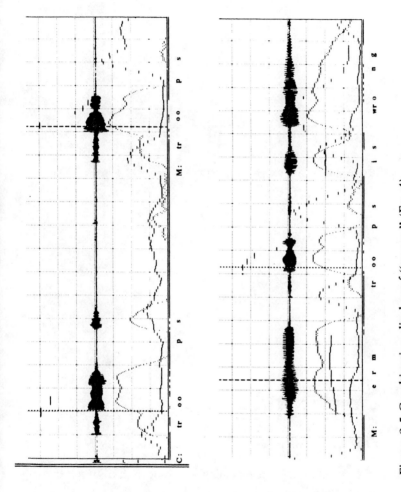

Figure 9.5 Combination display of "troops" (Ex. 4)

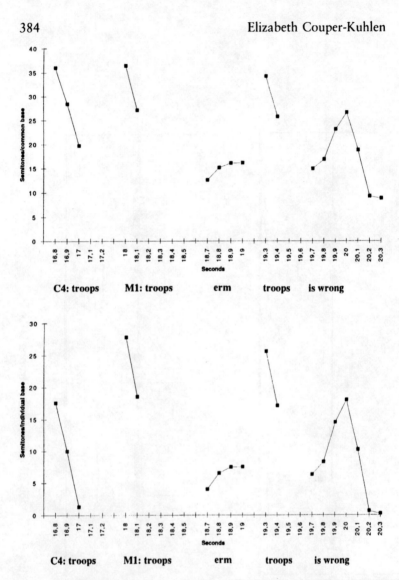

Figure 9.6 Absolute register matching in "troops" (Ex. 4)

⇒   Mı: "rabble" (0.5)
           er:
           no it isn't (.) h
           it isn't rabble (.)
           no way is it rabble
           how do you- how do you work out rabble
     C6:   oh me dad to:ld me °h°
     Mı: did he
           he's a daft dad i'n't he

In terms of syllable-level prosody the moderator's repetition of *is it
a spring* in example (5) is not a perfect copy of the caller's utterance:
his rendition of *spring* is somewhat longer than hers and lacks the
rise–fall in tone (see Fig. 9.7). However, in terms of overall register,
it is a very good absolute copy: both utterances begin at between 18
and 21 ST, rise to between 26 and 27 ST and terminate at approximately 21 ST above 50 Hz (upper half of Fig. 9.7). In order to
achieve this, the moderator must adjust his natural register
upwards: instead of using his base of 83 Hz, he must adopt the
caller's base of 135 Hz.

Example (6) illustrates a case with even more tonal modification
(see Fig. 9.8). Here the peak values which the caller and the moderator reach on the first syllable of *rabble* are within 2 ST of each
other; yet the moderator ends his contour approximately 12 ST
lower than the caller (upper half of Fig. 9.8). Despite the tonal
modification, however, this can be considered a case of absolute
register matching because the two speakers have approximately the
same upper-level (topline) pitch. Moreover, as the lower half of
Figure 9.8 shows, this is not an artificial product of naturally
similar pitch ranges; because the moderator's and the caller's
bases are quite different, the same values do not have comparable
locations relative to each individual base. The moderator's pitch is
relatively speaking much higher in his voice range than is his caller's
(identical) pitch. In other words, here too the moderator's absolute
pitch register repetition is an achieved production: in order to
reproduce the caller's peak of 26 ST, he must shift from his base
at 83 Hz to the caller's at 182 Hz.

It might be argued now that such examples could just as well be
treated as cases with little or no *relative* register matching. This
would accord with the claim that it is only relative pitch which

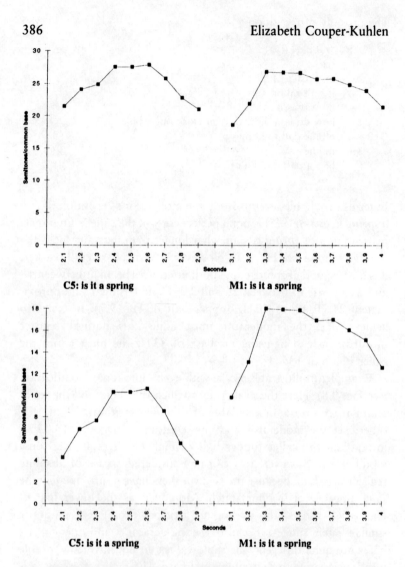

Figure 9.7 Absolute register matching in "is it a spring" (Ex. 5)

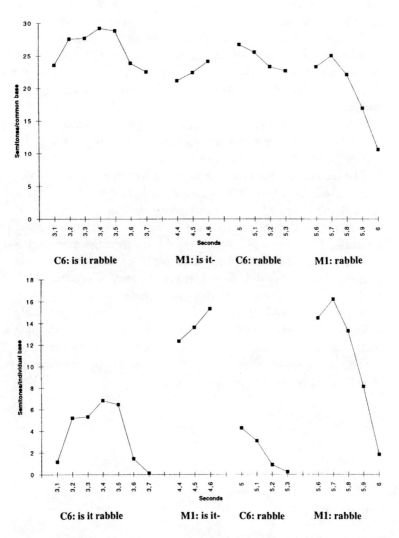

Figure 9.8 Absolute register matching in "rabble" (Ex. 6)

counts in speech and it would avoid the introduction of an additional analytic category. However, two arguments speak against such a stance. First, what is significant about the phenomenon of absolute register repetition is not just that there is a less-than-perfect match on a relative scale, but, more importantly, that there is a close-to-perfect match on an absolute scale. The latter is something of a feat. Folk linguists may think of it as a talent which only born singers possess. Yet in fact, everyday conversationalists use absolute register matching regularly: and they exploit it for specific interactional purposes (see below).

The second and even more compelling reason for treating absolute register repetition as a separate analytic category is that a sequential analysis of the contexts in which it occurs reveals that conversants orient differently to it compared to relative register matching. In excerpts (4)–(6), callers do not treat the moderator's repetition with absolute register matching as an attempt at eliciting confirmation. If they did, their next turns would be occupied with confirming or disconfirming the moderator's 'understanding' of their guess.[20] Instead, although the moderator's repeat is routinely followed by a pause, it receives no uptake from callers. Assuming that these are complete turn-constructional units (and the tonal configuration suggests as much), the sequential development in (4)–(6) could be represented as follows:

(4′) C4:   °.h- .h troops
            (0.5)
      M1:   "troops"
→   C4:   (0.1)
      M1:   erm

(5′) C5:   is it a spring
            (0.2)
      M1:   "is it a spring"
→   C5:   (0.1)
      M1:   no it isn't

(6′) C6:   "rabble"
            (0.3)
      M1:   "rabble"
→   C6:   (0.5)
      M1:   er:

This mode of presentation suggests that callers could have come in following the moderator's repeats but did not. If this is so, then the fact that there is no response here, in comparison to (1)–(3), may mean that something different is going on interactionally. This serves as additional justification for recognizing absolute register matching as a separate and significant kind of prosodic repetition.

But what *is* going on interactionally in these sequences? The key to the answer lies in what absolute register repetition involves, in particular for speakers with naturally different voice ranges. To match another speaker's absolute pitch values means in a sense taking over that speaker's base and producing a pitch interval with approximately the same number of ST steps above an 'alien' base. In cases where a speaker with a naturally low base takes over a much higher base, the transposition is particularly noticeable because it involves switching into falsetto register. That is, in order to repeat a pitch which is produced by a caller with middle voice register, the moderator on numerous occasions abandons middle and shifts to head voice register. This accounts for why his voice sounds unnatural, artificial, disguised in these examples.[21]

Absolute register matching can be thought of as a kind of prosodic *mimicry*. In a Goffmanian framework we could say that the moderator becomes the animator of the caller's utterance but, significantly, he animates the words with a borrowed voice. In citing a caller, he not only repeats the words but also imitates the way these words were said. This use of non-natural prosody can be seen to cue a shift in frame, if we understand 'frame' in the Goffmanian sense of interpretative schema (1974:21). It signals that the words themselves are not the speaker's own and are not to be taken 'seriously':

When a speaker employs conventional brackets to warn us that what he is saying is meant to be taken in jest, or as mere repeating of words said by someone else, then it is clear that he means to stand in a relation of reduced personal responsibility for what he is saying. He splits himself off from the content of his words by expressing that their speaker is not himself or not he himself in a serious way.   (Goffman 1974:512)

In conjunction with a high degree of verbal repetition, mimicry comes close to what Bakhtin described as *parody*:

with parody, as in stylization, the author employs the speech of another, but, in contradistinction to stylization, he introduces into that other speech an intention which is directly opposed to the original one. The second voice, having lodged in the other speech, clashes antagonistically with the original, host voice and forces it to serve directly opposite aims. Speech becomes a battlefield for opposing intentions. (Bakhtin 1929, 1978:185)

Just as parody is related to direct quotation because both entail the reporting of another's speech, so prosodic mimicry is related to prosodic quotation. In both cases some prosodic parameter of a speaker's utterance is repeated, or 'reported', in another's utterance. However, with prosodic quotation as in (1)–(3), the reported register is adapted to the reporting speaker's natural voice range, whereas with prosodic parody as in (4)–(6), the reporting speaker's register is modified to match the voice range of the reported speaker. In both cases the reporting voice can still be heard: it may seem more audible with quotation adapted to its individual base, but it may ultimately be just as noticeable in parody if the foreign base being assumed is naturally a quite different one.

The two sets of examples discussed so far have in common that the speaker whose words and prosody are being reported is not only co–present with the reporter, but that the report is immediately adjacent to its source. The producer of the source is at the same time the recipient of its report and therefore in the sequential position of responding to it in some way. The fact that an immediately adjacent repeat with absolute register matching meets with silence (rather than eliciting confirmation, as does a repeat with relative register matching) provides an indication that recipients interpret it as mimicry. One of the distinguishing features of mimicry, or parody in Bakhtin's words, is the passivity of its object:

It is indeed a fact that in . . . parody the other speech act is completely passive in the hands of the author who avails himself of it. He, so to speak, takes someone else's speech act, which is defenseless and submissive, and implants his own intentions in it, making it serve his new aims. (Bakhtin 1929, 1978:190).

When the object of mimicry is a co-present conversational partner, this passivity may transfer as a lack of response to the mimicking turn.

However, if the moderator's verbal and prosodic repetition counts as an instance of mimicry, it still remains to determine why he would choose such a format for his turn. Recall that relative register matching on repeats in similar sequential environments functioned as a staging device to increase interest and heighten suspense. Because of their sequential placement, the repeats in (4)–(6) clearly also have a delaying effect. As in (1)–(3), they are preceded by pausing. Thus they give both the moderator and the radio audience time to examine the proposed solution for its appropriateness. Yet a repeat with elements of prosodic mimicry also arguably carries an additional message: by imitating his caller's words *and* pitch, the moderator can be heard to draw attention to and indirectly criticize the guess and/or the way it is produced. In the case of (4), where absolute register matching entails the use of falsetto, the criticism implied seems to pertain to speaker's current pitch level. Indeed, C4 uses higher relative pitch on her guess – it is 17 ST above her individual base – than do C1, C2 and C3, who are not mimicked by the moderator.[22] In the case of (6), on the other hand, the point of criticism appears to be less the height of caller's voice (it is, relatively speaking, much lower than C4's, being only 5–7 ST above her base) than the 'daftness' of her guess: cf. his query *how do you work out rabble* and subsequent commentary *he's a daft dad i'n't he*. In both cases, however, the moderator is using indirect non-verbal means to imply criticism of a face-threatening nature. At the same time he is exercising social control over his callers, from whom he appears to expect 'normal' pitch of voice and intelligent guess work.

Yet it should not be forgotten that the interaction between moderator and caller takes place on the radio and that the success of the programme in which it is embedded depends crucially on audience interest. Conceivably, one of the ways audience interest can be maximized is by enlarging the participation framework such that mere overhearing listeners can be made partners in the communicative process. The moderator's prosodic mimicry is one subtle way of doing precisely this. Indeed, the implicit commentary which he makes by imitating the caller's voice is arguably directed as much to the radio listeners as to the caller. In other words, his message is not only 'Your voice is too high' or 'Your guess is daft', but also 'Her voice is too high' and 'Her guess is daft'. This type of personal criticism, made in the presence of the object criticized and via a mimetic rendition of the criticizable itself, has the undeniable attraction of turning listeners into voyeurs: they become silent witnesses to a socially emboldened act. It also establishes an axis of collusive communication between listeners and moderator. The radio audience thus serves as the occasion and the excuse for the moderator's parody: without an appreciative audience, this kind of mimicry would be aimed too pointedly at the object of criticism and might no longer be socially acceptable in everyday conversation. At the same time personal criticism of the caller, if expressed too baldly, would have the effect of discouraging other potential callers and would ultimately be counter-productive for the moderator's programme. Thus his choice of prosodic mimicry rather than explicit verbal criticism is a resourceful and well-motivated strategy.

4.3 Absolute and relative register matching in other sequential environments

The discussion so far has focussed on guessing sequences in the *Brain Teaser* data. This should not be understood to mean, however, that relative and absolute register matching occur only here. Absolute register matching, for instance, is also found accompanying verbal repetition in the following:

```
(7)  MI:  have you got all the wor:ld with you there as normal
     C3:  well: yes me mum's just come in actually (.)
          she's been out on the razzle
     MI:  oh she been out-
          is she rat-legged again
     C3:  yes ⌊again
     MI:      ⌊is she
          ev:ery night that we speak to you (.)
          she's rat-legged ⌊i'n't she
     C3:                   ⌊it's terrible
     MI:  every time we ⌊speak to you
     C3:               ⌊((he he))
→    C7:  excu:se me:
⇒    MI:  "excu:se me:"
     C3:  ((ha ha ha))

(8)  MI:  you can say:
          you can say: hello to the wor:ld while you're on
     C8:  well I'd just like to say hello t' (1.0)
          parents (1.0)
          girlfriend
          Janet Banks h (.)
```

```
            Margret Banks
            Al Banks
  →         Kathy Banks (.) h
  →         Ron Sterling
     M1:    mhm
  →  C8:    Lou Rather
  ⇒  M1:    "river banks"
     C8:    ((he he |h:))
     M1:              |((he he h |he hi))
     C8:                        land the friends
     M1:    ((he h he)) it was good that wudn't it river banks
     C8:    ((he he |he-))
     M1:              |((he he |he ha ha ha))
     C8:                        |((he he h he .h.hh))
```

Here although conversants are occupied with activities other than proffering/evaluating an answer to the riddle, we find the moderator using absolute register matching when repeating a prior turn by a co-participant. In (7) his repeat of *excu:se me:* by the caller's mother (C7) achieves not only a good match of pitch register but a fair match of syllable-level prosody as well (see Fig. 9.9).[23] In (8) his *river banks* is a close imitation of both syllable and phrase-level prosody in the last item of the caller's list *Lou Rather* (Fig. 9.10).[24] In both cases the effect is one of mimicry, which M1 seems to use here with humorous intent: see his follow-up comment in (8) *it was good that wudn't it river banks*. Callers acknowledge their recognition of this intent by snickering or laughing in subsequent turns. Since they are the brunt of his joking, however, their merriment may be somewhat subdued[25] compared to that of the radio audience. Here too then the moderator can be seen to achieve collusion with his hearers at the expense of his callers, who are not only the recipients of his jokes but also their objects. In sum, the pattern of distribution attested for absolute register matching in guessing sequences seems to carry over to other sequences as well: when it accompanies a high degree of verbal repetition and a moderate to high degree of syllable-level prosodic repetition, it appears to contextualize mimicry.

Surprisingly, however, the reverse of this distributional pattern does not appear to hold true: not all cases in which there is interactional evidence of mimicry necessarily have absolute register matching. This is apparent from examples such as the following:

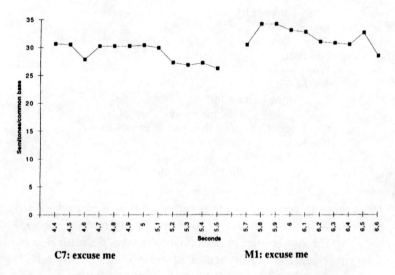

Figure 9.9 Absolute register matching in "excuse me" (Ex. 7)

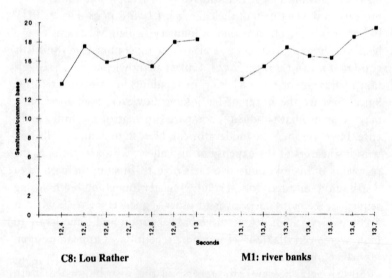

Figure 9.10 Absolute register matching in "river banks" (Ex. 8)

(9) MI: then we go to Hardwick (.)
           and there we get (.) h sexy Sharon
           hi
           (0.4)
→   C6:   hello
           (0.1)
→   MI: "hello" (0.1)
           how are you Sharon
           (0.1)
     C6:   alright |thanks
     MI: |oh: cheer up dear
     C6:   ((he hh))
     MI: cheer up for goodness sake
           don't put me in a bad mood
           at (.) one o'clock

(10) MI: .hm er Louise Hillman
           who lives in Wigan
           hi Louise:
           (0.3)
→   C9:   hi
           (0.2)
→   MI: "hi (0.1) how are you"
           (0.6)
     C9:   fine thanks
     MI: oh: do enjoy yourse:lf
           it's not the end of the worlld:
     C9: |(hhe)
     MI: it's only you and me on the radio
           cheer up (.)
           goodness .h
           are you unhappy
     C9:   no not really
     MI: you sound unhappy:

Based on an exclusively verbal analysis of the exchange of greetings
in (9) and (10), it might appear that these are routine sequences and
that no repetition is involved: callers acknowledge the moderator
with one greeting token and moderator returns the greeting with
another (lexically identical) token. Yet if this were the case, it would
be difficult to account for why the moderator's subsequent turns are
aimed explicitly at getting his callers to cheer up. This indicates that
something less than routine is going on interactionally. In fact, there
are cues, primarily of a non-verbal nature, which suggest that the
moderator is *repeating* the caller at the same time as he is returning

the caller's greeting. Note, to begin with, that the choice of the same greeting token as his caller (*hello–hello, hi–hi*) may not be accidental, given the fact that there is a whole set of items for him to choose from. Yet not only does the moderator use the same greeting token, he also imitates the caller's syllable and phrase-level prosody on that token. Notice, however, that in both cases caller's register is matched only on a relative scale (see Figs. 9.11 and 9.12). Placed on a common scale (upper halves of figures), the moderator's voice is significantly lower than that of his callers; but scaled with respect to individual bases, he can be seen to adjust his relative pitch to that of his callers (see in the lower half of Fig. 9.11 his pitch on *sexy Sharon* vs that on "*hello*" and in the lower half of Fig. 9.12 his pitch on *hi Louise* vs that on "*hi*").

Yet despite this relativity, it can be argued that the moderator is doing more than merely prosodically quoting his callers in (9) and (10): he is at the same time mimicking them. Two observations argue for such an interpretation. One is that in both cases the prosody of the caller's prior greeting is marked, in the sense that it does not conform to what would be interactionally expected. Rhythmically, for instance, the timing of the callers' greetings is off: their tokens come noticeably late with respect to the moderator's prior rhythm and tempo (see the discussion in Couper-Kuhlen 1993:230ff). But also melodically, their voices are relatively low with respect to their individual voice ranges: C6's pitch in (9) is between 3 and 4 ST above her base, C9's pitch in (10) is between 1 and 2 ST above hers. The moderator is arguably expecting more animation of his callers' voices. This he makes explicit several turns later with remarks such as *cheer up dear* (9) and *do enjoy yourself* (10).

The second observation which supports an interpretation of mimicry is a sequential one. Note that the moderator's rather pointed directives to his callers to cheer up come only after their follow-up turns to his repeat. Significantly, in these turns (*alright thanks* (9) and *fine thanks* (10)), callers use the same low pitch as in their greetings. Thus there appears to be an implicit message in the moderator's repeat, e.g. to the effect 'Your voice is too low', which the callers do not pick up on in their next turns.[26] If so, this provides a nice explanation for why the moderator becomes verbally

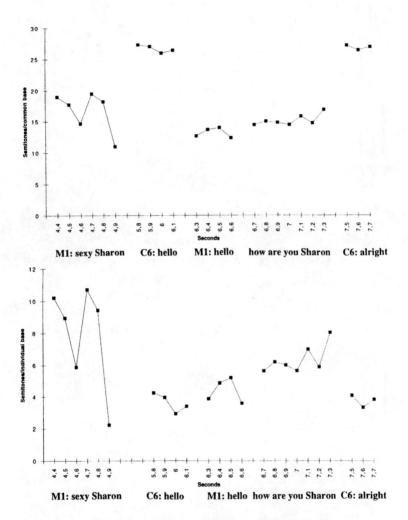

Figure 9.11 Relative register matching in "hello" (Ex. 9)

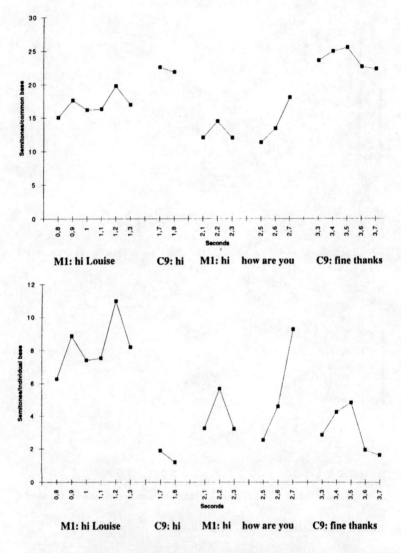

Figure 9.12 Relative register matching in "hi how are you" (Ex. 10)

explicit only now, after callers have not reacted to his prosodically contextualized, indirect hint.

Compared to the use of relative register matching (quotation) vs absolute register matching (mimicry) in the guessing sequences examined above, the moderator's strategy here is one of mimicry. It carries a critical message aimed at the caller personally; in other words, it is doing something to, not with, the caller. Like in (4)–(6) above, the moderator is exercising social control over his callers here: his criticism implies that he expects different voice behaviour from his callers, presumably more cheerful animation in order to make his programme lively and interesting for the radio audience. Yet the prosodic means used to achieve this criticism and social control are different. Rather than taking on the caller's base and pitching his repeat at an identical number of semitones above it, the moderator retains his own base, placing the repeat noticeably low in his own voice range. Why should he refrain from absolute pitch matching with its directly iconic display of the problem? The answer appears to be quite simple. Giving a repeat with absolute identical pitch here would have involved fundamental frequencies of approximately 230 Hz in (9) and 189 Hz in (10). For this moderator (M1), with a natural base of 83 Hz, these frequencies would be perceived as *high*, not low in his voice range. Therefore, they would have cued the wrong message.

On a somewhat more general level: when speakers have recourse to prosodic repetition for the purpose of indirectly passing comment on some behaviour in a fellow speaker, they must signal (i) that there is an implicit message, and (ii) what this implicit message might be. In the cases at hand, where the object of imitation has natural high pitch and the imitator has natural low pitch, and it is the relative low pitch of the object which is to be commented on, absolute register matching would call attention to an implicit message (i), but it would be misleading with respect to the thrust of the message (ii). Relative register matching, on the other hand, cues the presence of an implicit comment and analogically suggests what its content might be. Under the given circumstances, relative pitch is better suited than absolute pitch for the achievement of the interactional goal in question.

A final point concerns the fact that, in the majority of cases encountered in the *Brain Teaser* data, it is the male moderator who imitates a high-pitched female caller. This may of course be an artificial product of role distribution – the moderators are male, the callers are (typically) female – and the asymmetric relation between interactional partners, the moderator bearing clear responsibility for the organization and success of his programme. However, there may also be a wider social issue at play. To take someone else's words (and prosody) into one's own mouth is to lift a 'text' out of its original context (decontextualizing it) and place it in a new one (recontextualizing it). In one sense doing so amounts to a display of social power:

> To decontextualize and recontextualize a text is . . . an act of control, and in regard to the differential exercise of such control the issue of social power arises. More specifically, we may recognize differential access to texts, differential legitimacy in claims to and use of texts, differential competence in the use of texts, and differential values attaching to various types of texts. All of these elements . . . are culturally constructed, socially constituted, and sustained by ideologies, and they accordingly may vary cross-culturally. (Bauman and Briggs 1990:76)

The fact that the moderator's appropriation of his caller's 'text' is viewed as legitimate, can be put to self-serving use, and is culturally valued as a skilful performance contributing to audience pleasure and merriment – all of this suggests that as a controller of the decontextualization and recontextualization of discourse the (male) moderator is thereby constructing and sustaining a position of authority over the original producer of the discourse, his (female) caller. Note furthermore that it is he who constructs and reconstructs social norms concerning how his (female) callers' voices should be: if they are too high or too low, they are sanctioned with mockery. No similar sanctioning of male callers' voices is encountered in the data.[27] In the event, this absence – as well as that of female speakers exercising similar authority and power over male interlocutors – may be less of a coincidence than initially appears.

5 Conclusion

This study of pitch register in various types of interactional sequences in a corpus of British phone-ins makes two points clear with respect to relativity. First, the repeated and systematic use of absolute pitch matching as found here suggests that the classical tenet concerning pitch relativity in speech needs some refinement, if not correction. Speakers apparently do sometimes have recourse to absolute pitch when repeating utterances or parts of utterances by other speakers. They use this kind of prosodic repetition together with a high degree of verbal repetition to imitate, and at the same time critically comment on, another speaker. The nature of the comment to be passed, as well as the natural starting points of the model and the copier, influence whether the pitch imitation is accomplished on a relative or an absolute scale.

Second, the study casts some light on the question of relativity in prosodic contextualization. There continues to be some debate about how prosodic contextualization cues function, i.e. whether both arbitrarily and conventionally like knots in a handkerchief, signalling merely that some (unspecified) inference should be made, or rather non-arbitrarily, as natural and iconic cues to what the inference might be (see Auer 1992:32ff). The present study would appear to tip the scales in favour of the latter. The choice of prosodic contextualization cue, e.g. here relative vs abso-lute register matching, appears to depend in part on the nature of the inference to be triggered. To comment on an inappropriately high voice, speakers use cues involving high pitch. To comment on an inappropriately low voice, speakers use low pitch as a cue. However, when speakers with quite different natural voice ranges are involved, the former case will involve matching on an absolute scale, the latter, matching on a relative scale (provided it is the commenter who has a naturally low voice range).[28]

In this sense, relative and absolute register matching can be viewed as different contextualization cues for the same interactional task, that of mimicry. The choice of one as opposed to the other, however, is not arbitrary but depends on the natural voice ranges of the speakers involved. Contextualization may thus rely – at least on occasion – on iconically motivated cues. This does not mean that conventionalization is thereby excluded. Iconicity can be repressed or overridden by cultural convention. Yet presumably because mimicry itself is an inherently iconic activity, it is heavily dependent on the direct or indirect iconicity of prosodic cues in speech.

402   Elizabeth Couper-Kuhlen

Notes

An earlier version of this paper was presented at the 7th SAUTE Symposium on Repetition in Language and Literature held at the University of Zürich in May 1993. I am grateful to Peter Auer, Susanne Günthner and Margret Selting for helping the present version along.

1 The prosodic feature of pause may appear to be an exception, but it can be conceptualized as the *absence* of one or more syllable-sized speech-like units.
2 Tannen (1989) makes a similar point.
3 *Register* as found in descriptions of tonal downstep (see, e.g. Ladd 1990) is a different, unrelated use of the term. Chest, middle and head (or falsetto) *voice registers* (see Crystal 1969:107) are related but not identical concepts (see below).
4 In intermediate and larger domains it is also meaningful to distinguish durations of intervals between selected prosodically prominent sylla-bles, a dimension which relates to rhythm and tempo (see Auer, Couper-Kuhlen and Müller (to appear)). Here too one can envisage repetition.
5 These differences in voice range are partly physiological but also partly social in origin; for a discussion, see Graddol and Swann 1989.
6 I am grateful to Peter Auer for making this data and the transcripts available to me. Proper names have been changed to preserve speaker anonymity.
7 Crystal (1975) points out, however, that the relativity hypothesis in intonation analysis does not preclude – and in fact may require – a framework of absolute values.
8 'Absolute pitch values' as used here refers either to raw Hertz measure-ments or to their perceptual counterparts when converted, for example, to a musical scale.
9 To avoid excessive r-alliteration, the term *matching* will be used inter-changeably with *repetition*. Its intentional overtone should be ignored for the time being but will prove relevant later in the discussion.
10 The analysis was carried out on a Kay Elemetrics digital sonagraph using the stored pitch extraction algorithm in combination with a time-aligned wide-band spectrogram for segmentation purposes.
11 One Hertz value (f_1) may be expressed as a semitone interval (D) above another Hertz value (f_2) by use of the following formula ('t Hart, Collier and Cohen 1990:24):

$$D = \frac{12}{\log_{10}2} \cdot \log_{10} \frac{f_1}{f_2}$$

12 This value was determined on the basis of all the utterances by a given speaker in the recorded material.

13 The final rise on *Bible* in the moderator's repetition can be thought of as forming a transition between the repetition and the second part of his utterance *is wrong*.

14 The Russian term for reported speech *čužaja reč*, which also translates as 'other speech', aptly expresses this alien element (Titunik 1973:191).

15 See, however, the discussion in Clark and Gerrig 1990.

16 By the same analogy, prosody could be said to be mentioned here, or used reflexively (see also Lucy 1993).

17 It would require systematic contextualization analysis to determine exactly what affective component is added by the prosodic variation in the moderator's repetition in (2) and (3). A first guess, however, would be something akin to surprise.

18 Riddles have been compared to examinations: both involve 'questions' which demand an 'answer'. And the questions have 'right' answers, in the sense that the answers are known in advance by the questioners; candidates provide evidence of their knowledge of the answer by attempting to 'find' the 'right one' (see Jolles 1974:126ff).

19 Some listeners reportedly hear M1's pitch here as *higher* than C4's. This perception may well be based on the unmarked expectation of relative register matching.

20 In fact, in (6) repair on the caller's guess has already been initiated and carried out *before* the sequence in question.

21 It is conceivable that if a female speaker were prosodically mimicking a male speaker, an equally noticeable shift to chest voice register would be necessary. However, this case does not occur in my data.

22 Only C1 approaches a high pitch comparable to that of C4 on the proffered guess (15–16 ST above her individual base), but this appears to be motivated by the fact that her guess is formatted as a question. C4's high pitch, by contrast, does not have this motivation.

23 For instance, the tones used in original and copy are roughly comparable, although the moderator uses rise–falls rather than falls on *ex-* and *me*.

24 This is one of the few cases in which M1 noticeably uses absolute register matching with a male caller.

25 Note, for instance, that in (8) M1 must work to elicit sufficient appreciation from C8.

26 In (9) the moderator can actually be heard to demonstrate what he has in mind when he uses noticeably higher pitch on *how are you Sharon*.

27 In the one example in which absolute register matching of a male caller is noticeable (8), the criticism appears to be aimed not at the caller's voice but at his rather insistent and repetitive listing.

28 The reverse situation would hold if the commenter had a naturally high voice range. To mock inordinately high pitch, relative register matching would be appropriate; to mock low pitch, absolute register matching would be used but would be subject to physiological limits, the bottom of one's voice range being less expandable than the top (Liberman and Pierrehumbert 1984).

404   Elizabeth Couper-Kuhlen

References

Auer, P. 1992. Introduction: John Gumperz' approach to contextualization. In P. Auer and A. di Luzio (eds.) *The Contextualization of
Language*. Amsterdam and Philadelphia: Benjamins, pp. 1–38.

Auer, P., E. Couper-Kuhlen and F. Müller (to appear) *Language in Time:
the rhythm and tempo of spoken interaction*.

Bakhtin, M. M. 1929. Discourse typology in prose. In L. Matejka and K.
Pomorska (eds.) 1978, *Readings in Russian Poetics. Formalist and
stucturalist views*. Ann Arbor: University of Michigan Press, pp.
176–196.

   1934–1935. Discourse in the novel. In M. Holquist (ed.) 1981, *The
Dialogic Imagination. Four essays by M. M. Bakhtin*. Austin:
University of Texas Press, pp. 259–422.

Bauman, R. and C. L. Briggs 1990. Poetics and performance as critical
perspectives on language and social life. *Annual Review of Anthropology*, 19: 59–88.

Brazil, D., M. Coulthard and C. Johns 1980. *Discourse Intonation and
Language Teaching*. London: Longman.

Chafe, W. L. 1988. Linking intonation units in spoken English. In J. Haiman and S. A. Thompson (eds.) *Clause Combining in Grammar and
Discourse*. Amsterdam and Philadelphia: Benjamins, pp. 1–27.

Chatman, S. 1965. *A Theory of Meter*. The Hague: Mouton.

Clark, H. H. and R. J. Gerrig 1990. Quotations as demonstrations. *Language*, 66: 764–805.

Couper-Kuhlen, E. 1993. *English Speech Rhythm. Form and function
in everyday verbal interaction*. Amsterdam and Philadelphia:
Benjamins.

Crystal, D. 1969. *Prosodic Systems and Intonation in English*. Cambridge
University Press.

   1975. Relative and absolute in intonation analysis. In D. Crystal *The
English Tone of Voice. Essays in intonation, prosody and paralan-
guage*. London; Edward Arnold, pp. 74–83.

Fry, D. B. 1979. *The Physics of Speech*. Cambridge University Press.

Goffman, E. 1974. *Frame Analysis. An essay on the organization of experience*. Cambridge, Mass.: Harvard University Press.

Graddol, D. and J. Swann 1989. *Gender Voices*. Oxford: Basil Blackwell.

Hart 't, J., R. Collier and A. Cohen 1990. *A Perceptual Study of Intonation.
An experimental-phonetic approach to speech melody*. Cambridge
University Press.

Jolles, A. 1974. *Einfache Formen. Legende, Sage, Mythe, Rätsel, Spruch,
Kasus, Memorabile, Märchen, Witz*. (5th edn). Tübingen: Niemeyer.

Ladd, D. R. 1990. Metrical representation of pitch register. In J. Kingston
and M. E. Beckman (eds.) *Papers in Laboratory Phonology* I. Cambridge University Press, pp. 35–57.

Liberman, M. and J. Pierrehumbert 1984. Intonational invariance under changes in pitch range and length. In M. Aronoff and R. T. Oehrle (eds.) *Language Sound Structure*. Cambridge, Mass.: MIT Press, pp. 157–233.

Lucy, J. A. 1993. Reflexive language and the human disciplines. In J. A. Lucy (ed.) *Reflexive Language. Reported speech and metapragmatics*. Cambridge University Press, pp. 9–32.

Schegloff, E. A. 1972. Sequencing in conversational openings. In J. J. Gumperz and D. Hymes (eds.) *Directions in Sociolinguistics. The ethnography of communication*. New York: Holt, Rinehart & Winston, pp. 346–380.

Sweet, H. 1906. *A Primer of Phonetics*. Oxford: Clarendon Press.

Tannen, D. 1987. Repetition in conversation: towards a poetics of talk. *Language*, 63 (3): 574–605.

1989. *Talking Voices. Repetition, dialogue, and imagery in conversational discourse*. Cambridge University Press.

Titunik, I. R. 1973. The formal method and the sociological method (M. M. Baxtin, P. N. Medvedev, V. N. Vološinov) in Russian theory and study of literature. In V. N. Vološinov *Marxism and the Philosophy of Language*, trans. by L. Matejka and I. R. Titunik. New York: Seminar Press, pp. 175–200.

Uhmann, S. 1992. Contextualizing relevance: on some forms and functions of speech rate changes in everyday conversation. In P. Auer and A. di Luzio (eds.) *The Contextualization of Language*. Amsterdam and Philadelphia: Benjamins, pp. 297–336.

Vološinov, V. N. 1926. Discourse in life and discourse in art (concerning sociological poetics). In V. N. Vološinov 1976, *Freudianism. A marxist critique*, trans. by I. R. Titunik. New York: Academic Press, pp. 93–116.

1930. Reported speech. In L. Matejka and K. Pomorska (eds.) 1978, *Readings in Russian Poetics. Formalist and structuralist views*. Ann Arbor: University of Michigan Press, pp. 149–175.

10

Working on young children's utterances: prosodic aspects of repetition during picture labelling

CLARE TARPLEE

1 Introduction

Within that tradition of child language research that has been concerned with a characterization of the speech with which adults address young children, attention has often been drawn to the frequency with which adults reproduce the utterances of the young children with whom they are conversing. The most commonly cited kind of adult reproduction is the *expansion* (coined by Brown and Bellugi 1964), where adults 'fill out' the child's 'telegraphic' speech, rendering a syntactically well-formed version of what the child is perceived to have been trying to say. Somewhat less extensively documented, although still commonly mentioned in this literature, is a phenomenon whereby adults produce straight, unexpanded repetitions[1] of the utterances of their child conversants. It is the prosodic characteristics of a subset of these repetition utterances which are the focus of analysis in this chapter.

These repetitions and other kinds of adult reproduction of children's utterances have invoked an extensive terminology and a wide range of overlapping formal definitions in the literature on 'child directed speech'. *Imitation, echo, partial imitation, recasting* and *modification* are just some of the terms which have been used, and which have appeared (with no small degree of arbitrariness and imprecision) as coding categories in quantificational analyses of adult–child interactional data. It is notable that the structural distinctions drawn between these categories have been largely restricted to the lexico-syntactic domain: the phonetic relationships between the child's original utterance and the adult's reproduction have tended to be ignored. One exception is a study by Snow,

Arlman-Rupp, Hassing, Jobse, Joosten and Vorster (1976), who suggest that unexpanded (lexico-syntactic) repetitions can be regarded as 'phonological expansions', since a repetition of a phonetically deviant child production will typically be produced as 'a correct phonological model' (1976:11). However, the fine details of the phonetic relationship between child and adult versions are passed over in this study, just as they are in this literature more generally. Nor, typically, is consideration given to the sequential context in which these objects occur, or to the nature of the child production which is reproduced. It is clearly pertinent, in considering these adult–child repetitions, to pay careful attention to the formal features which characterize them.

With regard to the functional characteristics of these objects, here too the literature presents a mixed and somewhat confusing picture. Adults' reproductions of children's utterances have been variously regarded, for instance, as corrective (Moerck 1974), interpretative (Ryan 1974), and confirmatory (Slobin 1968). It would seem quite feasible to propose that these utterances perform a whole host of interactional functions; yet rarely has analysis been detailed enough to tease out the intricacies of these different kinds of work. In order to do this effectively, an analysis must obviously take account of the details of the interactional context of each occurrence of the phenomenon, so as to avoid the tendency to assume that a collection of formally similar objects are a functionally cohesive set.

The analysis presented in this chapter focusses on a collection of adults' repetitions of children's utterances, produced in a particular interactional setting – where the children are engaged in labelling from picture books. It employs conversation analytic techniques in an attempt to uncover some of the interactional accomplishments associated with different repetition turns which are distinguished by their phonetic, and particularly prosodic, design. Specifically, features of pitch and of pausing are found to be implicated in delicate ways in the accomplishment of phonetic repair work on the child's articulations – and it is apparent that the children under investigation here are orienting to these cues at a very early age. By making a detailed analytic progression through a small set of repetition sequences, the chapter aims to illustrate something of the procedure, as well as the findings, of this kind of analysis, and to highlight the kinds of interactional evidence on which it relies in its attempt to relate in a warranted fashion the forms and functions of linguistic objects.

1.1 Picture book labelling

The labelling of pictures from books is an activity which figures prominently in the homes of many young children. It is also an activity which frequently plays a part in the assessment and remediation of speech and language disorders. On both counts, the management of the picture labelling activity is a social accomplishment which is worthy of research attention. One characteristic of the talk which accompanies, and indeed constitutes, this activity, is that it has features in common with other instructional modes of talk, and is bound up specifically with working, in various ways, on the child's linguistic skills (see Tarplee 1993). A distinction can be drawn between two kinds of linguistic ability in the child which receive explicit attention in this talk. First, labelling predominantly tests the child's lexical knowledge and word-finding abilities. Yet in addition, labelling requires the child to display articulatory abilities, and these phonetic skills are sometimes directly addressed in labelling talk. (In other words, for the child engaged in a labelling task, there is not only the issue of getting the right word: there is also the issue of getting the word right.) Work on both these areas, the lexical and the phonetic, will be seen to be implicated in the adult repetition turns which are the focus of the analysis presented in this chapter.

1.2 The data

The labelling sequences which form the basis for analysis are taken from three recordings of children engaged in picture labelling with their care-takers. The children range in age from 1;7 to 2;3.

1.3 The phenomenon

A characteristic of picture labelling talk is that it displays a similar three-part structure to that which has been identified in other modes of instructional interaction (e.g. Mehan 1979, McHoul 1978, Drew 1981). A labelling sequence typically opens with some kind of eli-

citing turn from the adult, which is followed by a labelling utterance
from the child, which is in turn followed by a receipt of some kind
from the adult. This third position receipting turn takes different
forms, but one recurrent turn shape found in this position is an
exact repetition[2] of the child's prior labelling utterance.

Of interest for the concerns of this chapter is the fact that different instances of this particular shape of turn appear to have different consequences for the trajectory of the talk which follows them.
On occasion, these adult repeating turns end a labelling sequence
and appear to accomplish affirmatory work in relation to the child's
choice of label (see example (1); the phonetic symbols in this and the
following examples are those recommended by the IPA). Here, there
is a five-second pause following the adult's repetition, and the child
then moves on to label a next picture. No further attention is given
to the *lion* label following the repetition.

(1)   adult :   o{ oh } who's th<u>a</u>t
             child :   {[ëh]}

                            (1.0)

             child :   li̱: on
→   adult :   l̲:i̲::on

                            (5.0)

             child :   °norah°

On other occasions, however, an adult's repetition of the child's
label results in the child taking reparative action with regard to
phonetic aspects of the prior labelling turn, as in example (2).
Here the child has another go at articulating the label following
the adult's repetition.

(2)   child :   [tˑʰa̱dɪˈə̣θ]
→   adult :   [tʰi̱:əθ]
→   child: [ti̱:jəʰ]

                            (.)

             adult :   where's <u>tho</u>mas's <u>tee</u>:th

An adult repetition in third-turn position in a labelling sequence can therefore do two quite contradictory kinds of work. In cases like (1), it does the work of an affirming receipt which puts an end to the sequence. In cases like (2), it is followed by a further child version – a version which is phonetically repaired; that is to say the adult's turn is treated by the child as a model, which encourages a further attempt at the label.

The intriguing question posed by this concerns just how an adult's repetition of a child's label is displayed to do these two different kinds of work. How are these two kinds of repetition distinguished in their design, such that the child may appropriately infer their implications? Put another way, just how is phonetic repair work on the child's labelling articulations understood, inter-subjectively, to be a relevant next action in the talk, and thus how is this kind of work collaboratively achieved? The remainder of this chapter is addressed to exploring this question, by taking a careful look at some instances of these two classes of repetition, in order to identify the linguistic – and particularly the prosodic – exponents of these differentiated interactional accomplishments.

2 Reparative repetition

2.1 Some examples of reparative repetition

In tackling this task, attention is first of all drawn to sequences which take the shape of extract (2), that is:

child: label
adult: repeated label
child: phonetically repaired label

Consider again extract (2) above. The child's first attempt here is phonetically quite deviant from the adult form, particularly in having an open and front vocalic portion after the utterance's consonantal beginning, and in having alveolar closure in the middle of the utterance. The later vocalic portion, [ɪ'ə] corresponds quite closely to the vocalic portion in the adult form, in beginning with a close, front, unrounded quality which becomes centralized -- although it begins less front and less close than the adult's form, and more swiftly takes on a central quality. The child's second attempt brings his version more closely in line with the adult's. This time there is no alveolarity and no closure in the middle of the utterance, and the vocalic portion begins more close and more front. The duration of this utterance is also brought into line with that of the adult's version.

A second example is extract (3).

(3)   →   child :   [p'ɛ̃ə̃ʔːtʃ ɪ]

(1.2)

→   adult :   [pʰɛ̃n·s·ə̰ə̰ɫ]

(.)

→   child :   [pæ̰̃ə̰s·ə̰ʷ]

(.)

adult :   good boy

Here, the most striking difference between the child's two utterances is the introduction of alveolar friction, [s·], in the middle of the child's second version, in place of glottal and alveolar closure, [ʔːt]. This second version also comes into line with the adult's, by having a vocalic portion at the end with a central quality and with lip-roundedness, where the ending of the first version was characterized by unroundedness and a more front quality. The differences between the child's first attempt and the adult model in this sequence can usefully be seen in terms of differences in 'phasing', in the sense of Kelly and Local (1989). In the middle part of the child's first version, [p'ɛ̃ə̃ʔːtʃɪ], there is nasality [ɛ̃ə̃], closure [ʔːt], alveolarity [t] and friction [ʃ]. In the adult model, there is, likewise, nasality and closure [n·], and alveolarity and friction [s·]. It is in the relative phasing of these features that the two versions differ. What the child is doing in producing his second version, [pæ̰̃ə̰s·ə̰ʷ], consists, in large part, of rearranging the phasing relationships between these features.

Both these examples, then, illustrate a pattern whereby a child's second attempt which follows an adult repetition is not only hearably different from the first attempt in its articulatory characteristics – but different by virtue of being closer to the adult version.

That is to say, phonetic repair has taken place. The issue to be tackled, then, is to assess whether this reparative action on the part of the child is being projected or invited by some feature of the adult's repetition. As a first approach, these sequences will be compared with a second set – cases where an adult repetition of a child's label does not result in a further attempt by the child.

2.2 Some examples without repair

Two sequences to be presented here follow this kind of a pattern, where no repair work ensues:

child: label
adult: repeat
(no repair work)

(4) → child : [d̡ʲʷʊˑkʼ]

     → adult : [dʒʊˑg̊ʰ]

                        (.)

        child : [danɪʔˑdʑʊə̣ˑkʼ]

        adult : is that jaːnet's jːug

Here the child clearly does not treat the adult version as a model for improving his performance: he moves straight on to elaborate on the picture (*janet jug*).

In considering this sequence it might be noted that the child and adult versions have many phonetic similarities. Both begin with closure, alveolarity, palatality and voice, and have orality throughout. The vocalic portion of the two versions is very similar in both quality and length, and at the end of both utterances there is velar closure with no or little voicing, and with markedly audible release. One very plausible possibility, then, is that the child in this sequence is able to hear for himself that no repair is necessary, on the basis of perceiving the lack of discrepancy between the two turns. This claim would lead to the converse suggestion that, in those sequences where the child does produce a second version, this repair work is motivated by the child's own monitoring of the differences between her or his own production and the adult model.

However, example (5), which follows the same format, casts doubt on this kind of claim.

(5) →   child :   [ʔʲaˑɪðe̞ˑ]

     →   adult :   [lɐˑdǝ˞ˑ]

                       (0.8) ((sound of turning pages))
         child :   [dǝ̞ˑgɪˑ]

Again the child does not take the adult's repetition as a model: he goes on, after a pause in which pages are turned, to label the next picture. But here the phonetics of the two versions are hearably different. At the beginning of the child's version there is glottal closure and palatal approximation: there is no alveolarity or laterality. The first vocalic portion ends up close and front, and in the middle of the utterance there is friction and dentality, and neither the closure nor the alveolarity which characterize the adult's version. The second vocalic portion has a front, unrounded quality, unlike the adult's. Phonetic repair work, then, is hearably an option. One might expect any monitoring of the two turns by the child to point up marked, repairable articulatory differences. However, repair is an option which is not taken up in this sequence.

In (4) and (5), then, we have two cases where an adult repetition is not treated by the child as a model for repair – one case where the child's version conforms closely to the adult's, and a second where the child's version is hearably repairable. However, it is apparent that instances such as these have limited evidence to lend to an investigation into the different kinds of work accomplished by adult repetitions in this sequential position. The problem with examples such as (4) and (5) is that they do not eliminate the possibility that repair work was being in some way projected by the adult's turn, but happened not to result simply because the child, for whatever reasons, chose not to take up that option. In (5), there is some evidence to support the notion that the adult, as well as the child, is orienting to the sequence-final nature of her own labelling turn, in that the sound of page-turning follows swiftly from the end of this turn, before there has been an opportunity for a further child version. However, this very feature may, in preference to any implicit characteristic of the adult's turn, be the feature (or at least a contributing factor) which signals sequence-termination to the child. In (4), there are no clues as to whether or not the adult expected a further version from the child. A simple comparison, then, of sequences where the child follows an adult repetition with self-repair, and sequences where the child does not do this, does not supply us with the kind of evidence that we need to make claims about the status which these turns have for the adult.

2.3 Uncovering the sequential implications of an adult's repetition: an example

The sequence in example (6), by contrast, gives ground to analytical claims which have not been possible in the sequences considered thus far.

(6)

1   child :   [d̥ə̣ˑgɪ]

2   adult :   [mə̃ŋ k↓h↓ mə̃ŋˑkʰɪ̯]

3   child :   [ʁï̈ç]

4   →   adult :   say [mə̃ŋkʰɪ]

5   child :   [mə̆kɪˑ]

6   adult :   [mə̃ŋkʰɪ]

7   (0.5) ((sound of pages))

   In this extract, the adult's version of the label in line 2 is not followed by a further child version. The child's utterance [ɐ̈ɪç] in line 3 is short and produced high in the pitch range, and whatever its signification it is quite clearly not any kind of acceptable version of *monkey*. Of particular significance, however, for the investigation at hand, is the adult's response to this turn in line 4, *say monkey*. With this kind of a turn, which explicitly prompts the child to repeat the label, the adult displays orientation to the absence of a child version in line 3, and can be heard to be spelling out the sequential implications of her earlier turn in line 2. Hence, this turn supplies evidence that the adult's label in line 2 was indeed intended as a model. Analysis of this sequence can therefore proceed with good grounds for an assumption that the adult's labelling turn in this case represents, not an affirmation which projects the end of the sequence, but an invitation to self-correct.
   Investigation can therefore focus on the design of the turn which is accomplishing this work. In this case, the turn is marked by a 'false start'. The adult breaks off in the middle of a production of *monkey* – and then goes on to produce the word in full.

Interestingly, when she does this, the adult changes no aspect of the articulatory phonetics of the utterance: the first part of the word when it is uttered in full turns out to be just the same, in articulatory terms, as it had been when it was broken off. Now while it has been demonstrated (Schegloff, Jefferson and Sacks 1977:363) that there need not be hearable error for repair to take place in talk, it is nonetheless striking that, while these two versions are articulatorily similar, they differ quite markedly in their pitch contour. While the original utterance started with a mid-to-low fall, the repaired version starts high, rises, and falls to low. A candidate analysis for this shape of turn, then, is that it represents an instance of a repair in pitch.

Now, the concept of a repair in pitch is one which presents a particular difficulty for analysis.[3] The difficulty lies in positing prosodic features as the *object* of repair when they are themselves the *vehicle* of that repair, since the work of correction seems often to be marked by particular prosodic patterns. Local (1992:295) has observed certain prosodic features associated with *self*-corrections (within a turn), whereby the correction is routinely 'produced louder than the preceding talk and with a higher pitch which falls'. All of these features are evident in the adult's second *monkey* in line 2, and, while it may be that these prosodic features are characteristic of more kinds of correction in talk than the self-corrections considered by Local, there is nonetheless a difficulty in ruling out a possibility which might be suggested here – that these prosodic features in the second part of the turn are themselves doing some self-corrective work, and are involved in correcting the broken-off utterance which immediately precedes the full version of *monkey* in the same turn. Nonetheless, I think this possibility *can* be ruled out in this case, on the basis of other prosodic properties of the turn. Local observes that the self-corrections in his data are also marked by a change in rhythm and tempo, such that speakers accelerate and arrive at a repaired version with a syncopated timing. Line 2 in extract (6), on the other hand, comes off quite differently. At the transition from cut-off to the full version of *monkey*, there is a slow, audible voiceless release of velar closure during inbreath, with a slight pause before the full version. In rhythm and tempo, then, this turn is not characteristic of an interruptive self-correction (and this is supported by the absence of any repair in articulation across the two versions). It is therefore consistent to suggest that prosodic features here are the object of repair, and that this turn constitutes an example of a repair in pitch.

In order to come some way towards uncovering the motivation for a repair in pitch in this position, it will be informative to consider the interactional work which each of the adult's two versions in this turn, differentiated in their prosodic design, appears to be directed towards. It has already been suggested that the second, repaired version of *monkey* is presented as a model, projecting a further version from the child. This is suggested by the adult's turn, *say monkey*, in line 4, which is produced when such a child version is not forthcoming. It can be observed that this work is here accomplished with a version of the label which has a high rise–fall pitch contour which falls to low – a pitch contour which stands in contrast to that of the child's labelling turn in line 1 (a low to high rise), to which it is addressed. It may be, then, that this second adult version is marked as inviting a further child attempt (that is, as doing corrective work) by virtue of the contrastivity which it shows in relation to the child's version, and that an important part of this work of contrastivity is carried by the pitch contour.

The adult's first, interrupted, version of *monkey*, on the other hand, begins with a low fall – displaying, as far as it goes, no prosodic contrastivity with the child version. While it is of course impossible to predict the melodic shape which this utterance was taking before it was broken off, a compelling possibility, suggested by other sequences in a larger corpus, is that this first version was on course to follow the pitch contour of the child's version. Example (7) shows a sequence where just this kind of pitch matching happens. In this sequence, the adult's turn, matching the rising pitch contour of the child's version, comes off, not as an initiation of repair inviting a second attempt by the child, but as an affirming receipt which ends the sequence and is followed by page-turning to a next labelling event.

(7)   (1.4) ((sound of pages))

child :   [ɓɔbʌ·l]

adult :   [bˑɔːɵł]

                         (1.8) ((sound of pages))

Of course, the suggestion that the adult's broken off *monkey* in line 2 of extract (6) was the start of an affirming receipt of the kind evidenced in (7) is conjecture. However, it is conjecture which is supported by other details of the sequence. Presented with a picture of a monkey, the child has produced [də̣ˈgɪ·]. Such a turn may well be hearable at first as an attempt, albeit phonetically wayward, at the target label *monkey*. As such it might invite affirmation. Now, whether or not the child was indeed producing a version of *monkey*, his utterance [də̣ˈgɪ·] could also be heard as a version of the wrong label, namely *doggie*. And a slight delay in that second hearing, on the part of the adult, who may have first heard the child's utterance as lexically appropriate if phonetically deviant, could motivate just the kind of repair, from an affirming receipt to an invitation to correct, which is being suggested here.

2.3.1 Contrastivity

The point which arises from analysis of this extract is that an adult repetition of a child's label which invites reparative work on that label from the child (and essentially amounts to a correction) is marked as such by doing some work of 'contrastivity' in relation to the child label. This observation points up something of the complexity of repair in general and correction in particular. Any correction *y* of a preceding utterance *x* needs to do two, apparently contradictory, kinds of work. It needs to display itself as different from *x*, different enough to warrant being proffered as a 'replacement' at all – not to be hearable, that is, as an imitation of *x*. At the same time it needs to bear enough similarity to *x* to be heard to fill the same slot that *x* filled, to be speaking in place of *x*, and not to be an independent contribution to the exchange. That is to say, it needs to be not just different, but contrastive. This contrastivity may be displayed in a number of ways. If one hears the child's turn in line 1 of this sequence as being a version of *doggie*, then one can argue that the adult's following turn is marked as a lexical correction by being lexically contrastive. *Doggie* is replaced with *monkey*. However, it would appear that lexical contrastivity alone may not be sufficient to signal that correction is being done. The adult's *monkey* is marked as being lexically contrastive by virtue of also being prosodically contrastive with the child's turn. The details of this sequence, in comparison with those of (7), suggest that an absence of prosodic contrastivity in such a position would eliminate lexical contrastivity – would treat the child's *x*, that is, as having in fact been an instance of *y*.

To support this, attention can be drawn to the end of extract (6), where there is a further instance of an adult repetition of the child's label. When, in line 5, the child does produce a repaired version[4] in response to the adult's prompt, this version is receipted in line 6 with a repeat from the adult which is matched in pitch (a fall from mid to low), and which ends the sequence. There is nothing in the prosody of this adult turn which suggests that contrastivity is being done, and the turn comes off as an affirmation, being swiftly followed by the turning of pages to a next labelling issue.

It would seem, then, that some adult repetitions of child labels solicit further labelling turns from the child by being marked as being 'corrections', and that one feature which marks a turn as carrying this status as a correction is that it displays some level of contrastivity (prosodic as well as articulatory[5]) with the 'corrected' turn. This analysis is supported by a return to extract (2), the first of the two examples cited earlier as cases where the adult's repetition of the child's label was followed by a phonetically repaired attempt from the child:

(8)[6]

                            ‿ ⌢

→   child :   [tʲʰa̠drʲə̞θ]

                            ┐

→   adult :   [tʰi̠ːə̞θ]

                            ┐

    child: [tḭːjəʰ]

                        (.)

    adult :   where's tho̲mas's tee̲ːth

It has already been seen how the articulation of the child's turn differs from the adult's subsequent model: the adult's turn, in other words, displays phonetic contrastivity in articulatory terms. But in addition, it may be noted that the pitch contours of the child and adult turns stand in contrast. While the child's first version has a rise–fall contour in mid range, the adult's begins level and high, and falls to low (as does the child's subsequent version).

Correction status may be marked in part, then, by lexical or articulatory phonetic contrastivity (as the adult corrects the child's choice of word or the child's pronunciation), but the preceding examples show how this contrastivity may be highlighted and interpreted by prosodic contrastivity, and specifically by contrastivity in pitch. Pitch contrastivity, then, can be pointed to as one feature which is associated with adult repetitions which invite phonetic repair work on the part of the child.

2.4 Reparative repeats without prosodic contrastivity

Other sequences in the corpus, however, show that the child may sometimes produce a phonetically repaired version of a label following an adult repetition which does not display this kind of contrastivity in its prosodic relationship to the child's turn. The start-ing-point for analysis here is extract (9) which, in rather the same way as extract (6) above, provides the analyst with a warrant for treating the adult's repeat as an invitation to the child to self-correct.

(9)

1   adult :   [kwç·ɔn]

2   (.)

3   child :   [ʔˠiə̰n]

4   (1.2)

5   adult :   [kwç:ə̰n]

6   child :   yea

7 → adult :   say it

8   child :   [ʔi:ə̰n·]

9   (.)

10   adult :   thomas say it

11   (1.0)

$$\overline{\diagup}$$

12   child :   [kiːɔ̃nˑ]

$$\overline{\diagup}$$

13   adult :   [kwɔ̰ˑçn]

14   (1.1) ((sound of pages))

This sequence is initiated with an adult production of the target label. After the child's attempt in line 3, the adult repeats the label and the child responds with *yea*. The adult responds to this with a prompt, *say it*. Two particular points can be illustrated off this response. Firstly, it illustrates how an adult's production of the target label at the opening of a labelling sequence can still carry the force of an elicitation of a label from the child: *yea* is treated as an insufficient response. Secondly, *say it* suggests that the repeat which came before it was intended as a prompt or model. In just the same way as the adult's *say monkey* in extract (6) was seen to do, the adult's *say it* here can be seen to spell out for the child the sequential implications of a prior turn which has not been met with an acceptable response. Once again, then, a warrant is drawn for treating the adult's repetition (in this case the adult's *queen* in line 5) as a correction/model/prompt – at all events a turn which, for the adult, projects a further version from the child.

The adult's repetition in extract (9) thus looks to be accomplishing similar work to the repetitions in (6) and (8). Unlike those examples, however, there is no evidence of pitch contrastivity at work in this sequence. A similar pitch contour – a rise or fall–rise which starts mid or low and rises to high – is common to all versions of *queen* uttered by both participants. However, a feature of the repetition in line 5 which attracts attention is its timing. Rather than following immediately from the child's version, it follows a 1.2 second pause. Can a case be built for the significance of this kind of temporal delay as a feature of some adult repetitions which project phonetic repair work?

2.4.1 Temporal delay

Three pieces of evidence will be presented to support the suggestion that the timing of these repetitions may play a part in the interactional work which they accomplish. The first derives from a comparison of the repetition in line 5 of extract (9) with the ending of that sequence, at lines 12 and 13. Here, the child produces a version of the label which is met with an adult repetition. This repetition, like that at line 5, matches the rising pitch of the child turn which precedes it. Unlike the adult repetition at line 5, however, it follows directly from that child turn, without delay. This adult turn in line 13 does not invite child repair. It ends the sequence and coincides with the start of page-turning to a next label, and thus comes off as an affirmation. One feature which distinguishes the adult turns in lines 5 and 13, in the absence of any salient difference in the pitch relationships which they hold with their priors, is their temporal placement in relation to those prior turns. It is therefore consistent to suggest that this feature is associated with the differential interactional work which the two adult turns are seen to be doing.[7]

A second piece of evidence to bring to bear on this claim is found by returning to extract (3):

(10)[8]

→ child :   [p'ɛ̃θʔːtʃɪ]

→   (1.2)

→ adult :   [pʰɛ̃nˑsˈθθɬ]

              (.)

child :   [pæ̃ə̃sˈθʷ]

              (.)

adult :   good boy

Again, as in (9), there is no clear contrastivity displayed here in the
pitch configuration of the labelling turns of child and adult in lines
1 and 3, both being produced with a short mid or mid-to-low fall,
followed by a rise to high. But, just as was the case in (9), the adult's
repetition follows a 1.2 second pause.

A third, and final, piece of evidence derives from extract (11).
This sequence is a little more messy, on account of some latching
and overlap, but here too, as in (9), there are two instances of adult
repetitions of child labels – one which is preceded by a pause and
appears to come off as a model, and one which follows its prior
turn directly and comes off as an affirmation. As was the case in (9)
and (10), the pitch configuration across all labelling turns is similar.

(11)

1	adult :	[ɹɪˈŋːg]
2	1→ child :	[jrŋ]
3	1→	(0.7)
4	1→ adult :	[ɹˈɪŋːg] =
5	child :	= what
6		(0.6)
7	2→ child :	{ [j ī ŋ }ˈkʰ] =
		{ }

8   adult :   {(what)}

                          ⌣∕

9   2→   adult :   = [ɹ ɪ̣ŋːg]

10   (2.2)

11   adult :   [ǂ]   su-

The adult's opening label in line 1 is met with a child version in line 2. After a pause of 0.7 seconds the adult repeats the label. This turn is not accompanied by page-turning and does not appear to orient to a completed sequence. Although the child does not imme-diately produce a repaired version of his label, producing instead a turn which sounds like *what*, it can be noted that the adult waits until he does repair his label (after a further 0.6 seconds) before she takes another full turn. In line 8, an adult turn which appears to begin with *what* is broken off to give way to the child's repaired label. There is evidence here too, then, that an adult label which follows a child label and a pause is one which is presented as a model to project further work. By contrast, the adult's version of *ring* in line 9 coincides with the turning of pages, is followed by a next labelling sequence, and comes off as an affirmation. And, far from being delayed, it is latched to its prior. In other words, it follows directly from the child's turn without even minimal pause.

These three sequences, then, support the contention that the timing of an adult repetition may be a salient factor in distinguish-ing the interactional work which it does. In considering the length of the pauses which precede these repeats, it is interesting to note that Jefferson (1989) has identified a possible 'metric' for conversa-tion which allows for a 'standard maximum' silence of approxi-mately one second. That is to say, a pause of around one second appears regularly to represent a kind of tolerance level beyond which speakers will attend to that pause as signifying something problematic and will undertake some kind of remedial activity. A particularly clear example from her data is the following (Jefferson 1989:173):

[W:PC:III:1:1] (telephone)
Sue: Hello:?h
                        (1.0)
Sue: Hello::,hh

On the basis of hundreds of similar examples, Jefferson suggests that there may be a systematicity to the occurrence of pauses in talk which measure around 0.9 to 1.2 seconds. With this in mind, it is apparent that the pauses in the sequences considered above, measuring 1.2, 1.2 and 0.7 seconds, cluster (loosely) around this one-second figure.

   Now, just what may be made of this in the context of the present data is unclear. One may want to suggest, for instance, that a pause of this length is being treated here by the adult as indicating that an option available to the child for initiating self-repair on a prior turn is not being taken up, and thus is giving the adult warrant to initiate repair her- or himself. In support of this, it can be noted that in those couple of instances in the corpus where it does seem as if the child might be undertaking articulatory repair uninvited, such repairs are carried out well within this time frame. However, if these repetitions were to be viewed as corrections[9] which are simply delayed to provide an opportunity first for self-initiated correction, it might still be expected that the correction when it happens would carry certain prosodic characteristics associated with repair. We might expect high, falling pitch and loudness. In fact these turns all match the rising pitch of their priors, and are not noticeably louder than the surrounding talk. The way they come off is not as corrections, but as re-elicitations. By avoiding doing contrastivity, and by being delayed, they appear to 'try again' – to give the child an opportunity to have another go – without explicitly indicating that the child's first attempt was problematic. In this way, they seem to manage the work of repair in a particularly subtle fashion.

3 Affirmatory repetition

The alternative class of repetitions being considered here – those which have no reparative outcome but which serve to affirm the child's choice of label and terminate the labelling sequence – were exemplified earlier in extract (1). In order to characterize this class of repetitions more fully, they can be compared with the reparative repetitions just considered. Extract (1) and some further examples of affirmatory repetitions are therefore presented here for this kind of comparison:

(12)[10]   adult :   o{ oh } who's th<u>a</u>t

                        {   }

            child :   {[ëh]}

                         (1.0)

            child :   [nʲaːïn]

    →   adult :   [lːɐːːɪən]

                         (5.0)

            child :   °norah°

(13)   adult :   't 're th<u>oː</u>sːe

                         (1.9)

            child :   [nʔkʲgɘˑɤ̈ʔtɕˑ]

                         (0.5)

child :   [gʊˈeˑɪʔt̪'̥{sʲ]

                              {‗‗‗‗‗
                              {‗‗‗‗⁀
→   adult :   {[gɵɪˈɕˈɪpʰ]

                    (2.0)

child :   ·h hhh hhh

                    (0.6)

child :   ·h o̲rˈng:e

(14)

child :   [tʰa̲ t̪ʲʰeɪt̪ʰɔːʷ]

adult :   [t̪ʰëɪt̪ʰɵʷ]

(15)   adult :   ri̲:ght 'n' what's tha̲:t

                    (0.5)

child :   [ʰɐʊʔq]

                    (.)

adult :   wha̲t

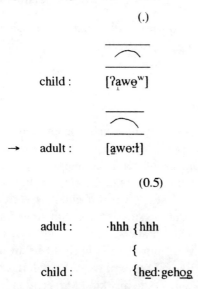

(.)

child :   [ʔa̱we̱ʷ]

→   adult :   [a̱weːɫ]

(0.5)

adult :   ·hhh {hhh
                       {
child :   {he̱d:geho̱g

Bearing in mind that two features in particular were found earlier to be associated with corrective adult repetitions – namely that they were delayed in the turn space following a child's label, and that they displayed contrastivity with the child's turn by means (most saliently at least) of their pitch contour – consideration of the extracts presented above reveals that these repetitions are different on both counts.

Firstly, all of the adult repetition turns in extracts (12)–(15) above occur without delay, immediately following the child's production of the label (and in (13), the adult's turn is even slightly incursive into the child's (second) labelling attempt). While phonetic work has been seen to be projected by a delayed adult repetition, adult repetitions in the corpus which come off as affirmations and suppress phonetic work are never delayed.

Secondly, an examination of the pitch contours of the child and adult labels in (12)–(15) shows a marked lack of contrastivity operating between the two turns in each sequence. In each case, the pitch contour of the adult's repetition shadows very closely that of the child's turn which went before it. In all cases that contour is some kind of rise–fall, but the sequences display different shapes of rise–fall pitch, and it would seem much more likely that it is the relativity of the two pitches in each sequence, rather than some value of a rise–fall pitch *per se*, which is important here.

3.1 Minimizing contrastivity

This issue of contrastivity, the way in which it is effected, and its association with correction, raises interesting questions for the analysis of this kind of data. One problem for the analyst working with talk from children of this young age lies in drawing the boundaries around what 'counts' as correction, when a child's speech is so unadultlike that child and adult versions of 'the same thing' necessarily differ (sometimes quite dramatically) in their phonetic shape. An adult 'repetition' of a child utterance is likely to be an object which is formally distinct from it in several ways. Indeed, this is not only a problem for the analyst. To do any kind of repetition in talk runs the risk of being heard to be doing a correction, if any differences are hearable between one's own version and its prior. A potential problem for the adult interactant here, then, lies in managing to produce a repetition of some part of the child's talk without it coming off as a correction.

Looking again at sequences (12)–(15), it can be seen that while a striking feature of the adult repetition turns in each case is their echoic pitch contour, pitch is not the only prosodic feature in which similarities are observable between the child and adult turns. Take (12) for example. Here, not only is the rise–fall pitch contour of the child's turn matched in the adult's, but the adult version also has a markedly long open vocalic portion which matches it in rhythm to the child's turn. In (13), similarly, there is some rhythmic matching between the child and adult turns, as well as a narrow high rise and fall to low pitch contour in common to both.

Articulatory features, in addition to prosodic ones, may also be matched, as is the case in (14). Both child and adult versions here are marked by two instances of alveolar plosion which is tense, quite heavily aspirated and laminally articulated. There is marked lip-rounding at the end of both versions. In addition the rhythm of the two turns is closely matched, and a tense voice quality in the utterance of the adult mimics that of the child. And, in (15), the disyllabic structure of the child's version of *owl* – with a labial glide and following vocalic portion with rounded and central quality – is retained in the adult's repetition.

Contrastivity in these examples is being neutralized not only through the feature of pitch contour (which is perhaps most salient), but through a complex of phonetic features (both articulatory and prosodic) by which the adult's utterance is brought into line with that of the child. What these examples suggest is that one way of doing a repeat in talk without it coming off as a correction, is to minimize all phonetic differences between one's own version and its prior.

4 Summary and discussion

The investigation presented in this chapter has centred on an attempt to differentiate between instances of what superficially appears to be a single linguistic object in one particular sequential position – that is, adult repeating turns following a child's attempt at labelling a picture. It has been found that these repetitions can be distinguished in terms of their interactional accomplishments, and in terms of their prosodic design, suggesting caution in the inter-pretation of the somewhat superficial treatment of a class of objects like 'repetitions' which appears at times in the child language lit-erature. Even single-word repetitions occurring in the same position in sequence can be seen to be quite disparate objects. Fine details in the prosodic construction of these turns can be associated with significant diversity in the consequences they hold for the trajectory of the talk which follows them.

Two features in particular have been found, through this inves-tigation, to be associated with adult repetitions which are reparative in orientation. Some reparative repetitions are marked by a pitch contour which, like that associated with the self-corrections identi-fied by Local (1992), is high and falls to low. Whether this kind of a pitch pattern is more generally associated with corrective work in talk, or whether it here does that work by virtue of contrasting with the pitch contour of the child's turns and thereby underlining the work of contrastivity which is inherent in the activity of correction, is a question which would merit further research.

A second class of adult repetitions which accomplish similar reparative work with respect to their priors have been seen to be

designed rather differently. Here, a temporal delay in the placement
of these turns appears to disguise their corrective character by
bringing them off as re-elicitations. This finding raises two particular points for discussion. First, some parallels can be drawn with
other work which has been carried out on correction. Jefferson
(1987) has described certain ways in which correction can be
'embedded' in conversation, and accomplished in particularly dis-
creet ways without ever being brought to the surface of what speakers are dealing with in their talk. Similarly, Couper-Kuhlen
(1992:354) has identified a rhythmic kind of 'prosodic camouflage'
(rather different in form from the phenomena being described here)
by which speakers can soften certain reparative utterances, and
Local (1992:295) has uncovered a kind of 'prosodic disguise'
which characterizes certain self-corrections in speakers' turns.
What is suggested by all of these findings is that, while repair
in talk is often oriented to as an activity which is challenging or
threatening in some way, speakers nonetheless have at their disposal various delicate resources by the use of which they may
disguise or euphemize their corrective actions.

Second, an important methodological point is raised by a comparison of this class of delayed corrective/re-elicitative repetitions
with those which similarly match the prosodic characteristics of
their priors but are produced without delay and come off as affirmations. Much has been gained in conversation analytic work from
a consideration of the precise timing of speaker's turns relative to
one another (e.g. Jefferson 1973, Jefferson and Schegloff 1975),
particularly in the area of overlap and incursion. It would seem
to lend even more weight to the importance of a fine-grained
sequential analysis to consider a phenomenon whereby the members of a class of formally (including prosodically) non-distinctive
objects, occupying the same *position* in sequence, can be interactionally quite different objects by virtue of their *temporal placement*
within that position.

In addition, the findings of this investigation in relation to the
design of non-reparative, affirmatory repetition in this data is
suggestive. Since repetition in this kind of talk is so heavily implicated in the work of correction, there is a very real problem here for
the adult who chooses not to pursue phonetic refinement from the
child. By the nature of young children's speech, an adult repetition

of a child's label is likely to express a certain amount of contrastivity with it in articulatory terms. However, it would seem that, in order not to be heard to be a correction, a repetition may minimize contrastivity along other parameters – may become, in other words, a kind of imitation of the child's turn. One account for the observation that adults are often heard to 'mimic' young children's utterances is suggested by the possibility that when adults repeat young children's utterances they very often opt to do it in an expressly non-corrective format.

Notes

1 See Couper-Kuhlen (this volume) for a more detailed explication of different categories of *repetition*.

2 In the terms of Couper-Kuhlen (this volume) these are verbal repetitions.

3 Treatment of prosodic repair in the literature (e.g. Cutler 1983, Fromkin 1977) seems to have dealt principally with repair of focus misplacement (shifts in lexical stress and sentence accent). The issues raised here by an instance of a repair in pitch contour extending over a single word utterance without a shift in stress are somewhat different.

4 Note the bilabiality and nasality at the beginning of the utterance.

5 Throughout this chapter, a distinction is drawn between *articulatory* and *prosodic* phonetic properties of the talk. The motivation for this terminology is to avoid terms like *segmental* and *non-segmental* or *suprasegmental* which impose, inappropriately, a phonological interpretation on phonetic events. It is recognised that this distinction is not wholly satisfactory: some phonatory features such as voice/voicelessness, for example, may be most appropriately included under the umbrella term *articulatory*, and some features which we would want to call prosodic – duration, for example – are strictly speaking matters of articulation. Nonetheless, these terms avoid the danger of adopting a pseudo-phonological stance. For the same reasons, care has been taken throughout the analysis to describe phonetic events, wherever possible, in non-segmental terms.

6 This is extract (2) with additional transcription of pitch.

7 It can be noted that this kind of delay is not a feature of the repetitions in extracts (6) and (8).

8 This is extract (3) with additional transcription of pitch.

9 An 'invitation to self-correct' of this kind amounts to a correction, since the adult, in articulating the label, supplies the correct version.

10 This is extract (1) with more phonetic detail.

434   Clare Tarplee

References

Brown, R. and U. Bellugi 1964. Three processes in the child's acquisition of syntax. *Harvard Educational Review*, 34: 133–151.

Couper-Kuhlen, E. 1992. Contextualizing discourse: the prosody of interactive repair. In P. Auer and A. di Luzio (eds.) *The Contextualization of Language*. Amsterdam: Benjamins, pp. 337–364.

Cutler, A. 1983. Speakers' conceptions of the functions of prosody. In A. Cutler and D. R. Ladd (eds.) *Prosody: Models and measurements*. Berlin: Springer, pp. 79–91.

Drew, P. 1981. Adults' corrections of children's mistakes: a response to Wells and Montgomery. In P. French and M. MacLure (eds.) *Adult–Child Conversation*. London: Croom Helm, pp. 244–267.

Fromkin, V. A. 1977. Putting the emPHAsis on the wrong sylLABle. In L. M. Hyman (ed.) *Studies in Stress and Accent*. Los Angeles: University of Southern California, pp. 15–26.

Jefferson, G. 1973. A case of precision timing in ordinary conversation: overlapped tag-positioned address terms in closing sequences. *Semiotica*, 9: 47–96.

1987. On exposed and embedded correction. In G. Button and J. R. E. Lee (eds.) *Talk and Social Organisation*. Clevedon: Multilingual Matters, pp. 86–100.

1989. Preliminary notes on a possible metric which provides for a 'standard maximum' silence of approximately one second in conversation. In D. Roger and P. Bull (eds.) *Conversation: an interdisciplinary perspective*. Clevedon: Multilingual Matters, pp. 166–196.

Jefferson, G. and E. A. Schegloff 1975. Sketch: some orderly aspects of overlap in natural conversation. Paper delivered at the Meeting of the American Anthropological Association, December 1975. Mimeo., Department of Sociology, UCLA.

Kelly, J. and J. K. Local 1989. *Doing Phonology: Observing, recording, interpreting*. Manchester University Press.

Local, J. K. 1992. Continuing and restarting. In P. Auer and A. di Luzio (eds.) *The Contextualization of Language*. Amsterdam: Benjamins, pp. 272–296.

McHoul, A. 1978. The organisation of turns at formal talk in the classroom. *Language in Society*, 7: 183–213.

Mehan, H. 1979. *Learning Lessons: Social organisation in the classroom*. Cambridge, Mass.: Harvard University Press.

Moerck, E. L. 1974. Changes in verbal child–mother interaction with increasing language skills of the child. *Journal of Psycholinguistic Research*, 3: 101–116.

Ryan, J. 1974. Early language development: towards a communicational analysis. In M. P. M. Richards (ed.) *The Integration of the Child into a Social World*. Cambridge University Press, pp. 185–214.

Schegloff, E. A., G. Jefferson and H. Sacks 1977. The preference for self-correction in the organization of repair in conversation. *Language*, 53: 361–382.

Slobin, D. 1968. Imitation and grammatical development in children. In N. S. Endler, L. R. Boulter and H. Osser (eds.) *Contemporary Issues in Developmental Psychology*. New York: Holt, Rinehardt and Winston, pp. 437–443.

Snow, C. E., A. Arlman-Rupp, Y. Hassing, J. Jobse, J. Joosten and J. Vorster 1976. Mothers' speech in three social classes. *Journal of Psycholinguistic Research*, 5: 1–19.

Tarplee, C. 1993. Working on talk: the collaborative shaping of linguistic skills within child–adult interaction. D.Phil thesis, Department of Language and Linguistic Science, University of York.

11

Informings and announcements in their environment: prosody within a multi-activity work setting

MARJORIE HARNESS GOODWIN

Linguistic anthropologists have long been fascinated by the complex ways in which intonation plays a critical role in the production of 'non-casual' speech (Voegelin 1960). Typically prosodic features have been examined in the domains of ritual speech (DuBois 1986, Fox 1988, Voegelin 1960) and verbal art (Briggs 1988). However, recently attention has turned to the examination of more secular domains in which specific alterations in the production of ordinary speech occur: for example, radio sports announcements (Ferguson 1983),[1] auctioneering (Kuiper and Haggo 1984), horse-race calls (Horvath 1991, Kuiper and Austin 1990), and public community announcements (Kroskrity 1993, Tedlock 1983). As argued by Tedlock (1983:190), in both ritual and secular contexts systematic stress and pitch inversion 'attracts more attention than ordinary delivery and implies that what is being said is "important"; the speech event in question "is not ordinary" and will take precedence over any other speech event that may already be in progress'.

This chapter will investigate intonation as a constitutive feature of two related types of speech actions used for the transfer of information about the arrival of incoming planes in a mid-sized American airport: (i) informings within the Operations room (the coordination center for ground operations) and (ii) subsequent announcements from Operations to the Ramp (where baggage is loaded and unloaded). Through analysis of the prosody of these related types of information transfers, I examine how talk gets tailored for a target audience and the space that they inhabit.

Both the Operations room and the Ramp are extremely noisy areas. Within the Operations room, a multi-activity work setting in the airport, workers are faced with a barrage of incoming messages from various sources: radio scanners which transmit conversations between pilots and air-traffic control, other radios that connect various parts of the airport (for example, the gate area, the Ramp or baggage area, lost luggage, catering, fuel, etc.), telephones, computer print-outs, computer monitor displays and face-to-face communication. Distinctive intonation contours are useful for cutting through the sonic soup that constitutes the auditory environment of Operations. In the Ramp area, crew chiefs, responsible for seeing that their crews meet incoming planes to unload them, deal not only with the noise of incoming and outgoing planes, deafening without earplugs, but also radio calls from other areas of the airport. Radio announcements from Ramp Planners to crew chiefs on the Ramp, not unlike utterances of Hopi chanters signalling the start of a rabbit hunt (Voegelin 1960:61), perform the function of calling recipients to action, through use of a specialized register (Ferguson 1983).

1 The ecology of work situations in the airport

Figure 11.1 situates the two information transfers that are the focus of this paper within their ecological setting.

Updating co-workers in the airport about the arrivals and departures of planes is an important part of the Operations room's work. The radio scanner next to Flight Tracker's work station broadcasts conversations between incoming pilots and either tower or ground control (number 1 in fig. 11.1). Though this talk is not designed for them, it can be overheard by personnel in the Operations (Ops) room; this has implications for a whole set of others in the airport.[2] A person in the position of the Flight Tracker, overhearing a directive regarding parking from ground control to a pilot (e.g. *Sixteen seventy five contact ground point seven*) on a scanner next to her, relays the information that a plane is *on the ground* to the Ramp Planner through *informings* (number 2 in fig. 11.1). Subsequently through an *announcement* (number 3 in fig. 11.1), Ramp Planner relays the information that a plane has arrived to crew chiefs on the Ramp, whose job it is to organize their crews to meet a plane and unload baggage.

Utterances are parts of action chains which set in motion a set of next actions that mobilize people. Once the tower/pilot exchange

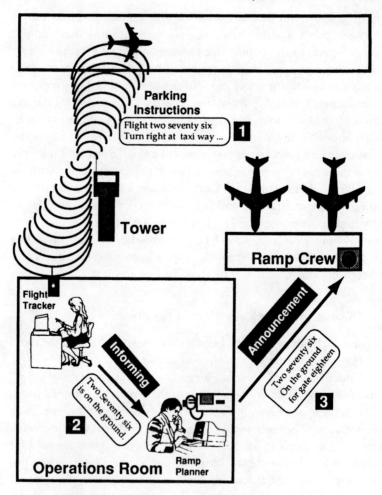

Figure 11.1

has been overheard, there are systematic modifications in the talk as
it gets passed through the system. Intonation is not incidental, but
rather a constitutive feature that frames talk in information transfer
sequences. Speakers must be able to produce hearable utterances in
the midst of competing talk; in the organization of this action
sequence, monitoring or listening is equally as important in the
sequence, of activity as talk itself. Producing a next action in a
chain of actions means participants must be closely attending

talk, even though it is not specifically addressed to them, for its relevance to their activity.

The Ops room, as a 'center for coordination' (Suchman 1992, and in press), provides the possibility for coordinated action around a single focus; however, the room is arranged such that persons in each of four different work stations can also be occupied with their own focus of attention which involves work groups in other locations as well. The multiple distributed participation framework (Goodwin 1995) that is particular to this work setting differs from that assumed in most analyses of *encounters* (Goffman 1961:17),[3] in that it entails both co-present participants (the Flight Tracker and the Ramp Planner), who are positioned *back-to-back* rather than face-to-face, and work groups who are spatially distributed (workers in the Operations room and those on the Ramp). Ramp Planners, with their announcement, provide a single action relevant simultaneously within *two participation frameworks*; they both ratify that they have heard the informing from Flight Tracker and initiate an action prompting Ramp crew chiefs to meet a plane.

Among experienced Ops workers monitoring is carried out with relative ease by participants situated next to each other; with little more than a gesture or a glance, persons side-by-side may be cued that they should initiate a next projected action in a sequence (for example, placing a call to another service division). Though unproblematic for oldtimers, newcomers complain at length of the incredible effort that attending multiple messages demands. As one new Ramp Planner trainee reports:

(1)   RP Trainee: It's like I have fifteen people on the radio
                          trying to get ahold of me.
                          And I can only answer one.
                          And not many people know how to stand by.
                          Three people talking at once.
                          It doesn't work on that. It breaks up.
                          And then you have all the different commotion
                          going on inside Ops. So it is a difficult job.

Newcomers to the position of Ramp Planner may in fact experience so much difficulty in attending simultaneous messages that they have to be physically summoned by Flight Tracker. In the following example, upon noticing that the novice Ramp Planner has not pro-

Figure 11.2

duced an appropriate next move to his informing about an incoming flight, Flight Tracker (in right front) swivels and taps Ramp Planner's chair to create a focus of mutual attention. In the video freeze-frame (fig. 11.2) we see Ramp Planner (on the left) turning as he says *I'm sorry?* requesting repetition of the Flight Tracker's informing (transcription conventions appear in the appendix).

(2)   FT: Eleven **twen**ty's on the ground.
              A little bit earlier.
              Than expected.
->   RP: I'm sorry?
       FT: Eleven twenty's on the ground.
              For gate twenty.

In informing sequences, Flight Tracker, who initiates the informing, is seated diagonally opposite Ramp Planner. Yet Flight Tracker generally manages to relay the news about an incoming plane *without* an address term or change in facing formation. In the midst of simultaneous activities, speaker displays that talk is designed for Ramp Planner without interfering with the talk of others in the room. The next part of this chapter will deal with how this is accomplished.

2 Informings

Informings vary depending upon the level of activity in Ops. However, they frequently take the form of a declarative statement:

> FT: Flight X is on the ground.

Expert Ramp Planners constantly monitor their computer screens for news of the status of incoming planes, and have ways of readily accessing relevant information. However, for less experienced planners, the informings of Flight Trackers serve as important prompts. As one trainee put it:

> (3)   Ramp Planner Trainee: If I'm in the computer and I'm pulling loads or something, weights and balance, I sometimes can't get into who's on the ground, who's taxiing, who's going out. So if they tell me 'four forty six or whatever flight number it is, is on the ground, taxiing to this gate' I can just automatically just turn to the radio and say 'the flight number is on the ground, holding or taxiing to this gate'. It's much simpler than having to change DECS, that's weights and balance, and then pull up who's on the ground.

During periods of relative calm, Flight Tracker may wait briefly for a silent period between competing talk and then relay the message to Ramp Planner without a marked intonation shift, using falling intonation:

> (4)   FT: Four **sixty's** on the **ground**.

However, in the midst of densely occurring interaction, for example, when the intended recipient is involved in simultaneous talk,[4] Flight Tracker may modulate his/her voice in order to be heard over other talk in the room. The following informing occurs when Ramp Planner has been providing brief comment into ongoing talk with co-workers:[5]

> (5)   FT: Two seventy **si:x** is on the **gr:ound,**

The most important information being conveyed in the informing utterance is the naming of a specific flight. This is positioned in the initial part of the utterance, and is accented. In producing her

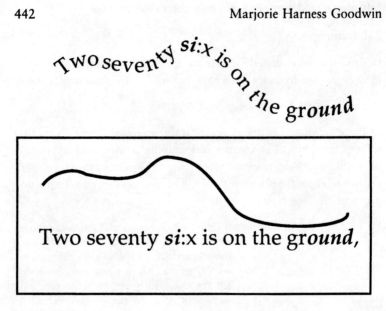

Figure 11.3

informing, this Flight Tracker uses an intonation contour which remains high over each of the numbers of the plane, the important information in the utterance (see fig. 11.3). The words *two* and *six* are produced without the characteristic deep 'sag' \/ that usually occurs between pitch accents. The phonetic interpolation rule used to get from one high-pitched sound to another is not applied to this instance and this indicates that scaling values or the pitch ranges are being manipulated for a specific effect.

Specifying that the plane is *on the ground* also provides useful information for Ramp Planner. Simply stating that a plane *is here* does not provide Ramp Planner with sufficient information to proceed with an announcement. For example, in the following when Passenger Planner (PP) states that a plane is *here*, RP requests clarification that the plane is actually *on the ground* before proceeding with her announcement to crew chiefs on the Ramp:

(6) Radio: Wagon. Four seventy five. // (   )
     PP: **Holey mack**erel. Four seventy **five** is here. ((looking
            first at computer and then at his watch))
     RP -> On the ground?
     PP: Yep.

RP: Four seventy **five**'s
       on the ground.
       For gate **fifteen**.

Intonation varies across speakers and even within a single speaker's repertoire. For example, some informings, as in the following examples, are produced with what could be called a 'stylized falling' (Ladd 1978:520), 'vocative chant' (ibid: 525), ' spoken chant' (Pike 1945:71) or 'call' contour (Gibbon 1976:274–287) – a chanted intonation pattern which steps down from one level pitch to another with an interval of approximately a minor third.

(7)   FT: **Three** sixty **three**'s on the ground,

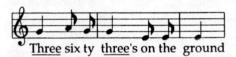

Three six ty three's on the ground

(8)   FT: **Six ninety one**'s here **now**::

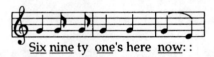

Six nine ty one's here now: :

A drop of a minor third as over the word *now::* in example (8) is usually associated with such everyday American English calls as 'Johnny', 'Dinner's ready', or 'Ally ally all in free all', used during the children's game of hide-and-seek.

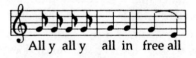

All y all y all in free all

Amidst periods of extremely dense interaction the contour will be even more pronounced and address terms may be appended after the informing. For example, the following occurred when the intended addressed recipient, Ramp Planner, was hearably engaged in extended talk with his co-worker:

(9)   FT: Four **sixty**'s on the **ground Mark**,

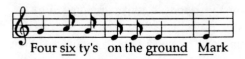

Four six ty's on the ground Mark

Informing statements delivered amidst dense room activity are characteristically produced with raised volume, higher pitch than other talk in the room, and an intonation contour which often sounds more like song than speech. Instead of dropping as in a normal declarative contour, tonal targets are sustained as in chanting or singing. In the one chanted contour which appeared 'in the clear' of simultaneous talk so that a pitch track could be attempted (*three sixty three's on the ground*), the shift in contour was so rapid that it could not be accurately tracked by the computer.

Under normal circumstances Flight Tracker uses neither a summons nor an address term to get the attention of a co-worker, and rarely even makes a turn of the head in his or her direction to direct talk towards a colleague. Instead the chanted intonation *frames the talk* as distinct from other ongoing talk and thus permits it to stand out from the hubbub of other activity in the room (while not, however, conveying any sense of emergency about a plane's arrival).

Ladd (1978:520)[6] describes vocative chants as signalling a certain predictability or stereotype in the message. Discussing the ritualized nature of this contour Ladd (1978:520) argues it conveys a 'flavor of everyday domestic life': 'What is signaled by this intonation is the implication that the message is in some sense predictable, stylized, part of a stereotyped exchange or announcement.' For Ops workers this 'call' signals that an expected, unremarkable event has occurred; it prompts the Ramp Planner that a scheduled flight has in fact arrived while conveying the sense that business is proceeding as usual. The construction of the utterance as a declarative statement (without an explicit address term or form of summons) does not demand that addressee abandon concurrent activity, or elicit a direct response from Ramp Planner to Flight Tracker. Informings are produced without the initial establishment of a framework of mutual orientation. As Gibbon (1976:280), Abe (1962:522) and Pike (1945:187n) argue, call contours are used when physical distance separates the interlocutors. In the Operations room the multiple, competing foci of attention as well as distance between work stations which are diagonally opposite make listening difficult. Flight Tracker relies on Ramp Planner being positioned to receive the message in the work space he or she habitually occupies and on the chanted intonational contour to carry the message over the ongoing talk in the room.[7] This intonation provides a way for Flight Tracker to mark for recipients that new updated information about a routine work activity is available.

3 Announcements

In informal settings, confirmation of the receipt of an informing or 'new news' in conversation is achieved through a return action to prior speaker, for example an assessment of the news (Terasaki 1976:7–8).[8] In the Operations room, by way of contrast, no talk whatsoever by Ramp Planner is addressed to the prior speaker, the Flight Tracker who relayed the message about the arrival of a new flight. As participants are located within a web of interlocking distributed participation frameworks, the appropriate next action is, instead, delivery of an announcement to crew chiefs in the bagroom, whose job is to meet incoming flights. This action carries out the projected next move in the chain of activity, thus providing a powerful demonstration of understanding of the import of Flight Tracker's informing. Through the Ramp Planner's announcement Flight Tracker knows that his/her talk has been received and properly taken into account.

The following provides an instance of how Ramp Planner's announcements (lines 2–4) typically follow an informing from Flight Tracker (line 1):

```
(10) 1 FT:     Three sixty three's on the ground,
        RP:    ((goes to mike, then looks through papers, checking for
               number of gate))
               (0.4)
     2         Three six three
     3         On'th'ground
     4         F'ga'eighteen.
     5 Radio:  Thanks Mary.
```

Whereas Flight Tracker in her utterance (line 1) describes only the flight number of the plane that is on the ground, relays by Ramp Planner (lines 2–4) note both the flight number and the gate. Through her complex sheet (a print-out of expected times of incomings and outgoings for planes) and computer monitor Ramp Planner has access to information regarding the gates at which planes will arrive. By constructing her relay as she does, Flight

Tracker delivers in as concise a fashion as possible what is new
news[9] for Ramp Planner – that a particular plane has arrived on
the runway and is now *on the ground*, omitting information that
Ramp Planner already has accessible.

An orientation towards the sequential implicativeness of the
initial informing for Ramp Planner's next course of action is observable in examples where Ramp Planner (RP) does *not* take stock of
Flight Tracker's informing to produce an announcement of the
plane's arrival to the ramp. If, while Flight Tracker monitors RP's
talk, Flight Tracker does not hear this next projected move in the
action chain, she will repeat her informing, making use of a more
insistent informative intonation and a more direct statement about
the plane's arrival, until RP displays some recognition of receipt. In
the following example (11), Flight Tracker's informing of a plane's
arrival (line 5) is recycled (lines 11, 13, 29, 32, 35) until she receives
a display of recognition that Ramp Planner has heard and acted
upon her delivery of it (line 36). Below, the participation frameworks between Flight Tracker and Ramp Planner are highlighted by
shading. A box is drawn around talk over the radio between Ramp
Planner and a crew chief, and marked with a walkie-talkie icon.
Other talk within Ops is not marked.

Though the Ramp Planner's announcement, like other
announcement sequences (Terasaki 1976:7), is formulated as a
declarative statement, it has far greater significance than a mere
description of events. As a prompt for relevant subsequent action,
it alerts crew chiefs in charge of meeting incoming flights. Should
this announcement not be made (as was done once as an Ops-
initiated experiment), crew chiefs on the Ramp will radio Ops
with messages such as *What's going on? We're not hearing arrivals.*
and meeting the plane could be delayed.

3.1 The structure and intonation of announcements

Acoustic analysis of announcements confirmed initial auditory analysis[10] of the sequences, showing that they are segmented into three
separate *intonation units.*[11] Schuetze-Coburn, Shapley and Weber
(1991:216) define an intonation unit as 'a stretch of speech by a
single speaker uttered with a "coherent intonation contour" (Chafe,
1987, p. 22)'. According to Schuetze-Coburn, Shapley and Weber

(11)

Ramp Planner:	Oh: *okay* uh: ***There*** we go.	1
	=Ruh is Jason the: (.) (uh) transfer driver?	2
Radio:	*yeah.*	3
Ramp Planner:	Uh: can you have him go over to gate uh:m	4
Flight Tracker:	Five seventy *eight*'s on the grou:nd ((chanted))	5
Ramp Planner:	((looks down at papers, holds finger on page))	6
	tch! Sixteen when five seven eight gets in?=	7
	It'll be in about ((*looks at flight information*	8
	display screen)) thirty six *af*ter.	9
Supervisor:	Eagles okay?=	10
Flight Tracker:	=Here-	11
Ramp Planner:	And uh:, you've got ((looking at papers))	12
Flight Tracker:	It's on the ground now:, ((leaning her head back	13
	in direction of Ramp Planner over her shoulder))	14
Ops B:	((shakes head)) Uh: the next thing probably start	15
	callin in in about ten minutes.	16
	(0.5)	17
Ramp Planner:	*Wh*at'a'we got here.	18
	You've got about ***twelve people*** come to you	19
	so you got *ba:*gs comin off that flight.=	20
	Can you pick em up?	21
Radio:	I sure *will* Mike.	22
Ramp Planner:	Kay. That's on gate *six*teen.	23
	Be in about ((looks toward the Flight	24
	Information Display)) thirty six *af*ter,	25
	((starts looking for a pen or pencil on the surface	26
	of his desk and in his drawer as Radio responds))	27
Radio:	Gate *six*teen. *I co*py.	28
Flight Tracker:	It's *here*	29
Ramp Planner:	((The Ramp Planner is looking in a drawer	30
	displaying disengagement from the radio call))	31
Flight Tracker:	*It's here.*	32
Ramp Planner:	It's here? ((looks in direction of Flight Tracker	33
	and at screen with a quizzical look))	34
Flight Tracker:	It's here.	35
Ramp Planner:	Okay. It's on the ***ground*** right *now:*	36
	It'll be coming in to sixteen ((looks at monitor))	37
Radio:	Yeah buddy.	38

(1991) prosodic cues which are used to determine intonation unit boundaries include cues related to the pitch pattern of the utterance and cues related to timing:

> The perception of coherence in the pitch pattern is influenced by at least two factors: degree and direction of pitch movement on a stressed syllable and change in pitch relative to the speaker's preceding utterance (pitch reset). Timing cues which contribute to perceived IU unity include an acceleration in tempo on initial unstressed syllables, prosodic lengthening of the final syllable(s), and a noticeable pause (0.3 second or greater) between IUs.

All three intonation units of announcements are produced with falling pitch. The pitch range declines throughout the production of each intonation unit of the three-part utterance (which is part of what makes it appear a cohesive unit).

(12) RP: **Two:** seventy **si:x**
     On'th'ground.
     F'ga'eighteen.

(13) RP: Six ninety **one.**
     On'th'ground.
     For'gate **fifteen.**

(14) RP: Two two **five.**
     On'th'ground.
     Gate six**teen.**

(15) RP: Eleven **twenty**'s.
     On'the'ground.
     For gate **twenty.**

The announcement has a three-part structure. In the stereotypical announcement sequence the first intonation unit contains the flight number of the plane, the second, the phrase *on the ground*, and the third, the gate that the plane will be arriving at:[12]

> Flight X   ((flight number of plane))
> On the ground   ((state of plane))
> For gate Y   ((gate destination))

Three separate pieces of information are presented in the intonation units making up a turn at talk.[13] The information is produced in one turn at talk and is delivered as a single package by fitting it into one *declination unit* (Schuetze-Coburn, Shapley and Weber 1991:212), a period of speech sharing a common declination line, or gradual falling-off of pitch during an utterance. By packaging information in this way it can be received intact and the pieces can be assembled into a whole. The following figure provides a diagram[14] of the pitch track of a typical announcement sequence:

(16) RP: **Two:** seventy **si:x.**
            On'th'**ground.**
            F'ga'eigh**teen.**

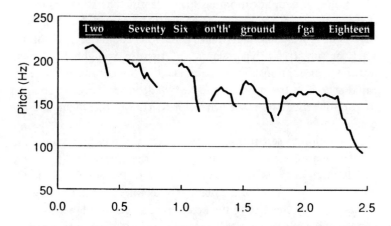

The *new* information in the utterance is the announcement that a particular *flight* has in fact arrived. The flight number is relevant for a particular set of individuals, those responsible for unloading baggage from it and fueling it. It implicitly functions as an address term, alerting those responsible for servicing a particular flight number that 'it's showtime'.[15] Other information in the announcement is highly predictable. Through information on documents called complex sheets, hard-copy versions of the day's schedule, as well as computer displays on monitors positioned in the bag-room, Ramp personnel (crew chiefs, as well as transfer drivers for whom the announcement is relevant) have access to the expected times of arrival of planes at particular gate destinations.

Salient information is highlighted throughout the turn. The flight number is positioned right at the opening of the announcement, in the first intonation unit. Not only is it delivered with relatively high pitch, but it also takes up roughly half of the turn. The time used to produce the flight number in the above example was 1.2 seconds out of 2.57 seconds for the complete declination unit.

The second intonation unit, *on'th'ground* produced with a small
reset, indicates the state of the plane. Accelerated and phonetically
reduced speech at the beginning of the utterance indicate the lack of
salience of this part of the intonation unit. Rapid speech is indicated
in the transcript through apostrophes separating words (indicating
the speech is elided); the spelling of *th*, eliminating the vowel from
the word *the*, indicates that the word *the* is barely discernible.
Shortening or simplification has been identified as a feature of registers such as sports announcements (Ferguson 1983:160). Note
that as in sports-announcer talk (1983:159) copula deletion occurs
after the subject, so that essential information is highlighted, as in
headlines or captions. This 'assimilated' (phonetically reduced) or
rapid speech in the production of *on'th'ground*, stands in contrast
to careful articulation over the words naming the flight and the
gate.

In addition to separating the two parts of the utterance containing information delivered with numbers, the phrase *on the ground*
stands in contrast to other sorts of identifications concerning the
whereabouts or 'state' of the plane. For example, similar announcements making reference to the position of a specific plane and gate,
use phrases such as *clear to land*, a formulation frequently used in
communications from tower to pilot.

(17) Tower to Pilot: (   ) clear to land.
    FT: Fifteen twenty **three**'s cleared to land.
    RP: Fifteen twenty **three**'s
->   clear to land
               for eigh**teen**.

Though the phrase *on the ground* was by far the most commonly
used phrase of the second intonation unit, alternative phrasings
include *just landed* or *on*.

(18) RP: Eight sixty **six**
        Just landed
        For gate **nine**.

(19) RP: Twelve o one
        Is **on**
        For Alpha **nine**.

Such phrases stand in contrast to others such as *cleared to land*,
which would indicate that the plane is still in the air. The informa-

tion within the second intonation unit is quite predictable, as most announcements concern the arrivals of planes. One Ramp Planner (who frequently showed disrespect for traditional announcement forms) eliminated this part of the turn completely, specifying only the flight number and gate:

(20) RP: Five **sixty**.
        For gate **nine**.
        Shut **up**.

Note that although *Shut up* was added, the three-part rhythmic structure of the turn was nonetheless preserved.

The third intonation unit of the turn specifies the gate the plane is coming into. Through complex sheets and the flight information display terminals in the bag-room crew chiefs already know scheduled gates. However, given that gates *can* change in the course of the day due to airplane swaps (Jordan 1990) such information is still relevant, confirming that the expected gate is the actual gate. In the production of this intonation unit the nonessential information *for gate* is greatly compressed. In example (16) above *for gate* is produced as *f'ga* with *ga* eliding with the *ei* of *eighteen*.

By way of contrast the actual number of the gate is produced clearly, in full form, and often accented (as indicated by the boldfacing in the text). This part of the utterance functions like an address term. As the Ramp is divided into different three- or four-person teams assigned to a particular gate, the gate number indicates the precise crew for which the utterance is relevant. In fact, in the third intonation unit, personal names designating for which crew chief the announcement is relevant, can occur *in place of* specific gates:

(21) RP: Two eighty **six**.
        Clear't'land.
->   Javi**er**.

(22) RP: Seven eighteen.
        Just landed.
->   uh **Mark**.

As these examples indicate, an optional feature of the announcement is the use of a personal name, placed at the end of the utterance. This also provides a form of address and serves to personalize the announcement.

(23) RP: That i:s
                 Six**teen** se**ven**ty **five.**
                 On'the'**ground.**
                 For'ga'**twelve**
                 Charles.
       Crew chief: **Thank** you **Joe.**

(24) RP: **Ni:ne** six **four**
          on'the'ground
          for gate **twenty**
          uh Freddy.

A pitch track of example (24) shows that the address term is produced as if a separate intonation unit:

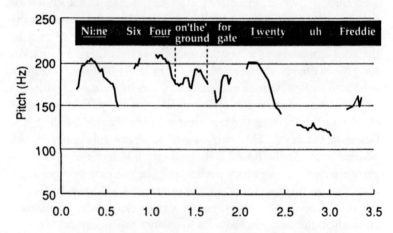

On the word *ni:ne* of *ni:ne six four* the pitch drops and there is a slight pause before talk resumes. The Ramp Planner gives this part of the utterance extra emphasis not only through accent on the numbers *nine* and *four*, but also through the high percentage of turn time devoted to it (1.2 seconds, almost half of the total time for the basic announcement). In contrast *on'the'ground* and *for gate* occupy minimal time during the turn.

Though optional elements, such as address terms, can be appended to the basic announcement turn, and it can take a variety of different forms, the announcement's rhythmic triplet structure is typically preserved:

(25) RP: Gate **five**.
           Dwight **L**ugeroff.
           It's **show**time.

Aviation textbooks explicitly instruct pilots in their communication with the ground or tower to 'State your intentions or your request for service – *briefly*' (emphasis in the original; Glaeser 1982:204). Such practices are carried over into less formal airport settings such as Operations. The announcement highlights important information; the aircraft flight number, which acts as a summons, is positioned in the initial part of the turn, and separate bits of information are conveyed in each intonation unit.

4 Conclusion

Talk about incoming planes in an airport gets changed as it is propagated through the system in different divisions of the airport. An overheard message on a scanner from air-traffic control to pilot about where to park is transformed into an *informing* (a prompting about the current state of the plane) to Ramp Planner and finally delivered as an *announcement* to the Ramp. Unlike the canonical single-focussed face-to-face encounter, in a multi-focussed setting such as Operations, speaker and hearer are not necessarily oriented to each other, so they may not have access to visual feedback. The problem posed is how to produce talk that can be heard above the 'sonic soup' noise of the Operations room. A solution which has evolved entails adapting the informing to the situation at hand through intonation contours, such as chants, which in Gumperz's sense (1982) contextualize talk as set apart from ordinary conversation. In the informing by Flight Tracker, the intonation contour as well as the specific words used vary from speaker to speaker and within a single speaker's repertoire. Informings are targeted for specific co-present others, and are adapted to the specifics of the interaction of the moment. For example, intonation contours can be more exaggerated – almost sung – and address terms appended when Flight Tracker perceives Ramp Planner to be engaged in talk which might impede hearing of the informing.

While a variety of types of signals and intonation contours may be used to summon a Ramp Planner in the informing, features of

454Marjorie Harness Goodwin

the *announcement* are much more routinized. Though intended for specific crew chiefs (who have radios on their person), they can be heard and easily interpreted by any Ramp person in the baggage area for whom they might be relevant. These are typically one-way interactions which, in contrast to informings, are produced where the local environment is not known in detail. Whereas informings are delivered as a single intonation unit, announcements are usually produced as three intonation units packaged within one declination unit. Each intonation unit contains information useful for prompting crew chiefs, the most important information receiving the greatest salience. The three-part structure allows recipients to easily process the information conveyed. By producing talk with a distinctive intonation contour the announcement stands out from other talk in the bag-room (one of the noisiest rooms in the airport).

The announcement exhibits certain features which resemble those of oral-formulaic speech or what anthropologists have described as 'ritual speech' (DuBois 1986, Fox 1988, Briggs 1988). According to DuBois (1986:317) ritual texts are uttered 'with a high degree of fluency, without hesitations, in a stylized intonation contour'. In the production of these utterances, in contrast to the more conversational talk, the speech is extremely fluent, and there is no hesitation (no *uhs*, *uhms* or sound stretches). In addition, the intonation contour of the announcements to the Ramp is quite regular across the talk of different speakers. Though generally the parallel elements characterizing ritual speech are found to be paired, semantically related lexical items or grammatical structures (Jakobson 1987:173–179; DuBois 1986:316; Fox 1977:78), here repetition exhibiting poetic features is achieved through intonation units with similar falling contours.

In ritual speech a form of 'authoritative voice' is conveyed through what DuBois (1986:330) describes as the 'obliteration of ultimate personal source'. For example, shifters, especially those which index the speaker as an individual, are avoided. As Olson (1980:103) states, the ritual orator does not express his personal views, but rather acts as a spokesman or messenger. He proposes that an important feature of establishing authority for ritual speech is to make it appear to be derived from a 'transcendental' source. DuBois (1986:330, 333) argues that an important feature of establishing authority for ritual speech is to make it appear to be of apersonal origin – that the words appear to be in some sense 'god-given', derived from some timeless source whose authority is self-evident. Following Turner (1967:19), DuBois (1986:314) states that he understands ritual as 'prescribed formal behavior for occasions not given over to technological routine, having reference to beliefs in mystical beings or powers'. Interestingly, in the announcement sequences examined here it is *over technologically mediated speech channels* with their feature of only one person speaking at a time that talk becomes routinized. Radio communication in particular seems to promote this ritualization.

DuBois (1986:333) argues that parallelism promotes the perception of the utterance as an artefact – a 'speech tool' rather than a 'speech act'. In a similar vein, Bruce and Touati (1992:457) argue that 'parallelism facilitates monologue processing by reducing information density and increasing redundancy'. The three-part format for delivering the announcement is a powerful way of conveying information. It is easily produced so that anyone can say it (examples 10 and 13–15 show novice Ramp Planners competently using it on the second day of the job), and it is very brief. While relayed informings can be tailored or adapted to take into account the targeted addressee's situation of the moment (by, for example, moving to chant in a particularly busy sound environment), announcements get their force from the highly regularized way in which they are routinely produced over and over for different audiences where the local environment is not known in detail. Simultaneously the special register of Ramp Planner's announcements unambiguously cues Ops personnel (Flight Tracker in particular) that prior information has been received and understood.

This chapter has attempted to describe the complex phenomena that must be attended to simultaneously by personnel in an airline's Operations room. Producing an informing requires not only competence in the prosodic production of talk which is distinctive, but also intensive monitoring of one's physical environment (computer screens which display information about incoming planes) as well as auditory environment (the scanner which broadcasts calls between pilots and tower). The historically constituted material world in which information is transferred is an essential part of the participation framework within which this talk occurs. In producing talk in its environment, participants do not merely sequence utterances, but, in addition, juxtapose a variety of resources – technologically mediated communication as well as written documents – to formulate appropriate next moves. The speech actions discussed here are constitutive parts of activity chains, which can rally a number of participants to assist in carrying them out. Participants must be able to juggle the simultaneous demands placed upon them, as the situation in the Operations room differs from the accepted view of encounters as single-focussed engagements (Goffman 1963; Kendon 1985). In producing parts of information transfer sequences, Ops participants must find solutions to the problem of targeting communication to co-workers which will carry over the other talk being attended, yet not place undue demands on them. The crafting of utterances within information transfer sequences provides strong evidence for the claim that language is a powerful social tool. Indeed language constitutes ongoing work in the Operations room workplace, and therefore, as argued by Malinowski (1959:312–313), should be considered 'a mode of social action rather than a mere reflection of thought'.

Appendix: transcription

Data are transcribed using the transcription system developed by Jefferson and described in Sacks, Schegloff and Jefferson (1974:731–733).

Punctuation symbols are used to mark intonation changes rather than as grammatical symbols. A period (.) indicates a falling contour, a question mark (?) indicates a rising contour, and a comma (,) indicates a falling–rising (list-like) intonation.

A dash (-) marks a sudden cut-off of the current sound.

A left bracket ([) marks the point at which the current talk is overlapped by other talk.

Double slashes (//) provide an alternative method of marking overlap.

Colons (::) indicate that the sound just before the colon has been noticeably lengthened.

The equals sign (=) indicates *latching*; there is no interval between the end of a prior turn and the start of a next piece of talk.

Rapid speech is indicated by an apostrophe (') between words.

Numbers in parentheses (0.0) mark silences in seconds and tenths of seconds.

Capitals indicate increased volume.

Underlining or bold face indicates accented syllables.

Low volume is indicated by a degree sign (°).

Material in parentheses ( ) indicates problematic hearings.

Materials in double parentheses e.g. ((nonverbal actions)), indicate nonverbal actions of speaker, or transcriber's comments.

Notes

Earlier versions of this chapter were presented at the 12th World Congress of Sociology (Madrid, 9 July 1990), the International Pragmatics Conference (Barcelona, 12 July 1990), and the invited session on 'Spacing, Orientation and the Environment in Co-Present Interaction' at the 89th Annual Meeting of the American Anthropological Association (New Orleans, 30 November 1990).

This report is part of a three-year fieldwork project on multi-activity work settings, *The Workplace Project*, organized by Lucy Suchman through Xerox PARC. I wish to thank my co-ethnographers, Françoise Brun-Cottan, Charles Goodwin, Gitti Jordan and Lucy Suchman for their collaboration in the fieldwork and analysis of this material. I am indebted to Elizabeth Couper-Kuhlen, Cynthia McLemore, Livia Polanyi, Margret Selting, Stephan Schuetze-Coburn and Malcah Yaeger-Dror, not only for their comments on earlier versions of this paper but also for their help in explaining features of prosody.

1 Though Ferguson (1983) notes that features of tempo, rhythm, loudness, intonation and 'other characteristics of voice' distinguish radio-announcer sports talk, his discussion of announcements is primarily concerned with syntax rather than prosody.

2 Linguists have looked at speech acts largely with reference to the underlying preconditions and intentions of a speaker. Here, however, talk between tower and pilot has relevance for an unintended audience. Though the message from tower to pilot provides no indication that it should be used by the Flight Tracker for relayed messages to the Ramp Planner, it has the possibility of being used in this way, as a resource for other planning. For a critique of speech act notions of intentionality from an anthropological perspective see Duranti (1988).

3 Goffman defines an encounter as 'a type of social arrangement that occurs when persons are in one another's immediate physical presence' (Goffman 1961:17).

4 Example (5) occurred during a conversation about an upcoming noon gathering; it involved several co-present people, including Ramp Planner (line 2):

((Flight Tracker is looking at her monitor, flight information display screen and at the row of monitors))
1   FT: Two seventy **si:x** is on the **gr:ound,**
                    [
2   RP: Probably have **food** there **too:.**

3   RP: **Thank** you. ((slight head bob as a 'take' of the prior
        message from Flight Tracker))
4   FT: **You're** welcome. ((typing on computer))
        (0.8)
5   RP: **Two:** seventy **si:x.**
6   On'th'**ground.**
7   F'ga'**eighteen.**

5   I am indebted to Cynthia McLemore for her help in providing an
    auditory analysis of this utterance.
6   See also Haiman (1991:59) for his description of chants as
    'quintessentially ritualised or stereotyped contours'.
7   Kroskrity (1993:4) describes Arizona Tewa announcements with
    respect to their 'attention-getting style', and states they involve not
    only increased volume but also a distinctive intonational contour
    which contrasts with the more general gradual intonational lowering
    from beginning to end in everyday speech. See Gibbon (1976:276–277)
    for a discussion of 'hailing', 'greeting' and 'formulaic shouting', which
    possess intonation forms similar to 'calling'.
8   See Heritage's discussion of change-of-state tokens in response to news
    (1984).
9   Terasaki (1976:21), citing Sacks, notes that '[t]he preference not to tell
    known news manifests itself in an apparent preference to, as Sacks
    [personal communication] has it, "undertell and over-suppose"'.
10 In their study 'Units of intonation in discourse: a comparison of acous-
    tic and auditory analyses', Schuetze-Coburn, Shapley and Weber
    (1991) showed that 99% of the acoustic unit boundaries coincided
    with auditory unit boundaries.
11 Couper-Kuhlen (1986:75–80) uses the term 'tone-unit', which she
    defines following Crystal as 'a stretch of utterance which has at least
    one prominent syllable with major pitch movement'. She argues that
    cues which establish the boundaries of a tone-unit include a short
    pause, and phonetic lengthening or aspiration at the end of the tone-
    unit (ibid.:75).
12 This format was also used in a computer airline, where Ramp Planner
    had to talk to (i) pilots of incoming aircraft, giving them parking
    instructions, and (ii) crew chiefs responsible for meeting incoming
    planes. In the initial part of the announcement, Ramp Planner distin-
    guished addressees by identification of a three-digit *aircraft number*
    (printed on the side of the aircraft) for Ramp, and *flight number*, fre-
    quently four digits, for pilots. In the second intonation unit, Ramp
    Planner either indicated the state of the plane for Ramp crew
    (through *here*) or provided a directive for the pilot (*Come in*). In the
    third intonation unit, Ramp Planner indicated the gate the plane was
    headed for, specified by words standing for letters (Delta=D) rather

than numbers as was customary for the larger commercial airline. For example:

> ((to Ramp crew chief))
> RP: Three sixty
>   here
>   for Delta.

Immediately following the announcement, the Ramp Planner provided parking instructions for the pilot:

> ((to pilot))
> RP: Fifty two fifty seven.
>   Come in
>   for Delta.

13 Quite similar components – specifications of addressed audience, information concerning location, and a directive feature – occur in Tewa announcements (Kroskrity 1993:14).
14 Stephan Schuetze-Coburn provided the pitch tracks for the acoustic analysis in this chapter and helped clarify many issues on prosody for me.
15 Alternative versions of announcements may use an explicit address term in the first intonation unit of the announcement turn, as in

> RP: Mamason.
>   Three o four
>   is on the ground.

References

Abe, I. 1962. Call contours. In A. Sovijäri and P. Aalto (eds.) *Proceedings of the Fourth International Congress of Phonetic Sciences, Helsinki 1961*. The Hague: Mouton, pp. 519–523.

Briggs, C. L. 1988. *Competence in Performance: The creativity of tradition in Mexicano verbal art*. Philadelphia: University of Pennsylvania Press.

Bruce, G. and P. Touati 1992. On the analysis of prosody in spontaneous speech with exemplification from Swedish and French. *Speech Communication*, 11: 453–458.

Chafe, W. L. 1987. Cognitive constraints on information flow. In R. S. Tomlin (ed.) *Coherence and Grounding in Discourse*. Amsterdam: Benjamins, pp. 21–51.

Couper-Kuhlen, E. 1986. *An Introduction to English Prosody*. London: Edward Arnold, and Tübingen: Niemeyer.

DuBois, J. W. 1986. Self-evidence and ritual speech. In W. Chafe and J. Nichols (eds.) *Evidentiality: The linguistic coding of epistemology.* Norwood, N.J.: Ablex, pp. 313–336.

Duranti, A. 1988. Intentions, language and social action in a Samoan context. *Journal of Pragmatics*, 12: 13–33.

Ferguson, C. A. 1983. Sports announcer talk: syntactic aspects of register variation. *Language in Society*, 12: 153–172.

Fox, J. 1977. Roman Jakobson and the comparative study of parallelism. In J. D. Armstrong and C. H. v. Schooneveld (eds.) *Roman Jakobson: Echoes of his scholarship.* Lisse: Peter de Ridder, pp. 59–90.

(ed.) 1988. *To Speak in Pairs: Essays on the ritual languages of Eastern Indonesia.* Cambridge University Press.

Gibbon, D. 1976. *Perspectives of Intonation Analysis.* Frankfurt: Peter Lang.

Glaeser, D. 1982. *An Invitation to Fly.* Belmont, Calif.: Wadsworth Publishing Company.

Goffman, E. 1961. *Encounters: Two studies in the sociology of interaction.* Indianapolis: Bobbs-Merrill.

1963. *Behavior in Public Places: Notes on the social organization of gathering.* New York: Free Press.

Goodwin, C. 1995. Seeing in depth. *Social Studies of Science*, 25:237–274.

Haiman, J. 1991. Motivation, repetition and emancipation: the bureaucratisation of language. In H. C. Wolfart (ed.) *Linguistic Studies Presented to John L. Finlay.* Algonquian and Iroquoian Linguistics, Memoir 8. Winnipeg, Manitoba, pp. 45–70.

Heritage, J. 1984. A change-of-state token and aspects of its sequential placement. In J. M. Atkinson and J. Heritage (eds.) *Structures of Social Action. Studies in Conversation analysis.* Cambridge University Press, pp. 299–345.

Horvath, B. M. 1991. The empirical study of texts: horse race calls. Unpublished ms., Department of Linguistics, University of Sydney.

Jakobson, R. 1987. *Language in Literature.* Cambridge, Mass.: Belknap Press of Harvard University.

Jordan, B. 1990. The organization of activity and the achievement of competent practice in a complex work setting. Paper presented at the Congress on Research in Activity Theory. Lahti, Finland.

Kendon, A. 1985. Behavioral foundations for the process of frame attunement in face-to-face interaction. In G. P. Ginsburg, M. Brenner and M. von Cranach (eds.) *Discovery Strategies in the Psychology of Action.* London: Academic Press, pp. 229–253.

Kroskrity, P. V. 1993. Arizona Tewa public announcements: form, function, and linguistic ideology. Ms. Department of Anthropology, UCLA.

Kuiper, K. and P. Austin 1990. They're off and racing now: the speech of the New Zealand race caller. In A. Bell and J. Holmes (eds.) *New*

Zealand Ways of Speaking English. Clevedon: Multilingual Matters, pp. 195–220.

Kuiper, K. and D. Haggo 1984. Livestock auctions, oral poetry and ordinary language. *Language in Society*, 13: 205–234.

Ladd, D. R. 1978. Stylized intonation. *Language*, 54: 517–540.

Malinowski, B. 1959. The problem of meaning in primitive languages. In C. K. Ogden and I. A. Richards (eds.) *The Meaning of Meaning*. (10th edn). New York: Harcourt, Brace and World. [1923], pp. 296–336.

Olson, D. R. (ed.) 1980. Some social aspects of meaning in oral and written language. In D. R. Olson (ed.) *The Social Foundations of Language and Thought: Essays in honor of Jerome S. Bruner*. New York: W. W. Norton, pp. 90–108.

Pike, K. L. 1945. *The Intonation of American English*. Ann Arbor: University of Michigan Publications.

Sacks, H., E. A. Schegloff and G. Jefferson 1974. A simplest systematics for the organization of turn-taking for conversation. *Language*, 50: 696–735.

Schuetze-Coburn, S., M. Shapley and E. G. Weber 1991. Units of intonation in discourse: a comparison of acoustic and auditory analyses. *Language and Speech*, 34(3): 207–234.

Suchman, L. 1992. Technologies of accountability: of lizards and airplanes. In G. Button (ed.) *Technology in Working Order: Studies of work, interaction and technology*. London: Routledge.

(in press). Constituting shared workspaces. In Y. Engeström and D. Middleton (eds.) *Cognition and Communication at Work*. Cambridge University Press.

Tedlock, D. 1983. On praying, exclaiming, and saying hello. In D. Tedlock (ed.) *The Spoken Word and the Work of Interpretation*. Philadelphia: University of Pennsylvania Press, pp. 178–193.

Terasaki, A. 1976. Pre-announcement sequences in conversation. Social Science Working Paper 99. School of Social Sciences, Irvine, Calif.

Turner, V. W. 1967. *The Forest of Symbols*. Ithaca: Cornell University Press.

Voegelin, C. F. 1960. Casual and noncasual utterances within unified structure. In T. Sebeok (ed.) *Style in Language*. Cambridge, Mass.: M.I.T. Press, pp. 57–69.

Subject index

absolute pitch values 402
accent, *see also* pitch accents 234
  domains 361
  placement 291, 363
  unit 68, 70
  vs. stress 362
  emphatic 327
  sentence 97
acoustic analysis 330, 362, 372, 402,
  446, 458f., 459
acknowledgeable 140, 144f., 152
acknowledgement tokens 5, 38, 134f.,
  148, 156, 158, 160
  as precursors 148
  'in time' 160
  'out of place' 158
  'out of rhythm' 160
  'out of tune' 148f., 156
  affiliating with 140
  solicitation of 153
  'spontaneous' placement of 156
  weak vs. strong 135f.
activity, multi- 436f.
activity type 3, 6, 305
  and intonation 232
  distinction 264, 266, 272, 281
  constitution of 5, 239
address term 440, 443f., 449, 451f.,
  459
adjacency pair 304
affect 6f., 18, 20, 23, 26, 28, 299
  display 339, 346, 359
affiliation 5, 32, 131, 133, 178, 366
afterthought 81
amplificatio 287, 297, 300
anacrustic syllables, *see* syllable,
  anacrustic
announcements 9, 436ff., 445, 458f.
  vs. informings 455

  three-part structure of 446ff., 452,
    454f., 458f.
apologies 288, 299
argument, obligatory 61, 65, 70, 82
argumentation 275
assessable 304
assessment 7, 154, 303f.
  sequences 304, 315
    structure of 318
  signals 304, 358
  sounds 304, 339, 346, 359
  'concluding' 315
  concurrent 341f., 359
  'confirming' 334
  downgraded 306, 312
  prosodic salience in 155
  'same' 306, 312
  summary 140
  temporal organisation of
    sequences 310
  upgraded 306, 312, 336, 358
  location of in conversation 332
  second, in German 313, 319, 357
astonishment, *see* surprise
asyndetic appositionals 67, 77, 94

back channel 139, 171
Beat
  Addition 321ff., 330
  Deletion 321ff., 325, 330
  Insertion 321f., 328
  Movement 321 ff.
beat clash 7, 303, 319, 321ff., 325
  as a contextualization cue 327,
    332, 354, 363
  in assessments 326 (*et passim*),
    346, 357
  in informings 337ff.
  in news deliveries 337ff.

Subject index

Index of names

Printed in the United Kingdom
by Lightning Source UK Ltd.
100204UKS00001B/1